DEMOCRATIC BRAZIL

**PITT
LATIN
AMERICAN
STUDIES**

Billie R. DeWalt, General Editor

Reid Andrews, Catherine Conaghan, and
Jorge I. Domínguez, Associate Editors

Democratic Brazil

Actors, Institutions, and Processes

Edited by
Peter R. Kingstone
and
Timothy J. Power

Foreword by Thomas E. Skidmore

University of Pittsburgh Press

Published by the University of Pittsburgh Press, Pittsburgh, Pa. 15261
Copyright © 2000, University of Pittsburgh Press
All rights reserved
Manufactured in the United States of America
Printed on acid-free paper
10 9 8 7 6 5 4 3 2 1

An earlier version of the Weyland chapter was published in the *Journal of Interamerican Studies and World Affairs,* 39, no. 4 (winter 1997–1998): 63–94. Copyright © *Journal of Interamerican Studies.*

CONTENTS

FIGURES AND TABLES

Figures

Tables

ACRONYMS AND INITIALS

ABEIP   Argentine-Brazilian Economic Integration Program
ABONG   Associação Brasileira de Organizações Não-Governamentais
ANC   Assembléia Nacional Constituinte
BDMG   Banco de Desenvolvimento de Minas Gerais
BNDES   Banco Nacional de Desenvolvimento Econômico e Social
CEBRAP   Centro Brasileiro de Análise e Planejamento
CEBs   Comunidades Eclesiais de Base
CEF   Caixa Econômica Federal
CJP   Comissão de Justiça e Paz
CMN   Conselho Monetário Nacional
CNBB   Conferência Nacional dos Bispos Brasileiros
CNI   Confederação Nacional da Indústria
CONAMA   Conselho Nacional do Meio Ambiente
CSN   Companhia Siderúrgica Nacional
CUT   Central Única dos Trabalhadores
DECEX   Departamento de Comércio Exterior
DIEESE   Departamento Intersindical de Estudos Econômicos, Sociais e Estatísticos
DOPS   Departamento de Ordem Política e Social
EAP   Economically Active Population
EMFA   Estado Maior das Forças Armadas
EU   European Union
FIESP   Federação de Indústrias do Estado de São Paulo
FGU   Fundacão Getúlio Vargas
FPE   Fundo de Participação dos Estados
FPM   Fundo de Participação dos Municipios
FSE   Fundo Social de Emergência
IBGE   Instituto Brasileiro de Geografia e Estatística
IBOPE   Instituto Brasileiro de Opinião e Pesquisa
ICM   Imposto sobre Comercialização de Mercadorias
IMF   International Monetary Fund
INAMPS   Instituto Nacional de Assistência Médica da Previdência Social

INCRA Instituto Nacional de Colonização e Reforma Agrária
INDI Instituto Nacional de Desenvolvimento Industrial
IPI Instituto de Pesquisas Econômicas
IPTU Imposto Predial e Territorial Urbano
ISER Instituto de Estudos da Religião
ISI Import Substitution Industrialization
IURD Igreja Universal do Reino de Deus
MICT Ministério de Indústria, Comércio e Turismo
MMP Mixed-Member Proportional System
MOVA Movimento de Alfabetização de Jovens e Adultos
MST Movimento dos Sem-Terra
NGOs Nongovernmental Organizations
OAS Organization of American States
OP Orçamento Participativo
PBQP Programa Brasileiro de Qualidade e Produtividade
PC do B Partido Comunista do Brasil
PCB Partido Comunista Brasileiro
PDN Política de Defesa Nacional
PDT Partido Democrático Trabalhista
PFL Partido da Frente Liberal
PMDB Partido do Movimento Democrático Brasileiro
PMs Polícias Militares
PSDB Partido da Social Democracia Brasileira
PT Partido dos Trabalhadores
PTB Partido Trabalhista Brasileiro
SADEN Secretaria de Assessoramento de Defesa Nacional
SAE Secretaria de Assuntos Estratégicos
SEJUP Serviço de Justiça e Paz
SIVAM Sistema Integrado de Vigilância da Amazônia
SMDP Single Member District Plurality
SNI Serviço Nacional de Informações
SRF Secretaria da Receita Federal
SUDS Sistema Unificado e Descentralizado de Saúde
TSE Tribunal Superior Eleitoral
UNCED United Nations Conference on Environment and Development
(Rio de Janeiro 1992)
URV Unidade Real de Valor

FOREWORD 〠

A New Test for Brazilian Democracy

Thomas E. Skidmore

The potential reader of this volume is in luck. What follows in its pages is an exceptionally clear and informative handbook for understanding how another "emerging country" fell victim to the perils of globalization. What makes the Brazilian case noteworthy is that it had seemed since 1994 to be so successful under a widely praised economic stabilization plan. Why was the government of Fernando Henrique Cardoso not able to adapt to changing economic circumstances? Most observers agree that the problem was fundamentally political, or, more accurately, it was a problem of political economy. And it is on the latter dimension that *Democratic Brazil* is an invaluable guide.

The twentieth century has been hard on Brazilian democracy. Constitutional rights have been suspended twice (1937–1945 and 1964–1985) when authoritarian governments have seized power. Both times it was the military that took the initiative and provided the institutional base for arbitrary rule. When the latest episode ended in 1985, hopes were high that Brazil could finally begin a long-lasting democracy. It has proven difficult, as the contributors to this volume make abundantly clear.

The new democratic era began with a stroke of bad luck. President-elect Tancredo Neves had fallen ill on the eve of his inauguration and died before he could take office. This event robbed the republic of a highly popular politician who had seemed the ideal figure to preside over renewed civilian rule. His successor, Vice President-elect Jose Sarney, fell far short of that description.

Sarney was a traditional, patronage-oriented politician from Maranhão, one of Northeastern Brazil's most backward states. His lackluster record was appropriate for the vice presidency, a ceremonial post with little power, but now he was president. His term (1985–1990) did have one major accomplishment: the maintenance of democracy. This was no mean achievement, given recent Brazilian history.

The major political event was the writing of a new constitution by the Constituent Assembly of 1987–1988, an assembly dominated by a desire to reverse the political centralization imposed by the military regime. Most important, the constitution's authors diverted an increased share of federal revenues to the states and *municipios* without any corresponding shift in spending responsibilities. This proved to be a formula for chronic federal deficits and irresponsible spending sprees by states and *municipios*. Yet there were also some bright spots in local and state administration, as Alfred Montero clearly demonstrates. The new constitution was also highly progressive in guaranteeing civil liberties and social rights (job security for federal bureaucrats, etc.). It was the longest and most liberal constitution of the six Brazil had adopted since 1824.

The major economic trend of the late 1980s was the ruinous inflation that followed the failed Cruzado stabilization plan of 1986–1987. That plan had begun with high hopes, briefly realized during 1986 as prices were frozen and retail sales boomed. By early 1987, however, the plan had collapsed. Thus began the years of the highest inflation Brazil had ever experienced, reaching over 1,000 percent by early 1990. Meanwhile, the much-needed modernization of Brazilian industry and economic infrastructure was put on hold. Nor was there any improvement in Brazil's notoriously unequal distribution of income. It was left to the numerous nongovernmental organizations (NGOs) and a few politicians (primarily of the Workers' Party [PT]) to publicize the country's social ills and demand action on them. In his chapter William Nylen ably describes the party's notable successes in governing at the local level. But lack of steady economic growth, corrosive inflation, and the inefficient state apparatus (especially in health and education) left few resources with which to attack the pressing needs in education, health, housing, and such infrastructural areas as communications and transportation. One bright spot in the economic record was the creation of Mercosur, the economic union of the Southern Cone. As Jeffrey Cason carefully explains, this new link was most important with Argentina, Brazil's traditional diplomatic rival.

Sarney was followed in the presidency in 1990 by Fernando Collor de Mello, the first popularly elected president since 1961. Collor was a telegenic young politician from Alagoas, another backward northeastern state. Collor burst on the scene as a crusader against corruption, offering a combination of moralistic policies and neoliberal economics. His first nine months seemed successful as inflation succumbed to a price and wage freeze, an end to indexation, and an impounding of private financial accounts. At the same time, the government started privatizing major state enterprises, deregulating the domestic economy and opening it to world competition by reducing tariffs and simplifying trade regulations.

This economic policy offensive miscarried in early 1991, however. Inflationary expectations returned as it became clear that the wage, price, and asset freeze had been based on no longer-range plan. Public confidence rapidly collapsed, and the Collor government's subsequent stabilization attempts never had a chance of succeeding. The privatization campaign also stalled as the defenders of the state enterprises (such as the PT and affiliated unions) rallied to protect the swollen public payrolls.

Yet Collor might have survived his presidential term had it not been for his political maladroitness. Rumors had long circulated that the Collor government was demanding exorbitant financial kickbacks from government contractors (i.e., beyond the "normal" percentage collected by all politicians). The press pursued the story relentlessly in 1992, documenting details about pay-offs to the president. Collor was extremely vulnerable to such charges because of his previous denunciation of corruption and his arrogant refusal to cultivate links to the Congress and the political elite. The axe fell in September 1992, when the House of Deputies impeached him, and the Senate voted to expel him from the presidency. Collor had granted the new democracy one favor: he was the first Brazilian president to be forced from office by normal constitutional procedures.

Collor's demise brought another nondescript vice president to the presidency. Itamar Franco had been a senator (from Minas Gerais) with a vaguely nationalist reputation. He was generally seen as a provincial politician with few qualifications for national leadership. He served out the remainder (1992–1994) of Collor's term by making one significant move: choosing Fernando Henrique Cardoso as his finance minister in early 1994. Cardoso in turn chose a first-rate economic team, which formulated and launched the *Plano Real* stabilization program. By 1998, it had reduced inflation to a post-1945 record 2 percent a year. This process is ably analyzed in Peter Kingstone's chapter.

Fernando Henrique capitalized on his stabilization success to run for and win the 1994 presidential election. Lula, the PT candidate who had narrowly lost to Collor in the election of 1990, now lost again, not so much to Fernando Henrique as to the immensely popular *Plano Real* (Real Plan). The new president moved quickly to implement a comprehensive neoliberal economic policy. Priority was given to continuing the *Real Plan*, which included high interest rates, a (gradually sliding) pegged exchange rate, and intermittent pressure on Congress to reduce the federal deficit. The Cardoso government hoped thereby to satisfy what it thought was every Brazilian's fondest wish: stable prices.

A further neoliberal measure was privatization, begun under Collor but slowed by Itamar Franco. It was now accelerated and the government succeeded in auctioning off all the largest state sectors, including the giant telephone industry. But the Cardoso government's real emphasis was on attracting the foreign investor. That was the logical result of the government's belief that it could not mobilize sufficient domestic savings and its reliance on the overvalued foreign exchange rate as the "anchor" for the Real Plan.

The anchor did not hold. In July 1998 Brazil began to hemorrhage foreign exchange reserves, which then stood at $70 billion. By the end of the year the reserves had fallen to $38 billion. In January the dike burst, as the capital outflow accelerated. The government devalued once and then had to let the Real float. By the end of January its value had fallen by 40 percent. The prospect was for renewed inflation (perhaps 10 percent in 1999) as Brazil grappled with an enormous fiscal deficit (8 percent of the GDP). The collapse of the Real Plan created a serious crisis for Brazil's reborn democracy.

As of late January 1999, one could begin to recognize the origins of the latest crisis. First, the post-1985 political and constitutional system were both badly designed to deal with long-term economic problems, as is made clear in Kurt Weyland's chapter. The constitution's reallocation of revenues produced prodigious fiscal deficits and the electoral rules created by the fragmented party system allowed politicians to escape accountability. Second, Cardoso and his economic team failed to modify the Real Plan while there was still time. The Real (overvalued by some 20 percent when it was created in 1994) should have been devalued while confidence was still high, probably in 1996. That was also the time for a maximum attack on the federal deficit. Instead, the president chose to spend his political capital in a costly effort to amend the constitution so that he could do what no other president had dared since Getúlio Vargas in 1937: succeed himself. He won the amendment and reelection in 1998, but the price has been high.

To insure his victory he relied even more on the Real Plan, gambling that its continued success (and his resulting popularity) would keep him in the presidential palace. Despite warnings even before the November election, he was convinced that he would have time later to modify his economic policy. For a while, he seemed to be right. Within days of his inauguration in January, however, disaster struck. Suddenly no one knew where Brazil was headed. Renewed inflation? Recession? Default on the internal or external debt? More cutbacks in government attempts to meet pressing social needs, such as health, education, and housing? What about the political results? And these questions would have to be answered in a demographic and social context very different from the pre-1964 era, as Timmons Roberts and Timothy Power explain in their jointly authored chapter.

At the least, we know that Brazilian democracy is in for another severe test. An ill omen is the continued fragmentation of the party system and the resulting disarray in political decision making, as is made clear by Timothy Power. Accountability of elected politicians, long thought essential for successful democratic systems, has become difficult if not impossible as federal deputies change labels at will. The heavy overrepresentation of the least populous states in the Chamber of Deputies has also meant that the majority of Brazilian voters could and were negated by smaller electorates from the north and northeast. Any reform of the currently highly permissive electoral system (with minimal requirements for declaring candidacy for federal deputy) depends on a vote by members of the Congress, who are beneficiaries of the present system. Not surprisingly, reform has made little headway.

Another factor affecting Brazilian democracy is the decline of the nongovernmental organizations that seemed so influential in the 1980s. Many opponents of military rule had hoped that the NGOs would stimulate a recovery of initiative in civil society and thereby strengthen the reborn democracy. Two obstacles intervened. One was the structure of the NGOs, many of which depended heavily on foreign financing, especially from the United States, Canada, and Western European nations. As this financing shrank, Brazilian sources did not replace it and the NGOs were weakened, although they remained an important force, as Kathryn Hochstetler convincingly argues. The second obstacle was the rapid resurgence of the traditional clientelistic political culture. Concerned citizens increasingly turned to the old-fashioned political brokers, who knew how to dispense favors and consolidate the kind of patronal networks that had long dominated citizen-state interaction in Brazil. Meanwhile, the Catholic Church, previously a key source of opposition to the military regime, was struggling to respond to the rapid growth of Protestantism, as Kenneth Serbin relates in his perceptive chapter.

There are exceptions to this dreary scene. In Ceará, a dynamic political movement (PSDB) won control and put through a far-reaching reform of state and municipal government. Similar examples of positive change took place in Paraná under Mayor Jaime Lerner, in the Federal District's school attendance program under Governor Cristóvam Buarque, and in the reforms of the educational system of Minas Gerais. But these successes pale in contrast with such other examples as the clientelistic housing policies in Paulo Maluf's São Paulo, the opulent federal tax subsidies for the Manaus Free Trade Zone, and the endemic corruption in the school system of virtually every state and *município.*

A final feature of the period since 1985 was the learning process among economic policymakers. In the late 1980s and under Collor, Brazil had the reputation of being the major Latin American nation most reluctant to adopt neoliberal economic reforms. Fernando Henrique had the opportunity to begin anew. His economic team, which included technocrats who had drawn up the failed Cruzado Plan, formulated the *Real Plan,* one of the most technically sophisticated anti-inflation programs ever attempted in Latin America. Thanks to Cardoso's smashing victory in the October 1994 presidential election, the Real Plan economists could count on political continuity. As a result, Brazil enjoyed a stable currency and cheap imports until the bubble burst in January 1999.

⁂

What had been expected when democracy was restored in 1985? Brazilians who had the means to allow them to think about the luxury of political democracy wanted the end of arbitrary rule. (The rest were still hoping for a decent job and a living wage for their family.) Now, the police would have to honor habeas corpus (if the arrestee could afford a lawyer). In short, it was expected that civil liberties would be fully restored. That would require a real retreat by the military, which Wendy Hunter has well documented. Unfortunately, however, human rights are still often violated by the police, as Anthony Pereira describes in chilling detail.

Second, politically active Brazilians expected a more open, democratic political system—an end to arbitrarily imposed electoral rules and "bionic" senators. It should also mean less government interference in elections. Some even hoped for a reformulated system of representation, removing the geographical distortions imposed by the military regime and establishing stricter rules for party loyalty. On the *municipio* and state levels, many politicians hoped to reverse the extreme centralization of power and finance in the federal government.

Finally, some Brazilians hoped that a restored democracy would make a speedy start on correcting the country's shocking social and economic inequalities. Brazil continued to exhibit the most unequal income distribution in the world (by World Bank data). Would there now be an attack on such causes of poverty as the archaic educational system, especially at the primary level, and the overloaded health care system? Would civilian leaders now recognize their moral obligation to tackle these social needs in a way that the military had failed to do?

What has happened to these expectations? Is this the democracy the opposition dreamed of? Hardly. But should this surprise us? Brazil's experience with a mass democracy before 1985 had been exceedingly short. It got only a brief start between 1934 and 1937 and resumed between 1946 and 1964—a total of only twenty-one years since Brazilian independence in 1822. Thus the civilian architects of restored democracy in 1985 inherited institutions and a public with far less experience in mass democracy than the North Atlantic nations on which Brazil is modeled.

Fortunately we can look to this new generation of Brazilianists, all of whose penetrating research can help us understand Brazil's return to democracy. The chapters in this volume offer proof of the sophistication of these authors, all with extensive field research in Brazil and all of whom have given us in-depth analysis of post-1985 Brazil. All have received their graduate training since 1985. They are also a scholarly cohort which has developed a close rapport among themselves. They are proof that the growth of U.S. scholarly interest in Latin America no longer depends on the Cold War for its justification. On the contrary, there are new problems which will keep these scholars busy for many more years.

ACKNOWLEDGMENTS

In 1996–1997, a group of young scholars began discussing the need for a comprehensive evaluation of Brazilian democracy. Nearly a decade had passed since the publication of Alfred Stepan's edited volume, *Democratizing Brazil,* the last major study of this type in English. Moreover, Brazil itself had recently commemorated its tenth anniversary as a democracy. In that crucial decade, Brazil had witnessed important changes that defied earlier expectations about democratic transitions and challenged conceptual discussions of democratic consolidation. A working group of young Brazilianists, all of whom had conducted field research as foreign doctoral students in Brazil in the 1990s and to whom the post-1985 democracy was the natural frame of reference, felt strongly that the time had come for a collaborative appraisal of the regime. The result is this volume.

The editors are particularly grateful to a number of people who have helped us produce this collection. First and foremost, we would like to thank the contributors for their efforts. Each contributor, in addition to his or her own chapter, anonymously reviewed one other chapter, so that each chapter was subjected to multiple rounds of comments. As a consequence, the volume reflects a truly collaborative effort. We would also like to thank a group of more senior scholars whose comments and criticisms were particularly invaluable. *Democratic Brazil* began as a pair of linked panels at the Latin American Studies Association in Guadalajara, Mexico, in April 1997. We were very fortunate to have Douglas Chalmers, Frances Hagopian, Margaret Keck, and William C. Smith as our discussants on the initial panels, and their insightful observations have added tremendously to the quality of the final contributions. We are also grateful to a distinguished scholar who has done more than anyone to advance Brazilian studies outside of Brazil, Professor Thomas Skidmore, for contributing the Foreword to this volume.

Those of us who are foreign scholars of Brazil are especially blessed in that we can draw substantially on the support of Brazil's diverse and talented scholarly community. All of the writers were helped significantly in their research by Brazilian scholars without whom our research would have been impossible. We would like to take this occasion to thank them for teaching us about Brazil. In Brazilian alphabetical order, they are Fr. Dr. Alberto Antoniazzi, Bolivar Lamounier, Brasílio Sallum, Celecino de Carvalho Filho, Celso Barroso Leite, Celso Castro, Fr. Celso Pedro da Silva, Claudio

Couto, David Verge Fleischer, Eduardo Gomes, Eduardo Viola, Eliézer Rizzo de Oliveira, Fernando Abrúcio, Francisco Weffort, Geraldo Lesbat Cavagnari Filho, Glaucio Ary Dillon Soares, Henrique Rattner, Janina Onuki, João Paulo Cândia Veiga, João Paulo Peixoto, Jorge Zaverucha, José Álvaro Moisés José Roberto Ferro, Lourdes Sola, Luciano Coutinho, Luiz Pedone, Marcelo Viana Estevão de Moraes, Marco Antônio da Rocha, Maria d'Alva Gil Kinzo, Maria do Carmo Campello de Souza, Maria Helena Moreira Alves, Otávio Dulci, Paulo Mesquita Neto, Ronaldo Porto Macedo Júnior, Rubens Figueiredo, Rui de Britto Alvares Affonso, and Ruth Corrêa Leite Cardoso.

All of our contributions grow out of our initial doctoral research on Brazilian politics, history, and society. Therefore, we would like to take this opportunity to thank the scholars who contributed most to our professional development by supervising our doctoral theses and otherwise mentoring us in graduate school. *Aos técnicos da seleção:* Stephen Bunker, Douglas Chalmers, David Collier, Ruth Berins Collier, Gary Cox, Jorge Domínguez, Paul Drake, Bud Duvall, Peter Evans, Maria Patricia Fernández-Kelly, Frances Hagopian, Mark Kesselman, Scott Mainwaring, Guillermo O'Donnell, Leigh Payne, Philippe Schmitter, Kathryn Sikkink, Barbara Stallings, Alfred Stepan, and Eric Van Young.

Peter Kingstone would like to thank the Institute for International Studies at the University of California, Berkeley, and the University Committee for Research and Scholarship at the University of Vermont for supporting field research relating to this project. He is also grateful to the College of Arts and Sciences Dean's Fund for supporting travel related to editorial work for this volume. Finally, he would like to thank his wife, Lisa, and his children, Ben and Lara, for their love, encouragement, and many suggestions for book jacket colors.

Timothy Power would like to thank the Comissão Fulbright and the Department of Political Science, University of Brasília, for helpful institutional support during his visits to Brazil. He is grateful to his department chair at Louisiana State University, Dr. Cecil L. Eubanks, for committing travel resources to facilitate the editors' work on this project, and also to his research assistant at LSU, David Gauthier, who helped prepare the volume for final publication. He would also like to thank his wife, Valéria, for her unfailing support ever since the day he first met her in the romantically named Annex No. 4 of the Brazilian National Congress.

Finally, Kingstone and Power would like to thank the editors and staff at the University of Pittsburgh Press, particularly Eileen Kiley, for their exceptional guidance and support.

DEMOCRATIC BRAZIL

Still Standing or Standing Still?

The Brazilian Democratic Regime
Since 1985

**Peter R. Kingstone and
Timothy J. Power**

The Promise of Democracy

When José Sarney donned the presidential sash on March 15, 1985, Brazil ended twenty-one years of military rule and embarked on a new experiment in democracy. The dynamics of Brazil's 1964–1985 military republic have been widely debated, and that regime's slow post-1974 demise is also one of the most intensely studied political transitions in recent memory. In 1985, scholars turned to analyzing democracy in practice. As they began their efforts, they were fortunate because as a result of the accumulation of literature on the military regime and the democratic transition, analysis could begin from excellent empirical and theoretical baselines on Brazilian politics, economy, and society.[1] But from these baselines emerged decidedly mixed opinions about the prospects for the democratic New Republic after 1985.[2]

On the positive side, some analysts identified trends throughout the late 1970s and early 1980s that appeared to support democracy. These included the preeminence of the main opposition party to military rule, the Partido do Movimento Democrático Brasileiro (PMDB), which at the time enjoyed strong social democratic credentials; the development of *novo sindicalismo* ("new unionism"), a new form of trade unionism that for the first time was independent of the state; a number of social movements and popular organizations that had emerged during the transition; the emergence of grassroots Catholicism as a force for justice and human rights; the rise of the Workers'

Party (PT), a leftist party that rejected traditional politics and espoused a participatory ideology; the development of a "modern" segment of business elites that supported democracy; a generalized "resurrection of civil society" that coincided with the military withdrawal; and secular changes in the social structure that seemed to be more conducive to democracy.

However, observers also pointed to some towering challenges to the new democratic regime, including widespread poverty combined with the world's worst distribution of income; the unprecedented economic crisis of the 1980s, including massive foreign debt, erratic growth, intractable inflation, and falling real incomes; the persistence of various authoritarian enclaves throughout the state and the specter of military tutelage; a legacy of weakness in the main representative institutions, such as political parties and Congress; the aftermath of a negotiated transition to democracy that was favorable to the military's civilian supporters; and the persistence of traditional, nonaccountable political practices—such as personalism, clientelism, and patrimonialism—that the elites carried with them into the New Republic.

These were the concerns of scholars in 1985. Over the next decade and a half, neither the most optimistic nor the most pessimistic scenarios materialized. The democratic regime in Brazil has not broken down, but neither has it "consolidated" (to use a contested term that is discussed later). Thus, Brazil falls into what Philippe Schmitter (1995) calls "the excluded middle" of the set of postauthoritarian regimes. These are cases in which neither consolidation nor breakdown occurs, but which probably represent the most frequent outcome in the aftermath of democratic transitions.

"The excluded middle" presents an analytical challenge in the study of new democracies. If we focus on the polar opposites of outcomes—regime breakdown versus an ideal type of democratic consolidation—we tend to undertheorize the *kind* of postauthoritarian regime that is actually unfolding. But if we downplay these outcome-oriented assessments in favor of disaggregated work on institutions, actors, and processes (a pragmatic research agenda for "the excluded middle"), we still need to identify the overall direction, magnitude, and pace of political change. As Schmitter has argued (Schmitter 1992), studying "the excluded middle" requires us to recognize that democratic consolidation is a multifaceted process that takes place at different speeds, with democratization in some "partial regimes" moving faster than in others. Thus, an appraisal of Brazilian democracy requires simultaneous analysis of key players, rules, and patterns of interaction, measuring change within each unit in relation to its 1985 baseline. Only then can we move beyond the observation that Brazilian democracy is "still standing" in order to ask, But is it also "standing still"?

Nearly fifteen years of democratic experience allow us to attempt such an updated appraisal, revisiting and reevaluating some of the initial hypotheses about the New Republic. How has democracy fared in Brazil? What is the record of the New Republic? Which actors, institutions, and processes have most critically impacted postauthoritarian politics? In which areas has the New Republic succeeded in meeting the expected challenges, and in which areas has it been less successful? Have there been new, unforeseen challenges to democracy, and if so, how has the regime responded to them? In general, where has Brazilian democracy been and where is it going? The chapters in this book address these questions.

Evaluating Democracy

What Samuel Huntington (1991) calls the global "third wave" of democratization is usually dated as beginning in 1974, the same year in which Brazil began its political liberalization. The third wave has spawned a vigorous debate over the nature and definition of "democracy" and its "consolidation," but the debate has not provided clear answers. As has been noted often, democracy is an essentially contested concept. Individual scholars interpret and define democracy in different ways depending on their normative preferences and/or theoretical purposes. As a result, there is more than a little tension over definitions and evaluations in the literature.

Most scholars accept a minimal procedural approach—such as that innovated by Robert Dahl (1971)—as a base definition of democracy. Dahl's concept of "polyarchy" emphasizes two basic dimensions, participation and contestation. In this view, democracy is based on elections that feature effective competition for all positions of government power, held at predictable intervals; the right of individuals and groups to participate in those electoral contests without major proscriptions; and the existence of basic civil and political liberties that guarantee both contestation and participation. Because many scholars would like to say even more about democratic regimes, broader conceptions of democracy have proliferated as analysts have coined adjectives to modify the term (Collier and Levitsky 1997). These definitions often incorporate more stringent standards on procedures, substantive results, or some mix of the two, but they often measure democracy on widely differing variables, which can and does lead to very different results. Thus, individual analysts may reach widely divergent conclusions about the "quality" of democracy.

Similarly, debates about democratic consolidation (a field that Philippe Schmitter termed "consolidology") have also led to widely divergent interpretations based on contested definitions, and those different definitions reflect differing normative and theoretical preferences. Some scholars have criticized consolidation literature for that reason and have also accused it of drifting into both tautology (Schneider 1995) and teleology (O'Donnell

1996). For example, Guillermo O'Donnell has noted that many scholarly notions of consolidation emphasize the need for "institutionalization," but on closer inspection the yardstick for "institutionalization" is based on nothing more than the author's preferred institutional set, a *telos* of which the author approves.

As a solution to the problem, several scholars, notably Philippe Schmitter and Ben Ross Schneider, have argued in favor of disaggregating the concept of democratic consolidation. In this view, regime consolidation is simply too highly aggregated a concept to capture the most meaningful causal interactions of postauthoritarian politics. Democracies have both formal and informal rules of behavior. Democratic governance entails decision making at the level of the national state. However, a great many important interactions occur at the state and municipal levels, in the workplace, in courts of law, and within civil society. Really existing democracies may fuse a whole range of democratic, undemocratic, liberal, illiberal, universalistic, and clientelistic practices, and all of these elements may interact with each other in different ways at different times and in different loci or domains—Schmitter's "partial regimes" of democracy. Given the current state of the consolidation literature, analytical disaggregation is pragmatic and warranted and is the strategy followed in this book.

Research Questions and Findings

Each of the contributors to *Democratic Brazil* examined a critical area of Brazilian democracy after 1985. No yardstick of "democracy" or "consolidation" was imposed: to do so for a group of twelve authors would have been not only unworkable but intellectually dishonest. Each contributor problematized democracy in the ways that best fit his or her theoretical purposes, and as a result, the authors as a whole cast a broad net over the New Republic. Some paid particular attention to formal institutions and rules; others were more concerned with substantive results. Yet these emphases were not mutually exclusive, as most of the contributions encompass both procedural and substantive (or "quality") concerns. The book that has resulted reflects and incorporates some of the tensions over defining democracy that exist throughout the social sciences.

Nevertheless, the authors all followed a unifying set of questions that link the chapters in this book. The contributors framed their chapters by asking what has been the impact of democratic rule on their specific area of interest and then reversed the question to ask how their specific area of interest has shaped Brazilian democracy since 1985. Despite applying different standards (i.e., based on procedural or substantive criteria of democratic success), the majority of the authors point to mixed results. The New Republic has not lived up to the normative promises inherent in the concept of democracy, to the expectations its defenders held at the time of the transition, or to the standards provided by advanced industrial democracies. Brazilian democratic institutions remain controversial and problematic, as do many of the public policies emerging from them. Brazilian society remains highly unequal and elitist, and the rule of law has not been effectively extended to the lower-income segments of the population. Groups and movements that were intriguing in the early 1980s now seem less vital or more ambiguously prodemocratic. Formerly authoritarian elites are alive and well, and many have never been dislodged from their positions of power. Clientelism remains pervasive.

However, neither has Brazilian democracy been as disappointing as some analysts have suggested. In fact, the large majority of the chapters in this book point to two general observations. First, Brazilian democracy and Brazilian democrats have been remarkably adaptive. Much of the literature has focused attention on the shortcomings of Brazil's formal democratic institutions and rules, but politicians and social actors have found ways of working within this institutional setting, albeit in an uneven, stop-and-go fashion. As a result, a significant number of positive changes and trends have taken place at the national level, particularly since 1994, including significant reforms in economic policy and enhancements of state autonomy and capacity. Important changes have also occurred below the level of the national state. Creative governance by the Workers' Party has fostered participatory democracy at the municipal level, and the federal-level fiscal crisis has pushed states and municipalities into experimenting with new social policies. Labor and capital have developed new, more cooperative ways of negotiating without the state and to some extent in spite of it. Social movements have matured in ways that have allowed them to work with the state while still challenging exclusionary conceptions of citizenship. Thus, despite many obstacles, Brazilian democracy has been dynamic in a way that static depictions or definitions of democracy might not capture.

Second, in accord with Schmitter's theoretical expectations, the analyses presented in this volume also document wide variations in the rate and degree of change across "partial regimes." These subcomponents of the larger regime represent alternative arenas, formal and informal, in which decision making and conflict resolution can take place. There is no uniform model for how these subregimes may cohere, or for how much importance each subregime may acquire (or lose) as a decision-making arena. The notion of partial regimes is helpful in that it points to the fact that democracy is a complex system, which means that the constituent parts and processes may develop in sharply different ways without a necessary point of convergence.

The chapters in this book clearly lend support to Schmitter's multispeed conceptualization of democratic change. Reform of political institutions has proceeded at a glacial pace, but social actors have changed markedly and rapidly over the course of the New Republic. Similarly, economic policy has changed gradually and incrementally, but stabilization, economic liberalization, and privatization have led to a rapid restructuring of business and fueled changes in labor-capital relations. Regional economic integration has advanced impressively, but the land tenure system remains highly unjust. Political decentralization has picked up steam under democracy, but the legal environment has barely changed at all. Brazilian democracy may endure for a long time and may achieve striking gains in a wide array of areas, yet society and the rule of law are likely to remain overwhelmingly unequal. The chapters in *Democratic Brazil* document the varying rates of social and political change—and thus point to the uneven crystallization of an imperfect democracy.

Organization: Institutions, Actors, and Processes

The book is organized into three parts. Part 1 focuses on the institutional design of the New Republic and its influence on national policy making. The basic formal design of Brazilian democracy remains contested and subject to almost continuous debate, but policymakers have still managed to adapt to their institutional environment. As a consequence, in spite of shifting, unstable coalitions owing to the fluidity of political institutions, the policymakers have managed to implement an array of vital policy reforms. Thus, the authors of the chapters in Part 1 point to some cautiously optimistic conclusions despite the New Republic's uneven progress toward a satisfactory institutional framework.

Timothy Power examines the design of political institutions, such as the electoral system, the party system, and the presidential system of government. He suggests that a number of institutional choices made by legislators during the National Constituent Assembly (1987–1988) have hampered governability and that rules such as open-list proportional representation combined with presidentialism have exacerbated political personalism, forced presidents to rely on ad hoc measures such as decree authority, and debilitated party organizations. In particular, Brazil's electoral system weakens the accountability of parties and legislators and thereby increases the influence of narrow, particularistic interests. At times, this disturbing cluster of traits has been blamed for political immobilism, which raises questions about long-term governability in the absence of real institutional reform. The question of political reform is always on the agenda, but fear of its "instrumental" appropriation leads to mutual recriminations about the motives of actors, thus creating an equilibrium centered on a very unsatisfactory status quo.

On quality grounds, the constitutional design appears deeply flawed, facilitating neither effective performance nor greater social justice.

By contrast, Kurt Weyland reaches a more moderately optimistic conclusion in his study of state capacity, particularly under presidents Fernando Collor (1990–1992) and Fernando Henrique Cardoso (1994–present). Democratization initially weakened the Brazilian state, but democracy also later produced leaders who sought to recover state capacity. Collor's rule by imposition and Cardoso's rule by negotiation both generated some room for the state to act independently of narrow, particularistic interests. Thus, to some extent, there was an upward trend toward the recuperation of state autonomy in the 1990s. Under Cardoso, that stability came at the price of preserving clientelism, as Cardoso traded short-term benefits to politicians in return for long-term improvements in state capacity. Cardoso's conscious tradeoff did not generate sufficient autonomy to permit real advances in equity-enhancing policies, but it did permit an incremental improvement in the state's capacity to manage its own finances and thereby address long-standing fiscal problems.

Alfred Montero's study of political decentralization finds piecemeal improvements in policy performance, despite continued instability in the rules of the federal pact. Montero notes that decentralization remains a controversial issue in Brazil, particularly with reference to fiscal and monetary control. Nevertheless, over time, the central authorities have gained increasing leverage over decentralized actors and thus have acquired greater control over fiscal imbalances. Furthermore, as the federal government has retreated or failed in critical social policy areas, innovative solutions have emerged at the state level. Thus, although the "new federalism" has at times hindered effective governance (particularly with respect to social policy) and has left crucial issues on the negotiating table, continuous adaptation at both the federal and subnational levels have led to pockets of effective performance.

David Samuels's chapter endeavors to explain the recent emergence of municipal governments in Brazil as important—and relatively autonomous—providers of government services. Samuels argues that the political consequences of urbanization and military rule set the stage for the significant transformations in intergovernmental relations that the members of the 1988 constitutional convention introduced. However, despite a significant decentralization of resources and power to municipal governments, and despite the opportunities for political entrepreneurs to implement innovative new programs at the local level, Samuels, like Montero, argues that significant obstacles remain to improving the responsiveness of local government to popular demands. In particular, given the retraction of the central government from the provision of social services, and the imprecise division of responsibilities in the 1988 constitution, municipalities across Brazil lack the resources and the expertise to adequately meet the needs of Brazil's citizens.

Part 2 revisits a set of political actors that were central to the democratic transition and evaluates their role in the New Republic after 1985. Two of the chapters examine the role of "old" actors—the military and the Catholic Church—while the other two examine "new" actors—social movements and the Workers' Party. All of the chapters acknowledge that observers have been disappointed with these critical actors, but nevertheless, each author points to continuous changes in their roles that tend to support democratic durability and quality.

Wendy Hunter focuses on changes in the role of the armed forces, which governed Brazil from 1964 to 1985. Military elites were well ensconced in the government of José Sarney from 1985 to 1990, but beginning with Fernando Collor, successive presidents have redefined the role of the military in ways that have increased civilian control. Simultaneously, political pluralism and the ascendance of civilian politicians have revealed that Congress prefers pork-barrel appropriations to military spending, which has led to downward pressures on military budgets. As a consequence, the presidents of the 1990s were able to shunt the military further and further from the center of politics. Nevertheless, the armed forces remain an important factor in evaluating the transparency of democracy. Specifically, the military retains discretion over critical areas, such as intelligence gathering and the Amazon, and appears only partially reconciled to civilian authority. Thus, although civil-military relations changed notably from the 1980s to the 1990s, the gradual retreat of the military has not translated into an unqualified success.

William Nylen's chapter on the Workers' Party (PT) offers an optimistic assessment of the party's performance and its contribution to democratic quality. The PT has prospered, despite sharp internal cleavages and its defeats in the 1989, 1994, and 1998 presidential elections, particularly at the local level as it has substantially increased the number of municipalities it has governed since 1985. Nylen argues that the PT's expansion has deepened democracy in several critical ways. The party has consistently reached out to marginalized voters in Brazil, it has tried to socialize poor Brazilians into democratic politics by opening new channels of participation, it has made room for potentially antidemocratic left-wing critics of the regime, and it has steadfastly criticized and exposed undemocratic practices in the political system. Thus, the PT has upended many of Brazil's historical traditions and has compensated, at least partially, for the skewed character of political representation in the New Republic.

Kenneth Serbin's study of the emerging religious pluralism in Brazil notes that the role of the Catholic Church has changed substantially since the 1970s when it was the vanguard of the prodemocracy movement. The church has had to respond not only to an internal conservative retrenchment but also to the external challenge of the rise of Pentecostal Protestantism, and as a result, religious organizations are a weaker force for social justice than they were at the outset of the New Republic. The conservative resurgence has muted the church's more aggressive efforts at progressive social change while Pentecostals have embraced clientelistic politics as part of their effort to win political breathing room in an overwhelmingly Catholic country. Despite this conclusion, Serbin suggests that religious pluralism has several possible benefits. First, competition in a "religious marketplace" may revitalize the Catholic Church, which has suffered from overconfidence and bureaucratic inertia. Second, the Pentecostals' overt political strategies have helped intensify the role religious organizations play in mediating the relationship between the poor and the state and in building civil society. Finally, as the Pentecostals mature as a religious force, they may choose to join the Catholic Church in highlighting redistributive issues.

In her chapter on social movements, Kathryn Hochstetler finds that, contrary to the prevailing view, popular forces remain robust in Brazil. She argues that social movements follow a cyclical pattern of behavior so that the strategies and struggles that define movements endure even as specific movements wax, wane, or vanish. Thus, many of the diverse movements under the New Republic look very little like the vocal prodemocracy movements that helped hasten the demise of authoritarianism. In fact, the New Republic's social movements have tended toward cooperative strategies and access to the state far more than in earlier periods. Nevertheless, they remain effective participants in the political process as they continue to challenge Brazilian conceptions of democracy and citizenship. One clear example in the 1990s was the rise of the Landless Workers' Movement (MST), which aims to push agrarian reform toward the top of the national agenda in coming years.

Part 3 looks at a set of emerging social and political processes and considers how they have affected democracy in Brazil. These processes—economic management, regional integration, human rights prosecution, and demographic change—are crucial for both democratic quality and stability. As in Parts 1 and 2, the conclusions in Part 3 tend to be mixed. Three of the four chapters suggest that the basis for significant democratic deepening rests on trends within the areas under study. However, the pace of change has varied substantially as actors have or have not taken opportunities to advance democratic causes. Thus, while processes like labor-capital negotiation and the increasing density of civil society have helped advance democracy, poverty, inequality, and human rights abuses still remain as disturbing challenges.

In his analysis of economic management, Peter Kingstone finds that successive presidents have improved economic policy incrementally, despite deep flaws in the constitutional design. Poor constitutional design has repeatedly undermined stabilization efforts, and as of 1999, this poor design remains an obstacle to a long-term resolution of Brazil's fiscal problems. However, the democratic process has allowed each new president to build on the efforts of his predecessor, and as a result, gradual achievements in stabilization and growth policies have led to substantial economic reforms. In turn, economic reform has tended to strengthen democracy by rapidly weakening elements in the business class that might prefer military intervention.

In the New Republic, regional economic integration has been seen as a way to bolster both democracy and domestic policy reforms. In his chapter on Mercosul, Jeffrey Cason notes that the negotiating partners explicitly viewed the formation of the regional trading bloc as a way to weaken the military and promote democracy. Mercosul succeeded in thrusting civilian leaders to the center of regional debates on economic reform and foreign policy, but despite the democratic impulse behind Mercosul's creation, the integration scheme has not fared well on participatory grounds. For the most part, interest groups have complained that the government negotiators excluded interested parties and (much like critics of the European Union after Maastricht) have begun to speak of an inertial "democratic deficit" in Mercosul's institutions. Thus, although Mercosul was negotiated to strengthen *regional* commitments to democracy, it has done so at the expense of *domestic* participation by placing foreign economic policy outside the democratic debate.

Anthony Pereira raises perhaps the most disturbing questions of the volume in his chapter on military impunity with regard to human rights issues. Pereira notes that the rule of law remains pointedly elitist in Brazil, and more important, there appears to be little momentum toward correcting that fact. Human rights activists did gain limited compensation for the victims of military abuses during authoritarian rule, but that victory primarily benefited middle-class activists. Furthermore, the military police continues to abuse both rural and urban poor with only limited public interest or support for correcting the problem. Thus, in this area, Brazilian democracy has yet to deliver significant results.

In the last chapter, Timothy Power and Timmons Roberts examine demographic and societal trends over the course of the New Republic and note that the socioeconomic structure of Brazil's modern democracy has changed dramatically from the earlier democratic period (1946–1964). Among several of the new developments are much higher rates of urbanization and industrialization, a significantly larger electorate, comparatively higher rates of literacy, a relatively robust civil society (defined as the proliferation of secondary associations), and the rapid diffusion of television. Many of these trends could potentially support democratic deepening and durability. However, the authors also point to some disturbing social continuities, including pervasive poverty, drastic inequalities in income and wealth, and unequal access to education. The authors suggest that an increasingly complex Brazilian society has become difficult to govern by authoritarian means and that a base exists for building a stronger, higher-quality democracy. But Power and Roberts also illustrate a number of powerful incentives toward inertial inequality in the New Republic, none of which has been successfully attacked by previous regimes but which the New Republic must resolve in order to distinguish itself from its predecessors.

The chapters in *Democratic Brazil* illustrate that the New Republic of Brazilian democracy has proved remarkably durable and adaptive in its nearly fifteen years of existence. In some respects, the quality of Brazilian democracy has improved, albeit slowly, but in other respects, democratic deepening has lagged appallingly. Brazilian democracy is "still standing," but it is *not* simply "standing still"—even if its movement is imperceptible and unsatisfactory to many observers. If this book yields any prescription, it is for more disaggregated studies of postauthoritarian politics. If it yields any prediction, it is that the practitioners of Brazilian democracy will continue to adapt to their circumstances in ways that surprise us, defy our expectations (both negative and positive), and generate creative responses to a constantly evolving regime.

PART I

The Institutional and Policy-Making Context

ONE

Political Institutions in Democratic Brazil

Politics as a Permanent Constitutional Convention

Timothy J. Power

n assessing the performance of Brazilian democracy since 1985, issues of formal institutionalization are paramount. Recent research on Brazilian politics follows one of the dominant streams of literature in comparative politics, the debate on the institutional design of democracy, and Brazil has both benefited from and contributed to that debate. There are few countries in the world where an academic debate on constitutional design has so decisively influenced the journalistic and partisan arenas as the debate in Brazil has since 1985, and fewer still where public debate is so sensitive to perceived deficiencies of the existing institutional arrangements. The Brazilian experience has also proved extremely conducive to comparative academic analysis, and Brazil has become a favorite case study of "new institutionalists" who are conducting research on parties, legislatures, electoral systems, and executive-legislative relations.

By the mid-1990s, researchers had produced a significant body of theoretically and comparatively informed work on the institutional architecture of Brazilian democracy, and now is an opportune moment for an assessment of this literature and some reflection upon its findings as they relate to the underlying theme of democratization. The purpose of this chapter is threefold: to explicate the underlying justifications for the institutionalist approach to Brazilian democracy, to review the main institutional variables and evaluate the main arguments in the literature that has appeared to date, and to place these arguments in broader perspective with respect to the consolidation of political democracy in the New Republic.

In the first section, I outline some theoretical and background issues and sketch out a brief periodization of "the institutional debate" in Brazil. Subsequent sections condense and critique the arguments revolving around four key institutional and constitutional variables: presidentialism and executive politics, the national legislature, the political party system, and the electoral system. I conclude with some observations about institutions, governability, and democratic consolidation at the close of the 1990s.

The Travail of Institution Building

Since the advent of the New Republic in 1985, a major aim has been how to anchor Brazilian democracy constitutionally and institutionally—i.e., on how to devise more or less permanent "rules of the game" that would make the regime a sustainable one. "Sustainable" in this sense means not only enduring but also functional, and a recurring problem in institutional design derives from the subjective understanding of these two facets of sustainability and the implicit tradeoffs between them. Even if all actors prefer the maintenance of a democratic regime (which is not always true), they are certain to prefer different outputs. The institutional set that is minimally agreed to by N players may permit the regime to survive but not "perform well" in the eyes of any single actor, and conversely the institutional set preferred by a given actor may stimulate the regime to "perform well" but not allow it to survive. The arrangements that are eventually settled upon reflect sundry second- and third-best alternatives and are frequently disappointing and mediocre in the eyes of many—including political scientists. I raise this point as an initial disclaimer concerning the dissatisfaction that pervades much academic analysis of institutional choices in nascent polyarchies.

Thus, institutional design in new democracies presents a collective action dilemma, and there are three ways in which collective action problems are typically overcome in the early years of a regime. The first is a "restoration" strategy in which the democratizing forces agree to adopt an institutional set that existed in the past: for example, they might agree to resurrect a defunct constitution. Second, the outgoing authoritarian regime might impose institutional rules that cannot easily be changed and which hamstring the new democracy. This scenario, which exists in post-Pinochet Chile, is undesirable in many ways and has been justifiably criticized, yet it undeniably "resolves"—if only in the short run—the collective action problem of institutional redesign. Third, collective action problems can also be overcome when the transition is led by a majoritarian, coherent, and decisive democratizing coalition that moves immediately to marginalize antidemocratic actors, to hammer out institutional arrangements, and to implement those arrangements swiftly and unequivocally. This scenario could result from liberal revolutions that fill a power vacuum (such as in Costa Rica and Czechoslovakia) or in the wake of "pacted" transitions like those in Venezuela and Spain.[1]

Post-1985 Brazil does not correspond to any of the three ideal-type "solutions" to the institutional design problem. Rather, it presents a fourth, indeterminate outcome. There was never a possibility of restoring the constitution of 1946, as from the 1970s onward, the democratic opposition had demanded a constitutional convention to write an entirely new document. This antirestorationist view was consistent with earlier regime transitions in Brazilian history. The current charter, written by the National Constituent Assembly (ANC) in 1987–1988, is the country's eighth since independence. Between 1985 and 1988, the military-imposed constitution of 1967 was followed, and in contrast to Chile's, it was easily amendable and did not unduly tie the hands of reformers. It is more important that Brazil was handicapped by the muddled circumstances of the 1984–1985 transition, which produced a democratizing coalition championed by everyone and captained by no one. In an early appraisal of the New Republic, Mario do Carmo Campello de Souza criticized its "invertebrate centrism," which she defined as a "vast center whose boundaries . . . are unknown" (Souza 1989, 355). Guillermo O'Donnell (1992) has argued similarly that the transition never clearly established which actors did or did not belong to the democratizing coalition and described it as a "coalition of all for all."

Several actors could claim paternity of the New Republic, yet in the 1980s, none of them—including the party that seemed to have the best chance to do so, the Partido do Movimento Democrático Brasileiro (PMDB)—succeeded in imposing a clear agenda, whether in institution building or in any other aspect of democratic consolidation. Although the coalition charged with building democracy lacked definition, coherence, and decisiveness, it was united by the desires to reestablish competitive elections, reoccupy executive power, and wield it (Power 1991). In the first two to three years of democracy, institution building was relegated to a secondary place—even in the Constituent Assembly *(Assembléia Nacional Constituinte)* of 1987–1988, which quickly became a free-for-all of parochial and sectoral demands and produced a document reflecting its chaotic politics and ad hoc procedures (Rosenn 1990). With short-term, individualistic concerns prevailing over longer-term, collective ones, and with a constitution that reflects sectoral demands, it is no surprise that there has been virtually nonstop tinkering with the institutional arrangements of Brazilian democracy. The continuous nature of this process invites a comparison with Sidney Blumenthal's famous characterization of American politics as "the permanent campaign" (Blumenthal 1982): post-1985 Brazilian politics might be characterized as "the permanent *Constituinte*."

In the first decade of democracy, institutional design never disappeared from the national agenda, but there were four clear spikes or "institutional moments" of paramount importance.[2] The first of these came in May 1985, only two months into the new regime and only weeks after José Sarney was confirmed as president after the death of Tancredo Neves. Congress approved Constitutional Amendment No. 25 to the military-dictated charter of 1967, attacking what then-Senator Fernando Henrique Cardoso nicknamed "the authoritarian debris" *(entulhos autoritários)* bequeathed by the military. This amendment reestablished direct elections for all levels of government, legalized Marxist political parties such as the Partido Comunista Brasileiro (PCB) and the Partido Comunista do Brasil (PC do B), abolished party fidelity, erased most barriers to the formation of political parties and to their representation in Congress, and allowed multiparty alliances in elections. Within several years the extreme liberalization of the party arena would come to be viewed as a mistake, but in 1985 party fidelity and barriers to party formation were widely viewed as *casuísmos* (casuistry) of the military regime. The somewhat overcompensating antiauthoritarian reforms typify what Scott Mainwaring (1999) calls the "democratic libertarianism" of the Brazilian transition: democratization was identified with a form of institutional permissiveness demanding the removal of any and all barriers to the personal latitude of individual politicians.

The second "moment" of activity in institutional design, the National Constituent Assembly (ANC), actually lasted twenty months. The ANC had a controversial genesis, for in 1985–1986, politicians had rejected the idea of an "exclusive" assembly comprised of jurists, notables, and representatives of societal organizations. President Sarney convened an advisory commission chaired by the eminent former foreign minister, Afonso Arinos, and it produced an initial draft constitution that was promptly shelved. Finally, Congress decided that the Senate and the Chamber of Deputies to be elected in November 1986 would serve simultaneously as the ANC.

The *Constituinte* convened in February 1987 and concluded its labors in September 1988, and the current constitution was promulgated on October 5. For almost two years, then, the ANC dominated Brazilian politics. First came months of committee work, which became a target for lobbyists and interest groups; a first draft was approved in July 1987; then came thousands of amendments, proposals, and popular petitions that led to a second draft; and 1,021 roll-call votes on final amendments between June and September 1988 finally led to a final document of no fewer than 245 articles.[3] Although the macroeconomic articles of the constitution have earned much notoriety and are the current focus of the Cardoso government, the politico-institutional articles have also proved controversial.

The battles of the *Constituinte* were fierce, and some of them were resolved by postponing difficult decisions. After first opting for a "parliamentary" (actually semipresidential) system of government, the ANC backtracked in 1988 and chose to maintain the historic system of pure presidentialism.[4] But this decision was so controversial it led to a compromise that scheduled a plebiscite to be held in five years to decide not only the system of government (presidential or parliamentary) but also the form of the regime (republic or monarchy).[5]

The period preceding the plebiscite in early 1993 was the third institutional moment of the New Republic. Newspapers were filled with op-ed pieces; dozens of books and voters' guides were sold at every newsstand; and the presidentialist, parliamentary, and monarchist "fronts" received free daily television time for sixty days prior to the election. What was interesting was not so much the predictable arguments over the relative merits of presidentialism and parliamentarism (which in televised commercials were often distorted beyond recognition), but the way in which the debate branched out to incorporate broader issues of institutional design such as the party system, the electoral system, and the role of the national legislature. The presidentialist forces easily triumphed, receiving 55 percent of the vote compared to only 25 percent for parliamentarism (Lamounier 1994, 215–16).

The 1988 constitution provided not only for the subsequent reopening of the question of presidentialism but also for a top-to-bottom revision of the constitution to commence five years after promulgation.[6] The idea was to simplify the normal amendment procedure by allowing Congress to sit in a unicameral session (thus diluting the power of the smaller, more conservative Senate) and pass amendments with an absolute majority of the total membership. By 1993, the very concept of constitutional revision had become ideologically polarized. The center and right parties believed the revision would be an opportunity to remove perceived constitutional obstacles to neoliberal adjustment (which Fernando Collor had already attempted with his *Emendão* [Big Amendment] strategy of 1991–1992), but the leftist groups saw the revision as a plot to reverse the *conquistas* (social conquests) of the 1988 charter.

The *Congresso Revisor*, which finally convened in March 1994, was the fourth main institutional moment of the New Republic. The revision was paralyzed by a major corruption scandal involving twenty-nine congressional members (Fleischer 1994; Krieger, Rodrigues, and Bonassa 1994). Investigations dragged on into the middle of the year, by which time the election campaign of 1994 had already begun to heat up, so congressional leaders were forced to abort the special assembly and thus end five years of hopes for constitutional reform (Martínez-Lara 1996, 185–89). Of the 30,000 proposals presented in the *Congresso Revisor*, only 5 were enacted as constitutional amendments, which would seem to indicate that this exercise in institutional design had only a minor effect. However, one of the outcomes—the decision to reduce the presidential term from five years to four while maintaining the ban on immediate reelection—provided for political drama during the Cardoso administration in 1997 when Cardoso fought for and won a constitutional amendment permitting the immediate reelection of executives.[7]

To draw attention to these four "institutional moments" does not imply that institutional issues receded at other times. Rather, these four moments were simply the spikes or high-water marks of what was more or less a continuous process after 1985. The 1989–1992 period, which coincided with President Sarney's last year in office and Collor's entire short-lived administration, appears to have been the least dramatic years for two reasons. First, these years marked a period of adjustment to the new constitution. The document required numerous items of subsequent enabling legislation, plus the establishment of precedent in a few gray areas, which meant that institutional concerns were diffused across many issues and (with the partial exception of presidential decree powers) did not converge on any single one. Second, most actors believed that the major institutional controversies would surface again in 1993.

Four Arenas of Democratic Institution Building: Debates and Controversies

The most efficient way to understand the problems of institution building and relate them to democratic consolidation in Brazil is to examine the four areas that comprise the most important variables of representation and governance in any polyarchy: the system of government (in Brazil, presidentialism) and its repercussions, the electoral system, the political party system, and the national legislature. In stark contrast to the 1980s, a substantial amount of literature now exists on each of these four aspects of Brazilian politics. My discussion of each will be brief and introductory, only condensing and assessing the major insights of recent research. For more information, and for the fully nuanced arguments, the reader is referred to the works cited. As will be demonstrated, it is difficult to discuss any one of these institutional variables in isolation from the other three.

Presidentialism

Since 1985, presidential democracy has been the subject of spirited academic debate. Juan Linz's now-classic essay argues that presidential democracy is inferior to parliamentary democracy for several important reasons. Presidentialism is a winner-take-all system in which losers are excluded from power for long periods; there is no mechanism to resolve competing claims of democratic legitimacy made by the executive and the legislature; the fixed term of office means it is more difficult than under parliamentarism to replace bad governments or respond to crises; and it is generally an inflexible system in which crises of government are prone to become crises of regime, thus making presidentialism an especially unattractive option for new, untested democracies (Linz 1994; see also Shugart and Mainwaring 1997). Building on Linz, Mainwaring argued that multiparty systems tend to exacerbate the problems of presidentialism, for multipartism promotes ideological polarization, makes interparty coalition building more difficult, and contributes to immobilism in executive-legislative relations (Mainwaring 1993a, 1993b). These provocative hypotheses not only inspired a growing secondary literature (e.g., Stepan and Skach 1993; Power and Gasiorowski 1997) but were discussed publicly during a number of democratic transitions, including Brazil's (Lamounier 1994).

Unfortunately, many of the most telling criticisms of presidentialism found resonance during the first decade of Brazilian democracy. The failed first president, José Sarney, turned out to be a poster boy for parliamentary rule— Sarney would never have come to power in a parliamentary system, and as prime minister he would never have lasted the sixty months in office that he enjoyed as president. Sarney overruled economic advisers and caused the failure of the Cruzado Plan, he intervened repeatedly in the Constituent Assembly, he overtly distributed patronage to his political cronies, he backed military prerogatives against civilian demands for accountability, and he wasted most of his political capital in order to secure a presidentialist constitution and an additional year in office for himself.

Sarney was followed by the populist Fernando Collor, whose presidency did equal violence to institution building. Collor ran as an outsider whose personalistic party held only 3 percent of the seats in Congress, he antagonized elites and attempted to govern "above" the parties, he implemented a draconian stabilization plan without prior negotiation, he repeatedly abused presidential decree authority, and he was eventually impeached on corruption charges (Weyland 1993). Both presidents epitomized the neopatrimonial, unaccountable style of rule that characterizes "delegative democracy" (O'Donnell 1994).

The diagnosis of Brazilian presidentialism under Sarney, Collor, and the early Itamar Franco (1992–1994) was therefore alarming. One question is whether the problems resulted from personal qualities of these leaders, from the web of institutional incentives imposed by minority presidentialism, or from some combination of these two factors. Authors such as Sérgio Abranches (1988) and Scott Mainwaring (1993a) have emphasized the institutional setting: Brazilian presidents have lacked consistent party support in Congress, which has forced them to form and re-form cabinets and legislative coalitions on a mostly ad hoc basis, which, in turn, has led to erratic and unpredictable policy outcomes.

In a series of articles, Argelina Figueiredo and Fernando Limongi (1995a, 1996) question the idea that presidents cannot govern in such an environment. They find that presidents usually get what they want in Congress and claim that "parties matter, and presidents negotiate with parties and not with [individual] legislators and/or supraparty groups" (1996, 29), that "behavior on the legislative floor *(plenário)* is predictable and consistent" (1995a, 516), and that "minority presidents possess the means to obtain legislative support through negotiations with the parties" (1996, 33).[8]

However, their methodology of using roll-call votes suggests that their conclusions should be qualified. The traditional legislative game is played alongside at least three others: a "decree game," in which presidents legislate via iterated decrees that often spend months in a parallel universe before being put to a vote (Power 1998); an "appointment game," in which cabinet posts and other nominations are used to influence party support in Congress (Amorim Neto 1995); and a "patronage game," in which pork-barrel legislation, government concessions, president-governor relations, debt forgiveness, and other policies are "massaged" to effect the desired legislative outcome (Ames 1995b). All three games frequently entail foot-dragging, blackmail, and brinksmanship on the part of parties and individuals. The simultaneity of these games means that the nature, scope, and content of legislation may change significantly between presidential proposal and legislative ratification, and the final floor votes do not capture this dynamic. Until we have a more holistic view of executive-legislative relations in Brazil, the conclusion that legislative behavior is predictable and consistent seems a bit premature, and the environment is probably less propitious for presidents than Figueiredo and Limongi suggest.

The Afonso Arinos Commission, the Constituent Assembly, the policy failures of Sarney and Collor, the accession to power of two vice presidents in the space of seven years, the diffusion of academic critiques of presidentialism, the demonstration effect of foreign parliamentary transitions (particularly the Spanish), and the plebiscite of 1993 all ensured that the presidentialism debate was carried on nonstop. As Bolivar Lamounier (1994) has documented, the debate was somewhat bifurcated: support for parliamentarism was always stronger among various segments of the national elite (especially in the National Congress, where it enjoyed overwhelming approval) than among the mass public.[9]

Mass attitudes in the late 1980s and early 1990s did, however, move toward an increasing awareness of and support for parliamentarism, although this trend was quickly reversed when the plebiscite got under way. In their free television spots, both the Parliamentary Front and the Presidentialist

Front distorted the ideas of the opposing side, but the presidentialist propaganda was far more effective (the concept of presidentialism being more accessible to the average voter). Presidentialists charged that parliamentarism would deny voters the right to choose the head of state. This charge was irresponsible, since the Parliamentary Front actually endorsed semipresidentialism with direct election of the president, but the accusation was devastating in that the right to vote for president—absent in Brazil during two decades of military rule—had only recently been won. The plebiscite turned out to be a yawner.

A great deal of political, academic, and journalistic energy was expended between 1985 and 1993, but the debate is now over. Presidentialism triumphed. The decision may have been the wrong one (Linz and Stepan 1996, 181), but the debate should now be directed toward a different issue: how Brazilian presidentialism can be improved within the system the people elected. Most of the proposed remedies actually concern Congress, the party system, and the electoral system, but there are two outstanding issues that relate to the presidency per se. The first is the existence of the *medida provisória* (provisional measure), a kind of presidential decree that is supposed to expire after thirty days unless Congress converts it into law. Presidents view this privilege as an invaluable tool—and since 1988 they have expanded their paraconstitutional decree power—but legislators view it as abuse (Power 1998), and numerous reform proposals are being discussed, including limiting the president to one reissue of a decree.

The second main issue concerns the presidential term of office. In the ANC, Sarney had a five-year term written into the constitution; in 1994, the *Congresso Revisor* reduced the term to four years and did not alter the ban on immediate reelection. Cardoso, following a regional trend, succeeded in removing the ban in 1997 and was successfully reelected in October 1998. There are persuasive arguments on both sides of the reelection issue: those opposed claim that Brazilian executives will abuse the power of the state to secure reelection while those in favor say that a single four-year term is too short and that the possibility of reelection allows voters either to reward or to punish their leaders. After Cardoso's victory in late 1998, a number of political parties—including Cardoso's own Partido da Social Democracia Brasileira (PSDB)—expressed interest in reaching a multiparty accord that would reestablish the ban on immediate reelection.

The Electoral System

Brazilian election laws have undergone substantial change during the years of the New Republic. Suffrage is now universal, with illiterates receiving the vote in 1985 and the voting age being lowered to sixteen in 1988. Voting is compulsory for all but illiterates, sixteen- and seventeen-year-olds, and persons over seventy, and the potential electorate is now more than 100 million. In the first decade and a half of democracy, the voters had plenty of chances to exercise their rights. Direct elections for mayors of major cities were held in 1985 and for all cities in 1988, 1992, and 1996; senators, deputies, governors, and state legislators were elected in 1986, 1990, 1994, and 1998; and presidential elections were held in 1989, 1994, and 1998. Including runoffs and the 1993 plebiscite, voters in large cities could have been called to the polls as many as seventeen times between 1985 and 1998.

There are different arrangements depending on the political office in question. Presidents are now elected in a two-round majoritarian system, with the top two finishers advancing to the second round. The same procedure is followed in electing governors and mayors of the largest cities, but senators are still elected in first-past-the-post contests. These arrangements are mostly noncontroversial, but the electoral system used for the Chamber of Deputies (that is, 513 of the 594 national legislative seats) and for state assemblies has generated heated debate in the New Republic.

In most proportional-representation (PR) systems, parties present closed and ranked lists of candidates for a given number of available seats, and the voters choose from the names on the party lists. Seats are awarded to the parties according to the proportion of votes received. In the Brazilian variant of PR, known as "open-list PR," parties do not rank their candidates, and the electorate votes for individuals rather than for parties.[10] The individual votes are totaled to determine the number of seats won by each party (or coalition of parties), and the election of a given candidate depends upon his or her performance in relation to other members of the same party or coalition.

There are several implications of this system. First, when there is no party list, the role of the party organizations is weak. The system promotes intraparty as much as interparty competition, and individualism predominates over programmatic concerns (Mainwaring 1991). After election, legislators are likely to behave in a undisciplined manner because they do not feel that they owe their mandate to their party (Power 1997a). Although legislators frequently represent informal bailiwicks or nonterritorial constituencies (Ames 1995a, 1995b), they are all elected at large within the states, which means there is substantial confusion regarding the identifiability and accountability of the elected representatives. Laws that permit coalitions of parties to run more candidates than the number of seats available further distort the process, as they make it difficult for all candidates to have access to free television time and for voters finally to settle on a single candidate (Nicolau 1993, 108). The confusion results in huge numbers of blank and spoiled ballots, approaching 40 percent of all votes cast (Power and Roberts 1995). In sum, open-list PR appears to weaken the parties, undermine linkages of accountability, and alienate voters.

The prospect of reform has sparked a growing literature on electoral systems in Brazil.[11] The main alternatives to the current system are: party-list PR, which would reduce electoral personalism and strengthen the role of party organizations; the single-member district plurality (SMDP) system, used in the United Kingdom and the United States, which increases identifiability and accountability; and the German-style mixed-member proportional (MMP) system, which combines elements of both PR and SMDP but retains the proportionality principle overall. The German system has consistently won the most support from the elites in Brazil. In 1997, 56.3 percent of the federal legislators supported the mixed system, 34.8 percent supported PR, and only 8.9 percent supported SMDP.[12] However, when asked, If Brazil maintains a system of proportional representation, would you prefer that the order of candidates on the list be determined by the party, or would you prefer an open list (as exists now)? some 64.5 percent of respondents preferred the open-list variant of PR.[13] This result strongly suggests that if the mixed system is imported from Germany, the proportional side of it will likely be adapted to the Brazilian tradition of electoral individualism.[14]

If the current open-list PR system is so vilified, why hasn't it been changed before now? The explanation lies partly in missed opportunities and partly in collective action problems. Departure from the status quo generates tremendous uncertainty among politicians, and the leftist parties and small parties fear that their candidates may not be competitive in single-member districts (as is the case in the United States). They also fear that opening the door to electoral reform could pave the way for the adoption of a German-style electoral threshold, which would exclude small parties from the Congress. Candidates whose vote-getting patterns are spatially dispersed, such as media personalities, or who have nonterritorial constituencies, like Pentecostal ministers (Ames 1995a), are understandably fearful of single-member districts. There is generalized uncertainty about how district lines would be drawn and to whose advantage. Finally, although candidates may favor alternative systems in the abstract, they may balk when it comes to tampering with a system that, despite all its defects, at least got them elected the last time around.

Apart from open-list PR, there are three other aspects of the current electoral system that have generated controversy in the New Republic. The first is a set of incentives conducive to extreme multipartism—these are discussed in the next section in the context of the party system. The second is the scandalous disproportionality in the distribution of seats in the Chamber of Deputies, for the smaller states are overwhelmingly overrepresented while São Paulo—the most populous—is underrepresented by some forty or so deputies. In 1989, for instance, the vote of one inhabitant of Roraima was worth that of thirty-three residents of the state of São Paulo (Nicolau 1992, 229).

Because the small states have a built-in majority in Congress, this situation is virtually unalterable.[15]

The third issue of note is compulsory voting. The growing weariness of so many elections and the mounting totals of invalid votes have led to calls to make voting voluntary. Elite views on this issue appear to be deeply personal and do not overlap with any obvious cleavage within the Brazilian political class.[16] In the 1990s, however, there was a slowly growing acceptance of voluntary voting, and that policy may well be adopted in the near future. Recent elections and polling data suggest that this change could have important political implications, for under voluntary voting, the "effective" electorate would likely be more educated and urban, which would weaken traditional conservatives and populists and possibly strengthen the left and center-left.[17] But the decline in participation would be undesirable from the perspective of normative democratic theory (Lijphart 1997).

The Political Party System

Of all the institutional variables in Brazil, it is the party system that has generated the greatest dissatisfaction and the loudest calls for reform, for Brazil is an extraordinary case of party weakness.[18] In a comparative study of twelve Latin American party systems, Scott Mainwaring and Timothy Scully (1995) used four main variables to measure the comparative degree of system institutionalization: the stability of patterns of party competition, the depth of partisan roots in society, the degree of legitimacy accorded to parties in determining who governs, and the cohesiveness of party organizations. Brazil received the lowest possible score on three of the four indicators, and the composite index of its party institutionalization placed it near the bottom in Latin America (Mainwaring and Scully 1995, 17).

The main problems usually cited in Brazil are the degree of party system fragmentation and the internal weakness of the parties, and to a large extent, these problems are a product of the permissive electoral system. There is no national electoral threshold, and multiparty alliances are permitted, so it is easy for small parties to attain representation in Congress. In combination with the predominantly regional and local bases of Brazilian politics (Hagopian 1996), the low barriers to party formation encourage the emergence of parochial, personalistic, and machine-based parties. Open-list PR is fratricidal, and the electoral system contains other features that weaken the authority of party leaders over their candidates (Mainwaring 1991). The practice of party switching is rampant among elected officials (Nicolau 1996a, 1996b; Schmitt and Araujo 1997). Party fidelity was abolished in 1985 and is now voluntary; the only major party that now practices it voluntarily is the PT (Keck 1992; Figueiredo and Limongi 1995a).

To some extent, the permissiveness of party and electoral rules is a reaction against the former military dictatorship, which forced politicians to join "artificial" parties and imposed draconian fidelity rules (Power 1997a). But there is now a widespread consensus that the reformers overcompensated in instituting such a permissive environment. The number of parties represented in Congress increased from five in 1983 to eleven in 1987 to nineteen in 1991, and approximately one in three federal legislators switched parties in the 1987–1991 and 1991–1995 legislative sessions. President Collor's party was a piece of personalistic fiction, President Franco did not belong to one, and electoral volatility is staggering in comparative perspective (Coppedge 1995; Mainwaring and Scully 1995). For all these reasons and more, party system reform has been under constant discussion since the late 1980s.

Despite the well-known reputation and defects of the Brazilian parties, it is important to remember that they are not all alike, nor are they irrelevant. Antiparty orientations are much stronger on the right and in the center while the smaller leftist parties exhibit far greater degrees of internal cohesion and discipline (Mainwaring forthcoming 1999). The PT in particular is impressively organized (Keck 1992), and even the catch-all parties do at times behave like parties. Barry Ames (1994) demonstrated the importance of local party networks in the 1989 presidential election, and Figueiredo and Limongi (1995a, 1996) have shown that parties do have consistent ideological profiles in legislative voting. Parties do matter, but they could clearly matter more.

The main remedy for the party system, as suggested earlier, would be an overhaul of the electoral system that would remove some of the main antiparty incentives. In June 1995, apparently believing that Congress was too distracted by Cardoso's economic agenda to concern itself with political and electoral reform, the independent Supreme Electoral Tribunal (TSE) took the unprecedented step of announcing its own package of party-strengthening proposals. These included a German-style mixed electoral system with a national threshold, a return to party fidelity, and sanctions against politicians who change parties. This sweeping agenda was never viable in toto, but it did stimulate legislative debate, and three months later, Congress passed a new political parties statute (Law 9096 of September 19, 1995) that contained several minireforms.

As a result of that law, parties can no longer be legally chartered without demonstrating national penetration *(caráter nacional)*, which is defined as the winning of at least 0.5 percent of the national vote for the Chamber of Deputies (with at least 0.1 percent in one-third of the states). This requirement is still permissive in comparative terms, but it will eliminate some of the *legendas de aluguel* (literally, "parties for rent") that spring up at every election and award their nominations in exchange for money or votes. To win official recognition in Congress *(funcionamento parlamentar)* which is necessary for leadership and committee privileges, parties must now win 5 percent of the national vote with at least 2 percent in one-third of the states. Legislators who switch parties will now automatically lose their parliamentary privileges (but not their seat). As for party fidelity, the new law authorizes sanctions against transgressors but does not make those sanctions mandatory.

Although this law does not go nearly as far as the original TSE proposals, it does represent an advance over the extreme permissiveness in the party and electoral arenas that prevailed between 1985 and 1995 (Porto 1995). But there is a limit to how far Brazilian politicians will go in delegating power to parties: even if the mixed electoral system is adopted, which now appears to be likely in the near future, the proportional side will probably remain open-list. The two key remaining reforms are the ones that the TSE proposed and Congress ignored: party fidelity and a national vote threshold for legislative representation. But such a threshold would have little effect on party fragmentation if the law maintains the current practice of allowing multiparty alliances in PR elections (Nicolau 1993, 108). As Cardoso's proposed political reform amendments are only now taking shape, it is too early to speculate on these provisions. In the meantime, however, most Brazilian observers continue to believe that the party system as currently constituted can effectively neither represent or govern.

The National Legislature

The final institutional arena to be discussed is the National Congress. If it is difficult to discuss any one of the four institutional arenas in isolation, this problem is perhaps most obvious in the case of the national legislature. The Brazilian Congress is in many ways a product of the three foregoing variables: presidentialism, the electoral system, and the party system.[19]

On balance, the performance of the National Congress was disappointing during the first decade of democracy. The one major exception to this was in the Collorgate scandal of 1992 when Congress demonstrated impressive competence in amassing evidence of Collor's corruption, removing him from office, and swearing in his successor—all in a democratic and constitutional manner (Weyland 1993). Apart from this moment of glory, however, Congress has received poor marks. The complaints are many but can mostly be reduced to one basic concept: inefficiency. Congress is slow and unproductive, and most (approximately 75 percent) of the legislation it eventually approves originates in the executive branch.

The inefficiency derives from both external and internal factors. The dominant presidency and the abuse of decree power mean that Congress is saturated with a legislative agenda that is not really its own. Its internal agility is handicapped by the internal weakness of the larger parties, which in turn results from the electoral system. Legislators themselves are the product of this electoral system, and as such they often tend toward extreme individualism. These factors cause inefficiency, which in turn causes executive impatience, which in turn causes presidents to use decree authority and divide-and-conquer strategies. Prior to the Cardoso government, which is adept at negotiation and has achieved undeniable successes in economic reforms since 1995, executive-legislative relations took the form of a vicious circle.

Congress has routinely been excoriated by frustrated presidents, but it is also true that legislators themselves are dissatisfied. Academic research and public symposia on the Brazilian Congress (CEBRAP 1994; Abreu and Dias 1995) have shed light on some of the reasons for parliamentary dissatisfaction. These range from the media (perceived as hostile and unfair), to internal rules, to the inevitably oligarchical power structures in the two chambers, to the city of Brasília itself. A valuable insight is offered by Figueiredo and Limongi (1994a, 1994b, 1995b), who have argued that politics in the New Republic has featured two simultaneous and competing national agendas. The agenda of the executive branch has been macroeconomic stabilization; the agenda of the National Congress has been social action. This bifurcation is especially dissatisfying for legislators because the executive agenda always takes precedence: the president either gets what he wants (Figueiredo and Limongi 1995b) or at the very least, dominates the legislative calendar (Power 1998). The profound individualism of Brazilian legislators (Mainwaring 1991; Novaes 1994; Ames 1995b) leads to collective action problems that intensify this perception of powerlessness.

It is important to recall that Congress has a dual image: it is the outstanding symbol of popular sovereignty in any democratic regime, but it is also the symbol of the political class. The image of the political class impacts the image of Congress, and vice versa, and in Brazil, as polling results consistently show, both images are overwhelmingly negative. Whatever capital Congress gained through its handling of Collorgate was lost a year later when a scandal involving the Budget Committee ended in the expulsion of eighteen legislators. Congress's approval rating is consistently low, and support is lowest among the young and college-educated citizens.

The crisis of Congress is not merely an abstract issue of institutional design, for it has important implications for democratic legitimation. Support for the legislature is clearly associated with support for the regime. In a survey conducted in 1993, José Álvaro Moisés (1994) found that citizens' evaluation of the performance of the National Congress was the second-best predictor of overall satisfaction with democracy, which he found to be low (see also Linz and Stepan 1996). The only stronger independent variable, among the two dozen he tested, was the approval rating given to the incumbent government of Itamar Franco. This is an interesting finding, because normally one would expect a more instrumental evaluation of democracy, one based on individual-level economic satisfaction, as in the "specific support" concept of political culture theory. The centrality of the National Congress in Brazilians' assessment of the political order suggests that institutions "matter" not only in constitutional design but also on the broader plane of symbolism and legitimation.

Unlike the other three institutional arenas, there is no obvious reform agenda for Congress that is properly an internal, legislative matter. Rather, the renaissance of the Brazilian Congress depends more than anything on exogenous variables, including the curbing of presidential powers (especially decree authority), the reduction of party fragmentation and the strengthening of party organizations, and the adoption of an electoral system that would restructure political recruitment to attract less-individualistic, more-accountable politicians to the national parliament.

Brazil 1985–1999:
A Decade and More of Dysfunctional Institutions

Brazil spent the first fifteen years of democracy in a virtually continuous debate about the design of its political institutions, and three initial observations can be made. First, many of the main national political institutions are dysfunctional: they have objective deficiencies that have been pointed out repeatedly not only by academic political scientists but also by the politicians who use and inhabit these institutions. Second, debate over how to redesign these institutions consumed an extraordinary amount of political energy in the early years of democracy, and third, reform was minimal in relation to the energy expended. These observations in turn generate three concluding questions. If there is so much dissatisfaction with current institutional arrangements, why has there been so little change? What are the implications of underdeveloped and/or suboptimal political institutions? and Where does Brazil go from here?

As for the first question, institution building was clearly relegated to a secondary place in the first two to three years of the New Republic, a crucial time for any democracy. In a clear case of overcompensation against the confining party and electoral laws of the military dictatorship, the politicians gave high priority to tearing down authoritarian-era institutions that impinged on their personal freedom and less thought to building sustainable replacements. Having been excluded from most of the powerful executive posts for two decades, the politicians were intent on reoccupying the state apparatus and wielding state power. Within several years, the newly permissive institutional environment became difficult to reform, as many entrenched interests—especially personalists, populists, members of small conservative parties, and members of the large catch-all parties—came to prefer the status quo. The new democracy quickly spawned what Douglas Chalmers (1977) called a "politicized state," a political system in which political institutions are viewed instrumentally. This is an environment in which mutual mistrust of motivations leads to collective action problems, and in which institutional reform—if it occurs—is likely to be characterized by incrementalism and re-crimination. The *Congresso Revisor*—which was obstructed, postponed, and then died with business still pending—is a prime example of such an environment.

The second question concerns the costs of delayed institutionalization. Were there any such costs? Without specificity in this regard, the problem of weak institutions in Brazil could become a "cause in search of an effect," so it is necessary to ask what problems in the New Republic can reasonably be attributed to political institutions. We do not have to look very far to see the causal effects. One could cite the comparatively weak legitimacy of democracy in Brazil (Linz and Stepan 1996), which seems causally related to the dismal public image of the political parties and Congress (Moisés 1994, 1995). Or one could cite the failure of Congress to enable *(regulamentar)* many of the important articles of the 1988 constitution. One could also cite failures and delays on many substantive reforms—including agrarian reform and the updating of labor legislation (Hagopian and Mainwaring 1987), taxation, and social policy (Weyland 1996a)—many of which are traceable to unstable legislative coalitions or to high turnover at the ministerial level.

However, as Peter Kingstone demonstrates in Chapter 9, the best evidence of the effects of weak institutions is found in macroeconomic performance. Economic management in 1985–1994 was a slide into near collapse, a slide punctuated by seven failed stabilization plans. During this period, Brazil had the world's highest cumulative inflation rate, personal incomes were stagnant or declined, and growth was negative in the 1990–1992 years. Most diagnoses of the Brazilian disease pointed to the lack of political conditions for macroeconomic stabilization, and analysts began to speak of a crisis of governability. The weak party system and the inefficient Congress seemed to preclude the building of the kind of political and societal support that would be necessary for stabilization and renewed growth.

Fernando Henrique Cardoso's adroit implementation of the *Plano Real* in 1994 showed that the crisis could be tamed by negotiation, enlightened leadership, and patience; however, eight years of potential progress had been lost. And when inflation was brought under control in 1994–1995, the executive simply turned its attention to other macroeconomic issues, not to issues of political institution building. The focus shifted from short-term economic stabilization to long-term economic reform via constitutional amendment in a prolonged effort to rid the constitution of many of its statist provisions. This is the sad irony of the "permanent *Constituinte.*" Most of the political capital in 1987–1988 was spent in the making of a new constitution; in the 1990s, most of the political capital was spent trying to unmake the same document.

Concerning the third question—Where does Brazil go from here?—what are the prospects for reform of the main national political institutions? Speculation is difficult. On the positive side, in both academic and political circles there is heightened sensitivity to the importance of institution building, and sustainable democracy is now seen as being contingent on reforms of the party and electoral systems. There is evidence, for example, that in the 1990s, politicians modified their attitudes and became more favorable to party-strengthening reforms (Power 1997a). Also on the positive side, the advent of moderate economic growth with low inflation may provide a more hospitable environment for political engineering. But it remains to be seen whether the Cardoso government and legislative reformers will seize this window of opportunity. In 1995 and 1996, economic reforms drove the national agenda, and in 1997, the reelection amendment was added. A package of institutional reforms (the *reforma política*, in current parlance) slowly took shape via consultations among the government, the Congress, and the TSE. But reelection, social security, administrative and other constitutional amendments had higher priority, so the *reforma política* was postponed to Cardoso's second term. The postponement of institutional reforms, which has occurred previously in the New Republic, has rarely led to much that is good.

In an interview published in *Jornal do Brasil* on September 9, 1998, shortly before his reelection victory, Cardoso admitted that if the *reforma política*—especially party fidelity—had been approved prior to the third year of his first term in office, his package of macroeconomic constitutional reforms would have moved much more quickly through Congress. The president conceded: "I wish I had been able to finish the [economic] reforms some time ago. We should have dedicated ourselves more to the approval of the *reforma política.* Now we see clearly that it was fundamental for the passage of the [other] reforms we were trying to make. . . . We cannot continue with a truncated electoral system, with weak parties."

Another reason to maintain low expectations about the *reforma política* should by now be clear: there are important interrelationships among the main variables of institutional design. Reform of the party system depends on reform of the electoral system; the willingness of presidents to surrender legislative prerogatives depends on the increased efficiency of Congress; congressional reform, in turn, depends in part on a reduction in party fragmentation and alteration of political recruitment patterns; and so on. Because all of these variables are linked, an effective package of institutional reform would have to address all of these arenas *simultaneously*, a challenging task. But if there is a master key to all the various doors of the *reforma política*, it probably lies in electoral system reform, which—if it successfully attacked the corrosive effects of open-list proportional representation—would quickly reverberate throughout the institutional architecture of Brazilian democracy.

Supporters of Brazilian democracy must guard against complacency. In the years that Fernando Henrique Cardoso has dominated Brazilian politics, his impressive leadership skills and the resulting economic turnaround have caused "the G-word"—governability—virtually to disappear from the political lexicon. That is a mistake. It is undeniable that beginning in 1995, the president has stitched together a working political majority and has won major victories in (macroeconomic) constitutional reform. But the underlying political structures are no different than they were in 1993, when Brazil had apparently reached the end of its rope and rumors of a coup abounded (Linz and Stepan 1996, 178). Without deep and meaningful reform of the national political institutions, Cardoso's governing majority remains a house of cards—one that has been built over the fault lines sketched above. The lost decade of economic development may be over, but the lost decade of institutional development has now gone into overtime.

TWO

The Brazilian State in the New Democracy

Kurt Weyland

ow has Brazil's transition to democracy affected its state?[1] This question is of great importance given the crucial role that the state has played in the country's economic, social, and political development. Did democratization help institutionalize the state and make it more autonomous from established social forces, or did it further corrode the internal unity and undermine the strength of the state? In the theoretical debate on this issue, scholars have advanced divergent conjectures. Some authors expect a democratic transition to turn the state into a more autonomous and powerful Leviathan while others foresee a Gulliver tied down by an ever denser web of particularistic links to narrow social groupings.

The first set of arguments claims that democratization gives the state a higher level of institutionalization, makes its organizational apparatus more cohesive, and makes it more autonomous from powerful social classes and groups. Democracy enhances the transparency of decision making, for intensified control by civil society induces state officials to assume a more unified posture and refrain from constant bureaucratic infighting (Hintze 1981, 142–56). Increased accountability also eliminates the shady influences that private groupings commonly exert on the state under authoritarian rule, and since democratization opens up channels of interest representation for mass actors, it also makes political participation less skewed in social terms. The affirmation of political equality permits the "popular" sectors to demonopolize the access of privileged groups to the state. As a result, the state achieves more autonomy from dominant groups and classes and greater internal unity.[2]

Democratization may also strengthen the state by turning politicians away from clientelism. When electoral politics continue under authoritarian rule, as in Brazil, politicians are excluded from policy decisions and remain confined to winning support by advancing demands for special favors to the state bureaucracy. With democratization, politicians regain the power to make central policy decisions. They may therefore come to care more about program issues than about special favors. This turn away from clientelism allows state agencies to fulfill their administrative tasks without the constant interference of scores of patronage-hungry politicians. It also enables the public bureaucracy to institute more merit-based recruitment and promotion systems, which improve the competence of state officials and enhance the cohesion of the state apparatus.

Other authors, by contrast, expect democratization to corrode the state's cohesion and autonomy by allowing interest organizations and clientelistic politicians to enhance their influence and capture public agencies. According to this view, the extension of rights of democratic participation favors privileged social groups, who take better advantage of the new opportunities and further increase their influence in and on the state. Indeed, to the extent that "popular" sectors gain influence, state cohesion diminishes even more. Instead of balancing elite influence and thus giving the state greater autonomy, popular sector groups capture state agencies that affect their special interests and use them for their own benefit, often to the detriment of their less well-off brethren (Malloy 1987). Rather than making the state more cohesive, this diversification of outside influences exacerbates "bureaucratic politics."

Furthermore, democratization may extend clientelism, not eliminate it. The unfulfilled basic needs of many poor people, the long-standing weakness of political parties, and the persistent control of technocrats over crucial public decisions may induce clientelistic politicians to retain their principal strategy of political sustenance (Mainwaring 1992–1993, esp. 691–706; also see Weber 1976, 839–64). The requirements of electoral competition may prompt even politicians who had previously not relied on patronage to adopt clientelistic tactics, and the increased number of patronage-hungry politicians may cause a takeover of public agencies that had before been shielded from clientelistic machinations. Such a proliferation of clientelism further corrodes the internal unity and administrative capacity of the state (O'Donnell 1993).

Which of these divergent conjectures accounts better for the evolution of the Brazilian state since the return of democracy? In this chapter, I advance a dialectical argument that combines the two opposing viewpoints.[3] Initially, the trend toward a further erosion of state autonomy and capacity predominated, yet this deterioration of the state exacerbated Brazil's economic and political problems, discredited established sociopolitical forces, fueled popular discontent, and allowed reformers to win presidential office. The crisis, which was aggravated by the initial decline of the state, thus triggered a response that has produced an uneven and halting, yet noticeable, resurrection of state capacity. By facilitating the expression of discontent and by allowing reformers to win strong electoral mandates, democracy itself has been crucial to this trend reversal.

Further State Corrosion Under the Sarney Government

Toward the end of military rule, the Brazilian state resembled a "divided Leviathan" (Abranches 1978). Even while intervening in vast areas of the economy and society and thus having tremendous importance as a structure, the force of the state as an actor diminished,[4] and it was becoming ever less capable of attaining its goals. The very growth of the state apparatus, which had accelerated under military rule (1964–1985), made internal coordination and central control more and more difficult (Weyland 1998). As a larger number of public agencies had overlapping responsibilities, squabbling and infighting (bureaucratic politics) became endemic and undermined state cohesion. The state agencies involved in these conflicts often sought support from powerful interest groups, especially business sectors (other social sectors, especially those of lower status, had minimal access to the state). State agencies and officials therefore established innumerable links to business groups, both through associational and personalistic channels, or "bureaucratic rings" (F. Cardoso 1975, 181–84, 206–9). All these internal divisions and outside connections increasingly weakened the state (O. Lima and Abranches 1987).

Furthermore, clientelistic politicians penetrated many public agencies. They managed to have their cronies appointed to administrative positions, and those cronies then used their influence over resource allocation to channel benefits to their patron's followers and withhold them from the supporters of his adversaries. This clientelistic interference made the politically appointed public officials indebted to and dependent upon nonstate actors and thus weakened the bureaucratic hierarchy and undermined the internal cohesion of the state apparatus. Although many public agencies with economic responsibilities were shielded from clientelistic penetration, it pervaded the government's social agencies.

Did democratization prompt the Brazilian state to acquire greater autonomy and strength, or did it reinforce the tendencies toward fragmentation and capture that had been at work under the military regime? During the early years of the incipient democracy (1985–1990), fragmentation and capture clearly were the predominant trends. As clientelistic politicians, "rent-

seeking" interest groups, and patronage-hungry local and regional governments enhanced their clout, the autonomy and institutional capacity of the
Brazilian state diminished.

In the emerging democracy, clientelism did not decline; on the contrary,
it expanded (Hagopian 1996; Mainwaring 1992–1993). The long-standing
weakness of political parties and the control of technocrats over crucial policy
decisions induced politicians to focus, not on program debates, but mostly
on their own political survival. Because of the poverty and low educational
level of many of the voters (exacerbated by the extension of suffrage to
illiterates in 1985), the distribution of small-scale benefits continued to yield
considerable electoral dividends. As traditional politicians kept using
clientelistic means, representatives of the former opposition who had been
excluded from patronage under the authoritarian regime felt an irresistible
incentive to adopt the same means as their competitors (O'Donnell 1988).
As a result, a larger number of politicians with more diverse orientations
now came to beleaguer the state with incessant demands for patronage. This
extension of clientelism undermined the administrative competence and internal unity of the state in several ways.

The heightened demand for clientelistic benefits hindered recruitment
and promotion based on merit in state agencies and public enterprises that
had previously been shielded from clientelistic interference, and to control
patronage, clientelistic politicians sought to nominate their cronies to public
posts. The military regime had shielded parts of the state from such pressure
to ensure competent administration, but with the return of democracy,
intensified clientelistic competition broke down many of the barriers. The
Ministry of Social Security, for instance, which had been administered by
technocrats under the government of Ernesto Geisel (1974–1979), relied
more and more on "political" appointments during the democratization process.[5] Similarly, politicians captured Telebrás, the state telephone company,
during the Sarney administration (1985–1990).

Furthermore, a wider range of political forces managed to win clientelistic
appointments under the incipient democracy. While ideological commitment
is low among most Brazilian politicians, this increased political diversity exacerbated conflicts inside and among state agencies. For instance, the more
conservative wing of the PMDB, the main government party, controlled the
Health Ministry during much of the Sarney government, whereas its more
progressive element dominated the Ministry of Social Security. This difference intensified the unending conflicts over the administration of health
care, responsibility for which was shared by both ministries. This power
struggle triggered the Ministério da Previdência e Assistência Social's (MPAS)
rash, unprepared decision in 1987 to decentralize health care, which caused
innumerable complications in later years (Weyland 1995, 1705–6). Thus,

the diversification of clientelism hindered competent public administration.

These clientelistic conflicts came to pervade the whole state apparatus, and in order to regulate tensions, politicians negotiated formal agreements concerning the distribution of spoils. In this way, factions of the two main governing parties (PMDB and Partido da Frente Liberal [PFL]) appointed a vast range of public servants, from top officials to low-ranking staff members. For instance, the right to nominate the representative of the social security system who controlled the distribution of benefits in outlying areas fell to the parliamentarian who had gained the highest vote in each of those areas and who had voted for the winning ticket in the electoral college in January 1985.[6] Since the concession of social benefits was crucial for "buying" votes, these representatives frequently departed from administrative guidelines and committed innumerable irregularities in order to favor their clientelistic patrons.

In general, the people who owed their public positions to clientelistic machinations were much more accountable to their political benefactors than to their bureaucratic superiors. In addition to fueling conflicts inside public agencies, clientelistic appointments thus undermined the administrative hierarchy, and heads of agencies were often unable to guarantee the execution of their orders. For instance, the social security minister lacked effective control over the agency in charge of health care—which he was officially supposed to supervise—because he had little influence over the nomination of the agency's head. Both the minister and the agency head wasted much time and energy in the power struggle that this unclear line of authority provoked (Weyland 1995, 1706).

In sum, the extension of clientelism under the new democracy further undermined the internal unity of the state, subjected it to innumerable outside forces, and weakened its capacity to attain its own goals.[7] Rampant clientelism also led to a considerable waste of resources and caused a dramatic increase in expenditures. For instance, the federal government's spending for personnel exploded from 2.5 percent of the gross domestic product (GDP) in 1986 to 4.5 percent in 1989.[8]

At the same time, democratization did not eliminate the connections that business groups and some professional associations had established to state agencies and officials. Rather than counterbalancing these influences and thus giving the state greater autonomy, popular sector groups tried to capture those public agencies that most affected their own special interests. The return of democracy thus did not draw a clear borderline between state and society; on the contrary, it led to a more profound penetration of the state by social groupings.

Many of the bureaucratic rings that linked business sectors to state officials survived the regime transition or were re-created quickly. Lower-level bureaucrats who had served the authoritarian regime often retained important public posts in the incipient democracy, and many of the newly recruited top officials had fairly close ties to business groups. Even in some of the best-organized and most merit-based agencies, such as the Brazilian revenue service (the Secretaria da Receita Federal [SRF]), business people maintained the dense network of personal contacts that they had established under the military regime. This privileged access enabled entrepreneurs to influence decision making and implementation and thus win special favors.[9] Contrary to the democratic ideal of openness, these shady connections endured in the emerging democracy and continued to corrode state autonomy and capacity.

The recruitment of new state officials and the end of authoritarian restrictions on interest associations produced a diversification of these outside connections. Some of the new public servants had links to professional organizations or to popular sector groups that had lacked influence under the military regime. Nonelite sectors also took advantage of the end of authoritarian rule to put pressure on the state, and some of these associations achieved significant influence in certain issue areas. Trade unions, for instance, became a factor to be reckoned with in labor policy, and newly emerging, very active organizations of pensioners gained a say in social security policy.

Only in some areas, however, did these popular sector organizations counterbalance business influence and enhance the autonomy of state agencies. In health care, for instance, public officials had a very cozy relationship with private providers and profit-seeking hospitals under the military regime (Cordeiro 1984), but under the Sarney government, the recruitment of new, more progressive public servants and the increased activism of professional associations and popular sector movements broke some of these bureaucratic rings. As a result, the agency in charge of health care (the Instituto Nacional de Assistência Médica da Previdência Social [INAMPS]) gained the capacity to design redistributive health reform (Weyland 1995, 1702–8). The execution of such change, however, was greatly hindered by the connections that private groups retained with the lower levels of the bureaucratic hierarchy.[10] Thus, even in this case, state autonomy increased little and only for a short period of time.

More often, the expanding connections of professional associations and popular sector groupings did not strengthen the state but instead led to its further cannibalization. As outside links multiplied and diversified, public officials encountered more fetters on their activities than before, and tensions inside the state apparatus grew. For instance, the connections that pensioners' associations—mostly of the better-off sectors—established with the Ministry of Social Security hindered the pursuit of reforms benefiting the poorest groups and fueled conflicts with the Finance Ministry, which sought to limit public spending.

These outside links—especially the continuing connections of business groups to state agencies and officials—allowed special interests to increase state spending on their behalf and to limit resource extraction. For instance, expenditures for goods and services that the federal government bought from private contractors skyrocketed from 3.1 percent of the GDP in 1985 to 5 percent in 1989 (Varsano 1996, 4). At the same time, tax evasion—often facilitated by collusion between entrepreneurs and state officials—increased dramatically, as is indicated by the growth in the share of cash in M1 from 21 percent in 1985 to 39 percent in 1990.[11] The resulting loss of resources contributed to the reduction in the federal government's tax revenues from 7.8 percent of GDP in 1985 to 6.7 percent in 1989.[12] During the same years, public sector borrowing requirements rose from 1.2 percent of GDP to 4.3 percent (Varsano 1996, 7).[13] Thus, the connections between state officials and rent-seeking interest groups—combined with the extension of clientelism—exacerbated the severe fiscal problems that the Brazilian state was suffering as a result of the debt crisis.[14]

The revival of federalism further reduced the internal unity of the Brazilian state and aggravated its financial difficulties. Rather than leading to functional specialization and allowing the national government to concentrate on basic policy decisions, the move toward decentralization unleashed innumerable political conflicts and weakened the central state. Brazil's gradual regime transition, which avoided direct presidential elections for a long time, exacerbated this shift in power from the national to subnational governments. From early 1983 to early 1990, elected state governors confronted a president who lacked the legitimacy bestowed by direct popular election. This democratic deficit made it more difficult for the central government to resist the pressure of state governors and city mayors for the devolution of power and resources.[15]

As a result, Brazil's incipient democracy underwent drastic decentralization. Above all, the new constitution, promulgated in 1988, mandated a reduction of the federal government's share in total tax revenues from 43 percent in 1987 to 35.2 percent in 1993 while raising the shares of the state and municipal governments from 38.7 percent to 41.2 percent and from 18.3 percent to 23.6 percent, respectively (Rosa 1988, 118). Since this dramatic resource shift was not accompanied by a similar devolution of administrative responsibilities, it exacerbated the fiscal crisis of the federal government. To lower its expenditures, in 1989 the national government sought to devolve some of its routine tasks to the state and municipal levels *(operação desmonte)* but without any success (Bomfim and Shah 1994, 536, 539). The central state also attempted to reverse the revenue shift through technical tricks and later on, constitutional reform. All of these efforts led to innumerable conflicts, which further diminished the efficacy of the state.

In a context of low political accountability, the dispersal of power resulting from democratization also produced an increase in corruption. Whereas under military rule it was sufficient for business people to buy off officials in the executive branch, under democracy legislative politicians and agents of state and municipal governments, who gained significant influence over the allocation of public resources, also demanded "their share." As a result, the "going rates" of bribes rose from 8–12 percent of the value of public works contracts under the military regime to 15–20 percent under the Sarney government.[16]

In sum, democratization further reduced the autonomy of the Brazilian state from interest groups and clientelistic politicians, undermined its internal unity, and diminished its capacity to attain its goals. The Brazilian state increasingly resembled Gulliver, tied down by innumerable particularistic links to narrow social and political groupings. Yet instead of keeping the state prostrate, these problems paradoxically prompted efforts to rebuild and fortify the state.

State Reform by Imposition?
President Collor's Eventual Political Failure

The further deterioration of state capacity under democracy aggravated the acute economic problems that Brazil was suffering owing to a debt crisis and the exhaustion of import-substitution industrialization. Servicing the country's external obligations created an enormous fiscal drain, and the above-mentioned increase in budget spending and the simultaneous reduction in tax revenues intensified Brazil's financial crisis. These fiscal problems, in turn, fueled inflation and undermined several attempts at economic stabilization. As a result of all these difficulties, Brazil slid into a deep crisis in the late 1980s, marked especially by skyrocketing inflation rates of 981 percent in 1988 and 1,973 percent in 1989.

In the context of advanced democratization, this crisis prompted bold rescue efforts that were designed to stop further deterioration and put Brazil back on a path toward development. In the presidential election of late 1989, a majority of the citizens rejected established politicians and voted for outsiders who promised to turn the country around. The candidates of the two main government parties, the PMDB's Ulysses Guimarães and the PFL's Aureliano Chaves, won a meager 4.4 percent and 0.8 percent of the vote, respectively. The two most successful candidates were Fernando Collor de Mello, a young, brash upstart with few connections to the national political elite, and Luiz Inácio Lula da Silva, the leader of the socialist Workers' Party (Partido dos Trabalhadores [PT]), the greatest novelty in Brazil's party system (Keck 1992). The eventual winner, Collor, deliberately depicted himself as a newcomer who would embark on a sweeping housecleaning, moralize politics by combating favoritism and corruption, and save the country from its severe economic problems.

In a crisis situation, democratization thus permitted the accession to power of a bold outsider—something that would have been virtually impossible under authoritarian rule.[17] The regime transition also allowed the socialist left to grow and almost win the presidency. This threat indebted middle- and upper-class groups to Collor and initially gave the new president a free hand to pursue his own reform agenda. In these ways, the return of democracy opened the path for efforts to address Brazil's severe economic problems and revamp the state.

As promised, the new president made a determined effort to end Brazil's deep crisis and put the country back on the track toward development. Immediately upon taking office, Collor imposed the most drastic stabilization plan in Brazil's history, confiscating financial assets above a low limit (for savings accounts, approximately US$ 1,300 at the official exchange rate) for eighteen months. In addition, Collor initiated a wide range of structural reforms designed to give market forces freer reign. Yet while seeking to cut back state interventionism through deregulation, the privatization of public enterprises, and the dismissal of public officials, the new government in many ways sought to strengthen—not weaken—the state, precisely through a strategic retreat from excessive interventionism. Many of Collor's reforms constituted efforts at state building.[18]

For this purpose, Collor pursued a two-pronged strategy: he sought to fortify the core of the state through administrative and fiscal reform and at the same time shed peripheral areas of the state apparatus, which had been irremediably captured by social and political groupings. On the one hand, he wanted to centralize power in the presidency in order to enhance control over crucial agencies and thus increase the organizational cohesion of the state. In this way, he planned to recover the role of the state as the guiding force in Brazilian development (*Diretrizes* 1989, 10–15, 18–23). On the other hand, he sought to cut outside links that tied down the state. Since it seemed infeasible to eliminate the entrenched influence of special interests in many agencies, he wanted to privatize those agencies and thus amputate the privileged access of business sectors and professional groupings to public decision making (*Diretrizes* 1989, 17). This shrinking of the public bureaucracy was meant to reinforce, not destroy, the state. By giving up instruments of interventionism that could no longer serve to advance state goals (but instead undermined them), the nucleus of the state would gain greater autonomy and strength.

With these goals in mind, Collor initiated a sweeping administrative reform immediately after taking office. He united several ministries and incorporated others into the presidency as special secretariats. He announced the extinction of numerous state agencies, the privatization of public enterprises, and the dismissal of 360,000 of Brazil's approximately 1.5 million public officials. He also sought to clean up rule implementation, for instance, by dismissing the representatives of the social security system who were influenced by clientelistic politicians and who used their discretion to benefit their patrons.

During his first year in office, Collor also sought to keep interest groups and many clientelistic politicians at bay (Schneider 1991). In an unprecedented move, the new president's economic team did not consult with the most powerful business association, the Federação das Indústrias do Estado de São Paulo (FIESP), when drawing up the drastic stabilization plan of March 1990 (Amato 1992; Eris 1992; Kandir 1992; Mello 1995), and relations with many national business groups remained tense during the tenure of Collor's first economy minister, Zélia Cardoso de Mello (March 1990– May 1991).[19] In this way, the government cut many bureaucratic rings that had survived from military rule to democracy. This sudden exclusion, however, induced business people to seek access to decision makers through even more shady means, namely, bribes intermediated by the president's former campaign finance manager, Paulo César Farias—and it allowed Farias to raise "the going rate" of these bribes to 40–50 percent of the value of public works contracts.[20] In this way, Collor and his entourage were able to organize a huge corruption scheme, which, when discovered, would lead to the president's downfall.

In 1990, Collor also denied many petitions of clientelistic politicians for nominations to the public bureaucracy. Once again, the president sought to limit outside influences on the state in order to enhance his own control. Certainly, he followed technical criteria only in some of his appointments while nominating his own cronies and followers to many important posts. Yet for all these appointments, strict loyalty to the new president was a necessary condition. In this way, Collor sought to ensure his control over the state apparatus, making it more unified than it had been under the Sarney government.

Finally, Collor wanted to give the state a more solid resource base by raising taxes and limiting expenditures. Immediately after assuming the presidency, he enacted an emergency fiscal package that eliminated many tax breaks for important business sectors, and combined with the reduction in inflation that his stabilization plan achieved, these bold measures boosted federal tax revenues by almost 20 percent in 1990.[21] Collor also decreed strict budget austerity and instructed his economy minister to reject the pleas of special interests. By limiting spending on behalf of social groupings and clientelistic politicians and by raising revenues, Collor wanted to overcome the fiscal weakness of the state that had greatly restricted its capacity for directing Brazilian development.

Initially, Collor sought to attain all these reform goals through imposition (Power 1998; Schneider 1991). Invoking the legitimacy provided by the 35 million votes with which he had won the first direct presidential election in twenty-nine years, Collor decreed his comprehensive stabilization plan one day after taking office. Since rejecting Collor's program would have pushed Brazil into full-scale hyperinflation, Congress had no choice but to accept most of his drastic measures. Thus, the new president initially succeeded with his fait accompli strategy.

Soon, however, opposition resurfaced, and it grew stronger and stronger as Collor's efforts to eliminate inflation failed and price rises again inched up to the mark of 20 percent per month. The fact that the new president could not perform magic deflated his charismatic image. As a result, Collor's imperious style became less and less impressive and ever more annoying and, in the end, ridiculous. Clientelistic politicians and powerful social groupings, whom the president had initially kept at bay, voiced their demands for special favors in an ever more outspoken and insistent fashion. Congress, which Collor had steamrollered in the beginning, became increasingly unwilling to approve the government's controversial proposals, such as a comprehensive tax reform. The president had to make more and more concessions to these forces, for instance, by working ever more closely with the clientelistic PFL and by incorporating traditional patronage politicians into his cabinet. Thus, the obstacles that had weighed down the Sarney government rose up again and hindered Collor's efforts at rebuilding the Brazilian state.

As a result of these growing difficulties, the president's structural reform initiatives made only limited progress. Owing in part to the resistance of public employee associations,[22] which had gained great strength and assumed a militant posture under the new democracy (Boito 1991, 64–65), the privatization of public enterprises proceeded much more slowly than announced, and the Collor government managed to sell only fifteen firms, in exchange for US$ 5.874 billion (Matos and Oliveira 1996, 24). The plan to shrink the public payroll through widespread dismissals was successfully challenged in the courts and was transformed into a paid-leave policy.[23] In order to reduce expenditures, the government therefore compressed public sector salaries, which fell by approximately 40 percent from 1990 to 1992 (MARE 1996, 40). These income losses induced many well-trained, competent public officials to leave the administration, which seriously weakened the state.[24] Collor's efforts to strengthen the state thus not only failed to achieve their goals but actually backfired.

Collor's proposals for tax reform also had only fleeting success. Many of the measures enacted in March 1990 were of temporary application. After reaching 8.2 percent of GDP in 1990, federal tax revenues fell back to 6.4 percent in 1991.[25] In response to the threat of renewed public deficits, the government designed a profound overhaul of Brazil's fiscal system in order to raise more revenues from society and to regain part of the resource transfer to the state and municipal governments that had been mandated by the 1988 constitution. The idea was to strengthen the central state financially and to reduce the power and independence of the subnational governments. Advanced in different versions between early 1991 and mid-1992 (Brasil. Presidência 1991a; MEFP. CERF 1992; MEFP. SEPE 1991), this far-reaching plan always ran into insurmountable opposition.

Business associations rejected further increases in taxation and demanded instead a lowering of the fiscal burden, which raised their costs and thus weakened their competitive position vis-à-vis the newly liberated foreign imports. Clientelistic politicians defended tax breaks as well as the established social security system, whose overhaul was part of Collor's fiscal reform plan. Most important, state governors and city mayors flatly rejected any reversal of the revenue gains provided by the 1988 constitution. Their disposal of ample patronage gave them considerable influence over the congressional delegations from their domains, which they used to undermine support for the government's initiatives (Delfim 1992; J. Fernandes 1992; IEDI 1991). Since President Collor never managed to assemble a firm party coalition in support of his government, his proposals of structural tax reform were doomed to failure.

Mounting opposition blocked much of Collor's effort to revamp Brazil's development model. Since his attempts to strengthen the state jeopardized many powerful political interests, they especially made little headway. The growing sense of failure weakened the president, and his fate was sealed when evidence of massive corruption in his entourage surfaced. The president and his cronies had used their initially high degree of autonomy and distance from established interests to extract money from business groups, which were desperate to regain access to crucial policymakers. Standing in striking contrast to the president's rhetoric of moralization, these misdeeds completely discredited Collor and led to his impeachment in late 1992.

Nevertheless, Collor made some crucial contributions in combating Brazil's crisis. His government put state—and market—reform at the top of the political agenda; took the first important steps toward reform, especially through its initial fiscal measures and its trade reform; and elaborated many structural reform proposals that the administration of Fernando Henrique Cardoso has continued to pursue. Thus, Collor was an important reformer, despite his eventual political failure and his personal misdeeds. Nowadays, many observers—especially in Brazil—depict Collor as the incarnation of evil, but this vilification is problematic. In politics, there are few purely "bad guys" or "good guys." Instead, mixtures prevail: "Good guys"—such as President Cardoso— may need to use some "bad" tricks, and "bad guys"—such as Collor— do some "good" things. After the passions that Collor's defeat of Luiz Inácio Lula da Silva in 1989 and his impeachment in 1992 stirred up have receded, it will be time for an even-handed assessment of the Collor administration, one that considers Collor's political blunders and personal greed but does not deny his real accomplishments.

Prolonged Inaction: The Franco Government

During the interim government of former vice president Itamar Franco (1992–1994), an inept leader of mercurial temperament, efforts to rebuild the state came to a virtual standstill. During the first eight months, his lame-duck administration lacked clear direction and failed to make any headway in combating Brazil's severe economic and political problems. Only the privatization program continued with the sale of eighteen parastatal enterprises for US$ 5.561 billion from late 1992 to late 1994 (Matos and Oliveira 1996, 24). Despite Franco's skepticism, his economic teams pursued the sale of public firms that the Collor administration had prepared for privatization, but Franco blocked the initiation of new privatizations.

In May 1993, after months of simply drifting, Franco appointed as finance minister Fernando Henrique Cardoso, a well-respected leader of the moderate Partido da Social Democracia Brasileira (PSDB). During the remainder of Franco's term, Cardoso acted like a prime minister, even after stepping down from his post in April 1994 to run for president. Lacking the democratic legitimation stemming from an electoral mandate, however, Cardoso confined himself to temporary stabilization measures and refrained from pushing for structural reforms of lasting impact. Most important, Cardoso was unable to take full advantage of the opportunity provided by an attempt to revise the mandated constitutional review in late 1993 and early 1994.

During those months, the legislative quorum required for changing the constitution of 1988 was lowered, and the attempt to revise the document would have facilitated the adoption of structural reforms, such as an overhaul of Brazil's fiscal system. Because of the upcoming general elections of late 1994, however, many parliamentarians were unwilling to pass controversial measures and preferred instead to campaign in their home states. Chronically low attendance by the government's supporters and obstruction by the leftist opposition doomed the constitutional revision, and therefore none of the government's proposals for structural reform passed; most of them did not even come up for a vote (CN 1994b). The only success Minister Cardoso had was to win approval of a short-term fiscal stabilization plan (Fundo Social de Emergência), which for a period of two years raised taxes and limited constitutional restrictions on revenue use. This expedient temporarily alleviated the state's fiscal crisis but did not lead to a definite solution.

State Reform by Negotiation?
President Cardoso's Slow and Uneven Progress

Because of President Collor's political failure and President Franco's inaction, only limited progress was made during the early 1990s regarding the reorientation of Brazil's development model and the reconstruction of the state, and many of the country's underlying economic problems persisted. President Cardoso, who took office in January 1995, pursued reform goals that were similar to President Collor's,[26] but Cardoso had learned from Collor's debacle. He has therefore pursued his agenda, not through imposition, but through negotiation. Whereas Collor confronted—and antagonized—clientelistic politicians, rent-seeking interest groups, and powerful state governors, Cardoso has sought to bargain with them. Given the interest of these "veto players" in maintaining many aspects of the status quo, the progress of Cardoso's reform initiatives, especially in the area of state building, has been very slow and uneven. Although the Brazilian state is gradually regaining strength, for instance, through an increase in tax revenues, it is unlikely to achieve a high degree of autonomy from clientelistic politicians and business groups, who continue to have a strong influence on substantial parts of the public bureaucracy.

How has Cardoso managed to make any progress toward resolving Brazil's crisis by bargaining with actors that are responsible for many of the country's economic and political difficulties to begin with? Democracy once again has had a crucial impact. The new president assumed office in a position of extraordinary political strength while his adversaries, especially clientelistic politicians, were suffering from exceptional weakness. In October 1994, Cardoso gained the strongest electoral mandate in Brazilian history by winning a clear first-round victory with double the vote of his closest competitor. This success was mainly owing to Cardoso's stabilization plan of July 1994 *(Plano Real)*, which suddenly lowered runaway inflation without imposing drastic costs on large sectors of the population. Based on this feat, Cardoso's party also won the governorships of São Paulo, Rio de Janeiro, and Minas Gerais, Brazil's most important states. Finally, the president managed to assemble a wide-ranging, though loose, support coalition in parliament, which officially controlled about 60–70 percent of the seats in the lower house of Congress. Thus, an overwhelming democratic mandate seemed to give the new president enormous political strength. Cardoso has sought to keep this legitimation alive by appealing (usually via television) to "the people," over and above the heads of politicians, parties, and interest groups.

At the same time, clientelistic politicians and rent-seeking interest groups have been in disrepute. The budget scandal of late 1993 and early 1994 revealed a dense web of corruption that linked important political leaders with private contractors (CN 1994a), and the memory of this disgrace continued to weaken politicians and some powerful business groups. Thus, the scrutiny of public opinion, reinvigorated by democratization, debilitated potential opponents of Cardoso's reform efforts.

Furthermore, the threat of a (seemingly) powerful socialist left, which had grown in the course of democratization, helped to discipline established politicians and the private sector. Luiz Inácio Lula da Silva, the PT candidate, had been the clear front-runner in the presidential election until the government enacted the last step of the economic stabilization plan designed by ex-minister Cardoso's team, which introduced the Real as the country's new currency (Mendes and Venturi 1994). The menace from the left revealed the electoral weakness of established politicians, indebted rightist and centrist parties to the eventual winner, Cardoso, and induced them to look more kindly on his structural reform efforts (including the rebuilding of the state), which the new president depicted as necessary for sustaining his economic stabilization plan in the medium and long run. Thus, in a number of ways, the repercussions of democratization reinforced the clout of President Cardoso, debilitated his opponents, and improved his chances for enacting some state-building reforms.

The new president has also employed skillful political tactics. He has systematically sought to exploit divergences among the interests of clientelistic politicians, state governors, and powerful social groupings, reinforcing demands that coincide with his own reform agenda and providing compensation for demands he cannot satisfy. Cardoso's strategies for negotiating with each set of potential veto players differ slightly. In dealing with clientelistic politicians, Cardoso has tried to play their short-term interests off against their long-term goals.[27] Clientelistic politicians want to gain current patronage and maintain access to future patronage, but given the high level of uncertainty created by Brazil's electoral system of open-list proportional representation, which makes reelection unpredictable and leads to considerable involuntary turnover (Mainwaring 1991; see also Ames 1995a, 427–30), politicians tend to heavily discount the long run and focus on the short term. Cardoso has therefore offered patronage now in order to persuade politicians to accept state-building reforms that seek to limit patronage in the future.

The government has applied that tactic in areas such as administrative reform, seeking to restore the right of dismissing inefficient cronies of clientelistic politicians, and the privatization of public enterprises, by reducing political discretion over economic resources, i.e., the available mass of patronage. Although the success of the tactic is limited, it is the only one that holds any promise of success, as the rapid failure of Collor's confrontational strategy suggests.

The interests of state governors partly coincide with and partly diverge from Cardoso's reform goals. Although the subnational governments oppose any attempt at fiscal recentralization, they face an especially pressing need for administrative reform, which would allow them to slim down their bloated bureaucracies (MARE 1996, 51) and reduce their enormous financial deficits. The new president has therefore enlisted the governors as allies in his struggle for civil service reform as he tried to weaken the employment guarantee ("stability") reinforced and extended by the 1988 constitution (Moreira Franco 1996a; Santana 1996). Since state governors faced a legal obligation to reduce their personnel spending by 1999, they strongly supported Cardoso's efforts at administrative reform—and even dismissed about 300,000 civil servants on their own initiative.[28] In the area of fiscal reform, by contrast, Cardoso has had to offer compensation for any loss that the state governments would incur.

Private business groups have a collective interest in macroeconomic stabilization and state reform, but individually, they seek to avoid paying any of the cost for these improvements. Cardoso has sought to mitigate this collective action dilemma by welcoming the efforts of business leaders to create an encompassing, more cohesive organization of the whole private sector (Ação Empresarial [Business Action]). More important, the government has provided leadership and coordination in the reform effort (Cidade 1995) and has sought to ensure business compliance with and support for government goals by providing payoffs, such as selective protection from foreign competition or the financial bailout of bankrupt firms, most notably in the banking sector.[29]

With these clever tactics, the president has pursued his wide-ranging efforts at state reform. Through tax reform, the government has tried to guarantee the state a solid fiscal foundation and to stimulate investment by diminishing the fiscal burden on productive enterprises, which now face stiffer external competition (Presidência 1995; CD 1995b). Through profound administrative reform, including the "flexibilization" of the employment guarantee enshrined in the 1988 constitution, the government has sought to professionalize the public bureaucracy, make it more efficient and accountable, and limit clientelism (CD 1995a; Presidência. Câmara da Reforma do Estado 1996a). And through ambitious social security reform, the government has tried to reduce the enormous expenditures on behalf of retired state officials, whose privileged pension system provides exorbitant benefits, such as income raises at the time of retirement (CD 1996). Finally, the Cardoso administration has attempted to slim down the obese state apparatus through privatization and thus facilitate central coordination and control.

Yet despite President Cardoso's strong democratic mandate and his skillful tactics, the obstacles to state reform have remained enormous. Above all, the veto players have sought to minimize the costs they have to bear and extract a high price for any losses they may incur. In the area of fiscal reform, for instance, state governors have blocked any revenue shift from the subnational governments back to the central government.[30] In addition, clientelistic politicians have obstructed a lasting solution to Brazil's fiscal crisis and agreed merely to a temporary extension of the tax package adopted in early 1994.[31] The goal to maximize patronage governed this decision: every time the federal government has to win approval for a further extension, clientelistic politicians can extract new patronage. Thus, while rendering short-term expedients possible, clientelism has continued to hinder a permanent solution to the fiscal crisis of the state.

Similar difficulties have hindered administrative reform. Above all, many politicians have been unwilling to vote for any change—especially to make the job tenure of civil servants more flexible—that would appear antagonistic to the interests of "working people" and therefore be politically costly (Moreira Franco 1996a, 1996b). Public employees have been the most combative sector of "labor" in the new democracy, using the umbrella of the powerful socialist Central Única dos Trabalhadores to advance their own special interests, and their strong resistance has hindered administrative reform (as well as the privatization of public enterprises). Nevertheless, support from state governors and well-targeted patronage has allowed the Cardoso administration to marshal the necessary number of votes in Congress to lift the unconditional "stability" of civil servants,[32] but any large-scale dismissals would arouse too much opposition and are therefore infeasible (Santana 1996). The absence of the threat of dismissal makes it more difficult, in turn, to force improvements in the public bureaucracy. The constitutional reform was an important first step, however, and it could make further reform possible.

The Cardoso government's social security reform has also faced tremendous political obstacles as special interest groups supported by clientelistic politicians have fiercely defended their privileges (Weyland 1996b). Despite numerous setbacks and the elimination of many of its original proposals, the government tried to induce Congress through constant prodding and well-targeted patronage to preserve a few of its most basic goals, such as a (limited) reduction in new pensions conceded to better-off public servants.[33] Although Congress rejected these changes in May 1998, the government will probably use the financial crisis to achieve some reduction in expenditures, especially in the highly generous pension system for state employees, which has caused a rapidly growing budget drain in recent years (Presidência. Câmara da Reforma do Estado 1996a, 40).

In contrast to the slow advance of constitutional reform, privatization has picked up steam. Since President Franco had been reluctant to prepare new sales of public assets, privatization proceeded slowly at the beginning of the Cardoso government, which until December 1995 had auctioned off only five parastate enterprises worth a total of US$ 1.255 billion (Matos and Oliveira 1996, 24). The staff of these firms had resisted–concerned about their jobs, salaries, and generous fringe benefits–and the ministries supervising them– which were reluctant to lose power–have resisted privatization. In 1996, however, the government achieved greater success, netting US$ 5.359 billion through the sale of ten public enterprises (IESP 1997, 35–36), and in early 1997, it managed to overcome strong opposition and auction off the profitable mining firm Companhia Vale do Rio Doce, one of the crown jewels of Brazil's public sector. After completing the transfer of the state's industrial enterprises to the private sector, the government began to focus on privatizing infrastructure and services (Presidência. Câmara da Reforma do Estado 1997, 51–53), for instance, in the area of telecommunications, and in July 1998, it sold the telecommunications conglomerate Telebrás for an unprecedented US$ 19 billion, 64 percent above the minimum bid.

Overall, then, state reform has been slow and uneven, and the short-term price of the long-term initiatives has been high. The Cardoso government has had to dole out considerable patronage and other special benefits to buy off clientelistic politicians, powerful business groups, and state governors,[34] and even if further constitutional amendments–especially a limited social security reform–pass in the future, their real impact will be uncertain. The great strength of clientelistic politicians and interest groups is their pervasive, invisible, and therefore uncontrollable influence on decision implementation. By bending and distorting the execution of legal rules, these special interests can often undermine reform goals. Thus, the government's hope to buy restrictions on future patronage through the provision of current patronage will probably have only limited success. But given the dispersal of power in Brazil's new democracy, it is probably the only way to achieve any progress.

Cardoso's desire to win the right of reelection exposed him to further blackmail from patronage-hungry parliamentarians and–according to the available evidence–even induced some vote buying. The continued influence on public appointments and resource allocation that clientelistic politicians have demanded in return for their lukewarm endorsement of President Cardoso's reform initiatives has also kept state cohesion and capacity low. Similarly, the particularistic benefits that the government has had to provide to business sectors–such as selective protection and financial bailout–have called into question its commitment to the universalistic principles underlying the new, market-oriented development model. In addition to tarnishing the "modern," clean image of the Cardoso government, all these favors have also created heavy pressure on the public budget. For instance, federal personnel expenditures rose by a whopping 22 percent in 1995,[35] and total spending increases have exceeded the substantial rise in revenues produced by the temporary tax reform and the economic recovery beginning in 1993 (Varsano 1996, 2–9). The fiscal crisis of the Brazilian state has therefore not eased much. Indeed, Brazil's operational deficit reached a high 5.05 percent of GDP in 1995 (MF 1996, 18), 3.9 percent in 1996 (IESP 1997, 26), and 4.3 percent in 1997 (IESP 1998, 27) and contributed to the grave financial crisis.

In sum, the efforts of the Cardoso government to accomplish state reform through negotiation have had only limited success. Although President Collor's political failure revealed the impossibility of achieving drastic change through imposition in Brazil's new democracy, President Cardoso's negotiation efforts have advanced slowly and unevenly. If continued, however, these initiatives may add up to significant change in the medium and long run. Cardoso's nonconfrontational approach at least avoids the risk of drastic reversals. In other countries, state building also proceeded in a halting fashion. In the United States, for instance, it took decades to limit the spoils system and create a professional civil service (Skowronek 1982, chaps. 3, 6). Cardoso's reforms may be the first step in such a lengthy process of reconstituting the Brazilian state.

Conclusion

Democratization has had a contradictory impact on the Brazilian state. Under the government of José Sarney (1985–1990), it strengthened clientelistic politicians, rent-seeking interest groups, and subnational governments, who further undermined the internal cohesion of the state and diminished its capacity to attain its own goals. Yet the crisis that these corrosive tendencies exacerbated triggered efforts to rebuild the state, which gained in force through their democratic legitimation in the presidential elections of 1989 and 1994. Similarly, rampant clientelism and corruption discredited the forces that corroded the state and thus strengthened the reform impulse and weakened opposition.

President Collor's (1990–1992) efforts to impose state reform against patronage-hungry politicians, interest groups, and state and municipal governments failed because of the tenacious resistance of those veto players and the president's own misdeeds, which betrayed his campaign promise to moralize the state. Learning from Collor's debacle, President Cardoso

(1995–) has sought to attain state reform through negotiation. His bargaining with politicians, interest groups, and subnational governments has made some headway, but the government remains far from reaching its goals. Since Cardoso's compromise strategy requires cooperation with the forces that had undermined the state, the president is unlikely to attain any definite victory. Instead, he has to make many concessions, dole out innumerable payoffs, and frequently rely on clever expedients (*jeitinhos*), rather than achieving institutional solutions. However, he may manage to revert the trend toward further deterioration and take the first steps toward recovering state capacity.

What does this analysis suggest for the future of the Brazilian state? Given the divergent tendencies that democratization has unleashed, the state is unlikely to either remain a weak, tied-down Gulliver or turn into a powerful Leviathan. On the one hand, persistent deterioration is improbable because by pushing the country back into a crisis, deterioration would trigger new rescue efforts, especially under democracy. In fact, President Cardoso is likely to invoke the financial problems in order to push for a resumption of reform efforts in the areas of social security and taxation during his second term in office. On the other hand, President Cardoso's success in overcoming Brazil's acute economic problems, especially hyperinflation, limited the impulse for additional institutional reforms during his first term. And if the government succeeds in containing the economic challenges, any renewed reform effort is likely to peter out quickly. For these reasons, an ambiguous intermediate outcome is most probable in the foreseeable future, as has so often been the case in Brazil's history. The state will remain an agglomeration of incongruent parts, ranging from competent bureaucracies to agencies captured by business groups and patronage-hungry politicians. For the time being, the Brazilian state will resemble a disfigured, yet moderately effectual, Frankenstein.

Only a sustained expansion of universalistic values in Brazilian society could gradually beautify the ugly features of this Frankenstein. A growing commitment to equality before the law and a stronger adherence to neutral, clean procedures could result not only from the return of democracy but also from neoliberal reform. Fiercer domestic and foreign competition turns the machinations of clientelistic politicians and corrupt bureaucrats into unacceptable sources of inefficiency, and the ever-louder complaints of entrepreneurs about the cost of doing business in Brazil (CNI 1995, 1996) may help advance universalist norms.[36] This value shift, in turn, may gradually raise the standards of accountability for politicians and force greater transparency in public decision making, thus limiting the shady influence of clientelistic forces and special interest groups and undermining "the pact of impunity" that has so often protected politicians from prosecution for their misdeeds. Only such a sustained normative change could pave the way for a steady increase in state capacity and autonomy, and Brazil has a long way to go on this path toward reform.

How do the changes in the state that this chapter has documented affect the quality of Brazil's new democracy,[37] as indicated by the accountability and responsiveness of public decision makers, their accessibility to the public, and the participation of the citizenry (Schmitter 1983, 887–91)? The initial deterioration of the state further exacerbated the manifold problems that caused "low-intensity citizenship" (O'Donnell 1993) in Brazil. The greater penetration of the state by "invisible" forces, especially rent-seeking interest groups and clientelistic politicians, kept the accountability and responsiveness of decision makers to the mass public low, which reduced the beneficial direct effects of democratization. And while the accessibility of decision makers improved and mass participation in politics expanded with the return of democracy, the fragmentation of the state and the "capture" of many agencies by outside forces helped to keep citizens' opportunities for *effectively* advancing their interests low. Furthermore, the diminishing autonomy and capacity of the state weakened some of the preconditions for a flourishing democracy, such as the rule of law and the principle of equal citizenship. As long as the *senhores* and *doutores* can count on automatic privileges—including special jail cells in the unlikely case they are ever convicted—the minimal civic and political equality that democratic citizenship requires cannot flourish.

But in line with the dialectical argument advanced in this chapter, some of the most glaring problems of state weakness have helped to invigorate democracy. Brazilian society traditionally lacked a sense of indignation, a civic anger that insisted on compliance with procedural rules and their underlying principles. For instance, the corruption of political leaders was long shrugged off with a half-resigned, half-smirking *Rouba mas faz*—"he steals, but he gets things done." The cancerous growth of blatant corruption in the new democracy, however, intensified people's revulsion toward these misdeeds. More and more citizens came to reject the "pact of impunity" among politicians and state officials and to demand clean government. In general, citizens have increasingly responded to unresponsive and inaccessible government by protesting and mobilizing their fellow citizens, as the emergence of numerous social movements and public interest groups attests. Thus, by sparking indignation in society, the further deterioration of the state paradoxically has had a positive effect on Brazilian democracy.

An eventual recuperation of state capacity could further stimulate popular participation. When citizens face unresponsive and inaccessible bureaucrats and unaccountable politicians, only some of them protest; many others become resigned and withdraw into private life. By eliminating this dissuasive effect, an increase in state capacity could motivate more citizens to advance their interests and ideas through politics. Indeed, a stronger state could induce people to hold public officials and politicians accountable. For instance, if the Finance Ministry effectively combated tax evasion, citizens would probably insist on a more productive usage of the resulting revenue increase. At present, many people *pretend* to pay taxes, and the state *pretends* to provide services;[38] if the state actually *made* people pay taxes, they in turn would *make* the state provide services. Thus, a recovery of state strength may give rise to a new "social contract" that would improve the quality of Brazilian democracy.

THREE

Devolving Democracy?

Political Decentralization and the New Brazilian Federalism

Alfred P. Montero

M uch of the history of Brazilian politics has been dominated by swings between centralized and decentralized political rule, and Brazil's recent transition to democracy is no exception to this legacy.[1] The authoritarian regime installed in 1964 represented only the most recent attempt to centralize political control, and with the liberalization of authoritarianism, policy authority and resources were returned to the states. Brazil took a significant step toward democracy in 1982 when there were direct elections for governor, the first time such contests had been held since 1965. Along with directly elected federal deputies, the governors were strategically placed to extract new political authority and fiscal resources, and these politicians and the local interests they represented became key actors in the drafting of the 1988 constitution, which would further decentralize fiscal and policy resources to subnational governments.

In this chapter, I argue that the relationship between political decentralization and building democracy in Brazil is paradoxical. On the one hand, decentralization helped to fragment, and thereby weaken, the central state, for by strengthening the subnational governments' authority to tax and spend, political decentralization injected greater chaos into the central state's attempts to manage macroeconomic and social policy. On the other hand, the new federal order revealed a growing capacity to adapt to the problems of Brazil's nascent democracy. Many state governments engaged in economic reforms that improved public accounts, and in some cases, subnational government developed innovative responses to social and economic problems that national policies failed to address.

I analyze this paradoxical relationship between democratization and decentralization in Brazil as it evolved in three phases. Each phase was marked by an issue or a process that had a lasting impact on the way that decentralization and democratization would affect each other. This periodization is only a guide for events that partially overlap in time and regarding the third, and latest, period, are not completed but have clearly been initiated.

The first phase spanned most of the 1980s, and it was characterized by strong decentralization. During this period, the *sequencing* of political decentralization added to democracy's rough start and contributed to some persisting problems. The empowerment of the governors following the 1982 elections made those officials key architects of the new federalism, and before national democratic leaders could install a federal framework from above, the governors constructed one from below in ways that favored local political machines.[2] This situation strengthened local clientelism as a centerpiece of Brazilian politics and weakened the central state by fragmenting its resources and authorities. By weakening the central state, decentralization hindered Brasília's capacity to address crucial macroeconomic and distributional issues that were essential for improving the quality of the country's democracy during the 1980s.[3]

The second phase occurred during the early to mid-1990s and was a period of reequilibration of intergovernment authority. The decentralization wave stalled as the central state halted unsustainable patterns of fiscal devolution and subnational spending from the previous decade. In the fight against megainflation, for example, the Brazilian central bank had to threaten or actually intervene in the case of failing state banks to recapture control over public spending. Although decentralization created many of the problems such episodes of reequilibration were meant to redress, it also facilitated the central state's efforts to recover authority. Divisions among state governments vying for investments and hoping to correct fiscal accounts ruined by clientelistic politics during the 1980s shifted bargaining leverage to reformist presidents in Brasília during the 1990s, and as a result, central state agencies were able to extract reform concessions from weakened and divided states.

Nevertheless, reequilibration was only partial as it did not lead to a coherent national framework for requiring subnational compliance with federal reforms. Shifts in the interests of key subnational leaders consolidated reforms in some cases while others requiring additional federal prodding produced few changes. Overall, the haphazard reequilibration of intergovernment authority was a prerequisite in confronting sources of central state weakness and economic chaos that threatened the new democracy.

The third phase, which partially overlapped the second but concentrated more on Cardoso's presidency, was a period of receding decentralization and subnational consolidation of policy innovations. During this phase, the central state acquired access to previously devolved resources and authority and shifted spending responsibilities to subnational governments, reversing the gains made by the decentralizers. At the same time, many subnational governments pursued a wider range of policies to consolidate fiscal reforms initiated during the second phase and to produce new economic and social policies that were responsive to local needs. Where the influence of local political machines could be displaced or coopted by reformist political leaders, innovative policy experiments moved forward. These cases demonstrated that political decentralization could maximize federalism's "allocative efficiencies" and even improve on previous national policies.[4]

The periodization I have outlined has been referred to in the literature on Brazilian politics as "the new federalism," a term that often obscures more than it clarifies since it includes both the ascending and the receding phases of decentralization in recent Brazilian history. However, since my main argument in this chapter is that decentralization and democratization are related in both complementary and conflicting ways, references to "the new federalism" are useful for generalizing about a process that is both flexible and evolving.[5] This term contrasts with the term "federalism," which assumes the (re)emergence of a coherent, previously defined, model of intergovernment authority. Such a model has not existed in Brazil.

Both the dangers and the encouraging possibilities of the new federalism in Brazil are recognized by the theoretical and country-specific literature. However, most of those works tend to see either the negative or the positive aspects of political decentralization as endemic. Many scholars believe subnational politics to be hopelessly clientelistic so that political decentralization only reinforces the dominance of patrimonialism. Other scholars believe decentralization is a democratizing process, one that takes government "closer to the people," expands access to policy making, and increases the efficiency of policy implementation.

In this chapter, I argue that neither of these approaches is exclusively correct. After contrasting the two theoretical perspectives, I analyze the relationship between democratization and decentralization in Brazil during the three periods outlined above. In the first section, I focus on the sequencing of decentralization and democratization during the 1980s. The second section discusses the reequilibration of intergovernment authority during the early 1990s. The final section focuses on the experiences of some reformist states and cities, emphasizing that the third phase of the new federalism went beyond reequilibration to include policy innovations among subnational governments.

Two Contrasting Perspectives on
Political Decentralization and Democracy

In Chapter 2, Kurt Weyland argues that the relationship between state autonomy and democratization was dialectical in Brazil. I find that the same is true for the relationship between decentralization and democracy. Not surprisingly, the travails of state autonomy and capacity have accompanied changes in intergovernment relations in Brazil, and to be sure, reequilibration occurred on different levels.

Nevertheless, the crucial role decentralization played in the democratization process begs questions more specific than those addressed by a study of state capacity. Specifically, does political decentralization enhance Brazilian democracy or does it weaken it? Over the years, a number of scholars have advocated one or the other position, but few have reconciled the arguments into a coherent theory of decentralization and democracy in Brazil.

Arguments for the undemocratic effects of political decentralization in Brazil usually focus on how the dispersal of power fragments political organizations and the state. The most common argument is that decentralization empowers local clientelistic leaders who serve only themselves and not more universal concerns (Samuels and Abrucio 1997; Hagopian 1996).

Other authors, mostly those working from a comparative perspective and dealing with other countries or regions, argue that political decentralization can guarantee the most developed forms of democracy. For these scholars, decentralized government is more accountable, more accessible, more innovative, and generally more effective than centralized government. A common rationale of their work is that by being "closer to the people," subnational policy making reduces the cost of gaining access to government (World Bank 1997b). As a result, a subnational government must perform consistently and according to the expectations of regional economic groups and community leadership, and studies of subnational government show that local governments are often more willing than national leaders to respond to the demands of their constituency. The preeminent proponent of such an argument, Robert Putnam, even suggests in his study of the Italian regions that local constituencies apply a higher standard of performance to their local governments than they do to central government (Putnam 1993, 50–51). Therefore, political decentralization enhances the accountability of government by increasing its localization.

Studies of fiscal federalism address similar questions, but they focus on the efficiency of policy outcomes by specifying the optimal distribution of authority and resources between national and subnational governments. The best model of federalism is one in which allocative policies that require specific information about local demands are decentralized while distributive policies that depend upon a national perspective are centralized (Musgrave and Musgrave 1989; Oates 1972; IDB 1994, 178; IDB 1997, 153). As long as these "correct" principles of decentralization are followed, the efficiency of public functions is preserved.

Brazil's new federalism does not fit neatly into either one of the two perspectives reviewed thus far. The adoption and professional management of fiscal reforms and innovative new policies at the subnational level belies the view that all politics is clientelistic. On the other hand, no coherent, national model of efficient or accountable "good government" has emerged in Brazil. Rather, what is more apparent is that the new federalism is a product of conflicting policy interests at different levels of government, and any determination of how Brazilian democracy has been affected by this process must consider: (one) how the sequence of democratization and decentralization interacted during the regime transition to weaken the central state; (two) how the central state has reasserted its role in areas of critical importance to democracy, such as macroeconomic policy and distribution of wealth; and (three) why some subnational governments have developed innovative policies while others remain inept vehicles of patrimonial leadership.

The Politics of the Governors and the Fragmentation of Intergovernmental Authority

Political decentralization was both a tool of the larger project to initiate and deepen democratization and an outcome of the redistribution of access to power that was at the heart of the transition to democracy.[6] The two processes, however, did not overlap perfectly. The military initiated significant reforms that decentralized fiscal resources to subnational governments well before the generals began liberalizing the regime, and political decentralization accelerated *before* a democratically elected executive and a national constitutional system could be constructed. Consequently, local politicians and their clientelistic political machines had an inordinate amount of influence over the content of democratic institutions and national policies. Forced by the need to make alliances with subnational politicians, the first civilian government, that of President José Sarney (1985–1990), played to this panoply of parochial interests to strengthen Sarney's own political position, thereby further fragmenting political authority.

The Brazilian military, which embraced a formula of authoritarian centralism after the coup of 1964, decentralized new taxes and intergovernmental transfers through the 1967 fiscal reform. The act benefited the northern and northeastern states, where the military found a base of conservative support, so the 1967 reform served to counterbalance the power of the southern and southeastern states, where much of the opposition to authoritarianism first emerged (Selcher 1990). Yet the act also set a precedent for expanding subnational autonomy in perverse ways.

The reform allowed the state governments to administer the new Imposto sobre Circulação de Mercadorias (ICM, Tax on the Circulation of Goods) and the Imposto sobre Transmissão de Bens Imóveis (ITBI, Tax on the Exchange of Real Estate).[7] The federal government retained the other major tax on business, the Imposto sobre Produtos Industrializados (IPI, Tax on Industrial Products), another value-added tax. Since the ICM was a value-added tax on goods (and eventually, services, thus, ICMS), differences in ICMS rates across states created administrative confusion that aided tax evaders and allowed states to grant tax concessions in competition with each other. The latter tendency was partially controlled by the military government. Although the states retained new fiscal resources, the military governments controlled how the states and cities spent transferred resources, linking transfers to specific budget items (Arretche 1996, 52), and states seeking to increase expenditures were forced to depend upon the accumulation of debt to finance local development. By one estimate, in 1981, over one-third of Brazil's total external indebtedness was held by the state governments (Graham 1990, 87).

The combination of the fiscal crisis of the state during the 1980s, persisting disparities among the Brazilian regions, and the growing inability of authoritarian institutions to deal with these problems added to the forces behind the gradual transition to democracy. Many of these questions became the focus of distributional conflicts that drove the emerging federal framework (Afonso 1995, 321; Sallum 1996). As a result, the new federal order would be created on an ad hoc basis, led by intergovernmental conflict and divorced from any national program of decentralized democracy with demarcated rules and timetables.

The emergence of civilian leadership in state governments and the federal legislature during the liberalization process, particularly after the crucial governors' election of 1982, produced a group of nationally prominent subnational elites. Without a directly elected president, these subnational politicians were popularly identified as the leaders of the democratic transition (Kugelmas, Sallum, and Graeff 1989).

To be sure, the persistence of centralized authoritarian control over the process of democratization *from above* and the surprising acceleration of civilian penetration of the process in key states *from below* created a host of contradictions. Prominent among these contradictions was the continued control that the central state had over taxation and expenditures. Democratic leaders in the state governments could not, on the one hand, claim to be independent of the military government and, on the other hand, continue to depend upon the same government for fiscal resources. These constraints catalyzed a movement at the municipal and state levels in 1983 and 1984 to expand the size of and the states' control over the ICMS (Affonso 1988).[8] In preparation for the fight, the governors and the opposition municipal and federal representatives mobilized partisans through broad distributional and clientelistic networks at the subnational level (Abrucio 1994; Samuels and Abrucio 1997; Hagopian 1996).

National politicians strengthened subnational clientelistic networks by soliciting their support through the distribution of patronage. President Sarney attempted to woo the governors, federal deputies, and mayors by increasing nontax federal transfers to the states and municipalities 23 percent from their 1980 level. In this way, the weak president cultivated support among Brazil's governors and their local patrimonial machines in his campaign for a five-year term and the preservation of presidential rule on the eve of the drafting of the 1988 constitution (Serra and Afonso 1991, 49).

By the time the Constituent Assembly, the elected body charged with the responsibility of drafting the new constitution, first convened in 1987, regional interests were all but dominant in Brazilian political society. The assembly itself became a forum for subnational interests. These regional lobbies *(bancadas regionais)* were strengthened by the support of the governors and by demands at the local level for fiscal resources needed to redress social and economic problems. The states of the Northeast and North formed political alliances in favor of redistributive tax rules aimed at correcting regional disparities in wealth, and leaders from these states condemned Brasília's policies as reinforcing the continued concentration of industry in São Paulo (Rodriguez 1995, 437). In response, politicians from the southeastern and southern states moved to block these efforts and to expand their access to fiscal resources (Campos 1991).

Whatever their differences, the aggregate effects of the influence of the *bancadas regionais* were felt in the constitution of 1988, which gave Brazil a more fiscally decentralized federalism.[9] As Table 3.1 demonstrates, fiscal decentralization in Brazil decreased under authoritarianism but gradually accelerated during the transition. This phase was marked by the shifting of significant fiscal authority to subnational governments, especially municipalities. Increasing control over ICMS by the states explains the sharp recovery of their administration of tax revenues during the mid- to late 1980s. The figures also show significant gaps between tax collection responsibilities and public spending. Although the central state spent less than it collected in taxes between 1960 and 1994, the gap widened significantly following the 1988 constitution. The municipalities were the big winners as they were able to spend several times more than they collected.

The 1988 constitution served to lock in fiscal commitments to the states and municipalities by endowing them as democratic "rights." For the gover-

TABLE 3.1

Revenues by Level of Government Before and After Revenue Sharing
(in percentages)

Year	Tax Revenues Before Revenue Sharing			Final Disposition of Revenues After Revenue Sharing		
	Union	States	Cities	Union	States	Cities
1960	63.9	31.3	4.7	59.4	34.0	6.5
1965	63.6	30.8	5.6	54.9	35.0	10.2
1970	65.0	32.2	2.8	58.7	30.6	10.7
1975	70.8	26.1	3.1	64.8	25.7	9.5
1980	72.8	24.0	3.2	66.2	24.3	9.5
1985	70.4	27.0	2.6	61.0	27.3	11.6
1986	67.1	30.1	2.8	57.0	29.8	13.2
1987	69.9	27.4	2.6	60.7	27.8	11.5
1988	70.2	26.9	2.9	61.3	27.4	11.4
1989	65.4	31.7	2.9	57.3	29.8	12.9
1990	64.8	31.6	3.6	53.8	30.4	15.9
1993	68.0	27.0	5.0	58.0	26.0	16.0

Note: Figures may not total 100 because of rounding.
Sources: Serra and Afonso (1991, 45); Affonso (1995, 63–64); FGV (1996, 103).

nors and their supporters, the Constituent Assembly, "the representatives of the people," had bestowed upon the states and municipalities greater financial autonomy through these entitlements, which made fiscal decentralization a central aspect of the consolidation of Brazilian democracy (Sola 1995, 40).

Beyond having greater control over public revenues, the 1988 reform gave the states reasons to spend by delegating areas of policy that were not within the jurisdiction of the national state. The open-endedness of this provision granted the states virtual carte blanche to direct spending at an array of "development" needs, and this tendency was reinforced by large flows of intergovernmental transfers, more than 90 percent of which went unearmarked by Brasília (Afonso 1994, 356; Affonso 1995, 66). More than 30 percent of these transfers were considered "free" since they could be applied generically to elementary education and health, areas that could be more specifically defined by state and municipal governments (Afonso 1995, 318; Shah 1991).

The open-endedness of subnational fiscal authority, however, was also accompanied by a declining role of the federal government in social and economic policy making during the 1980s and 1990s, and in the wake of flagging federal efforts, states and municipalities were forced to assume greater responsibilities. Some Brazilian specialists have argued that the constitution of 1988 provided the states and municipalities with more fiscal resources but that it failed to also devolve official duties de jure to those levels of government. However, data presented by Rui Affonso (1995, 65) on the de facto effects of decentralization show that the state and municipal governments presently account for close to 80 percent of all public investment and 67 percent of current public consumption, excluding expenditures to national public firms. André Médici (1994, 63) notes that while federal spending on social assistance programs declined from 48.1 percent of the total in 1980 to 39.7 percent in 1990, the state governments' commitments in this area rose during the same period from 40.8 percent of the total to 44.6 percent. Municipal spending on social assistance also increased, from 11.1 percent of the total to 15.7 percent. Presently, subnational governments now account for 44 percent of all spending on health, 69 percent of all spending on education, and investments two times the size of those of the federal government (Affonso 1997, 15; Rezende 1995, 242–43; Medici 1995).[10]

Reequilibration of Intergovernmental Authorities

As part of the game of distributive conflicts that marked the process of political decentralization and democratization in Brazil, critical areas of macroeconomic and social policy were imprudently devolved to subnational governments. Without reequilibration, macroeconomic chaos and persisting social disparities promised to threaten the new democracy, and such reequilibration of intergovernmental fiscal authority depended upon an array of ad hoc political tactics by central state managers, shifting subnational interests, and changing economic contexts.

Distributive conflicts between the federal government, especially the central bank, and the state banks under the administration of the governors were at the center of a larger struggle over which levels of government would control macroeconomic policy. Besides the national public banks in Brazil—the Central Bank, the Banco do Brasil, and the Caixa Econômica Federal (CEF)—the states administer their own public banks, some of which are development banks. After the 1988 constitution, the right of the state governments to administer their banks was consecrated by their own state constitutions. These provisions prohibited the governors from "allowing" the central bank or the Conselho Monetário Nacional (National Monetary Council, CMN), the institutions designed to regulate the financial system, from intervening in the management of the state banks. These institutions protected what were, in practice, critical political assets of the Brazilian governors, and any attempt by President Sarney to wrest control of these resources would undermine his own base of political support (Sola 1994, 165).

During the 1980s, the governors made the state banks finance the expanding fiscal deficits of the states, often by issuing short-term, high-interest debt paper in domestic financial markets. The poor management of many of these banks and the equally inferior administration of the state budgets by the governors added to the deteriorating fiscal condition of the state governments. These processes worsened with democratization when the governors used the state banks to distribute public patrimony to political allies.[11] As the fiscal conditions of the state governments worsened, the central bank was forced to bail out the states annually in response to political pressures placed on national politicians by the governors and their secretaries of economy (Silva and Costa 1995, 270–72; Kugelmas, Sallum, and Graeff 1989). Thus, during the 1980s, a vicious circle developed in the fiscal order: The central state cut its budget to help deal with the external debt while the states spent irresponsibly and then rolled over their debt to the central bank, which worsened the central state's fiscal woes.

A secondary macroeconomic contradiction developed as the state banks issued currency to finance state spending (seigniorage), a practice that added to the astronomic inflation rates and helped scuttle consecutive national antiinflation plans. Lourdes Sola (1995, 48) insightfully describes this contradiction as the "regional fragmentation of monetary authority" and the concomitant weakening of the central bank and the CMN. This vicious financial and monetary circle *(ciranda financeira e monetária)* within the state spun out of control in the 1980s and generated a total $57 billion of debt among the states by 1991. This amount was almost half Brazil's total external debt and presented a clear threat to maintaining the financial stability of the new democracy.

Reasserting Central State Authority Over the Financial System

The dilemma presented by the *ciranda financeira e monetária* showed signs of improvement during the early 1990s because of a conjunction of different factors. First, the national monetary authorities of the Fernando Collor administration (1990–1992) forced the state banks to initiate adjustment programs under threat of central bank intervention.[12] In 1990, state governments were prohibited from rolling over their debt to the Banco do Brasil, a restriction that effectively scared away investors from state debt paper and placed tremendous pressures on the governors to either support federal tax reform efforts and state bank restructuring or face bankruptcy (Lagemann 1995, 336).

This game of chicken between the central and subnational governments improved the overall liquidity of the state banks after 1991, but not enough. Total liquidity minus debts and other obligations remained negative through the mid-1990s, and by 1992, the debt of the state banks represented almost twice their total liquidity. Financial pressures on the state banks increased with the advent of lower annual inflation rates under the Real Plan in 1994, as reduced inflation squeezed the profits of the state banks, which made financial adjustment more immediate and increased the leverage of the central bank. In the wake of these events, full enforcement of state constitutional provisions that defended the state banks from central bank intervention became politically and fiscally unsustainable.

The election of Fernando Henrique Cardoso and the financial impact of the Real Plan represented the high point for the recovery of central state leverage over the subnational financial system. As many state banks began to falter and state governments became increasingly dependent upon federal bailouts, Cardoso employed the leverage these factors accorded the federal government to force the governors to implement financial and fiscal reforms, privatize their utility companies, restructure and/or sell off their state banks, and initiate civil service reforms in return for federal help (Affonso 1997, 25).

Cardoso's pressure was reinforced by supportive federal legislation designed to coerce and cajole subnational governments into reducing bloated state and municipal payrolls. Empowering legislation called the *Lei Camata* (Camata Law) required that states and municipalities limit payroll expenditures to 60 percent of net revenues.[13] Under this new law, the federal government could even threaten to withhold federal transfers and loans from recalcitrant states.

Although the 1988 constitution forbade the old practice of using state banks to finance public expenditures, only the threatened or actual intervention of the central bank in the affairs of the state banks during the 1990s provided a stopgap against an unsustainable subnational spending spree. Other federal efforts kept the 1988 reform from generating additional fiscal problems. Losses of federal shares of tax receipts were partially compensated by increases in federal taxes not subject to transfer to the states or municipalities, and substantial increases in the collection of one of these sources of federal revenue—social security taxes—accounted for almost 40 percent of total federal income in 1994. Additionally, tax evaders were prosecuted more vigorously. The federal tax collection bureau (Receita Federal) was restructured and modernized, making it a more efficient state agency. Owing to countermeasures such as these, the federal government actually began to see a net increase in its total tax receipts.

The Fiscal War

Although certain aspects of federal regulation of state spending were accentuated, other aspects of centralized control dwindled. The constitution of 1988 kept the federal government from employing state tax incentives as it had in the 1970s and transferred that power to the state governments. As a result, fiscal incentives (mostly of ICMS) soon became the main weapon in attracting new, large investors away from other states, particularly São Paulo. The use of this mechanism by one state was often seen by neighboring states as an offensive that needed to be answered in kind.[14] The Brazilian popular press described the competition as a "Hobbesian fiscal war" among the states— a conflict that would ultimately create a series of problems for the tax system, for the internal market, and for the fiscal stability of the state governments themselves.

Despite these alarming trends, the overall fiscally destabilizing effects of "the fiscal war" have been greatly exaggerated. First, the argument that state tax incentives based on ICMS forced down tax revenues is based on mixed evidence, as long-range data show that fiscal incentives based on ICMS did not reduce total tax receipts. According to Eugênio Lagemann (1995, 340–43), the decline in ICMS receipts during the 1990–1993 period was the result, not of the fiscal war, but of a decline in the value of retail sales, a condition directly linked to the tremendous rise in inflation rates and the economic recession. In addition, the elimination of indexation, the rise of financial speculation, and widespread tax evasion also undercut ICMS receipts. All of these conditions emanated from the gradual failure of Collor's inflation control schemes. Conversely, there was a rise in ICMS receipts in 1994 precisely because the Real Plan stabilized retail prices and reduced the attractiveness of financial speculation and the Receita Federal, and the state governments cracked down on tax evaders.

Additionally, a number of informal constraints limited the Hobbesian nature of the fiscal war. During the 1990s, most state governments became unwilling to devastate their own fiscal accounts to implement social and economic policies. In fact, the most active "warrior states" in the fiscal war advanced the most in correcting for the poor budget administration of the past, privatizing state banks and utility companies, shrinking the civil service, and cracking down on tax evaders. Rio de Janeiro, a state that had recklessly exempted the ICMS under Governor Leonel Brizola (1990–1994), pioneered subnational privatization with the sale of Banerj, Rio's decaying state bank; Cerj, the state's electricity distributor; and Companhia Estadual de Gás and Riogás, both gas distributors. Rio also led the way in reducing redundant bureaucratic staffs with forced and voluntary dismissal programs. Minas Gerais followed suit with its own voluntary dismissal system and sales of going concerns such as Credireal (finance) and Cemig (utilities). Fiscal reforms in Minas also stabilized public accounts and led to increases in tax collection. Similar reforms were undertaken in Rio Grande do Sul and São Paulo.

In many of these states, fiscal incentive schemes continued to be used selectively as part of new subnational industrial policies, but their fiscal sustainability became a key factor governing their implementation. There is some preliminary evidence that the states involved in the fiscal war improved their tax collection functions to compensate for tax incentives to select businesses (Affonso 1997, 18). Moreover, "warrior" states such as Minas Gerais and Rio de Janeiro became reluctant to provoke their neighbors. These states granted strategic concessions to some firms but backed off from more aggressive policies. Governor Azeredo in Minas, for example, gave Mercedes fiscal incentives in 1995 to build a new plant in Juiz de Fora but was hesitant to extend the policy to automakers wishing to move from São Paulo. Moreover, Governor Azeredo, Governor Vítor Buaiz of Espirito Santo, and other state leaders became active in the campaign to create new national institutions to regulate fiscal incentive schemes.[15] In this way, the states developed incentives not to consume fiscal resources without regard for the welfare of the national fiscal structure and the fiscal structures of neighboring states. As subnational reforms move forward, these governments will overcome the tendency to embrace recalcitrant postures.[16]

Encouraged by growing support among the governors for new national rules, President Cardoso attempted to revisit his 1993 campaign for fiscal reform. This time, however, Cardoso faced state and municipal governments that, although not at Hobbesian odds with each other, were less inclined to form a subnational coalition against national reform after several years of fiscal war. Once again, the context for reform had changed, which allowed Cardoso to aggressively assert his proposals for institutional adjustments.

In 1994, Cardoso won passage of the Social Emergency Fund (FSE), an ad hoc measure that allowed the federal government to employ discretion over federal transfers constitutionally earmarked to go to state and municipal governments (the name was changed to the Fiscal Stabilization Fund [FEF] after it was renewed in 1995).[17] A similar strong-arm intervention by federal authorities into subnational fiscal policy was passed in November 1996. The Kandir Law, named after the planning minister, Antônio Kandir, removed ICMS taxes on exports to reduce Brazil's mounting trade and current account deficits. Through the FEF, the Kandir Law, the *Lei Camata,* and the transfer of additional responsibilities in health care, housing, and social policies to the state and municipal governments, the Cardoso government imposed a de facto reform of the fiscal structure without reform of the 1988 constitution. Of course, these were stopgap measures designed to rein in public spending while crucial reforms of the administrative and social security systems crawled through Congress.

Social Policy

If the central state began to reassert its authority over monetary and fiscal policy in the wake of the decentralization wave, Brasília clearly forfeited its role in creating a coherent national model of redistribution to counteract historical disparities among Brazil's regions. Despite decades of industrial deconcentration—the movement of firms from urban centers to interior regions and neighboring states—and several national policy experiments,[18] the distribution of economic activity in Brazil remains largely concentrated in the Southeast and South in general and São Paulo in particular (C. Diniz 1995). The southeastern states alone account for more than 60 percent of Brazil's GDP, and the per capita GDP of these states is three times that of the poor states of the Northeast (L. Neto 1995, 38).

Such geographic unevenness in income registers in the social indicators. Whereas 15 percent of the population in the Southeast subsists under the poverty line, more than 50 percent of the inhabitants of the Northeast are below that mark. The life expectancy of a *nordestino* (northeasterner), fifty-eight, is nine years below that of a *paulista* (a resident of the state of São Paulo), sixty-seven, and fifteen years below that of a *gaúcho* (a resident of Rio Grande do Sul), seventy-three.

Predictably, the decentralization of tax authority to the states and municipalities did little to reverse that legacy as the underindustrialized northern and northeastern states enjoyed a much smaller tax base than the industrialized southeastern and southern states (Rezende 1995, 250–53). In 1991, for example, the state governments of the southern regions received more than 85 percent of their revenues from state taxes whereas the northern states collected less than 35 percent of their income from state taxes (Barrera and Roarelli 1995). The poorer states continued to depend upon federal transfers, yet even here, distribution of such monies within the depressed regions was not equitable. Instead, distribution reflected the political importance of certain states. Thus, in 1988, Maranhão, the home state of the sitting president (Sarney), received 25 percent of the negotiated federal transfers to the North (Roarelli 1994).

The continued dependency of the poor northern and northeastern states on federal transfers severely limited their capacity to bargain with the federal government for national resources. More politically powerful states such as Bahia have the leverage of influential leaders like former governor, now federal senator, Antônio Carlos Magalhães and other key politicians. Yet most of the poor states of the North and Northeast have found it difficult to escape the constraints of their dependency on federal transfers and the superior leverage this gave Brasília to demand austerity. National reforms that force poorer states to adjust without social welfare compensation will have a regressive effect on the distribution of wealth in these regions in the years to come (Dain 1995).

The decentralization of key social policies also failed to improve the financing and overall quality of public services to the poor. One example is the performance of health care policy, the most decentralized social policy in

Brazil. The decentralization of health care under the Sistema Unificado e Descentralizado de Saúde (SUDS) led many states to reduce their own expenditures as new federal funds arrived. Municipal and state medical personnel also demanded the higher salaries of federal health care bureaucrats, and many local politicians unscrupulously misappropriated SUDS accounts. As a result, the decentralization of health care did little to promote either the quality of preventive medicine or citizens' access to policy making (Weyland 1996a, 174–75).

After Decentralization: Innovative Policy Experiments Among the Brazilian States and Municipalities

As noted earlier, shifts in the political interests of certain subnational governments were essential for moving national reform efforts forward. These dramatic changes in the subnational games of taxing, spending, and rolling over debt were owing to new economic and social priorities in state and municipal governments.

To be sure, there was plenty of evidence that patrimonialism persisted in subnational politics during the 1990s. One of the largest political scandals of recent years involved the distribution of kickbacks to important city and state officials from the sale of bond issues,[19] and given events such as that, it is easy to conclude that the enduring rule of Brazilian politics in state and municipal governments is the persistence of clientelism and illegal political transactions.

Despite such problems, many states and municipalities demonstrated a less commonly known trait of subnational government in Brazil: innovative leadership. During the 1990s, the expanding command over policy by the governors was, in part, a product of their capacity for producing innovative responses to persisting problems. Many of these so-called innovations from below *(novidades vindas de baixo)* appeared in the areas of health, education, housing, and industrial policy, areas that had been substantially decentralized during the 1980s and 1990s. In cases such as SUDS, however, decentralization did not improve the quality of services and only reinforced the clientelistic networks seen by many people as endemic in Brazilian politics. Under what conditions did the implementation of these *novidades vindas de baixo* serve Brazilians efficiently and under what conditions did these experiments decompose into "rent seeking"?

Recent studies of state and municipal policy in Ceará and Minas Gerais suggest that, in those cases, social and economic policies were implemented in ways that maximized allocative efficiency. Crucial to these experiences was the way in which the clientelistic tendencies of Brazilian politics were impeded by institutional innovations.

Judith Tendler's (1997) study of state programs in preventive health, public procurement, and agricultural productivity in the poor northern state of Ceará found a high level of professional dedication among the implementors of the policies, and Tendler outlines a number of reasons for the emergence of "good government" in Ceará. First, reformist governors, specifically Tasso Jereissati (1987–1991 and 1995–present) and Ciro Gomes (1991–1994), blocked parochial encroachments by political opponents by strengthening meritocracy in the state's civil service.

Second, through supportive publicity and the distribution of awards for meritorious performance, municipal workers, those most responsible for implementing many of Ceará's social and economic policies, were given incentives to develop working relationships with their citizen "clients" that were based on trust. Third, Ceará's inspired public servants cultivated multiple ties with nongovernmental organizations, citizen's groups, labor unions, business specialists, and other groups. These ties established mutual monitoring networks that buttressed trust between the public sector and its citizen clients. Multitask work (job enlargement) and a flexible problem-solving approach to service delivery increased the frequency of contact between public workers and social groups and thus expanded the system of mutual surveillance that kept both public and private interests from "shirking" their responsibilities. The result was a subnational policy system that proved efficient in responding to local needs.

In Minas Gerais, a state considered by some to be an exemplar of subnational clientelistic politics (Hagopian 1996), Alfred Montero (1997, chaps. 6–7) found a combination of political and institutional factors similar to those highlighted by Tendler in the state's industrial policies of 1989–1995. Once a prominent beneficiary of national industrial policy, especially in the public steel and mining sectors, Minas's economy fell on hard times during the 1980s when the central state became mired in a fiscal crisis. Patrimonial politics, particularly under the governorship of Newton Cardoso (1986–1990), almost destroyed the state's development agencies. Cardoso's exit and a concerted attempt by professional leaders of the Institute of Industrial Development (INDI) (Instituto de Desenvolvimento Industrial); the state development bank (BDMG) (Banco de Desenvolvimento de Minas Gerais); Cemig, the state utility company; and other agencies to redraw Minas Gerais's industrial policy in 1988 and 1989 produced new directives for the new governor, Hélio Garcia.[20] Garcia delegated authority over economic policy to a team of technocrats in the state secretariats of economy and planning, and the team emphasized policies that would reduce Minas's barriers for new investment and increase productivity among firms already in the state.[21]

One of the chief examples of the new industrial policy of Minas Gerais was public assistance to the Italian automaker Fiat, the state's largest private producer. During the early 1990s, Fiat attempted to launch a productivity-enhancing system that would place suppliers close to or inside the company's plant in Betim so that supplying firms could manufacture and install parts directly on the production line, which would obviate Fiat's costly system of maintaining an inventory of parts. Since most of Fiat's suppliers were largely inefficient Brazilian small- and medium-sized firms with little capital, the market alone could not guarantee that the multinational's new "just-in-time" system could be assembled. INDI, BDMG, Cemig, and other state agencies mobilized informational, financial, and infrastructural resources to move Fiat's suppliers. After the program had been completed, Fiat's productivity improved markedly, moving the firm from fourth position in the Brazilian market in 1989 to number one in 1994.

As in Ceará, industrial policy in Minas Gerais was enhanced by significant political support on the part of reformist leaders, but it was also made more efficient by an array of horizontal ties among the state's public economic agencies and secretariats and vertical ties between the public sector and private firms. Horizontal associations produced additional levels of political support by creating a broader constituency for industrial policy, and these ties also provided an interdisciplinary approach to policy by linking utility companies with financial and informational resources. Vertical associations fostered mutual monitoring networks that created additional barriers to rent seeking and reinforced trust between civil servants and firm managers. In subnational cases, such as Minas Gerais, where political support was strong and there was horizontal and vertical embeddedness (formal and informal ties between public agencies and private actors), industrial policy achieved a high level of allocative efficiency. When the mixture of political and institutional factors was either missing or malformed, in states such as São Paulo and Rio de Janeiro, Montero (1997, chap. 8) found that subnational industrial policies failed to achieve allocative efficiencies. These policies collapsed into widespread rent seeking and added to fiscal problems.

The cases of Ceará and Minas Gerais demonstrate that subnational politics in Brazil is not inevitably or endemically clientelistic, and the comparison shows that similar political and institutional factors in different areas of policy in very distinct regions of Brazil are responsible for the successful experiences. Replicating these factors in other regions throughout Brazil will be difficult. Nevertheless, William Nylen (1997b and Chapter 6) suggests that reformist parties such as the Workers' Party (PT) can take experiences with local-level governance and create a larger *modo (petista) de governar* "PT mode of governance") that is applicable to other jurisdictions. Other scholars who have studied progressive local governments in Brazil and Latin America agree that subnational innovations can be powerful models but find that the experiments depend on a sustained process of policy experimentation and learning (Jacobi 1995a; Winn and Ferro-Clérico 1997). That would be encouraging news for Brazilian democracy as it would enhance the notion that decentralization creates more accountable government over time.

The role of reformist political leadership is crucial to these experiences. By reinforcing the notion that governors and federal deputies were the leaders of the regime transition and the defenders of their regions in the Constituent Assembly, democratization enhanced the political standing of reformist governors (as well as nonreformists). The replication of experiments in "good government" will, in part, depend on whether these will become standards by which voters will judge their elected officials and demand a similar level of responsiveness.

Conclusions

The image of the new Brazilian federalism that emerges from this analysis is that of a mosaic of conflicting, flexible, and sometimes innovative institutions and political interests. During each of the three phases of decentralization, the process generated a mixed bag of implications for the country's new democracy.

During the liberalization of authoritarianism, decentralization played an important role in accelerating, even leading, the process of regime transition. However, the sequencing of decentralization before democratization reinforced subnational clientelism, which proved especially destabilizing for the new democracy as the fragmentation of political authority and fiscal resources led to irresponsible public spending and weakened the national state's distributive functions. Furthermore, the attack on the central state's monetary and financial authorities added to Brazil's megainflationary woes and threatened to push the country into economic chaos.

Reequilibration of intergovernmental authority was the only possible response to the problems generated by decentralization. Yet, consistent with the persisting paradox of the new federalism in Brazil, decentralization facilitated reequilibration. Central state authorities during the 1990s, such as the central bank and the Cardoso administration, made headway on fiscal and monetary problems with a combination of positive and negative sanctions on the states, and the credibility of these sanctions increased as subnational budgets and state banks fell on hard times. Additionally, the fiscal war helped divide subnational interests and eroded regional alliances formed during the 1980s. In this way, the leverage of Brazilian presidents increased, clearing the way for nationally imposed austerity.

In addition to changing contexts, shifting interests among governors also played a role in reequilibrating intergovernmental authority. Subnational efforts during the 1990s to improve public accounts and end the Hobbesian dangers of the fiscal war were critical to the success of federal attempts to reequilibrate intergovernmental authority and to remove the worst problems created by decentralization in the 1980s.

Continued reequilibration, however, rests on flimsy foundations. Current efforts rely too heavily on federal stopgap measures and continued compliance by governors. Brazil is far from attaining the thorough reform of the federal system and the constitution that it very much needs. The weakness of the national distributive policies is an indication that the central state must still recover significant authority and resources to face social problems that subnational government can only partially address. Although the new federalism proved itself adaptable in the face of the worse-case scenarios, it has yet to prove itself as a lasting framework for strengthening the central state.

Finally, in the current phase of reversing the gains of decentralizers and passing additional policy responsibilities on to subnational governments, evidence of innovative policy experiments is emerging in some parts of Brazil. Although these examples only highlight responses to local concerns and do not represent national solutions, these experiences rest on institutional and political innovations that can be replicated in other jurisdictions. Without one's denying the existence of patrimonialism in Brazil, these cases correct the all-too-facile assumption among scholars of Brazil that subnational politics is monolithically corrupt and clientelistic.

How can the new Brazilian federalism be understood? Endemic theories tend to overstate either the clientelistic tendencies of the country's politics or to imagine national systems of efficient federalism that are only partially borne out in practice. Neither approach sheds light on the mixed character of the Brazilian federal structure. This evolving process has enhanced democracy by limiting authoritarian centralism and promoting the allocative efficiency of some subnational governments, but it has also strengthened clientelistic circles in other subnational governments, weakened national political parties, and forced recent Brazilian presidents to resort to extraordinary measures in order to recover authority and resources once under the exclusive purview of the central state. Conversely, democratization has itself reinforced some of these tendencies. By empowering governors as historical leaders of the Brazilian transition to democracy, these subnational politicians have renewed their command over the country's politics. If the reequilibration of intergovernmental authority rationalizes the distribution of federal powers and resources, the new Brazilian federalism will become a force for strengthening democracy and the central state upon which social equity and macroeconomic stability depend.

FOUR

Reinventing Local Government?

Municipalities and Intergovernmental Relations in Democratic Brazil

David Samuels

razil's democratic transition has reinvigorated its federal institutions (see Chapter 3), and as part of that process, there has been a dramatically new development in the post-1988 period: decentralization of significant power and resources to Brazil's municipalities, the country's lowest level of government.[1] In this chapter, I address the questions, What explains the decentralization of political power to the municipal level, given the traditional dominance of national- and/or state-level political actors and institutions in Brazil? and What are the consequences of this development for democratic Brazil?"

Municipal politics in Brazil merits special attention because Brazil is not dominated by one "metropole" that also serves as the location of the central government, as is the case in Argentina and Mexico, for example. Instead, like the United States, urban centers are spread across Brazil's territory. Brazil is Latin America's most populous country, and the vast majority of Brazilians live in urban areas, where they have come to demand more from municipal government. All Brazilian politicians recognize that they dare not ignore the demands of the urban voter or municipal-government interests.

In addition, political and fiscal decentralization to municipalities gain in importance when we consider scholars' long-standing efforts to put a finger on "local power" in Brazil—whether under democratic or authoritarian rule. The debates range from the primacy of the local *coronel* (political boss) (Queiroz 1976), to the dominance of the central government over local power brokers (Faoro 1958), to the mutual dependence of local, state, and federal governments (Leal 1977). Recent scholarship continues to point to the political importance of intergovernmental relations in democratic Brazil (Abrucio 1994; Hagopian 1996; Samuels 1998), and several scholars have explored the municipalization of specific policy areas (e.g., M. Almeida 1994; V. Costa 1998; Arretche 1998). Yet despite the current political importance of municipalities, scholars have yet to provide an adequate explanation for their political gains in the democratic regime since 1985.

One answer, that democratization and decentralization go hand in hand, can be dismissed. Correlation is not causation, and democratization as a general concept cannot explain the extent and form of political decentralization in any given country. One must explore the particular context of each country's democratic transition to understand why decentralization occurs extensively in some countries and not in others.

In this chapter, I place post-1988 developments at the municipal level in the perspective of Brazilian history, separate out the distal and the proximal causes of increased municipal autonomy, and then discuss the consequences of this transformation for the functioning of democratic government in Brazil. I argue that the distal causes lie in demographic change and the unintended consequences of two policies the 1964–1985 military regime ostensibly adopted to *limit* municipal autonomy. Regarding the demographic change, as in other countries, urbanization shifted the mass of Brazil's electorate from the countryside to the cities, and this transformation has had far-ranging political consequences. In particular, given Brazil's electoral system, municipal interests were also largely rural interests up through the 1964 coup, but now almost all Brazilian politicians must focus on providing government services to urban voters.

Two of the policies the military adopted also resulted in favorable conditions for increased municipal autonomy after redemocratization. First, while the military rulers ended presidential and gubernatorial elections, gutted Congress's powers, and deliberately destroyed the pre-1964 party system, they maintained the schedule of municipal elections. Thus, aspiring politicians found that the best opportunity to "make a difference" was at the municipal level during the military regime, as opposed to the state or national level. Second, shifting from a long-established practice, the military regime deliberately attempted to sidestep the role of state governments as intermediaries between national and local governments and instead dealt directly with municipalities, in a less politicized and more bureaucratized fashion. This practice freed municipalities from state-government tutelage and, in combination with Congress's and the states' military-imposed debility, left municipal mayors as the only politicians able to "claim credit" for the implementation of government programs or projects at the local level.

Those two policies, together with the political consequences of urbanization, had important consequences after redemocratization. When free elections returned in the 1980s, voters continued to pour out of the countryside and into urban areas, and politicians realized that their own political careers depended more and more upon bolstering their ties with officials in municipal governments and with urban interests. In fact, by the 1980s, a surprising number of politicians wanted to make their political careers at the municipal level, for urbanization and the military's policies had made the position of municipal mayor a significantly more attractive political position than previously. As a result, after redemocratization, politicians decided not to return to the pre-1964 situation, when state and national governments not only dominated municipalities but political criteria largely determined whether or not a municipality would obtain funds.

Because municipalities had become a relatively more important part of every Brazilian politician's career, the members of the 1988 constitutional convention sought to cement municipal political autonomy into the new constitution. Thus, the proximal cause of increased municipal autonomy lies with Brazilian politicians' career motivations: given the social and political context, Brazilian politicians consciously made certain choices, based on their own self-interest, that resulted in significantly increased municipal autonomy under the 1988 constitution.[2]

In this chapter, I first briefly describe the political evolution of Brazil's municipalities and explore how the post-1988 situation significantly differs from that of previous eras. I then discuss three interrelated factors to explain this evolution and consider what the political rise of Brazil's municipalities implies for the prospects of local and national democratic consolidation in Brazil. I conclude that while decentralization allows increased opportunities to address local problems with local solutions, can improve democratic accountability and responsiveness, and allows for a broader inclusion of actors into the government process, Brazil's municipalities still face numerous problems that may limit the possibilities for deepening democratic consolidation at both the local and the national levels.

Municipal Autonomy in Brazil: Historical Evolution

Historically, the central and state governments have dominated Brazilian politics while municipal governments have lacked the autonomy to chart their own futures. Under the Empire (1822–1889), municipalities were completely subordinate to provincial (state) presidents (Mello 1955, 10), but since at least the late nineteenth century, prominent Brazilian politicians have championed the idea of *municipalismo* ("municipalism"), which favors decentralizing political power to municipalities (Nogueira 1962, 136). Because of their efforts, municipal autonomy was even given lip service in

Brazil's pre-1988 constitutions. Nevertheless, even though the Old Republic's (1891–1930) constitution proclaimed municipal autonomy, state governors dominated politics within their states, playing municipal bosses off of each other (Castro 1987, 26; Brasileiro 1973, 6). Subsequently, although the 1934 constitution offered a window of opportunity, Getúlio Vargas's *Estado Nôvo* (1937–1945) quickly put an end to hopes for municipal autonomy and established the preeminence of the central government over both state and municipal governments.

The 1946 Constitution: The Failure of Municipalismo

With democratization in 1945, *municipalista* fervor reached new heights (Mello 1965), and rules prescribing increased municipal autonomy were inserted into the new constitution. Indeed, scholars concluded that Brazil's 1946 constitution boded extremely well for municipalities (Mello 1955, 29; Sherwood 1967, 38). For the first time in Brazilian history, a constitution mandated that all local officials be elected.[3] Municipalities also gained the freedom to organize services according to local needs and, most important, gained new sources of revenue from both the state and the federal governments. Since nearly all municipalities at the time lacked their own revenue sources, the new fiscal transfers promised municipalities "a large windfall" (Mahar 1971, 71), and municipal leaders believed that increased political autonomy would follow from the intended funding increases.

Unfortunately, despite the written rules, nearly all municipalities remained penurious and politically dependent because both state and federal governments ignored the constitution's revenue-transfer rules. In many years, the federal government delivered its payments late; in other years, it disbursed only part; and in some years, it disbursed nothing at all (Sherwood 1967, 124; Mahar 1971, 73). In addition, except for three relatively wealthy states, during the entire 1945–1964 period state governments *never* disbursed what they owed municipalities, and the three remaining states did so only "sporadically" (Mello 1965, 23) and according to political criteria that reduced municipal political autonomy (Ferreira 1965, 423). In short, efforts to increase municipal resources during this period failed, and municipalities remained politically subordinate to federal- and, in particular, state-government whims. Brazilian scholars observed this fact soon after Congress had promulgated the new constitution. One analyst wrote that state governments could neutralize the promunicipal constitutional rules (Xavier 1950, 222), and others argued that political connections, not formal rules, determined whether a municipality would receive the funds it was due (Mello 1955, 42–43; Brasileiro 1973, 105; Sherwood 1967, 38–39).

Municipalities also remained subordinate because the 1946 constitution failed to clearly delineate responsibilities among the three levels of government, and continuing a long-standing historical pattern, this ambiguity of policy responsibility allowed state governments to restrict municipal political autonomy (Mello 1955, 23). Diogo Lordello de Mello later concluded that "without demarcated functional frontiers and assigned responsibilities, municipalities lacked anything beyond a purely political role" during the 1945–1964 period (Mello 1971, 14).

In sum, despite a vocal *municipalista* lobby and promunicipal regulations, the 1946 constitution ultimately failed to benefit Brazil's municipalities. Instead, state governments regained powers lost under Vargas, and the federal government continued its expansion. Municipalities remained locked in their traditional role as passive recipients of government services—if their leaders had the right political connections. In 1946, *municipalismo* did not resound with a broad enough audience for its ideas to be put into practice. That would have to wait until 1988.

Military Rule: Municipal Circumscription

The generals who ended Brazil's democratic experiment in 1964 initially had no clear plan to modify intergovernment relations (Samuels and Abrucio 1997). In fact, soon after the coup, mayors from around the country met in Brasília to debate fiscal reform and other matters, believing they could lobby the military. Military President Castello Branco attended the meeting and listened to the local leaders' complaints. Given their lamentable experience under the 1946 constitution, municipal leaders proposed funding increases and the adoption of an automatic mechanism to transfer federal and state funds to municipalities (*Revista Brasileira dos Municípios* 1965, 205–06).

However the military government soon foiled the municipal leaders' goals. In 1967, with the promulgation of a new constitution, the military dramatically revised Brazil's fiscal system. The government created two "participation funds," one for states (Fundo de Participação dos Estados, FPE) and one for municipalities (Fundo de Participação dos Municípios, FPM). Ten percent of the income and excise taxes was to be pooled and then divided equally between the two funds. Although these transfers (as well as state-to-municipal transfer) were made automatically every month after 1967, and thus ought to have increased municipal funding, in 1968, the military soon reversed course and restricted municipal funding. The government halved (to 5 percent) the share of income and industrial products taxes that were to go to the FPE and FPM, transferred other state taxes to central-government control, and placed restrictions on how state and municipal governments could spend the funds they received or raised (Oliveira 1995, 22). Consequently, the municipal governments' share of total government expenditures declined by 14 percent from 1965 to 1975, and the funding reductions and spending restrictions also limited municipal political autonomy during the military period (Oliveira 1995, 29).

The 1988 Constitution: De Facto Decentralization

The 1946 constitution paid lip service to *municipalismo*, but municipalities gained little political autonomy under its aegis and were further constrained by military rule. In contrast, while the 1988 constitution also contains promunicipalist rhetoric, it has actually decentralized power. I now turn to the consequences of political and fiscal decentralization to municipalities; subsequently, I will explain *why* the members of the 1988 constitutional convention enacted a document that differs from previous efforts in both word and deed.

Under the 1988 constitution, for the first time in Brazil's history, municipalities gained legal status as federal entities, which eliminates the ability of the state and federal governments to interfere with municipal laws. Municipalities also gained exclusive authority to organize and provide local public services (largely public transportation), to organize municipal zoning laws, and to legislate and develop urban development plans (Articles 30 and 182 of the 1988 constitution). In other cases, such as preschool and primary education, social welfare, and health care, the constitution describes the municipality as the policy "executor" and states that technical and financial assistance is to be provided by the state and/or federal governments.

These changes give Brazil's municipalities greater relative autonomy compared to municipalities in other Latin American countries. For example, in Argentina, the provinces retain the power to organize municipalities, and of seven other major Latin American countries, only Brazilian municipalities currently have the power to pass legislation on their own. In the other countries, municipalities may be delegated powers, but this decision always emanates from another level of government. Therefore, Brazilian municipalities have a degree of formal autonomy that is unheard of in the rest of the continent (Nunes 1995, 196).

Brazilian municipalities also gained significant new resources under the 1988 constitution, mostly in the form of revenue transfers from state and federal governments, and Table 4.1 shows the shifts since 1960 in the relative balance of Brazilian fiscal federalism. Although the central government's share of total expenditures climbed following the 1964 coup, it began to decline in the 1980s. Since 1980, state governments have gained, but municipal governments have gained much more, almost a 100 percent increase in their share. Municipalities currently receive relatively much more (about 60 percent) than they did during the 1945–1964 period.[4]

The post-1988 fiscal decentralization has provided municipalities with an unprecedented degree of political autonomy because nearly all fiscal trans-

TABLE 4.1

Division of the Fiscal Pie in Brazil, 1960–1995 (percent of total expenditures)

Year	Central	State	Municipal
1960	59.5	34.1	6.4
1965	54.8	35.1	10.1
1970	60.8	29.2	10.0
1975	68.0	23.3	8.7
1980	68.2	23.3	8.6
1985	62.7	26.2	11.1
1990	58.9	27.6	13.5
1995	56.2	27.2	16.6

Sources: Rezende (1995); Varsano (1997), Tables 5 and 6.

fers continue to be made automatically.[5] Automatic fiscal transfers, as a percentage of the central government's budget, increased by 200 percent between 1978 and 1994 while "politicized" transfers were cut in half during the same period (Nogueira 1995, 28).[6] When politicians organized to decentralize resources to municipalities in the 1988 constitutional convention (and even earlier), they chose to increase automatic as opposed to discretionary transfers, a conscious choice to reinforce municipal autonomy and avoid a return to the pre-1964 situation (Samuels 1998, chap. 8). Members of the constitutional convention also removed nearly all restrictions on how municipalities could spend transferred funds (Affonso 1994). These changes have had important political ramifications, for increased automatic transfers (and decreased discretionary transfers) and the elimination of spending restrictions reduce the ability of state and central governments to meddle in municipal affairs and ought to allow municipal leaders greater leeway in making policy choices.

Currently, because of fiscal decentralization and Brazil's prolonged fiscal crisis, the central government lacks the resources to fund many policies adequately, and to meet its budgetary obligations, the central government in some cases has simply stopped providing services. This change has in effect resulted in significant policy decentralization to the municipal level, as municipal governments have stepped in where the central government no longer acts. J. R. R. Afonso and Serra argue that "as never before, municipalities have become extremely important in Brazil's public sector . . . municipalities have rapidly increased their expenditures and their basic governmental services such as education, health and sanitation, urbanism, and even public safety" (Afonso and Serra 1994, 21), and Fernando Abrucio and Cláudio Couto conclude that "contrary to the general impression of public opinion, states, and most of all, municipalities, have assumed the larger part of the responsibility for policies that generally [used to be] the responsibility of the federal government" (Abrucio and Couto 1996, 41). Municipalities have also begun to be active in totally new areas, such as implementing mini-mum-wage programs, job-creation programs, urban development plans, and participatory budgeting systems (Figueiredo and Lamounier 1996; Larangeira 1996; Z. Silva 1996).

This apparently empowering picture of increased municipal responsibil-ity, autonomy, innovativeness, and responsiveness to local popular demands is somewhat misleading because nearly all municipalities face a funding cri-sis that limits their autonomy. Despite the increased revenue transfers since 1988, most municipalities remain without *independent* sources of revenue, and even though the 1988 constitution shifted some taxes to municipalities as well as increasing fiscal transfers, municipalities must have some significant economic activity within their borders to generate tax revenue. Only if they generate tax revenue can they free themselves from depending on fixed amounts of transfers, and unfortunately, most municipalities lack valuable property and service-sector industries that can generate such tax revenue. Table 4.2 shows the distribution of municipalities according to their ability to raise their own revenue.

Almost 75 percent of Brazil's municipalities generate less than 10 percent of their total revenue from taxes and the problem is even more acute in smaller municipalities—almost 90 percent of the municipalities with 10,000 or fewer inhabitants depend on transfers for 90 percent or more of their revenue.[7] Not one municipality generates over half of its total revenue from its own tax base. In short, most municipalities in Brazil remain highly depen-dent on state- and federal-government transfers to pay salaries and provide services. Given this situation, these municipalities could never be expected to provide public services if they were made independent of state or federal government without a concomitant (and unlikely) additional decentraliza-tion of fiscal resources (or an increase in local tax collection).

TABLE 4.2
Distribution of Self-Generated Income by Municipal Population, Brazil 1993

Own Revenue as Percent of Total Revenue	Municipalities Grouped by Population			Total Number of Municipalities
	< 10,000	10,001–50,000	> 50,000	
0–10	2,012 (88.5%)	1,564 (69.8%)	117 (25.4%)	3,693 (74.2%)
11–20	261 (11.5%)	534 (23.8%)	223 (48.5%)	1,018 (20.5%)
21–50	0	143 (6.4%)	120 (26.1%)	263 (5.3%)
Totals	2,273	2,241	460	4,974

Source: Bremaeker (1995), Table 1.

In sum, while the 1988 constitution represents a significant advance in both word and deed for municipal autonomy, like Brazil's states (see Chapter 3), Brazil's municipalities face a paradoxical situation. On the one hand, the 1988 constitution decentralized resources and political power, which has allowed for municipal-level policy innovation and given municipalities a dramatically different historical role as a service provider for Brazil's citizens. On the other hand, given the gradual weakening of the central government, the pell-mell decentralization of policy making following the 1988 constitutional convention, and Brazil's agonizing fiscal crisis, municipal leaders now face a number of difficult problems. Moreover, the collapse of the "developmentalist" state makes it unlikely that the central government will generate a coherent plan to resolve the daunting challenges municipalities face. Still, these unmet demands create openings for individuals or groups to propose creative solutions—and the emerging importance of municipal leaders and municipal governments for resolving problems and providing services to Brazil's citizens means that for the first time in the country's history, municipal-level solutions to municipal-level problems are indeed a possibility.

Urbanization and Military Rule: Shaping the Context for Increased Municipal Autonomy

In the previous section I described the "reinvention" of local government in Brazil following the 1988 constitutional convention, and in this section I endeavor to explain this transformation. Prior to the 1988 convention, politicians held numerous "promunicipalist" meetings that attracted a good deal of media attention (São Paulo 1983; Quércia 1986; F. Oliveira 1986, 29; *Folha de São Paulo,* March 23, 1987, 10; *Gazeta Mercantil,* March 26, 1987, 7; *Jornal do Brasil,* March 26, 1987, 20; *O Estado de São Paulo,* March 26, 1987, 4),[8] and the *municipalista* lobby appeared prominently in the debates.

However, given that *municipalista* sentiment also ran high prior to the 1946 constitutional convention, the mere presence of such a lobby is an insufficient explanation for the changes that the members of the 1988 constitutional convention introduced. Increased municipal autonomy and power did not necessarily follow from democratization and/or from lobbying Congress. Why did these changes go much further on paper and—more important, in contrast to the aftermath of the 1946 convention—why have they stuck? In considering these questions, I focus on the distal causes of decentralization to Brazil's municipalities, two sets of forces exogenous to the constitutional convention: the political consequences of urbanization and of military rule. These factors set the stage for the transformations that the members of the constitutional convention would introduce.

The Political Consequences of Urbanization

Two demographic transformations define post-1945 Brazil: population growth and urbanization (see Chapter 12). Urban population growth increased most rapidly in the 1970s, growing faster than overall population growth, and in 1993, unlike other Latin American countries, which have few large urban centers, Brazil had 12 cities with a population of over 1 million and 196 cities with a population between 100,000 and 1 million (IBGE, 1998b). Moreover, mid-sized cities (population between 100,000 and 500,000) have been growing faster than the largest cities (M. Santos 1994, 81), and although the Southeast is the most urbanized region, the growth of mid-sized cities has begun to spread throughout the country.

Members of Congress have a strong incentive to pay close attention to municipal-level demands because they depend on connections with municipal government leaders and with local-level popular groups to advance their political careers (Ames 1995a, 1995b). This tendency is exacerbated by Brazil's electoral system, in which both federal and state legislators are elected in at-large electoral districts that conform to state boundaries. Moreover, voters can choose a candidate's name instead of a party label when voting. Given the statewide electoral district and the pressure for candidates to cultivate a "personal-vote" following, candidates for legislative office have tremendous incentives to campaign in urban areas where they benefit relatively more from media exposure and economies of scale in campaign advertising (e.g., relatively more voters will show up for a rally or see a painted wall in an urban area as opposed to a rural one). Consequently, even candidates with bases in rural areas also campaign in urban areas.

It is true that politicians during the 1945–1964 period also depended heavily on municipal bases of support (Ames 1987), but far fewer municipalities were "urban" during that period—the system that Victor Nunes Leal (1977) characterized as *coronelismo* operated in mostly rural municipalities. Still, what is important is not simply that there are more voters now and that more of them now live in urban areas but that residents of urban municipalities have different needs and present different demands than residents of rural municipalities. For example, housing and transportation are generally more expensive, and crime more rampant, in the urban areas. As the democratic transition progressed, such demands rang increasingly loud (Costa 1996, 115).

In addition, while many urban politicians still continue to seek votes by providing particularistic goods, urban voters are typically less well-integrated into clientelistic machines than are rural voters (see Chapter 12). For example, given the success of parties such as the PT in the larger cities (see Chapter 6), we know that urban residents are more likely to vote on policy issues than on whether they received particular goods such as jobs or money.

Thus, for politicians who are interested in building their reputation on re-sponding to broad popular pressures, holding municipal office provides such an opportunity. Even for those politicians who are interested in distributing particular goods, the apparatus of the municipal government is useful. In short, with more voters in urban areas compared to earlier periods, and with urban voters having different demands than rural voters, politicians increas-ingly have had to pay close attention to urban popular pressures.

The Political Consequences of Military Rule

Along with urbanization, two policies the military government adopted in-creased the benefits to an aspiring politician of holding a municipal-level position. First, the military continued to hold direct mayoral elections in all municipalities except state capitals throughout its rule.[9] As a result, while the military emasculated Congress's powers and reduced municipalities' fiscal resources, mayors continued to appeal to and depend on popular approval—and were closest to the citizens' day-to-day problems. Compared to the power of a federal deputy, during the military period the power of a municipal mayor increased, particularly after the 1974 election, when the military lost ground to the opposition Brazilian Democratic Movement (MDB) party and subsequently increased the distribution of patronage to its National Reno-vating Alliance (ARENA) allies at the local level (Medeiros 1986; Ames 1987). Throughout the military period, congressional deputies were cut off from access to the budgetary pork barrel, which meant that winning an election at the municipal level was more politically profitable during the military re-gime than winning an election to be a federal deputy.

Second, the political attractiveness of municipalities increased as an unin-tended consequence of the military's initial policy of restricting municipal (and state) autonomy. Under military rule, federal-government bureaucrats gained a freer hand to exclude subnational authorities from policy making and execution, and as a result, municipal participation in planning and ex-ecution of government programs was "minimal" during the dictatorship and municipal authorities were rarely consulted prior to a program's implemen-tation. Municipal officials often learned of new programs only by reading the official government newspaper. In short, resource allocation reflected the central government's priorities, not local-level needs or desires, even in highly populous municipalities (Instituto Brasileiro de Administração Mu-nicipal 1976, 37–8).

As part of this process of centralization, the military also deliberately cur-tailed state governments' historic role as intermediary between federal and local governments (Schmitter 1973, 220; Cammack 1982, 67; Medeiros 1986). Up through the 1964 period, state-level politicians had often "diverted" fed-eral resources, but by 1976, the central government had "blocked" state-government officials from interfering with federal-municipal contacts (Instituto Brasileiro de Administração Municipal 1976, 18). The military not only limited states' interference in municipalities, it also reduced states' capacity to politicize municipal-level resource distribution by making fiscal transfers to municipalities automatic. Although the military initially reduced the amounts transferred, automatic transfers assured municipal-level politicians that they would receive *all* funds they were allotted, without political interference. One Brazilian scholar concluded that "municipal governments' greatest conquest in the 1967 fiscal reform was not in the volume of funds, but in the certainty of receiving the federal quotas" (Mello 1971, 56).

Summary

Urbanization, the continuation of a degree of real political competition at the municipal level, and the circumscription of state governments' political powers made municipalities a better prize—a more profitable political investment—for an ambitious Brazilian politician during the dictatorship. Even though less money was coming into each municipality's coffers, at least during the dictatorship it came in automatically. Even if largely dependent on government transfers, municipal mayors still had the final say in hiring and firing and gained recognition for implementing public-works projects within the municipality. Thus, the reduction of "politics" in intergovernmental relations during the dictatorship meant that *only the mayor* could claim political credit for "getting the job done" in a municipality, given that federal-government bureaucrats were less interested in political credit and that the mayor did not have to compete with state officials or congressional deputies for public attention.

This transformation has had important consequences for democratic representation in Brazil, for it has reversed the historic role of mayors from being passive recipients of state- and federal-government largesse to active, creative problem solvers. Likewise, at the national level, the transformation also caused a change in federal deputies' roles. Currently, at least in the medium-to-large cities, mayors carry far more political weight than do federal deputies; deputies act as intermediaries on behalf of mayors by attempting to pry resources from federal and state governments.

Pinpointing the Political Causes of Increased Municipal Autonomy

The increase in the "supply" of municipal-level political positions during the dictatorship is a necessary but insufficient explanation for why politicians transformed intergovernmental relations in the 1988 constitutional convention. Despite this distal factor, when democratic elections were renewed, politicians could have chosen to revert to the pre-1964 situation, in which positions at the state and national levels had had relatively higher status. However, upon redemocratization, politicians instead decided to *augment* the power of municipalities relative to the other two levels of government. To understand why they did so, we need to explore the "demand" side of the equation. I believe that the proximal cause of increased municipal autonomy lies not only with the desire of many Brazilian politicians to solidify their support bases in urban municipalities but with their desire to build their careers on holding office at the municipal level—in particular, as mayor. Because of this desire, politicians have striven to increase the payoff for holding office at the municipal level.

Traditionally, Brazilian politicians have sought to build a political career in executive-branch positions in state and/or national government and have not typically sought a legislative career at any level of government (Samuels 1998). In the past, aspiring politicians might have held municipal office *prior* to holding office at the state or federal level, but recently, politicians have come to regard holding municipal-level office as a career goal in and of itself. Relatively more politicians seek the mayoral office because currently, the municipal executive has significant power—and the larger the city, the more likely it is that its mayor has a large budget and a large bureaucracy to control. Specifically, while municipal legislatures are very weak, the mayor is largely responsible for hiring and firing, the implementation of public-works projects, and the execution of various public policies.

On the other hand, federal deputies typically find that they play only a minor role in the national legislative process and, compared to the power of a mayor, that they have little access to politically useful government-provided goods. As one federal deputy stated: "In a Chamber of 513, a deputy can't stand out. It's rare, very rare. Many deputies don't feel that they have any power. Whereas a mayor, even of a medium-sized city, he's the boss. He is the power, he has the power of the pen. In the Chamber, nobody has the power of the pen! It's impossible for the average deputy to feel that he has any power."[10] Another politician argued: "From the point of view of a political career, a mayoralty represents a real advance. Many deputies say that winning the race for mayor of his principal city is the most important thing that could happen to him. It represents the crowning achievement of his career, his highest aspiration. It's almost as if the term as federal deputy was some kind of intermediate point in his real career, which is linked to the municipality."[11]

Not only do politicians *claim* that being mayor has become an attractive career option, political career-path data indicate the current relative prominence of municipal-level positions, as well as why these same politicians have chosen to endow municipalities with additional resources and power.[12]

For example, since 1945, many sitting congressional deputies have abandoned their seats soon after the election, *while* a legislature is in session, in order to take a political position outside Congress. Table 4.3 provides the percentages of sitting deputies who took a position outside of Congress from 1945 to 1998; legislatures elected under the military regime are italicized.

The percentage of deputies leaving for a municipal position began to increase in the late 1960s and proceeded throughout the military period (except for 1978)[13] and into the democratic period. The increasing desire of deputies over time to take municipal-level positions becomes even more pronounced when we include data on those deputies who not only *win* but those who *seek* election as mayor during off-year municipal elections. About 20 percent of all sitting deputies have run for mayor in each legislature beginning in 1987—and some untold higher number may have considered running (Samuels 1998, chap. 3). Obviously, the percentage of Brazilian federal deputies who see a municipal-level position as more enticing than a seat in Congress,[14] and are willing to spend the time and money to run for mayor instead of developing an "incumbency advantage" that might help them win the next legislative election, is significant.

Many deputies run for mayor *during* their term, but what do they do *after* serving in Congress? Elsewhere (Samuels 1998, chap. 4) I have shown that, as in the pattern evident in Table 4.3, deputies did not typically pursue a postcongressional career at the municipal level in the 1945–1964 period—only 5 percent of the deputies elected from 1945 to 1964 held a position at

TABLE 4.3

Percentages of Deputies Going to Municipal, State, or National Positions

Legislature	Municipal	State	National
1945	0.0	11.2	4.3
1950	0.3	5.3	3.0
1954	0.9	7.1	2.8
1958	0.0	7.7	7.1
1962	0.2	5.4	3.9
1966	*0.5*	*5.4*	*2.2*
1970	*1.3*	*1.6*	*0.0*
1974	*3.0*	*5.2*	*0.6*
1978	*0.7*	*8.8*	*0.7*
1982	3.6	9.0	1.9
1986	4.7	8.8	2.5
1990	6.8	11.1	3.0
1994	7.8	8.6	1.4

Note: Lines in italic indicate legislatures elected during the military regime.
Source: Samuels (1998), chap. 2.

the municipal level subsequent to their election to Congress. In contrast, nearly 25 percent of the deputies elected from 1982 to 1994 have already moved on to municipal-level politics. This change again confirms the recent growth in politicians' interest in municipal-level positions.

Clearly, Brazilian politicians' career ambitions have shifted since 1945. In the past, relatively more politicians sought a long-term career at the state-government level, or sought to land a permanent position in the national bureaucracy. Currently, many more politicians seek power at the municipal level, which indicates the dramatic transformation in the place of municipal government within the hierarchy of government institutions in contemporary Brazilian politics. When few prominent politicians seek to enter municipal politics, we can be relatively confident that municipal politics is a place for novices and that holding office at the municipal level is probably considered as a stepping-stone to higher office.

Currently, the situation is somewhat reversed. Municipal politics is now a place for seasoned politicians, and serving in state politics or in the national legislature may serve as a stepping-stone to holding office as mayor. In short, the most important change in the structure of political careers in Brazil following redemocratization was a revitalization not of national political parties but of politicians' increasing efforts to secure office at the municipal level. Given the context of urbanization and the unintended consequences of military rule, this desire has shaped how Brazilian politicians have acted in Congress. Acting in their own interests, instead of returning to the pre-1964 balance of intergovernmental relations after redemocratization, they have acted to institutionalize increased municipal resources and autonomy.

The Consequences of "Reinventing Local Government" for Democratic Brazil

I have already both described and explained the decentralization of political power and fiscal resources to Brazilian municipalities since 1988. Although a few studies of specific municipal administrations exist (Couto 1995; Abers 1998), we unfortunately lack evidence that decentralization has encouraged municipal authorities to be more responsive or accountable to local-level electoral pressures in general. In this section, I explore some of the benefits and problems of decentralization at the municipal level for Brazilian democracy.

The Benefits of Reinventing Government for Democratic Brazil

In 1988, municipalities gained constitutional status as federal entities, which has given them greater freedom to plan what works best, given local conditions. Municipalities have also gained dramatic funding increases and—more important—a guarantee that funds will reach their coffers. These changes allow municipalities to provide services where none were previously provided, and they also allow municipal leaders to now plan how to spend revenue. Local leaders—most notably but not exclusively from the PT—currently also have more leeway to implement creative service-provision and budgeting programs that attend to local needs (Abers 1998). In theory, the spread of such practices ought to improve the allocative efficiency of Brazil's scarce resources and promote local-government responsiveness to popular pressures, which in turn should improve democratic accountability. Given that fiscal transfers are automatic, if money comes in but service provision is poor, voters can "kick the bums out" with good reason—and politicians can campaign along those lines.

The expansion of municipal-government power also ought to improve democratic participation by dispersing and fragmenting political power, which offers opportunities for nontraditional and/or more-progressive actors to enter the political arena at the local level and influence policies that matter for people's day-to-day existence instead of directing all their efforts toward national-level politics. And, in fact, analysts generally agree that local government presents many examples of innovative leadership and creative solutions in such areas as health care, education, and housing (J. Costa 1996, 114; Abrucio and Couto 1996, 41; Figueiredo and Lamounier 1996). In addition, policy innovation at the municipal level provides a "demonstration effect" that promotes the spread of such creativity. It is to be hoped that in an effort to "reinvent" government at all levels in Brazil, both citizens and politicians will latch onto the positive experiences while also striving to end such practices as the use of the municipal bureaucracy for political purposes. In short, decentralization has opened the door for greater democratic accountability, responsiveness, and participation, but democratization at the local level faces a number of high hurdles.

Cartographer's Migraine: The Explosion of Municipalities in Democratic Brazil

One of the most important—and problematic—developments in Brazilian municipal government since the 1980s is simply the explosive proliferation of municipal governments. In 1988, Brazil had 5,500 municipalities, up from just over 4,000 in 1985, an increase of almost 40 percent in fewer than fifteen years. In Table 4.4, I divided Brazilian history since independence according to some prominent "breaks." Doing so demonstrates that the recent explosion in the number of municipalities is not historically unique: in fact, Brazil experienced a similar phenomenon following the promulgation of the 1946 constitution. During both the 1946–64 and 1985-present periods the number of municipalities added per year has exceeded one hun-

TABLE 4.4

Number of Municipalities in Brazil Over Time

Year	Total Number	Average Number Added Per Year, Previous Period
1822: Independence	174	
1890: Creation of Old Republic	842	9.8
1930: Ascension of Getúlio Vargas	1,275	10.8
1945: Overthrow of Vargas	1,645	24.7
1964: Military Coup	3,826	114.8
1985: Civilian Control Restored	4,040	10.2
1988	5,500	21.7

Source: Calculated from Instituto Brasileiro de Geografia e Estatística (1998a, 1998b).

dred. In contrast, for example, the 1964–85 military regime allowed very few municipal *emancipações*.

Unfortunately, the growth in the number of municipalities during the two democratic periods does not reflect popular pressure for more responsive local government. Instead, in both periods it was the result of politicians' desires to enhance their status as local political "bosses" by increasing the availability of government jobs and contracts. The 1946 constitution mandated that regardless of population, all municipalities (except state capitals) would receive equal shares of the 10 percent of the federal income tax that the national government distributed to municipalities. Similarly, the 1988 constitution mandates a minimum amount to be distributed from the central government, regardless of the municipality's size.[15] Thus, during both periods, politicians had incentives to seek out districts within municipalities that might qualify as independent municipalities, and then sponsor their *emancipação* (legal incorporation). Both constitutions encouraged the creation of municipalities with a low population, and as Table 4.5 shows, in 1993, Brazil had over 3,500 municipalities—71 percent of the total—with

TABLE 4.5

Municipal Population in Brazil, 1993

Population	Number in 1993	Number Created Since 1988
< 10,000	2,194 (44.1%)	650 (73.4%)
10,001–20,000	1,338 (26.9%)	180 (20.3%)
20,001–50,000	942 (19.0%)	41 (4.6%)
50,001–100,000	289 (5.8%)	8 (0.9%)
100,001–200,000	112 (2.3%)	5 (0.6%)
200,001–999,999	84 (1.7%)	1 (0.1%)
> 1,000,000	12 (0.2%)	0

Source: Calculated from Instituto Brasileiro de Geografia e Estatística (1998a, 1998b).

fewer than 20,000 inhabitants.[16] Moreover, of the 885 municipalities created in the five years after the promulgation of the constitution in 1988, almost 95 percent were smaller than 20,000.

The minimum-transfer rules in both the 1946 and the 1988 constitutions generated perverse incentives to create local governments where none were needed. For example, back in the 1950s, when the current president of the Senate, Antônio Carlos Magalhães (also a former three-time governor of Bahia and minister of communications), was starting out in politics as a state deputy, he worked to increase the number of municipalities in his state "so that [Bahia] would gain a larger share of the income tax reserved in the 1946 constitution for municipalities" (Beloch and Abreu 1983, 2019). Municipalities were even incorporated where no one lived. Politicians in the state of Amazonas created several municipalities that lacked demarcated borders and were also largely under water when the rivers would flood. In these "ghost municipalities," the mayor would arrive by boat, drop anchor, and declare his ship the city hall for a day (Mello 1965, 11). A subsequent state governor extinguished most of these literal ghost towns, but the problem in general remained.

Many politicians have continued that practice because they hope voters will perceive them as a municipal "founding father," to influence politics in the new town, and gain the votes that might come with such prominence (Machado 1968, 34; Mello 1965, 9; *O Estado de São Paulo,* September 9, 1996, A3). A new municipality means more guaranteed government jobs. For example, the creation of 1,000 municipalities means 1,000 mayors, 1,000 vice-mayors, over 10,000 city council members, and countless other municipal employees (*Veja,* August 16, 1995, 68–73). However, given that FPM funds are not unlimited, the creation of a new municipality means that less money is available for each municipality so that the (potentially) unnecessary creation of new local-level government structures is questionable in terms of service provision to citizens.

Problems of Reinventing Government for Democratic Brazil

Many of the municipalities' problems are structural and cannot be addressed through one-time policy changes, such as the weakness of social actors and political parties at the municipal level. Because they lack these agents of "social capital," many municipalities may continue to rely upon state- and federal-government agents to solve their problems instead of attempting to solve them on their own. Only in scattered instances (Tendler 1997; Abers 1998) have local governments been able to foster local "human capital."

Another outstanding problem is that fiscal decentralization has pushed the central government into attempting to recentralize resources; the *Plano Real* is an example of such an effort that has reversed municipal gains to some degree.[17] In addition, the proliferation of local governments reverses the effect of fiscal decentralization because it spreads municipal transfers more thinly and municipal leaders must, as a result, put additional pressure on the state and central governments for nonautomatic fiscal transfers. As with state-level leaders, many mayors find that personnel expenditures consume nearly all their resources, leaving little in the coffers for improvements in health care, education, or infrastructure. In the face of pressing fiscal shortfalls at all levels of government, it is therefore unlikely that municipal finances will improve in the short to medium term, which will continue to limit the local leaders' capacity to address local problems.

Still other problems are rooted in the absence of institutions that promote both horizontal and vertical intergovernmental cooperation. Apart from state government, Brazil lacks any institutions to foster intermunicipal cooperation on such critical issues as environmental cleanup efforts or, given that not every municipality needs or can afford a hospital, access to health care facilities. For example, the state of São Paulo has for years tried to create regional governments that have some autonomy, but municipal-government lobbies have consistently opposed such a move.[18] Policy decentralization, the lack of intermunicipal mechanisms for cooperation, and municipal proliferation since 1988 have strained the ability of municipalities to provide services and have limited their ability to solve pressing problems (Nunes 1995, 199).

Vertical cooperation is a problem because decentralization was not a conscious policy choice and did not involve a plan for states and/or municipalities to take over the provision of services. Instead, vertical cooperation resulted from the central government's sudden abandonment of the local governments (in every policy area except health care). Consequently, the principal characteristics of decentralization in Brazil are chaos and conflict between levels of government (M. Almeida 1994; Affonso 1994). The new constitution's vagueness in terms of each level of government's specific policy attributions exacerbates the difficulty (Abrucio and Couto 1996), and the lack of institutions to foster horizontal and vertical intergovernmental cooperation increases inefficiency. In contrast to Alfred Montero's conclusion in Chapter 3 that decentralization to the state level may have improved allocative efficiency, the same may not be the case for municipal decentralization. Moreover, intergovernment conflict decreases government responsiveness and diminishes democratic accountability.

Finally, the equal legal status all municipalities currently enjoy coexists with dramatic regional economic inequalities, and municipal capacity for the provision of welfare and/or local development services varies dramatically across Brazil. In the more-developed South and Southeast regions, more municipalities have the technical and financial capacities to undertake policy initiatives while in the poorer regions fewer do. This disparity suggests that national-level policymakers should adopt a more flexible decentralization of policy responsibilities across levels of government, yet no such plan is in the works. Addressing Brazil's stark socioeconomic inequalities is a major challenge in an era of decreasing federal government activity (Affonso 1996). Unless a national-level policy is devised, the chaotic nature of decentralization may perpetuate regional inequalities and leave the desperately poor regions to their own devices.

Conclusion

Reinventing local government has two faces in Brazil. On the one hand, municipalities today have more capacity to chart their futures than at any point in Brazilian history and are more independent of state- and federal-government political manipulation. Decentralization has provided more institutional and fiscal resources to municipalities, which has promoted greater responsiveness and has also opened the door for innovative local-level solutions to local-level problems. It has also allowed a wider variety of actors to affect the political process. In general terms, these changes all point to the benefits of municipalization for democracy.

On the other hand, while we can see the benefits of the decentralization of resources and power in theory, and in some places in practice, the impediments to democratic consolidation at the local level are more concretely obvious, and Brazilian scholars have proffered a generally pessimistic assessment of the municipalities' situation (C. Souza 1996). I conclude this chapter on a cautiously optimistic note, for it is not clear that democratization and decentralization are necessarily associated with increased allocative efficiency and increased government responsiveness at the local level. Nor do we know that Brazilian voters reward improved efficiency and responsiveness at the polls in local elections. In the interest of assessing whether Brazilian voters reward progressive strategies or not, I suggest that scholars direct their attention to the electoral consequences of policy innovation at the local level in Brazil.

The main problems facing municipalities are the lack of resources and the lack of incentives for intergovernmental cooperation. The lack of resources can be addressed by raising taxes, firing workers, or increasing tax collection, but raising taxes is most likely politically unfeasible, and firing workers is probably even less so. On the other hand, democratic reformers on all three of Brazil's levels of government might work together to attempt to increase tax collection. Although few municipalities raise their own revenue, municipal "dependence" on state- and federal-government transfers may result from either a lack of economic activity or a conscious choice not to collect municipal taxes. This situation could be reversed. At the municipal level, reformers might consider working together to increase the collection of the rural property tax and the service tax. In many cases (Bremaeker 1995), municipalities don't bother to collect taxes because the taxpayers have political connections. A solution to this problem could be for municipal governments to farm out the responsibility for imposing penalties on those who avoid paying municipal taxes to the state or federal government. That way, municipal leaders could claim that their "hands are tied" and that they can't "help" their friends. Such a policy would benefit all municipalities, and no taxpayer would feel singled out because a hostile local administration had entered office.

The lack of incentives for intergovernmental cooperation is rooted in the structure of local government, in which the executive dominates, as legislative weakness and executive strength are particularly pronounced at the municipal level (Couto and Abrucio 1995). Both within and across municipalities, executive dominance promotes individualistic political strategies on the part of local mayors. Although on the one hand this dominance might encourage mayors to be creative and might allow progressive politicians who win mayoral races to have a greater impact than if the legislature had more power, it also means that mayors seek resources for their municipality in a zero-sum game: If a neighbor gains resources, they see it as a personal political loss. Furthermore, executive dominance of municipal government perpetuates Brazil's traditionally individualistic and clientelistic style of politics, and many mayors continue to act as local "bosses," transforming the rural *coronel* based on ownership of land into a "municipal *coronel*" whose power is based on the personal "ownership" of municipal government. In some respects, therefore, developments at the local level parallel Frances Hagopian's (1996) claim that Brazil's transition to democracy at the national level has more elements of continuity than of change.

To address these problems, political reformers at all three levels of government could consider the creation of regional governments—and not just around the *grandes regiões* (major metropolitan areas) but in other areas as well. Brazil could learn from the experience of the United States, where the creation of subnational "special districts" such as school boards, water-management districts, transportation boards, and air-quality management districts has exploded in the twentieth century (Burns 1994). Regional governments ought to serve to resolve intergovernment disputes across existing government boundaries or to provide services where none exist. Not all regional governments in the United States are the result of efforts of progressive reformists; citizens, businesses, and property developers have created special districts with an eye to the inclusion of some citizens and the exclusion of others. As a result, the creation of cities and special districts in the United States has also meant increasing social segmentation along racial and class lines. The creation of municipalities in Brazil has not reflected similar goals, and given Brazil's dramatically different demographic and economic geography, Brazil might avoid some of the exclusionary aspects of the U.S. experience and gain the provision of collective goods that regional governments provide. For example, the creation of regional governments would force personalistic municipal leaders to cooperate with others, and perhaps encourage those leaders to develop and implement longer-term programs for addressing collective challenges.

The lack of clarity in Brazil's constitution regarding the responsibilities of the three levels of government should also be addressed, for it induces municipal leaders in particular to "pass the buck" and blame the other two levels of government when a policy failure is obvious. Amending the constitution to clarify the division of labor among the levels of government ought to increase governmental accountability and transparency. To do so, however, will require that Brazil's Congress "clear the slate" and pass extensive administrative and fiscal reforms—both of which appear unlikely at this time. Opposition to proposals such as these comes first and foremost from federal-government bureaucrats themselves (one of Brazil's most successful lobbies), who resist giving up their traditional prerogatives to design and implement public policy and also resist transfer of their positions to state and/or municipal governments. In addition, without additional resources, which is unlikely given the *Plano Real* and President Cardoso's efforts to recentralize fiscal authority, both state- and municipal-government leaders are likely to oppose restructuring Brazil's constitution to decentralize authority further.

I thus conclude that the "glass" of Brazilian democracy is only half full. On the one hand, many problems continue (and will continue) to plague the administration of municipal government in Brazil, and these problems will not fix themselves. Correction will require a concerted effort on the part of politicians at all levels of government. On the other hand, unlike previous periods of Brazilian history, decentralization provides opportunities for addressing local problems with local solutions, can improve democratic accountability and responsiveness, and allows for a broader inclusion of actors in the process of "reinventing" Brazilian government.

PART II

**Critical Actors in
the New Democracy**

FIVE

Assessing Civil-Military Relations in Postauthoritarian Brazil

Wendy Hunter

I n 1985, civilians returned to power after a twenty-one-year period of rule by the Brazilian military. The doctrine of national security that had guided the dictatorship of 1964–1985 held that the nation's security hinged on the development of a strong industrial capitalist economy, which could happen only if popular mobilization were held firmly in check.[1] This doctrine contributed to drawing the armed forces into a wide variety of political, economic, and social roles. In this chapter, I assess the evolution of civil-military relations in postauthoritarian Brazil after the military left power with considerable political clout and an ample array of institutional prerogatives intact. After addressing the following questions—To what extent has the balance of power shifted between elected civilian leaders and the military? Do the armed forces imperil the stability and quality of democracy? Have they adapted (and how) to the challenges presented by democratization and the international security environment of the post–Cold War era?—I conclude that progress has indeed been made in weakening the military's political influence but that more remains to be done to institutionalize current achievements, further depoliticize the officer corps, strengthen civilian control, and assign missions to the military that will keep them out of complicated and politically questionable domestic situations.

On the one hand, the civilian leadership's authority over the armed forces has expanded considerably, especially since the end of the presidency of José Sarney (March 1985–March 1990). Military influence over civilian decision making, especially nonexplicitly military issues, has weakened markedly, and the armed forces' institutional prerogatives have shrunk, as have the economic resources they control. Saber rattling, not uncommon during the Sarney years, is now rare, and military missions are beginning to be defined and regulated more clearly. Testimony to the low political profile of today's military is the paucity of attention it receives in the press, which pales in comparison to its "front-page presence" during the first few years after the transition back to democracy. Whereas meetings between the country's president and top brass in earlier years typically generated a host of speculation and rumors, they elicit scant media attention today.

The military's place in today's political system also differs greatly compared with the democracy of 1945–1964. During that period, different civilian actors frequently called on men in uniform to resolve political crises and standoffs, and there were coups in 1945, 1954, and 1964 in addition to coup attempts in 1955 and 1961. In the interventions prior to 1964, the military played the role of a *poder moderador* ("moderating power"), stepping aside after securing the removal of the executive it had deemed unfit to govern and overseeing the assumption of power by a new civilian executive (Stepan 1971). There have been periodic crises since 1985, the most serious one ending in President Fernando Collor's impeachment in 1992, but by and large, the civilians have not appealed to the military to resolve them. Neither has the military leadership appointed itself as an umpire.

Yet to assert that the armed forces have receded in political importance since the return to democracy in 1985 (and especially since the beginning of Fernando Collor's presidency in 1990) and have kept a lower political profile than in the period between 1945 and 1964 is not to imply that civil-military relations in Brazil are unproblematic. The general absence of overt contention with the civilian leadership does not mean that the armed forces have become just another state actor or that they have ceased to constrain the workings of Brazil's democracy over the long run. Serious gaps in civilian authority persist in some substantive policy areas, and officers harbor attitudes and occasionally act in ways that raise questions about their obedience to elected authorities. For example, the saber rattling they engaged in from mid to late 1993, the most crisis-ridden period of the Itamar Franco government, suggests that the military may not have retired unconditionally to the barracks and that it remains a force to be reckoned with. Finally, military roles need to be defined (and confined) more clearly in order to prevent dangerous forms of "mission creep."

It is thus important to ask whether the men in uniform continue to represent a fault line in the country's democracy. Will the military emerge from political dormancy should economic crisis and political polarization revisit

Brazil? Is the direction in which military missions are being redefined auspicious for extracting the military from the kinds of roles that politicized the institution and enmeshed it in the social, economic, and political fabric of the country historically? Have underlying attitudes within the officer corps changed in ways that are propitious for sustained democratic rule and enhanced civilian control?

In this chapter, I first present the basic components of civil-military relations in a democratic state, an ideal standard against which to assess interactions between officers and civilian officials in Brazil. Then I discuss the nature of the transition to democracy, which began in 1974, and the status quo that existed in 1985—providing an empirical baseline from which to judge developments since then. Next I analyze the progress that has been achieved since 1985 with respect to shrinking military influence and enhancing civilian authority, normalizing civil-military relations, and regulating military missions. Last, I examine some of the extant missions, attitudes, and institutional arrangements that remain problematic as far as the deepening of civilian control and the strengthening of democracy is concerned.

Civil-Military Relations in a Democratic State

The guiding principle of democracy is popular sovereignty, realized through the open competition for power via elections, and the oversight of state power by elected representatives or the officials appointed by them. When the armed forces exercise formal or informal veto power over civilian decision making, especially concerning issues outside the realm of defense, strictly defined, they limit and distort the sovereignty of citizens. Civilian control hinges on the development of institutions and norms that effectively confine the reach and power of active-duty officers.

Formal institutions that promote civilian authority include (but are not limited to) the following: strong legal restrictions on allowing the military to carry out internal security and domestic intelligence operations; a civilian-led ministry of defense to control and coordinate the defense sector; and legislative monitoring of issues such as defense expenditures, weapons systems, and military intelligence.[2] The norms and values that active-duty officers embrace in most fully consolidated democratic regimes serve to further limit the military's sphere of jurisdiction and independent authority. Officers in such systems tend to regard meddling in broad social and political issues as fundamentally inappropriate; accept civilian directives and scrutiny as a matter of course, even in strictly defense matters; and accept without condition that officers are accountable to the public rather than above the law.

Military Strength at the Inception of Civilian Rule

How closely did institutional configurations and officers' attitudes in Brazil reflect these characteristics at the inception of civilian rule? The military entered the new democratic era from a position of considerable political and economic strength. Having presided over a series of governments that conjured up positive associations in the minds of many Brazilians—namely, economic prosperity and social stability—the armed forces were able to remain fairly unified and to enjoy a strong bargaining position during the transition to civilian government.[3] The move away from authoritarianism was very gradual and began with the inauguration of General Ernesto Geisel as president on March 15, 1974, although some observers consider the transition incomplete until Brazilians went to the polls and directly elected President Fernando Collor de Mello, who assumed office on March 15, 1990. Clearly, the governments of 1964–1985 were led by a military organization with sufficient power to control the pace of the transition and demand a high price for extrication. The military used its strength to negotiate the retention of a vast array of political and economic prerogatives.

The ministries of the Army, Navy, and Air Force, whose chiefs had served in the cabinet since the 1920s, were maintained in place of constructing a unified, civilian-led ministry of defense to control and coordinate the defense sector, even though most advanced democracies in the world have unified ministries of defense led by civilians. The system of separate service ministries enhances the representation of active-duty officers in the cabinet and thus strengthens the voice of the military as a whole in executive decision making. The armed forces also managed to keep two other cabinet positions: the Military Household (Casa Militar) and the Armed Forces General Staff (Estado Maior das Forças Armadas, or EMFA). Both the Casa Militar and the EMFA gained ministerial status during the military regime of 1964–1985. The chief of the National Information Service (Serviço Nacional de Informações or SNI), an agency created in 1964 to collect domestic intelligence and carry out repressive operations against the antisystem left, occupied a sixth cabinet position associated with the military.

Another agency in which the military had had a central policy and personnel presence since 1964, the National Security Council (Conselho de Segurança Nacional or CSN), survived the transition to civilian rule. Under the dictatorship, the CSN assumed a central policy-making role toward issues broadly related to national security, including the cashiering of citizens' political rights, land tenure, the occupation and development of the Amazon, and Brazil's nuclear program. The CSN formed a crucial link between the civilian and military bureaucracy, and the same army general chosen to head the Military Household was in charge of the CSN. The latter was renamed but not fundamentally revamped with the promulgation of the new constitution in 1988.[4]

In addition to political prerogatives, the military had come to control important economic resources, such as state enterprises involved in the production of armaments, the management of high technology weapons, and influence over research and development policy, including nuclear research (Acuña and Smith 1995; Conca 1997). By the mid-1980s, Brazil was the only Latin American country able to compete as a full-service exporter of middle-level-technology arms. Military officers, together with civilian technocrats, were also squarely behind Brazil's attempt in the 1970s to create a domestic computer industry (Adler 1987; R. Nelson 1995). A reorganization of the informatics sector in 1979 strengthened the influence of the National Security Council over informatics policy, and this and similar measures in the nuclear area suggest the military's resolve to insulate defense-sector activities from civilian control and to preserve military autonomy in questions of technological development (Conca 1997, 199).

As for the military's outlook on the regime change and its role in the new democracy, direct statements by and the outward conduct of leading officers suggest that most of them saw distinct advantages to stepping down from direct power while retaining the capacity to exercise behind-the-scenes influence and veto power over civilian decision making. By ceding power, the "military as institution" would be less subject to public criticism and internal politicization and fragmentation. Furthermore, it could focus heightened attention on beefing up the country's external defense capabilities. At the same time, positions in the cabinet and control over two key agencies, the National Information Service and the National Security Council, promised to keep the military engaged in most of the major issues on Brazil's social, political, and economic agendas. In this connection, Army Minister General Leônidas Pires Gonçalves stated in 1986: "I am a military man, but I have a political aspect (*faceta*) and it is my right to express this aspect. . . I am a soldier, but I am a Minister; Ministers have political aspects and I think I have the right to say some things about political issues" (Stepan 1988, 105).

In short, because of the military's retention of important political and economic resources, it appeared on the eve of Brazil's return to democracy that the officer corps would retain decision-making control over defense and security policy in the country. Moreover, it seemed that the military would be able to continue to influence policies of broad social, political, and economic significance. The institutional bulwark the military had built around itself promised to allow leading officers to advance their goals without having to form close alliances with select politicians and their parties or to engage in visible forms of saber rattling or coups, as had occurred during the previous period of democracy. In other words, military tutelage could be exercised in a regular and routine fashion. Did these expectations turn out to be warranted?

The Decline in Military Influence and Normalization of Civil-Military Interactions in the Postauthoritarian Period

Brazil's armed forces enjoy far less political power, influence, and privilege today than they did in the initial period after the return to civilian rule. For example, whereas active-duty officers headed six ministries in 1985, they controlled four throughout most of the 1990s; this number dropped to zero when, in June 1999, President Fernando Henrique Cardoso implemented the decision to replace the three traditional service ministries and joint chiefs of staff with a unified ministry of defense led by a civilian. Similarly, while the military under the Sarney presidency interfered in civilian issues ranging from labor legislation to land reform, its current efforts to affect civilian decision making are confined primarily to corporate issues (e.g., salaries) and matters of defense (defined in a more restricted manner than in the 1960s, when quelling street protests was considered "defense"). In fact, a tacit pact seems to have emerged since the government of Fernando Collor (March 1990–September 1992): In exchange for basic political subordination, the military is allowed to enjoy substantial autonomy over its own corporate affairs and defense matters—subject to civilian control of the budget, which greatly affects issues like military salaries and defense projects.

In addition to the erosion of military influence, a normalization in civil-military relations has taken place over time, with disputes between leading politicians and officers in the immediate posttransition period typically reaching a more feverish pitch than now. The overt contention that marked earlier disagreements—as well as the potential gravity of those struggles for the stability of the government and regime—has definitely receded, and the military has long ceased to present an immediate threat to Brazilian democracy.

Given this normalization, the ever-pragmatic President Cardoso felt secure enough to pursue a policy that no one before him would have dared to for fear of military reprisal: to compensate monetarily the families of those people who died at the hands of the dictatorship. Included in the pool were the families of the guerrilla leaders Carlos Lamarca and Carlos Marighella. Given that Lamarca had been a military officer himself and hence was a mutineer in the eyes of the officer corps, as well as in objective legal terms, Cardoso's decision to compensate his family was particularly bold. The move provoked visceral military outrage, but in the end, Cardoso prevailed, which reveals the extent of the change that has taken place in civil-military affairs.[5] Financial compensation obviously falls far short of rolling back self-granted military amnesties and punishing officers through trials and prosecutions, but in a country where men in uniform have acted with total impunity historically, and state officials in general have not been accountable to the public, such a policy represents a tremendous advance.

What accounts for the weakening of military influence and the normalization of civil-military relations since 1985? One factor, of course, is the erosion of military influence, for which it is necessary to examine civilian as well as military factors. Electoral competition under Brazilian democracy has created incentives for politicians to reduce the interference of a politically active and influential officer corps. Politicians can be expected to contest the military when the latter's preferences and actions conflict with the former's capacity to gain widespread electoral appeal. Democratization, coupled with the diminution of internal security threats in the post–Cold War era, has led many politicians to regard the armed forces more as a competitor for political influence and economic resources than as a potential ally. For example, institutional prerogatives that enhance the military's clout can restrict the latitude of politicians to support popularity-enhancing policies that are often at odds with military preferences.

Also, resources consumed by the military, often on projects that have little electoral appeal, are thought of in terms of their opportunity cost. The pressures of electoral competition often motivate politicians to wrest resources away from the armed forces and put them toward civilian projects that will gain more votes among constituents. If electoral competition creates *incentives* for politicians to reduce the military's clout, winning elections, especially by margins that endow politicians with strong mandates, enhances their *capacity* to do so.[6] A military leadership that acts forcefully against a government with widespread popular support runs the risk of losing legitimacy, something most military organizations seek to avoid.

My analysis differs from that of several other scholars—e.g., Alfred Stepan (1988), Brian Loveman (1994), and Jorge Zaverucha (1993, 1994)—who question the ability of Latin America's civilian governments to make meaningful reforms in civil-military relations, especially in cases where the military maintained a firm hand over the transition to democracy. According to those scholars, the founding conditions of democratic rebirth in Brazil made it all but certain that the armed forces would place the political class under their own strict supervision. My analysis, by demonstrating that the terms of the transition receded in importance as democratic pressures took over and compelled politicians to consider their own fortunes above those of the military, documents the ability of even a weak democratic regime to expand its margin of autonomy vis-à-vis the military and rejects the historical institutionalist paradigm other scholars adhere to in favor of an approach based on rational choice premises.

Although part of the divergence between my rendition of civil-military relations in postauthoritarian Brazil and that of others is theoretical in foundation, another important aspect is empirical: the judgments of earlier works, which stress the persistence of military power, are based on a shorter time period. For example, Stepan (1988) draws conclusions about civil-military relations in the new democracy from the 1985–1987 period only, but my observations are based on seeing Brazilian democracy unfold from 1985 to 1999.

As for the military, most of today's active-duty officers have come to accept—at least for the time being—the need to take a back seat to civilian leaders as long as the latter respect basic corporate integrity. Most of the officers have little interest in returning to power, and unlike the 1950s and 1960s, when the military was inspired by the doctrine of national security, today's military lacks a hegemonic project or agenda.[7] Its ideas on economic policy making do not differ significantly from those of Brazil's recent governments, notwithstanding its preference that certain state enterprises not be privatized. Senior leaders are relieved that "the military as institution" is no longer subject to the politicizing and fragmenting effects of military rule and feel under pressure to mend the institution's image. Moreover, they deem that the strength of support for democracy among both domestic and international actors would preclude a return to military government in any case. Hence, in contrast to decades past, senior officers no longer spend large amounts of time fraternizing with, much less conspiring with, the country's economic elite against civilian authorities at places like the Escola Superior de Guerra (Stepan 1973).

Instead of trying to regain political power, leading officers are actively engaged in efforts to protect their salaries and budgets, reinforce conventional defense roles, and develop new and credible military missions in line with changes in the international security environment. Seeking to enhance the institution's professional standing via more advanced training, the modernization of weaponry, and in other ways and to guard against downsizing, the military leaders devote significant attention to lobbying elected officials for resources. In putting pressure on civilian officials, they generally try to avoid saber rattling, which they fear might turn public opinion against the military, which could then contribute to downward pressure on military salaries and budgets. Thus, in general, the current military leadership is selective in its fights and has generally been unwilling to "go to the mat" to combat the institution's eroding influence. All things being equal, members of the officer corps are less likely to stick their necks out and contest government leaders when the latter enjoy a high level of popularity and a strong mandate.

How has the normalization of civil-military relations come about over time? Essentially, civilian leaders have discovered when (and over what issues) it is possible to check military power and privilege and when such efforts provoke conflict beyond what they are willing to withstand. A process of mutual testing, and the gains and losses that have resulted from that process, have established precedents and expectations. For example, whereas the army has demonstrated consistently a willingness to give up claims to certain public resources, it is adamant about preserving an age-old constitutional attribution that legitimizes an internal security function for army troops. A more stable coexistence between civilian governments and military officers has developed through this process of mutual probing and the accumulation of knowledge that has resulted from it.

In the following pages, I outline the general dynamic of civil-military relations in each postauthoritarian government, highlighting the specific achievements and/or failings of each with respect to pushing back military influence. The progression I demonstrate can be summarized as follows. During Sarney's presidency, the military maintained the vast majority of its institutional prerogatives but experienced the beginnings of an erosion in its ability to influence civilian decision making over nonmilitary issues of electoral salience to politicians. President Collor went a step further and successfully contested some of the military's institutional prerogatives of greatest political import. Actual military influence over civilian decision making eroded further in this period, but Collor did not try to fundamentally redefine the role of the military, nor did he attempt to redirect the armed forces' attention and energy toward credible nonpolitical roles of mutual interest to civilians and soldiers alike. Instead, he allowed corporate autonomy to prevail over questions of defense and military missions.

The brief presidency of Itamar Franco (October 1992–December 1994) impeded the reformism that had gained momentum under Collor from continuing but did not reverse previous gains in any serious sense. President Cardoso (January 1995–) is taking moderate but deliberate steps to further shrink the military's presence in the state. By not only contracting military prerogatives but also trying to redirect (and confine) the institution's substantive focus, his efforts go a step beyond those of Collor. Whether or not these efforts will meet with success and become institutionalized remains to be seen.

The Sarney Administration: Formal Prerogatives Prevail While Informal Influence Begins to Fall

President José Sarney trod lightly on the armed forces. Even had he wanted to challenge them, the weakness of his mandate—starting with the nonelectoral route by which he came to power—impeded his ability to do so. Sarney, a former politician of ARENA, the progovernment party under the dictatorship, had initially been the vice-presidential running mate of president-elect

Tancredo Neves, who died before he could assume office in 1985. Sarney became even more beholden to the armed forces after December 1986 when his popularity plunged after the failure of the Cruzado Plan. The media regularly showed Sarney alongside his military ministers, who frequently issued public criticisms of civilian authorities and commented on broad-ranging topics. In the absence of public support, the president sought refuge in the shadow of the military.

For the most part, the military successfully defended its formal institutional prerogatives during the Sarney period, and debates in the National Constituent Assembly (ANC) in 1987–1988 were the scene of intense military lobbying to defend these corporate privileges. The armed forces succeeded in maintaining the separate service ministries in place of a unified ministry of defense, a situation that enhances the military's collective voice in the cabinet. The armed forces were also able to prevent the dismantling of the CSN and the SNI, and they preserved their own personal and policy presence within those agencies. Of special interest to the army, the military managed to preserve a legal basis for intervening in internal security. The fact that many members of the ANC did not seem to perceive these military prerogatives as a direct and immediate threat to their own political interests contributed decisively to their survival. Also important were a complex dynamic of logrolling and the pivotal role played by President Sarney—who allied with the armed forces in response to problems of governability—in influencing votes and manipulating outcomes.[8]

Notwithstanding the preservation of most formal prerogatives and the military's continued efforts to try to influence extra-military issues through organs like the SNI and the CSN, the effective influence of the officer corps over policies outside its immediate corporate sphere began to slip even under Brazil's first postauthoritarian government. In other words, officers appeared increasingly unable to use the institutions they controlled to wield actual political influence. The logic of electoral advancement, coupled with the growing powers of Congress (especially after the promulgation of the new constitution in 1988), led many civilian politicians to contest the military leadership when its policy goals conflicted with their own.

Two specific examples of this concern are the law regulating strikes and the use of budgetary appropriations,[9] and politicians successfully opposed the military in both of these areas at the end of the Sarney administration. For politicians, liberalizing labor laws after a long period of highly restrictive legislation made sense politically since labor represented a group of considerable electoral importance. Similarly, it made sense to start cutting the military budget to release funds that could be put to better use as patronage and for pork-barrel projects. In the military's view, labor mobilization—a potential threat to political and social stability—should be controlled, larger sums should be allocated to defense, and less money should be wasted fueling the clientelist networks of Brazilian politicians. The conflict of interests raised by these two issues, coupled with the demonstrated ability of Brazilian politicians to expand the right to strike (along with other labor rights) and start cutting the military budget, suggested that the military might not remain all-powerful in the country's new democracy, especially under a president who was less sympathetic to the institution. The Collor period bore this suggestion out.

President Fernando Collor: Military Prerogatives and Power Undergo Considerable Erosion

Fernando Collor, Brazil's first directly elected president in twenty-nine years, took bold steps to assert authority over the armed forces and shrink their sphere of influence, especially in the initial stages of his government, and he managed to do so without provoking much of a backlash. The significant popularity that Collor enjoyed when he instituted these measures was decisive in inhibiting the military's reaction. By edging the institution to the political sidelines, Collor was no doubt attempting to increase his own political autonomy, and he was rarely seen in public alongside his military ministers, a sure sign that men in uniform had lost standing in the inner circle of power. But perhaps the most eloquent testimony to how much the role of the military had changed was the conspicuous distance its members kept from the political negotiations conducted in the final months of 1992, the turbulent period preceding the impeachment of President Collor.

Going beyond efforts made in the preceding government to decrease military influence in a de facto sense, Collor began to strip the armed forces of institutional positions and prerogatives, especially those that kept the armed forces enmeshed in broad social, political, and/or economic issues. Likewise, President Collor confronted the armed forces' previous monopoly over nuclear issues by signing an agreement with Argentina that allowed inspections by the International Atomic Energy Agency. During his tenure, the military found it ever harder to insulate its pet high-technology projects from the vagaries of the broader domestic economy and global market forces (Conca 1997, chap. 6). Even more striking, the military came to intervene far less in extramilitary affairs.

The most noteworthy institutional changes Collor made were in connection with the national security council (renamed SADEN, Advisory Secretariat for National Defense, after the constitutional debates) and the SNI. Although Collor initially endorsed the creation of a civilian-led ministry of defense in lieu of the separate service ministries, he never acted on this stated goal. Perhaps he felt that taking on the three traditional service ministries, in addition to SNI and SADEN, would have tested the limits of the armed forces' tolerance. More specifically, it could have alienated the navy and air force, which fear that a unified ministry would subject them to undue army domination. Collor deliberately sought to keep on good terms with those two forces, anticipating that their support could help insulate him from the army, the most politically active branch of the services and hence the primary target of his reforms.

Dismantling SNI and SADEN—formidable enclaves of military power under the dictatorship—and replacing them with a unified civilian-led organ (Secretariat of Strategic Affairs or SAE) was part of Collor's broader strategy to rid the political landscape of obstacles to his own agenda and possible competitors to his own power. The SAE had less of a military profile and presence than its institutional predecessors; it also behaved in ways that were more compatible with democracy and the rule of law. For example, whereas the SNI kept a watchful eye over agrarian leaders and other leftist activists under the Sarney government, there is little evidence that the SAE acted similarly. Also, during the Collor administration, there were fewer denunciations by Brazilian civilians about intelligence agents meddling in their affairs. Clearly, however, not everything about the national security community changed with the formation of the SAE. That agency remained virtually exempt from regular congressional oversight, and traces of military influence within the organization persisted. All in all, however, the SAE did represent a reduction of the armed forces' political weight in the state.

In short, the reforms of the Collor period contributed to a shrinking of the military's sphere of influence and an expansion of civilian authority. However, the fact that Collor took former roles and sources of influence away from the military but did not replace them with new, less politically potent roles and activities to redirect the institution's attention and energies constitutes a serious omission in his government's attempt to restructure civil-military relations. Leaving a military without direction, that is, without a well-defined set of tasks to pursue, can prove hazardous, for in the absence of clearly specified roles, the armed forces can be expected to lose state resources and suffer low morale as a result. This situation, in turn, could prompt them to challenge civilian authorities in ways unacceptable under democracy.

An extreme form of that scenario occurred in Argentina under President Raúl Alfonsín (1983–1989) when junior officers rebelled after the government radically cut defense expenditures as part of an overall attempt to weaken the military after the extraordinarily repressive dictatorship of 1976–1983. Failure to assign clear nonpolitical roles to the military can also lead to "mission creep," a process through which roles antithetical to drawing the military out of the social, political, and economic fabric of the country can accumulate over time.[10] President Cardoso has been acutely aware of this danger, and consequently, he has sought to define the military's sphere of action more explicitly than any of his predecessors.

Itamar Franco: A Politically Dormant Military Rears Its Head

The administration of Itamar Franco was relatively uneventful as far as progress in civil-military relations was concerned, but it was important in another key respect, for it illustrated the *dormancy,* as opposed to the *extinction,* of the military's inclination to interfere in politics. Franco suffered from the same basic weakness as President Sarney. He did not come to power with an electoral mandate of his own but replaced Collor in the wake of a corruption scandal. Moreover, until the *Plano Real* was implemented in July 1994, tremendous economic problems wracked Brazil, including an inflation rate of nearly 30 percent a month. Economic crisis, coupled with a political crisis centering on the involvement of several important members of Congress in corruption dealings, put the beleaguered administration in a weak position to further its predecessor's efforts to assert control over the military. For most of his twenty-seven months in office, Franco was more concerned with surviving than with confronting established powers.

The military hierarchy took advantage of the situation by engaging in saber rattling in order to extract higher salaries and budgets. Immediately following a May 1993 *pronunciamento* decrying the sorry state of military pay, President Franco took steps to give the armed forces the maximum possible salary raise and to liberate funds for modernization and reequipment purposes (*Istoé,* May 26, 1993). The officer responsible for issuing the manifesto went unpunished. In a further move to placate the military, Franco appointed a retired general to head the Secretariat of Administration, a position central to making salary readjustments for public sector workers, including the armed services (*Veja,* May 26, 1993). Although the military's public visibility extended mainly to attempts to advance corporate goals, such as higher budgets and salaries, its influence did increase somewhat (though to a lesser extent) in other realms, including internal security, intelligence, and strategic planning. The crisis-ridden period from mid-1993 to 1994 was even punctuated by rumors, albeit unsubstantiated ones, that top-level executives and business leaders had asked the military to intervene.[11]

Needless to say, President Franco did not choose this period to cut down on military prerogatives or to make reforms advancing civilian control. Any deliberate governmental efforts to roll back military influence further would have to wait for a president with more political standing and clout. At the same time, however, it deserves underscoring that military influence under Franco's presidency did not rebound to pre-1990 levels.

The Cardoso Government: Moderate Progress in Instituting Civilian Control

Under the administration of Fernando Henrique Cardoso, military influence has eroded further. This result stems from deliberate (yet cautious) efforts by the president as well as from the overall popularity of the government, achieved largely through its demonstrated ability to stabilize and begin re-structuring Brazil's long ailing economy. Cardoso has tried to direct the military's energies in ways propitious for drawing its members out of poli-tics, and he has on occasion challenged the military and prevailed. Yet, in general, contrary to what his own past as a leftist academic and opposition politician under the dictatorship might lead one to expect, President Cardoso has assumed a moderate and pragmatic stance toward the military. He has been reluctant to ruffle feathers or to expend political capital over issues unrelated or only tangentially related to his number-one goal of getting Brazil back on its feet economically. Nevertheless, his presidency has been responsible for some advances in civil-military affairs.

Decisions announced in September 1996 and June 1997 to compensate financially the families of victims of the dictatorship[12] provide stark evidence that civilian power has expanded significantly since 1985 and that Cardoso feels secure in his command over the officer corps. Financial compensation obviously falls far short of military trials and prosecutions, yet it breaks with the tradition of total military impunity that has existed in Brazil and intro-duces some sense that state officials must be accountable to the public. Given the clout and immunity enjoyed by the military historically, and the weak-ness of human rights groups, the gesture represents progress. The idea that the Brazilian state would identify the dead as victims and not the perpetra-tors of terrorism was undoubtedly anathema to many active-duty officers, yet the public position of the military leadership was to accept the civilian directive to pay the families the compensation due them. Most officers were restrained in their reactions. Assurance by the government that the 1979 amnesty would be respected helped maintain military discipline, although one senior officer resigned in protest, nevertheless. Retired officers of the Clube Militar took the most active, but ultimately unsuccessful, steps to re-sist the measure (*Latin American Regional Reports–Brazil,* September 21, 1996).

In another departure from precedent, in November 1996 the Cardoso government set forth a new defense policy for the country, codified in a seven-page document known as the Política de Defesa Nacional (PDN). This policy represents the first real effort since 1985 to rethink the role of the armed forces. In fact, it represents the first time in Brazilian history that a civilian government has established guidelines of action for the armed forces, and the PDN has been likened to a "white paper" (FBIS-LAT-96-092, May 4, 1996; *Latin American Regional Reports–Brazil,* November 26, 1996).

First, the PDN emphasizes that civilian leaders, not military officers, are in charge of determining military policy and that the role of the armed forces is to implement the objectives specified by civilians. That is generally the division of labor carried out between civilians and the military in advanced industrial democracies. Second, the PDN specifies clear hypotheses of conflict and defense goals for the military, and it tries to reorient the armed forces toward external and not internal defense, in contrast to the doctrine of national security under the dictatorship. Notably, in listing the objectives of national defense, it makes no reference whatsoever to the preservation of social stability or internal security as a prerequisite to Brazil's ability to project and protect itself against other countries (Brazil. Secretaria 1996). This lack also constitutes a marked break from the doctrine of national security, which inspired and guided the Brazilian military from the late 1950s well into the 1970s. Third, the PDN negates the idea of Brazil's automatic alignment with the United States and makes explicit the end of a long moribund doctrine that envisioned as the main hypothetical conflict war against Argentina, with whom Brazil has recently participated in joint exercises and numerous international peacekeeping operations.

While pronouncing the end of conflict with Brazil's southern neighbor, the PDN endorses the occupation and defense of the remote and vulnerable Amazon region as Brazil's number-one defense priority. Although the Cardoso administration is trying to elevate the prominence of Amazonian defense within the mission profile of the armed forces, the emphasis on Amazonian defense started sooner, namely, under President Sarney with *Calha Norte,* a program initiated in 1985 for the purpose of establishing a military presence along roughly 4,000 miles of Brazil's northern border. And despite instituting a number of high-publicity measures to protect the rain forest, including blowing up airstrips used by gold miners and setting aside vast stretches of land for Indian reserves, Collor gave the SAE control over zoning the Amazon (Foresta 1992).

In line with the increased attention Cardoso has placed on Amazonian defense, the government has ordered the transfer of more troops from southern and southeastern Brazil, where they have been concentrated, to the Amazon region (FBIS-LAT-96-208, October 20, 1996). This policy makes sense insofar as it moves troops to a region that is far more likely to see border conflict. Also, by lessening the concentration of army troops in Brazil's major cities, it renders the army less apt to regress to an internal-security orientation, and a move away from involvement in the domestic arena is advisable from the standpoint of depoliticizing the armed forces and advancing civilian control.

Another concrete advancement under the Cardoso presidency concerns the decision to abolish the three separate service ministries in lieu of creating a unified ministry of defense. Nearly all Latin American countries formed defense ministries much earlier, but Brazil has remained an exception until recently. Beginning as early as late 1994, then-president-elect Cardoso charged the Armed Forces General Staff (EMFA) with carrying out studies on the issue. Among the motivations for collapsing the three ministries into one are a more-rational management of the budget, greater joint planning, and the facilitation of Brazil's candidacy to one of the five new permanent seats on the United Nations National Security Council (*Jornal do Brasil,* October 24, 1997).

Apparently, increasing numbers of Brazil's political class have come to support the idea over time. Timothy Power conducted three surveys—in 1990, 1993, and 1997—in which members of Congress were asked about their backing for a unified defense ministry. Whereas only 66.8 percent of those polled in 1990 expressed agreement with the establishment of such a ministry, the figure rose to 75.7 percent in 1993 and to 82.3 percent in 1997. The numbers opposed to implementing such a policy fell, therefore, from 33.2 percent in 1990 to 24.3 percent in 1993 to 17.7 percent in 1997. Interestingly, congressional members are less insistent that the new defense minister be a civilian. When asked if the minister should be a civilian if a defense ministry were established, 63.0 percent agreed in 1990, 63.3 percent in 1993, and 66.2 percent in 1997. A plausible interpretation of these figures is that a growing majority of politicians wants to further diminish the political power of the military (hence the support for reducing the number of cabinet positions enjoyed by the armed forces overall) but is somewhat willing to allow the institution autonomy within its own sphere of influence (i.e., external defense). President Cardoso created the ministry of defense in June 1999, naming a civilian, the conservative former senator Élcio Álvares, as the first minister.

In sum, civilians have indeed made progress in reducing military interference in politics since 1985. Both formal military prerogatives and the actual influence of officers over civilian decision making have fallen since 1985, and of late, the civilian leadership has even started to define and regulate more clearly the military's missions. At the same time, however, reduced military influence is not equivalent to democratic control of the armed forces. Nor does it imply that the proper role of the military has been fundamentally redefined, that officers have become unconditionally accepting of civilian directives, or that they have focused their activities squarely on the external arena.

Bases for Persisting Concern

Aspects of civil-military affairs in Brazil that remain problematic fall into the following categories: the presence of prerogatives that provide the military with legal legitimation and institutional bases for meddling in extramilitary matters, de facto military autonomy over corporate as well as defense and security issues, the persistence and/or emergence of military missions that keep the armed forces involved domestically, and undemocratic attitudes among military officers as well as civilians.[13]

Legal Prerogatives

A number of legal prerogatives still in existence contribute to the armed forces' capacity to function as a pressure group and to undermine the sovereignty of elected governments. Stepan argues that prerogatives equal power "if the exercise of these prerogatives helps to turn potential issues on the political agenda into non-issues, if their existence facilitates the appeal to their exercise by civilians who have interests to protect and thus want the military to remain strong players in the political system, or if the strong defense of the prerogatives prevents major political initiatives from being implemented once they have begun" (Stepan 1988, 106).

The constitutionally sanctioned right to intervene in issues of "law and order" (Article 142) is one of the most outstanding remaining examples of a formal military prerogative that defies the ideal of a military subordinated fully to civilian control and oriented strongly toward external defense.[14] All Brazilian constitutions heretofore have given the military a legal foundation to guarantee law and order, and historically, this power has been used to justify everything from quelling strikes to toppling governments judged incapable of securing social stability themselves.

Whether or not to maintain the military's right to intervene in matters of internal security proved to be one of the most inflammatory issues of the constitutional debates. In the end, the ANC preserved the armed forces' internal security prerogative but eliminated a previous qualification stipulating that the armed forces only had to obey the president "within the limits of the law." It also made the exercise of internal security conditional upon orders by appropriate civilian authorities, either executive, legislative, or judicial. Without further restrictions placed on intervention, however, the latter qualification is meaningless since the armed forces could almost certainly find someone to extend the invitation. The exact terms of how and when intervention is acceptable are not specified. No successive government has challenged the military's internal security prerogative—not even President Cardoso, a forceful advocate of its elimination when he served as an ANC member, has raised the issue directly.

The persistence of such prerogatives like the military's internal security attribution does reflect civilian weakness, but at the same time, it must be remembered that the mere availability of prerogatives does not mean that the armed forces necessarily use them, or succeed when they do. If formal prerogatives were all-powerful, the military would not have suffered some of the important policy defeats it has in recent years. Salaries and budgets would also be higher. In short, prerogatives make up only one component of influence, and the military's capacity and will to exercise prerogatives hinges on a host of other factors as well. For example, concerns about negative public reaction sometimes inhibit the hierarchy from using its legal attributions to gain political leverage.

De Facto Autonomy Over Corporate and Defense Issues

In addition to the legal attributions that enhance the potential political influence of the officer corps, a de facto military autonomy has remained pronounced over corporate matters and policies related to security and defense. Military education, training, and doctrine; defense organization; force levels; and the nature of weaponry rest largely within the purview of active-duty officers. Civilian politicians, who have not targeted these issues as priorities, are as much to blame for this situation as anyone else. Cardoso's Política de Defesa Nacional (National Defense Policy), while elevating the role of civilian authorities in general, does not specify precisely how they are to influence policy making in this realm. Most civilian politicians dedicate their attention to electorally strategic and immediately important goals, and corporate and defense issues are not among the highest concerns of most citizens. Politicians prefer to confront the armed forces over issues that carry greater resonance with the public (e.g., human rights and defense expenditures) and hence have a greater impact on their reelection potential. Beyond wanting to direct their energy where the votes are, most politicians are precluded from engaging in defense-related debates because they are ignorant about the subject. The Brazilian Congress features no Sam Nunns or John Warners. Instead, the only people who tend to know much about the military are former officers, a troubling situation from the standpoint of establishing genuine civilian control.

Permitting the military considerable autonomy in corporate and defense matters may seem innocuous enough, especially if it is in tacit exchange for political quiescence. Yet civilians need to make inroads into these residual spheres of military autonomy in order to extend popular sovereignty and consolidate democracy. For example, by neglecting issues like the location of troops in the country and the kinds of weapons they procure, civilians lose a crucial opportunity to influence the role definition and orientation of the armed forces, such as whether they focus on internal or external conflicts.

Similarly, by leaving issues like military education, socialization, and doctrine in the hands of uniformed officers—who are likely to be steeped in the undemocratic traditions of the institution—civilians ignore the possibility of reshaping the attitudes of people who could exert a critical impact on the future of democracy.

Both houses of the Brazilian Congress have committees whose approval is necessary for certain projects, such as the development of new military weaponry. These committees, however, rank low on the list of positions congressional members would like to hold—in fact, the Committee for National Defense is the only committee in the Chamber of Deputies that allows for simultaneous membership on another committee. Because most of the issues raised in the military-related committees tend to have low electoral salience, only the rare Brazilian politician wants to devote much attention to them. Yet the failure of civilians to assert authority over issues that are potentially debatable within this context may in fact contribute to keeping the armed forces firmly entrenched in patterns and practices that are unpropitious for the development of a more robust democracy in Brazil.

Military Missions

Democratization, the end of the Cold War, a decline of the radical left, neoliberal restructuring, and the resulting reduction of military participation in the economy have all called for a redefinition of military missions in Brazil, as well as the rest of Latin America. The precise missions that the military will develop will doubtless affect the extent to which it remains a political player. To give the armed forces a stake in the current democratic system and to break the recurring authoritarian-democratic cycle of governments, missions that are credible, honorable, and nonpolitical need to be defined. As much as possible, these missions should focus on strictly military functions and draw the military out of broader involvement in society, the economy, and politics.

Certain developments augur in favor of a contraction of the military's jurisdiction to external defense, strictly defined, as democratization and the widespread disappearance of guerrilla insurgencies and their external sponsors have rendered internal security missions for the armed forces less valid. Privatization and economic restructuring have reduced military participation in strategic sectors of the economy, and these developments will certainly contribute to reversing the trend toward the "new professionalism" of internal warfare and the expansion of the military's role that began in the 1950s, whereby some of the most technologically and organizationally advanced militaries of Latin America became drawn into politics as a result of assuming roles related to internal security and civic action (Stepan 1973).

Yet opposed to these developments are factors that complicate reform and the shrinking of the definition of the military's role. Many of the most immediate threats to national security in the 1990s were in "the gray area" between strictly defined military functions and law enforcement. Drug trafficking, indigenous conflicts, and environmental protection became more significant national security issues in a country whose traditional border conflicts have greatly diminished in importance and whose old rivals (e.g., Argentina) are now economic partners.[15] In all of these issues, "the enemy" is much more likely to be a nonstate than a state actor. Although positive for regional peace, economic integration and the resolution of border disputes deprive the military of credible external defense functions, but the use of the military in law enforcement is counterproductive from the standpoint of contracting the military's overall influence. The line between conducting such operations and staying out of broader social and political conflicts is a finer one than what is encountered when combating traditional external threats. The danger is that a military that engages in such functions often begins to conduct intelligence, to administer justice, and so on.

A similar problem may result from using military personnel in civic action roles. Officers do not regard civic action as a glamorous military mission, yet civic action enhances the army's organizational justification in an era when the decline of the state-led development model has attenuated the military-development connection. Civic action and development roles—like the provision of food and health services and the construction of infrastructure in poor and remote areas—make a useful contribution, especially in the absence of private sector or state-funded civilian initiatives. But a potential problem is well stated by Felipe Agüero: "Whereas a larger role for the military in development will result in a more encompassing concept of security, such an expanded conception, including development-related issues, will, in turn, tolerate larger military roles" (Agüero 1994, 244).

President Cardoso is no doubt aware of the hazards. The spirit of the new defense plan described earlier, the PDN, is to draw the military out of problematic internal roles and to focus its attention on Amazonian defense. This plan agrees nicely with many officers' inclinations at the present time. But Amazonian defense is currently a "gray mission" in and of itself. Although the precise nature of the enemy has varied over time, fears concerning the international penetration of the Amazon constitute one of the most constant features in Brazilian military thought. Foreign environmentalists and crusaders for indigenous rights, like the rock star Sting, are the most notable demons of "internationalization" today.

Yet various circumstances complicate and conspire against an unequivocal shift in the direction of guarding Brazil's remote borders. "Amazonian defense" currently includes fighting international drug traffickers who operate on both sides of the borders with Colombia and Peru and use Brazil as a route to the United States and Europe. The U.S. government is eager for the Brazilian military to become more involved in the war against drugs, and past resistance in Brazil—from both civilian and military circles—seems to be breaking down. President Cardoso has permitted an increasing involvement of the military in drug interdiction, and his government has also given the final go-ahead for Sistema de Vigilância da Amazônia (SIVAM), an expensive and controversial system of satellites, radar installations, and computers designed to detect drug trafficking, other forms of smuggling, environmental destruction, and other "irregularities" in the region.

The mission of civic action continues under President Cardoso as well. In fact, much of the PDN involves reviving and strengthening the "social action" aspects of the Amazon project *Calha Norte*. Besides merely building up military bases, the program calls for the military-led construction of health posts, schools, and the like. This policy reflects the geopolitical strategy articulated by General Golbery do Couto e Silva to fill the vast empty spaces of the Amazon in order to lessen Brazil's vulnerability to foreign attack (Silva 1967).

Beyond the nature of current threats, the multimission profile of the Brazilian military stems from a tradition of domestic involvement, a relatively favorable public opinion of the armed forces (in the absence of which the military might be banned from internal involvement), and the perceived need by the military leadership to enhance organizational justification. Historically, Brazil's armed forces played a leading role in developing the vast and resource-rich country and in quelling internal conflicts that threatened to disrupt the social and political order. The military continues to be viewed by many public officials and citizens as the appropriate institution to combat the most severe internal conflicts, including drug trafficking.

In 1994 and 1995, the army made raids into the favelas of Rio de Janeiro to root out gang violence, racketeering, and the trafficking of arms and drugs. These raids, which became known as Operation Rio, were initiated, not by the military, but by the state governor and President Franco after considerable planning and legal precautions had been taken (*Folha de São Paulo*, October 27, 1994). The raids into the favelas continued during the first year of the tenure of President Cardoso, who also enlisted the military's help in arresting the wave of kidnappings in Brazil's urban centers.

For the most part, public opinion has been favorable toward military involvement in drug and crime control. The first manifest sign of such support came when army troops guarded Rio de Janeiro for the Earth Summit held there in 1992, and after troops entered the favelas in late 1994, support for the army's intervention reached a high of 86 percent (*Correio Braziliense*, November 13, 1994). Although Operation Rio managed to establish a temporary calm in the city, it was unable to create a lasting foundation for social peace. Army leaders themselves were uncomfortable with the idea of maintaining a permanent or semipermanent presence, fearing that human rights abuses would eventually occur and turn public sentiment against the troops (*Folha de São Paulo,* December 2, 1994).

The issue of public security in Brazil indeed demands attention. The World Bank is starting to conduct studies on the economic impact of crime in the country and has stated that drug trafficking must be eradicated (World Bank 1997a). Yet from the standpoint of drawing the military out of the kinds of activities that led to its intervention in politics in the first place, civilian authorities would be advised to keep military personnel away from regular involvement in internal security as well as civic action roles. Instead, the authorities should develop civilian means of addressing these problems.

Military Role Beliefs and Attitudes

Military attitudes and role beliefs—beyond legal prerogatives, de facto autonomy, and specific missions—reflect and shape the extent to which the military remains an important political actor. Civilian control is on strongest ground when the officers believe that subordination to civilians is fundamentally appropriate and not only tactically necessary, when officers perceive themselves as accountable to civilian authorities and the public rather than above the law, and when they abandon notions about the superiority of their own subculture—with the priority it places on values like order and discipline—in relation to that of the civilian world.

With respect to the depth of the military's commitment to the democratic order, a distinction needs to be drawn between a conditional acceptance of political noninvolvement and an independent commitment to honoring the principles of political neutrality and subordination. If democracy is to thrive, the military's acceptance of the democratic order cannot be based on factors like the economic performance of a given government or the generosity of its policies vis-à-vis the military. Whether and to what extent the military remains obedient when political and economic performance is poor and/or defense expenditures and related resources are low constitutes the true test of the military's commitment to the rules of the democratic game. A military that adheres unconditionally to political neutrality and subordination does not react to national political crises by becoming politically involved or by trying to extract concessions from the government. A military that has no internalized norms of political neutrality and subordination may well engage in role expansion and saber rattling when government performance falters.

Similarly, the extent to which the military regards itself as "a moral reservoir" in wayward societies, "guardian of the nation," or watchdog against corrupt incompetent civilian politicians affects democracy's future. Such self-definitions, especially when shared by key sectors of the society, contributed to the military becoming one of the most powerful political players in twentieth-century Latin America. Have Brazilian officers set aside such notions, adopting instead a narrow, professional self-conception? Has society ceased to view the military as a guarantor of law and order?

The Brazilian military continues to manifest some unsettling attitudes. Although such attitudes were more evident in the 1980s, some officers nevertheless retain elements of their self-perception as defenders of "national values," champions of development, and guardians of social order. Conducting formal surveys within the armed forces would be an ideal way to understand the extent to which such attitudes persist, but few researchers could hope to gain this degree of access.[16] Though less direct and rigorous, evidence of prevailing attitudes can be gleaned through officers' outward behavior, and public criticisms on a number of issues of broad political and social significance—including the rampant corruption in Brazil's new democracy, the spiral of crime that afflicts Brazil's urban centers, the political views of many public school teachers, the nature of the country's television programs, and the public behavior of the president—suggest that the army has not entirely abdicated its role as a watchdog of the government (Hunter 1997, 144). By continuing to define "permanent national objectives," the officers show that they have not completely internalized the idea of political subordination.

The inconsistency of military obedience to civilian authority reflects a lack of fundamental adherence to the principle of subordination. When popular support for the president is weak, the military has proved quick to expand its visibility and make demands on the government. This dynamic was evident from mid-1993 until early 1994, the low point of the Franco administration. Revelations of widespread corruption among Brazil's political elite, coupled with military budgetary and salary restrictions, prompted high-ranking officers to make veiled threats and to extract salary concessions and funding for military projects from the beleaguered president (*Istoé,* March 9, 1994; March 30, 1994; May 26, 1993).

It should be noted, however, that important divisions within the armed forces exist with respect to attitudes as well as missions. The navy and air force have tended to be more liberal and internationalist, more concerned than the army in meeting narrow professional and technological needs. The army remains more attached to broader involvement in politics, society, and the economy, and it has been the army that has lobbied hardest to maintain the military's internal security attributions—for example, the constitutional right to intervene in questions of "law and order."

Civilian attitudes reinforce nondemocratic inclinations within the army. Opinion polls indicate that the public consistently ranks the military as one of the most trustworthy institutions in society, and the public by and large also applauds a greater role for the military in crime control and law enforcement. Data from a comparative public opinion project, *Latinobarómetro*, reveal the following. When asked which groups or institutions the respondents would like to see gain more power (up to three choices), 32.9 percent of the respondents in Brazil answered "the military." Other options included large firms (16.7 percent), unions (33 percent), small and medium-sized businesses (23.5 percent), banks (9.3 percent), political parties (12.2 percent), multinational corporations (7.4 percent), the government (43.6 percent), and Congress (19.5 percent).[17]

Data from major Brazilian polling firms presented by Juan Linz and Alfred Stepan (1996, 171–78) further reflect the ambivalence that many Brazilians have toward democracy. In a survey conducted in April 1989, 46 percent of all respondents rated the overall situation of the country as better under the military regime; 17 percent as better under the New Republic; 28 percent as equal in both periods, and 9 percent were unclear.[18] Even more troubling for democracy's prospects than the high regard that many Brazilians have for the past performance of the military is the fact that a considerable percentage of citizens continues to think that a return to military rule might improve governance in the future. In a 1988 survey, 40 percent of all residents polled in São Paulo agreed that "the country would be better off if the military returned to power." When asked the same question again one year later, 38 percent agreed, and only 45 percent disagreed.[19] Certainly, these questions need to be repeated in order to assess the persistence of these attitudes. Notwithstanding the hazards of arriving at general interpretations based on findings from one point in time, however, these findings do put in question the underlying commitment of Brazilians to a democratic order, with obvious consequences for the present and future role of the military.

Conclusion

This survey of civil-military relations in Brazil since 1985 points out where progress has been made and where more needs to occur. In it, I have outlined past developments and present trends, and I conclude by speculating on future prospects. More specifically, I have argued that military influence has contracted overall, especially over nonexplicitly military issues, and that relations between civilian governments and the armed forces have normalized. At the same time, there is still the problematic nature of certain military prerogatives (de jure and de facto), missions, and attitudes.

One's assessment of how far civil-military interactions have come (and how far they need to go) depends on the specific yardstick of progress being used. If the measure is whether leading officers have ceased to threaten the existence of Brazilian democracy, or even whether they have ceased to meddle in issues clearly outside their sphere of competence, it is fair to say that significant advances have taken place. If the measure is whether the officer corps has become apolitical and staunchly committed to the principle of civilian control—breaking decisively with its historical involvement in nation building, development, and internal security roles—it is appropriate to conclude that the status of the Brazilian armed forces falls far short of the democratic ideal. In this connection, Felipe Agüero asserts, "Success should be measured not by the absence of political interventionism but, rather, by the active affirmation of democratic civilian control and by the full integration and harmonization of the armed forces with the dynamics of democratic political regimes" (Agüero 1999, 93; translation mine).

Where will "the military question" go from here? Although it is difficult to say with certainty, I venture the following. In all probability, it will be more difficult for civilian leaders to cut out the remaining areas of military influence and to reform military practices and attitudes. Egregious departures from democratic norms—as existed in the immediate posttransition period—were arguably easier for civilians to restrain than the more subtle (but nonetheless important) ones that persist. Furthermore, civilians are more likely to check military power when it is so great that it interferes directly with their own ability to garner electoral support. Yet for civilian control and democracy to become more robust, politicians must be motivated for reasons other than tactics. Whether or not there is an underlying commitment to these goals on the part of a majority of the Brazilian politicians—let alone the construction of political institutions that reflect those goals—remains to be seen. Bearing out Douglas Chalmers's notion of the "politicized state" (Chalmers 1977), these largely self-interested actors may well continue to behave in ways that are most convenient, crafting and recrafting state institutions accordingly.

Notwithstanding the continuous waxing and waning of military power that this analysis suggests, overall and in the long run the military may well retreat further into the background, especially if civilian institutions that are capable of good governance develop. Even if military power recedes further, in light of the accommodationist tendencies for which Brazilian politics is well-known, men in uniform will doubtless remain part of the country's "living museum" (Anderson 1967). New actors with new goals and practices may gain strength but never completely displace the military.

SIX

The Making of a Loyal Opposition

The Workers' Party (PT) and
the Consolidation of
Democracy in Brazil

William R. Nylen

> *Democracy is not just a nice little extra. It's fundamental to our life as human beings.*
> —Interview with Luiz Inácio Lula da Silva, PT founder, June 20, 1996

ounded in 1980, the Partido dos Trabalhadores (PT, Workers' Party) was Brazil's largest opposition party by the 1990s. Its steadfast and vocal opposition, and its efforts to design and implement a "democratic socialist" alternative program have raised questions about its contribution to democratic consolidation in Brazil. On one side are the people who share the opinion of Amanda Sives that the PT's efforts to construct a more participatory form of democracy and a more "socially just" society make it "the only party which is attempting to be truly democratic in Brazil at the present time" (Sives 1993, 556). The other side argues that the party's "chronic opposition" blocks necessary political and economic modernization; that it is a "corporatist" and increasingly bureaucratized party concerned more with protecting relatively privileged and organized urban blue- and white-collar workers and its own party cadres than with defending the mass of Brazil's unorganized poor (Rodrigues 1990; Novaes 1993; *Folha de São Paulo* 1997e); and/or that infighting between radical and moderate factions of the party hinders its ability to govern (Couto and Abrucio 1993; C. Azevedo 1995; *Folha de São Paulo* 1997b).[1]

In this chapter, I argue that the PT has contributed positively to the consolidation of Brazilian democracy in at least three important ways. First, the

PT has helped to consolidate Brazilian democracy by acting within the boundaries of democratic "loyal opposition."[2] Although less democratic factions have always existed within the party, their minority status has allowed the PT to reject the orthodox Marxist-Leninist strategies of taking advantage of democratic procedures to undermine "bourgeois democracy" from within.[3] By the same token, the PT has so far avoided joining the list of progressive-sounding parties in Brazil that after entering office "have been successfully co-opted into the orbit of the patrimonial regime" (Roett 1978, 45) by succumbing to the siren song of clientelism and patronage politics.[4]

Second, the PT contributes to the legitimation of democracy by using the opportunities provided by formal democracy (e.g., electoral debate and campaign advertising, parliamentary debate, and concrete experiences of governing at the state and local levels) to openly oppose social and economic exclusion and the practices that perpetuate them and to champion more inclusionary practices and policy outcomes. For example, the PT's participation in elections that are otherwise dominated by a field of "nonprogrammatic parties" and "pork-oriented" politicians (Ames 1995b, 325, 337) gives Brazilian voters a real programmatic choice at the polls and not just a choice among personalities.[5] Similarly, electoral victories have allowed the PT to administer municipal and state governments and to design and implement programs that benefit nonelites to a degree and in a manner unlikely to be pursued by other political parties. Even when constituting a small minority within legislative bodies, PT legislators are noteworthy in their efforts to focus policymakers' and the public's attention on segments of the population that are excluded, on the one hand, by Brazil's traditionally unequal economic and social systems (patrimonialism) and, on the other hand, by contemporary neoliberal policies and structural reforms.[6] Numerous analysts have argued that such a concern for greater social and economic equality is absolutely necessary to enable formal democracy to become consolidated in any meaningful sense of the word.[7]

Third, the PT contributes to democratic consolidation by providing a nonviolent channel of participation for political activists and potential activists who reject Brazil's traditional fare of nonideological, patrimonial, and organizationally diffuse parties.[8] Such individuals will always exist, and they will act either within formal democratic rules (if they see them as efficacious) or against them (if they do not). Since the PT attracts such individuals and groups and allows them to express themselves and to pursue their goals with some degree of success or hope, these same individuals and groups move beyond mere "integration" into the political system (i.e., simply being allowed to participate) and become "socialized," which implies their acceptance and internalization of the rules of the political game. As the PT's opponents see them "working within the system," they, too, are encouraged to integrate and socialize themselves into the rules of democracy rather than react in fear of some perceived authoritarian predisposition of the left.[9]

After stating these three points, a qualification is in order. Instances of intraparty disputes and fragmentation have plagued the PT throughout its history. Although normal for leftist parties everywhere, these disputes have compromised the PT's ability to act coherently and, in some instances, to govern effectively. Whether or not this "qualification" fatally weakens my three arguments is a question that only time will answer.

The rest of this chapter provides historical data for my arguments. First, I briefly describe the PT's history, outlining its participation in elections; second, I discuss its experiences in municipal government and in the National Congress; and third, I discuss the problem of party factionalization as it relates to the party's commitment to democracy.

Historical Background

The history of the PT reflects a fundamental transformation of the Brazilian left in the final thirty years of the twentieth century. It has largely emancipated itself from state corporatism, and it has fully embraced political democracy. After Getúlio Vargas's *Estado Novo* (1937–1945), the organized left was repressed and the urban working classes integrated into politics "from the top down" by state-controlled corporatist unions (Erickson 1977; Rodrigues 1990, 46–76). The unorganized poor remained politically inert owing to traditional clientelism, literacy requirements for voting, and numbing poverty. During the postwar democratic period (1945–1964), nationalist-populist "parties of the state" (Mainwaring 1992–1993)—especially Vargas's Brazilian Workers' Party (PTB)—continued this legacy of state incorporation and control. In the charged atmosphere of the Cold War, however, political debate became increasingly polarized, and the PTB split between its moderate deal-brokering *Varguista* leaders and its more radical grassroots. The Cuban revolution in 1958 and 1959 seemed to present a viable alternative to the latter group's frustration with "bourgeois democracy": only violent revolution spearheaded by a small but dedicated vanguard party or guerrilla movement could bring forth social justice by eliminating capitalism and its democratic facade.

Subsequent events, however, took their toll on the revolutionary left. Communism and Marxist-Leninist vanguardism were relegated to the fringes by thirty years of failed armed struggle, brutal military repression of real and imagined opponents, an enormous growth of the urban working class as well as an intensive modernization of vast rural areas (both accompanied by rising wages and expanded access to social benefits), the collapse of the Soviet Union and Eastern European socialism in the late 1980s, and the subsequent decay of Cuban socialism. New post–Cold War leftist goals and strategies emphasized "democratizing democracy" (empowering citizens to participate more directly and independently in contests and governance) and "humanizing capitalism" (redirecting a significant portion of the economic surplus toward improving the quality of life and future prospects of nonelites).[10] Meanwhile, in Brazil, many people who had never considered themselves "leftists" or even political joined in opposition to the country's authoritarian and highly unequal style of capitalism to demand a return to democratic government.

In 1978 and 1979, massive strikes in the industrial outskirts of the city of São Paulo brought participating union leaders and sympathizers to the conclusion that union representation of members' demands for better working conditions, wages, and other benefits was not enough to ensure a better life for Brazil's working classes.[11] Workers were also citizens, with needs and interests outside of the workplace, and they needed to be represented as such in the national political arena. Even for workplace issues, unions were seen as highly vulnerable to state repression whereas a party might operate in multiple locations within and outside the state apparatus.

In supporting the idea of a workers' party, the recognized leader of the strikes, Luiz Inácio Lula da Silva, called attention to Brazil's history of "oligarchical" and "populist" parties of elites cutting deals among themselves while making grand promises to an inert mass of client supporters. Lula argued that a true workers' party could only be constructed "from the bottom up" *(basismo)*, acting as an umbrella organization for the political participation of urban workers and all others who felt unrepresented by traditional politics.

Lula's "new unionist" leaders formed the initial core of the PT alongside a small but significant number of longtime leftist activists and intellectuals, and they found support in the progressive wing of the Catholic Church and from numerous community-focused and identity-based social movements throughout Brazil (Rodrigues 1990, 12–14). The PT was officially founded on February 10, 1980. Party leaders agreed that the formal rules and procedures of democratic politics, flawed as they were, could be used as a means of publicizing the struggles of the party's constituent social movements, to expand and unify their respective following, and possibly even to "occupy spaces" of institutional power in order to eventually transform Brazil's unequal social structures (albeit in an as-yet ill-defined direction).[12]

The party entered Brazil's electoral fray in 1982 and presidential politics in 1989. In presidential elections, candidate Lula placed a close second in 1989 behind Fernando Collor, winning 16 percent in the first round of multicandidate voting and 46.9 percent against Collor's 53.03 percent in the second round. Although there was no second round in the 1994 and 1998 elections owing to Fernando Henrique Cardoso's overwhelming victories (54.5 percent and 53.1 percent, respectively), Lula's second-place results (27 percent and 31.7 percent) were almost double his first round showing in 1989. Table 6.1 outlines the PT's performance in all other arenas of electoral politics from 1980 to 1996.

At the party's founding in 1980, one incumbent senator and five incumbent federal deputies switched their party allegiance to the PT, and the first multiparty elections in 1982 resulted in eight PT federal deputies. That number doubled in 1986, more than doubled in 1990, increased by 40 percent in 1994, then increased again by 18 percent in 1998. Although it took ten years before the party elected a senator, it elected five in 1995 and added two more in 1998. In state politics, the PT elected its first governors in 1994, in Espírito Santo and the Federal District of Brasília.[13] Even though the PT lost the Brasília seat in an upset in the 1998 elections, in that year the party elected governors in the states of Acre, Rio Grande do Sul, and Mato Grosso do Sul. The party's initial twelve state deputies in 1982 almost trebled in 1986, then almost trebled again in 1990, and stayed at about that level in the 1994 and 1998 elections.

It was in municipal politics that the PT surprised many observers. Beginning with only two elected mayors in 1982 (and its first state capital mayorship—Fortaleza, Ceará—in 1985), the number of PT mayors increased to thirty-two in 1988, almost doubled in 1992, and more than doubled in 1996. By

TABLE 6.1

Election Results for the Workers' Party (PT), 1980–1998

National Legislature	1980[1]	1982	1986	1990	1994	1998
Senate	1/69	0/69	0/72	1/81	5/81	7/81
House	5/479	8/479	16/487	35/503	49/513	58/513

State Government[2]	1982	1986	1990	1994	1998
Governor	0/23	0/23	0/27	2/27	3/27
Legislature	12	33	93	91	90/1,045

Municipal Government	1982	1985[3]	1988	1992	1996
Mayor	2	1	32	56	115
Vice Mayor	n/a	n/a	35	70	142
City Council	78	n/a	1,015	1,148	1,892

[1] In 1980, national legislators were not elected under the PT label, but they changed their prior party affiliation once the PT was legalized.

[2] Includes the Federal District (Brasília).

[3] Municipal elections in 1985 were for municipalities previously excluded from electoral competition for "national security" purposes.

Sources: Keck (1992, 164); Branford and Kucinski (1995, 57); PT (n.d., 1996b); Moraes (1998); Toledo (1998).

1997, the party had governed or was governing in a wide variety of cities ranging in size and character from the tiny rural town of Agua Branca Amapari in the northeastern Amazonian state of Amapá, 2,320 inhabitants, to the highly urbanized and industrialized city of São Paulo, 9.5 million inhabitants.[14]

The PT first garnered truly national attention in late 1984 with its demand that direct popular elections *("Diretas Já!")* ("Direct Elections Now!") replace the military's plan for indirect presidential elections. Massive street rallies and demonstrations resulted. Paulo Baia notes this "irony of history" by which "a Left that gave little strategic value to democracy and that even frequently discussed its merely tactical utility ended up being the principal voice in defense of its full installation" (Baia 1996, 56). When the direct elections campaign was adopted and then abandoned by PMDB leaders as a means to get their candidate, Tancredo Neves, indirectly elected, the PT risked public censure by requiring its congressional delegation to abstain from voting for the popular Neves. Neves's death and the subsequent collapse of José Sarney's presidency into economic turmoil and corruption, led "many Brazilians . . . to see the PT as the only political force that had had the courage to stick to its principles" (Branford and Kucinski 1995, 58). The party's subsequent "outsider" image fueled its electoral growth in the late 1980s.

In spite of losing the presidential elections of 1989, 1994, and 1998, the PT's strong showings in those and in subnational elections further raised the party's visibility and credibility. When Fernando Collor's presidency collapsed in a wash of economic stagnation and corruption in 1992, the PT's opposition remained loud and consistent. Relations with Itamar Franco's interim presidency started off with hints of a tacit alliance, but the PT declined any formal participation in Franco's administration and moved squarely into opposition as he adopted a growing number of neoliberal reforms. The PT remained steadfast in opposing the government of President Fernando Henrique Cardoso (1995–), in spite of Cardoso's popularity and that of his flagship economic program, the Real Plan.

In 1998, the party was far from being the isolated voice of São Paulo trade unionism that some of its critics had predicted in 1980 that it would become. It had grown into a national organization with some 750,000 registered members nationwide and an impressive electoral record, a solid nationwide party preference of 17 percent–19 percent throughout the 1990s (the highest among all political parties),[15] and a growing number of experienced politicians and administrators.

But the PT has always considered elections (and formal democracy in general) as a means of achieving more "substantive" ends. In Lula's words, the party is dedicated to "showing to the population that institutional democracy is not enough" in a country of such glaring inequalities as Brazil.

"It's necessary, for example, to democratize the economy. To the Brazilian elite, democracy means that the worker can shout out that he's hungry. For us, democracy means that the worker has the right to eat" (Interview with the author, June 20, 1996).

This substantive conception of democracy also includes greater citizen participation. In the words of PT president, José Dirceu:

> The idea that guides the PT's ideological evolution is the idea of citizenship, and the idea of the public–public space, not "statized" space. In Brazil, private space exists, and the state's space exists, but the public space must come into existence increasingly, to become a reference point. Because while voting is fundamental in electing a legislative representative or the executive chief in each of the three levels of government, we want citizens to be increasingly organized to directly participate in public administration, not just in decisions but in deliberation processes. This idea has gone from being an ideology to being an instrument of participation and citizenship . . . of putting one more power in the traditional arrangement of executive, legislature and judiciary. (Interview with the author, June 11, 1996)

To fully understand these definitions of democracy, and to see how the PT's pursuit of these ideals has impacted the development of Brazilian democracy (and the party itself), we need to look more closely into the party's participation in what it calls "institutional politics."

The PT in Office—Local Politics: *"Inversão de Prioridades"* and *"Participação Popular"*

PT activists' growing experience in local government is both giving them a chance to put into practice some of their ideas and changing the way they see the world (Branford and Kucinski 1995, 87). Victories in local elections, and constitutional provisions for substantial fiscal autonomy for local governments, provided the PT with the opportunity to practice what it preached. Experience ultimately had a moderating influence on the party as a growing number of party activists found themselves weighing the ideals and strategies forged in years of union organization, academic theorizing, and social movement activism against the give-and-take negotiations and compromises inherent in democratic governance.[16] How much one should compromise became a divisive issue among party members, particularly between those actually in local government and those in leadership positions in constituent unions and social movement organizations.[17] In spite of these debates, and in part, because of them, a programmatic consensus emerged around the two basic goals of "popular democratic" administration: inverting priorities (*inversão de prioridades*) and popular participation (*participação popular*).

Inversão de prioridades means targeting public policy to favor the poor (e.g., improving public education, public health, public transportation, low-cost housing) while taxing the people and groups most capable of paying

(Bittar 1992; Abers 1996, 39). In São Paulo, for example, under the administration of Luiza Erundina (1989–1992),

Social spending reached 48.1 percent of total city spending, up from 33.8 percent during Jânio [Quadros]'s administration [1985–1988] and nearly 10 percentage points higher than it had ever been in the past fifteen years.... The only funding source that was readily available to the mayor's office was a direct tax on property [Imposto Predial e Territorial Urbano, or IPTU; Urban Building and Real Estate Tax]. Erundina increased the share of the IPTU as part of the total municipal income from 9.7 percent in 1989 to an estimated 20.8 percent in 1992. The PT administration was partly successful in adjusting real estate resale assessments to realistic levels and in making tax collection more progressive. (Kowarick and Singer 1994, 239–40)[18]

An objective analysis of the results of inverting priorities in PT-administered cities would require a comparative analysis of local government performance before, during, and after the PT (a task beyond the scope of this chapter).[19] A number of studies do exist, however, that suggest an overall positive assessment. Silvio Caccia Bava, for example, argues that "from an across-the-board reading of the results of the recent democratic administrations [i.e., PT-administered cities from 1989 to 1996], one can affirm that public services under the responsibility of these municipal governments have improved" (Caccia Bava 1995, 170). From an intensive study of five PT-run cities, Rebecca Abers writes that "many PT administrations have successfully eliminated traditional forms of clientelism and corruption, such as the widespread practice of farming-out public works projects to select businesses at exorbitant prices" (Abers 1996, 35).[20] My own work on small-town PT administrations in the states of Ceará and Minas Gerais suggests similar conclusions (Nylen 1997a, 1997b, 1998).

Such studies point to the seriousness of PT activists and administrators in translating party platform into actual practice, but they cannot gauge the citizens' subjective evaluations of PT performance (e.g., party identification) nor their subsequent evaluations of the legitimacy of democracy. PT leaders and activists make the following argument in that regard:

1. "Inverting priorities" means that PT administrations are more responsive to the needs of citizens who are ordinarily ignored and excluded.
2. As a result, a greater number among this majority of Brazilians have felt represented by the PT.
3. Therefore, many more nonelite citizens are willing to see the democratic system in a more positive light than would otherwise be the case.

Such an argument, however, is difficult to prove.[21]

First, it seems doubtful that a large number of the nonelites feel represented by the PT. The electoral record is certainly inconclusive. Many PT administrations have been voted out of office after just one term (e.g., in Fortaleza, São Paulo, and the Federal District of Brasília), yet a good many others have continued in office for two or three terms (e.g., in Porto Alegre, Santos, Diadema, and Betim). Although it is true that many voters see the PT as the most ideologically consistent party in Brazil, and the one with the fewest number of corrupt politicians, they also tend to feel it is too "radical" for their tastes.[22] Many PT victories have been the result of time-specific "protest voting" and/or split voting among center and right candidates and do not indicate long-term partisan or programmatic support (Moisés 1993).

The PT also suffers from the fact that many Brazilians in the late 1980s and 1990s, and the poor most of all, showed little knowledge of or interest in politics (Instituto Gallup 1995; Meneguello 1994; *Folha de São Paulo* 1998). Alongside the poverty and inadequate education that usually accompany and help account for such views, voter indifference allows practices of elitism, clientelism, and corruption to bias election results. Brazilian television, for example, where the vast majority of Brazilians receive their information about politics, routinely portrays PT administrations in a negative light,[23] and without large expenditures of public funds for "self promotion" (a practice long rejected by the PT but not by others) and lacking large campaign war chests, the party is particularly susceptible to media bias. As for the effects of clientelism and corruption, the literature is replete with studies indicating how machine politics and vote buying sway elections, especially among the poorest segments of the population—precisely those who receive the benefits of the PT's "inversion of priorities" and should be most grateful or interested (e.g., Hagopian 1993; Gay 1994; Nylen 1997a; J. Toledo 1996).

Being fully aware of these problems, and believing that activism begets political consciousness (which, in turn, constructs true democracy by breaking down the power of political elites), the PT's agenda for local governance has long emphasized the importance of encouraging citizen activism by opening up new channels of *participação popular* (Bittar 1992; Caccia Bava 1995).

The principal objective is to build direct and routine contacts between citizens and public institutions so that the latter must consider all interests and socio-political viewpoints in the decision-making process. . . . When one speaks of participation, one is explicitly speaking of a potential break with the distance that almost always exists between centralized power and the constantly changing and heterogeneous social realities. This distance highlights the limitations of existing political mechanisms—formal, vertical, corporatist and clientelist—constructed to exclude citizens from participating in public affairs. (Jacobi and Teixeira 1996, 3)

Participation was seen as a means of engendering "empowerment," a form of political consciousness at once critical of existing inequalities and injustices and yet, at the same time, aware of the promise of collective action in achieving progressive reform (Dagnino 1994; Friedmann 1992).

In pursuit of these goals, PT administrations set up municipal councils and popular councils *(conselhos municipais* and *conselhos populares)* to provide opportunities for citizens to meet together in familiar settings (e.g., neighborhood meeting halls or local school buildings) and express opinions on issues they themselves deemed important—and to channel those opinions directly into the formal decision-making processes of the administration and the city council (R. Cardoso 1992; Abers 1996, 38). In an effort to make the municipal councils truly "popular" (i.e., not just a place for fellow *petistas*, or PT militants and their organized allies), a strategy emerged in 1989 that captured attention and adherents both inside and outside of the party: the Participatory Budget (Orçamento Participativo, OP). Ricardo Tavares describes the way the OP functioned in the city of Porto Alegre in the state of Rio Grande do Sul.

Popular assemblies in 16 city zones bring together 10,000 people and 600 grassroots organizations to debate and vote on municipal expenditure priorities. From a general budget of approximately $465 million, about 31% is divided up in an open, public process involving large numbers of people and interests. As a result of this process, the city's residents decided the city should concentrate its resources on legalizing land titles, providing water and sewage to poor communities (almost 100% of households now have clean drinking water), transportation, and environmental clean-up. (Tavares 1995b, 29)

The success of Porto Alegre's OP in terms of growing levels of citizen participation and a clearly popular redistributive outcome of the entire process (capped by the PT's reelection in 1992 and again in 1996) generated great interest within the party for studying and duplicating the strategy.[24] Porto Alegre's PT seemed to have discovered a means of balancing ideological concerns for promoting citizen empowerment with pragmatic demands that voters perceive government programs to be in their own vital interests. Although experiments in other cities—São Paulo, for example (Singer 1995; Jacobi and Teixeira 1996, 6–21)—have not always been so successful, the OP quickly became a cornerstone of PT administration in virtually every PT-run city in the 1990s.[25]

The PT argues that the OP democratizes local democracy, as it disempowers traditional entrenched political elites by providing ordinary citizens with a new means of access to the most important decision-making process at the municipal level: spending the city's money. How does this argument stack up? On the one hand, "popular participation" turns out to not be very popular. Most Brazilians tend to see politics as "dirty" or foreign to their day-to-day lives (Meneguello 1994; L. Ribeiro 1994), and most don't care to participate beyond the act of voting, which is compulsory in Brazil. The 10,735 participants in Porto Alegre's fifth year of OP discussions (1993), for example, represented less than 1 percent (0.77 percent) of the city's 1.4 million residents.[26] Similarly, in Belo Horizonte, the 38,508 participants in the OP's third year (1995) represented only 1.83 percent of the city's total population of 2.1 million. The fact that middle- and upper-class residents and young people participated minimally in these instances suggests another dimension of their unrepresentativeness. Pointing out these low rates of participation, and an alleged overrepresentation of *petista* participants, critics argue that the OP illustrates the PT's wasteful and inefficient "utopianism" or "propagandizing."

Even many of the people who did take part in OP processes expressed disappointment. The most often-expressed complaint concerned the slow or negligent results of their labors (a fact that officials attribute to unrealistically high initial expectations on the part of nearly everyone involved): "In case after case, according to administration informants, the promise to attend to the demands collected followed by the implementation of only a fraction of them led to a dramatic drop in grassroots support for the administrations. This decline in support negatively affected future attempts at implementing participatory programs . . . a large portion of potential participants had lost faith in the capacity of the government to respond to their demands" (Abers 1996, 42). Contributing to the frustration was the fact that city councils—long-standing redoubts of clientelist politicians—retain the power to ignore, reject, amend, or otherwise impede the realization of OP priorities and longer-term goals.

Considering those and other critiques of the OP in practice,[27] I repeat an earlier argument in support of its inclusionary and empowering implications:

First, relatively few people can be expected to sacrifice their time and energy to participate in politics on behalf of any transformative agenda . . . (call it a problem of collective action and "public goods," if you must, but political activists are a rare breed); second, all effort must nevertheless be expended to provide ample opportunities and encouragement to all those who desire to participate and to those who may come to appreciate it but have never yet been given the chance. These will be the activists and the representatives of tomorrow. That they will come from the ranks of the non-elite rather than exclusively from the privileged classes will help to assure that [Brazil's] representative democracy may, someday, live up to its name. (Nylen 1997b, 446)

Subsequent research has only strengthened that earlier argument. The figures cited above referring to the number of participants in Porto Alegre's and Belo Horizonte's OPs, for example, may seem small relative to the cities' total populations; seen another way, however, they represent 10,738 and 38,508 citizens, respectively, who embraced the opportunity to participate in matters of direct concern to them and to their community in a way previously unavailable to them—and still unavailable to the vast majority of Brazilians. In the town of Betim, Minas Gerais, roughly 5 percent of the population (10,000 out of 200,000) participated in the city's second OP (4,000 more than in the previous year), and many candidates for city council in the 1996 elections (not all of them for the PT) had begun their political careers as OP participants (Nylen 1997a).

The findings of Mercês Somarriba and Otávio Dulci suggest that most OP participants are nonpartisan nonelites with little effective power or access to "normal" politics. They have low levels of education, are active in community organizations, and are not members of the PT or any other political party (Somarriba and Dulci 1995, 11, 14, 15). Evaluating interviews with a number of active participants in Belo Horizonte's third annual OP, the authors conclude that "the experience constituted for them a lesson in political leadership, one that they evaluated very positively. They believe that the OP, in those three years, has been a learning experience, teaching to them and the population a new way of dealing with the problems of each community, changing as well their way of thinking about possible ways of solving such problems" (Somarriba and Dulci 1995, 30). They also argue that even participants' and citizens' complaints about the slow delivery of public works that are designated as "high priority" by the OP process should be seen in a positive light: "On the one hand, construction delays are exploited politically as a means of opposing the municipal government; even, in some cases, as an indirect form of attacking the very idea of the OP. On the other hand, however, the OP's basic proposition is strengthened, since the criticisms take the form of calling on the government to fulfill its commitments as laid down in the budget" (Somarriba and Dulci 1995, 34).

In sum, in places where the PT has gained public office at the local executive level, its efforts to invert the priorities of public administration do seem to have generated significant benefits for the nonelite sectors of the population; at the same time, the efforts and the benefits themselves cannot be said to have generated any swelling of popular support either for the PT or for democracy in general. Most Brazilians, and most nonelites especially, remain cynical about or disinterested in all "things political," including the PT. On the other hand, the party's adoption of the OP as a cornerstone of the PT way of governing has had the salutary effect of bringing significant numbers of nonelite activists and organizations into local processes of democratic governance. Their numbers may be small compared to the total population, but they are significant in that they expand and diversify the ranks of politically aware and active citizens.

Just as local politics is often seen as the repository for traditional clientelistic politics, Brazil's National Congress has been maligned for being a "gigantic distributivist arena" and "a dispenser of patronage" rather than a lawmaking body of citizens' representatives (Ames n.d.; Mainwaring 1992–1993, 696), which has generated what some call a "crisis of representation" in Brazil. In mid-1995, for example, 85 percent of the respondents in a Gallup survey felt

"They do not feel personally represented by the current Federal Deputies and Senators" (Instituto Gallup 1995, 24). Only 12 percent said they did feel represented, and 3 percent didn't respond. In a 1998 poll, 90 percent of the respondents couldn't remember who they voted for in the last congressional election, which had taken place less than four years earlier (Petry 1998).

The PT in Office—Legislative Activity: Principled Loyal Opposition and "Ethical Politics"

In 1996, the highly respected congressional lobby organization for the labor movement, the Departamento Intersindical de Assessoria Parlamentar (Inter-Union Department for Legislative Assistance), identified the PT as the most active opposition party in its annual list of the hundred most influential deputies and senators (DIAP 1996). The party's congressional activism is best illustrated by its participation in the writing of Brazil's new constitution (1986–1988). Alliances with other left and center parties succeeded in opening the Constituent Assembly to full public view, strengthening Congress vis-à-vis the president, maintaining or increasing social benefits and labor rights, and maintaining certain privileges for national businesses (Baaklini 1992, 157–98; Keck 1992, 215–19). This experience indicated, at least to those in the delegation, that working within institutions even as unpalatable as the National Congress could generate real benefits for the party's core constituents (e.g., constitutional guarantees for workers against unwarranted firings and layoffs) while also providing opportunities to make the party's ideas more public.

Loyal opposition in Congress meant openness to negotiation and diminished radical rhetoric; it did not mean flexibility of the party's core principles. In the face of constant criticism from political opponents and from the media that the PT was showing its "corporatist" and "statist" foundations by opposing the neoliberal economic policies of Presidents Collor and Cardoso, the party's delegation fought privatization and defended the constitutional rights and privileges of public and private sector organized labor. These were, and are, the party's core constituents. Their defense was politically necessary, all the more so in the context of economic instability and rising unemployment which had hit blue-collar and lower-level white-collar workers especially hard in the 1980s. Opposition to President Cardoso, however, further weakened the party's claim to be a "popular" party as his Real Plan lowered inflation and provided greater economic security and rising real incomes for Brazil's vast majority of unorganized working poor.

Congressional delegates addressed these charges of PT corporatism, and criticism that the party was little more than a radical obstructionist party, by publicizing program alternatives to such government initiatives as social security reform, reform of the state bureaucracy, tax reform, educational reform, and privatization. A most interesting example is PT Senator Eduardo Suplicy's Programa de Garantia de Renda Mínima (Guaranteed Minimum Income Program), which called for the provision of welfare-type payments of 50 percent of the difference between an individual's monthly income and a base rate of about US$ 250 (Suplicy 1995). Approved by the Senate in 1991 but never actually legislated, the plan resurfaced in the PT administration of the Federal District of Brasília (1994–1997) in a program entitled *bolsa-escola* ("school fellowship"), which paid about US$ 125 to roughly 23,000 poor families who, in turn, pledged to keep their seven-to-fourteen-year-old children in school (Falcão 1997). The program's popularity and its entirely manageable costs caused the Cardoso administration to consider a similar program at the national level, albeit without paying tribute to its PT authorship (Suplicy 1997; Cantanhêde 1997).

In addition to corporatist and economic issues, the PT's congressional delegation increasingly focused on exposing and fighting corruption and paternalism in government. Thus, PT deputies were instrumental in initiating and participating in the 1992 congressional investigating commission that exposed rampant corruption in the Collor administration. They were equally active in initiating and maintaining multiparty negotiations and participating in the massive *Fora Collor!* ("Out Collor!") street demonstrations that ultimately led to President Collor's resignation under threat of impeachment.

Despite "orthodox" concerns within the party that such issues were a diversion from the more important struggles against economic and social exclusion, the emphasis on ethical politics was retained because, in the words of one member of the directorate, "We are a progressive party, and anticorruption is progressive in the eyes of the masses."[28] Indeed, with its congressional delegation so consistently at the forefront of anticorruption campaigns and investigations, and its members (and other PT officeholders) so conspicuously absent from the growing lists of the accused, the PT built up its image of being the one and only clean party in Brazil. Even the usually critical news magazine *Veja* praised the party's deputies in this regard: "The best thing about the PT delegation is that it does not have the same flaws as the others. Its members have never been caught committing improprieties and their names do not show up on the construction contractor's lists [of illegal bribes in public works bids]. The only reported case of corruption is that of Ricardo Moraes, of Amazonas, who was dismissed from PT ranks after an internal investigation" (*Veja*, 1994).[29]

It is entirely possible that the "ethical politics" as practiced by the PT's congressional delegation has reinforced the public's perception that the PT is the least corrupt of all Brazilian parties and that the party can be a positive force in reforming democracy along ethical lines. It is also entirely possible that the PT's muckraking made Congress—and democracy—appear all the more illegitimate in the eyes of the public. If the response is mass cynicism rather than anger expressed in the ballot box, the PT's enemies will stand to benefit the most from the subsequent withdrawal of public attention.

In sum, PT delegates have been exceptionally active in Congress, demonstrating that they take this arena of democratic politics seriously. Once again, on-the-job experience seems to have fostered a willingness among PT legislators to moderate some of the party's earlier *basista* grassroots principles in favor of building alliances, negotiating deals, and presenting "responsible" legislative proposals. Delegates remain firm, however, in defending their core constituents, regardless of critics' cries of "corporatism." A compensatory focus on ethical politics, while popular and commendable, could backfire in the long run. In the meantime, it has become one more contentious issue for *petistas* to argue about.

PT Ideology: The Struggle for the Meaning of "Socialist Democracy"

From the PT's very beginnings, internal debates over goals and strategies have been intense, and several prominent individuals and organized factions within the party have even been expelled for various transgressions of party rules and majority decisions. Party leaders point to these debates as evidence of the PT's "internal democracy" and its commitment to democratic debate and tolerance of diverse opinions. Similarly, the expulsions are explained as resulting from individuals' refusals to abide by democratically arrived-at party decisions. It is said that the party line is not handed down from the leadership to passively obedient members but democratically hammered out in state and national conferences *(encontros),* in which all factions and viewpoints are represented and open to public scrutiny.[30] Opposition politicians and the media regularly interpret these debates as evidence of the party's intense fragmentation and even imminent demise (Guidry and Probst 1997, 15, 27).

Implying that the "internal democracy" argument is best seen as making a virtue out of necessity, Paulo Baia (1996) and Carlos Alberto Marques Novaes (1993) each argue that practical concerns of maintaining party unity have always necessitated concessions to minority viewpoints.[31] These analysts suggest that, much like party platforms in the United States, the PT's official documents and declarations have been less useful for discovering the true meaning of socialist democracy, or for guiding the party's political action, than for papering over differences and mending fences among party factions.

Other observers are less sanguine. Clovis Bueno de Azevedo (1995), for example, asserts that the internal democracy argument masks irreconcilable contradictions between the principles of "orthodox" Leninists and "heterodox" reformist social democrats and that the party could eventually self-destruct if it does not come down definitively on one side or the other. Somewhat similarly, Margaret Keck (1992), Marcelo Cavarozzi (1992), and Cláudio Gonçalves Couto (1995) have each argued that the operative logic of playing by the rules of democratic politics (i.e., negotiating, compromising, and interest aggregating) contradicts the vision of *basistas* that the party should represent the needs and interests of its constituent grassroots social movements and support those movements' efforts outside the institutional arena of politics, even if that means compromising electoral prospects. Novaes (1993) adds a third dimension to the struggle: the party bureaucracy and support staff are capable of controlling party decision making and operations in the name of "party building," but they do so to the ultimate detriment of the party's vital grassroots basis and its electoral appeal.

Most of these writers were responding to developments surrounding the 1994 presidential elections. During that period, while PT candidates or *políticos* tried to figure out how best to get elected or reelected, repeated victories of leftist PT groups in state directorates translated into an orthodox majority in the party's national directorate.[32] But these so-called radicals were not Leninists, as Azevedo and the media at the time would have us believe. Rather, they expressed legitimate concern that the *políticos'* electoral alliances with "insufficiently progressive" parties, and their "nonideological" focus on good government and ethical practice, threatened to drive the party to abandon or fatally compromise what they saw to be the party's fundamental principles: first, to wage a frontal attack on poverty and extreme inequality; second, to transform Brazil's paternalistic political culture via nonelite political participation and empowerment; and, third, to promote and protect grassroots organizations that are carrying out these tasks in the realm of civil society (i.e., the party's core constituents).

If these orthodox groups were not the Leninists that their detractors painted them, neither were the heterodox groups that regained control of the party in the mid-1990s totally devoid of progressive principles and ideals. Heterodox-inspired party pronouncements regarding the economic dimension of socialist democracy increasingly approximated standard Keynesianism (i.e., an active state in leading sectors of the economy and in redistributive income policies), but with a newly minted commitment to administrative reform of the patrimonial state, primarily via greater citizen oversight (Baia 1996; Rodrigues 1997; C. Toledo 1994). The political dimension reflected a clear and unambiguous acceptance of the legitimacy of representative democracy, but with a renewed commitment to improving that democracy—and making it more acceptable to *basistas*—with additional channels and institutions of direct citizen participation.

In sum, a retrospective of the PT's ideology provides a complicated picture. On the one hand, there is a consistently heterogeneous mixture of orientations that span the center-to-left spectrum. On the other hand, there is an evolutionary development of hegemony from the late 1970s' rejection of authoritarian capitalism and an embracing of *basismo* (sometimes to the point of dismissing formal institutions of representative democracy) to the late 1990s' essentially social democratic vision (in all but name) of a reformist loyal opposition.[33]

Conclusion

Clearly, the PT has taken an active role and has performed well in Brazilian electoral politics. Its party program has increasingly valued democracy as a positive goal in and of itself. The fact that the most important leftist force in Brazil has committed itself to abiding by the rules of procedural democracy indicates a major step in the legitimation of democratic rules of the game.

The PT also contributes to the legitimation (and, therefore, consolidation) of democracy by actively opposing social exclusion—by placing popular concerns and interests on the public policy agenda, by directing some percentage of public funds toward alleviating material inequities, and by promoting greater citizen involvement in democratic processes. At a minimum, the PT makes political contestation in Brazil significantly more than competition among political elites who sound and act more or less the same. But when the PT champions such policies as those described under the headings *inversão de prioridades, participação popular,* and "ethical politics," the output of the democratic process itself can be seen to further regime legitimacy (although, admittedly, in an unmeasurable way). The PT's electoral growth over its history provides some evidence to support this claim. We must be careful to note, however, that all of these innovations are subject to such delegitimizing factors as the exclusionary neoliberal policies of the 1990s, Brazil's political culture of passivity, the indiscriminate politician bashing that is carried out by much of the mass media, partisan-inspired disinformation disseminated by the PT's political opponents, and perhaps even muckraking carried out by the PT itself.

The PT further contributes to democratic consolidation by providing a home for political activists who oppose the inequities of peripheral capitalism and patrimonial democracy. Many such individuals and groups have entered the PT, expressed and pursued their goals with some degree of success or hope, and have come to accept and to internalize the rules of democracy. Such "socialization" is visible in the growing numbers of experienced politicians and administrators who have filled the ranks of the party's leadership. We must also recognize, however, the concern expressed by some people that these apparently positive processes carry with them the negative effect of increasingly distancing the party's leaders and functionaries from the grassroots movements and local activists that has made the PT such a vital and strikingly different actor in Brazilian politics.

Be that as it may, by the end of the century, the PT had become the institutional expression of the overwhelming majority of the Brazilian left. The party presented to the Brazilian people a mixture of the "orthodox" leftist critique of capitalism (and its concern for greater equality and social justice) with a "heterodox" commitment to make democracy live up to its promise by working to reform the system from within. This mixture represented a three-part gamble. First, by giving up dreams of a socialist utopia (along with the inevitably violent means of attaining it), party leaders are betting that "playing the game" of formal democracy, no matter how flawed at the present time, means that progressive reforms are both possible and cumulative. Second, they are betting that Brazilian voters will see the logic and the necessity of such reforms—and vote accordingly. Third, they are gambling that their own ranks will not become thinned by fatigue and frustration with such a gradualist and long-term strategy. As long as playing the game continues to result in electoral victories in the municipal, state, and national arenas (giving leaders and activists significant opportunities to practice what the party preaches), the PT will continue to be a positive force in Brazilian politics. If such victories dry up, for whatever reason, the party could very well fragment, and Brazilian democracy will have lost one of its most precious assets.

SEVEN

The Catholic Church, Religious Pluralism, and Democracy in Brazil

Kenneth P. Serbin

he Roman Catholic Church, which gained prestige and power for helping lead Brazil back to civilian rule in 1985, has faced the difficult and
complex challenge of maintaining its influence in the increasingly pluralistic
society that has since emerged. The Church has also undergone a paradoxical shift. Between 1968 and 1985, it opposed the military regime and acted
as "the voice of the voiceless" by promoting human rights and social justice
for the poor through such structures as the renowned Comunidades Eclesiais
de Base (CEBs, or Grassroots Church Communities). After 1985, the Church
continued to work for change through support for democratic consolidation, political activism, and criticism of the government's failure to focus on
social justice. However, a reaction against Brazilian Catholic progressivism
also took place. Pope John Paul II and conservative bishops restricted the
clergy's political activities and cut back many of the innovations introduced
during the heady days of the dictatorship. The Church also refocused on
evangelization and spirituality at the expense of political action. This paradox is partially explained by a changing political climate, the Church's internal situation, and the need to safeguard privileges provided by the state. But
the key to understanding the paradox is the church's exercise of its traditional mission as moral tutor of Brazilian society.

The Church no longer holds a monopoly on power in the religious arena.
In the 1980s, democratization could be viewed largely from the standpoint
of the Catholic Church (Della Cava 1989), but today it is impossible to
consider democratic consolidation without studying the new religious plu-

ralism created mainly by the rapid growth of Protestant Pentecostalism.[1] Because of this emergence of Pentecostalism, religion is no longer an immutable social given but a private and nonpermanent choice.

For the first time in the country's history, the notion of an exclusively Catholic Brazil has been seriously challenged, for the Pentecostals have converted their religious success into social and political power by incorporating their followers into organized churches, electing members of humble origin to public office, and tapping into political networks and state patronage. Brazil has thus become a "pioneer: the first traditionally Catholic country in the world with a large Protestant electoral and parliamentary presence" (Freston 1993a, 67). When attention to CEBs and other Catholic-inspired social movements peaked in the 1980s, few people would have predicted that Pentecostalism would soon be a different kind of voice for the poor. Though often painted as conservative, quackish, and manipulative, the Pentecostals have achieved what the liberation theologians and others failed to accomplish: the attraction of millions of the poor into their flocks. As one pastor perhaps cruelly but not completely inaccurately put it, "The Catholic Church opted for the poor, but the poor opted for the evangelicals."[2]

The advent of religious pluralism represents significant social change, and religion and religious change can help shape democracy on different levels by affecting institutional politics and church-state relations,[3] voting patterns, and movements in civil society. At each level religion can have a positive, negative, or even mixed effect. I argue two points.

First, pluralism has not yet become a crucial factor in democracy from a top-down or macropolitical perspective. Brazilian politics is still largely an extremely conservative and elite affair that focuses much more on negotiation of interests than ideological or religious issues.[4] The Pentecostals are increasing political participation, but they are doing so in a conservative way. Their leaders have sought, not to alter, but simply to adapt to Brazil's socioeconomic structure and political system. Pentecostal politicians are especially known for seeking patronage and privileges. In Brazil, the poor do not want to revolt but to ascend the social ladder,[5] and the Pentecostal churches reflect this hope. Especially among the newer churches the primary concern of the leaders is power, and often their theologies are attuned to economic interests. The new churches have little concern with social justice on a national scale.[6]

However, from a bottom-up or micropolitical standpoint, religious pluralism reveals the maturation, growing complexity, and mobility of Brazilian society. Religious change is part of a long-term socioeconomic and cultural transformation that envelops politics and the process of democratic consolidation: the continued modernization of Brazilian society through ever closer integration into the world capitalist economy but with the country's traditions and colonial legacy always hanging in the balance. Religious change indicates important shifts in people's behavior and views of society, and most religious change in Brazil has occurred among the poor, where in the long run such factors have greater impact on their daily lives than the machinations of elite politicians. Because the Pentecostal churches have become politically active, religious pluralism also means that there are now more intermediaries between the people and the state. Such religious pluralism makes civil society more dense but not necessarily more democratic (Gaskill 1997). Nevertheless, it is a mirror of Brazilian democracy, which, though still highly ineffective, has incrementally improved people's awareness of politics and the political process.

Brazil's poverty and social exclusion are the common forces behind the quite different outlooks of Catholicism and Protestant Pentecostalism. Brazil continues to have one of the world's worst records of income distribution. The "lost" decade, economically speaking, in the 1980s was paralleled by a "feckless democracy" (Mainwaring 1995a) in which the elite failed to carry out many basic reforms, most notably, the redistribution of land (Brazil was outwardly democratic, but inwardly still oligarchical [Hagopian, 1996]). Social and economic conditions improved only slightly in the 1990s, and for the poor this situation means hunger, underemployment, inadequate housing, ramshackle schools, and a dilapidated public health system. In their respective utopias, the Catholic Church transforms or at least reforms this milieu while the Pentecostals offer ways to adapt to or escape from it.

The Catholic Church:
From "Moral Concordat" to "Moral Watchdog"

The Catholic Church's self-perceived mission as the moral tutor of Brazilian society provides the framework for understanding religion, pluralism, and democracy, and it is important to explore the development of that mission through institutional growth and political activism. Since the 1930s, the Church's political role, its relationship to the state, and its exercise of moral tutorship have gone through three quite different but not mutually exclusive phases. The first was the "moral concordat," the dominant phase that led to the others. Antidemocratic and antipluralistic, the roots of this first phase lie in the largely authoritarian, highly corporatist regime of the first presidency of Getúlio Vargas (1930–1945),[7] as he helped resuscitate the embattled Church as a national institution by granting it privileges and subsidies in exchange for political and ideological support. Close Church-state ties continued during subsequent, democratic administrations (1946–1964) and to a certain extent even during the military regime, when the bishops and the generals met secretly in the hope of continued collaboration.[8] The moral concordat led the Church to become a social arm of the state through the building of hospitals, schools, and other projects and led the Catholic bishops to become involved in the nation's drive for economic development.[9] Minus this last aspect, the moral concordat has served as a model for other Brazilian confessions that recently have tried to gain political influence.

After World War II, the Church underwent a political transformation that called into question its traditional support for the status quo—some bishops advocated agrarian reform, for instance—and in the early 1960s, the Catholic left advocated deep changes in the social structure. The important Second Vatican Council (1962–1965) opened Catholicism to dialogue with the modern world, other religions, and even Marxism. The Brazilian Church anticipated Vatican II and radicalized the council's regionwide sequel, held in Medellín, Colombia, in 1968. These changes occurred as Brazil's military regime was imposing a model of rapid capitalist accumulation and a highly repressive, anticommunist doctrine of national security. The security forces arrested and abused scores of priests, nuns, lay militants, and even bishops. The result was the worst Church-state crisis in Brazilian history.

The repression moved the Church into a second political phase: "moral opposition"[10] to the regime. The Conferência Nacional dos Bispos do Brasil (CNBB, National Conference of the Bishops of Brazil) criticized human rights violations and denounced social inequality. Progressive Catholics formed what was called the Popular Church (also the Church of the Poor and the Progressive Church), which gained hegemony within the Catholic Church as a whole and implemented a series of politically important innovations such as the CEBs and organizations to promote agrarian reform, the independent labor movement, and the rights of Amerindians. These groups fed into the popular movements that arose in Brazil in the 1970s and 1980s. The Popular Church's theoretical blueprint was liberation theology, which borrowed from Marxism and emphasized social transformation as salvation. The Brazilian Catholic Church became the most radical in the world and played a substantial role in the democratic *abertura* ("opening"),[11] which set the stage for the Church's latest phase, that of "moral watchdog."[12]

Conservative Reaction and the Catholic Retreat from Politics

When Brazil redemocratized, the Church receded from overt political activism for several reasons. First, the Church was not a political party and therefore encouraged other groups and movements to take the lead, and those groups assumed much of the work that had been carried out by the Church under the military (Mainwaring 1986a; Bruneau and Hewitt 1992). Although the Church was the glue that held together the left and other opposition groups before 1985, afterward the glue became the socialist Partido dos

Trabalhadores (PT, or Workers' Party). Significantly, the bishops did not want to jeopardize the legitimacy of the fledgling and fragile democratic government that they themselves had helped to foster (Gill 1998).

Second, a conservative reaction within the Church moved the clergy out of politics, rolled back many progressive innovations, and stressed the orthodoxy of the pre–Vatican II era. The reaction gained an important supporter in John Paul II, a staunch anti-Marxist, and under him, the Vatican punished liberation theologians, reprimanded progressive bishops, intervened in religious orders, censored publications, and divided the Archdiocese of São Paulo, a progressive stronghold. At the fourth continental assembly of Latin American bishops held in Santo Domingo in 1992, the Vatican ignored much of the progressive approach. Moreover, John Paul II appointed conservative bishops and curtailed the power of the CNBB, which had embodied the ecclesiastical nationalism of the 1970s and 1980s. Thus, in 1995, the CNBB elected Dom Lucas Moreira Neves, a cousin of Tancredo Neves (the president-elect who had died in 1985), as the conference's first nonprogressive president in twenty-five years.[13] A year later John Paul II made him a cardinal.

Third, the prestige of the Popular Church deflated as the political context changed. The collapse of communism and the retreat of the Latin American left (Castañeda 1993) discouraged Catholic progressivism, and disillusionment set in when the Popular Church failed to bring about a deep social transformation (Berryman 1996). Furthermore, the conservative reaction and the end of the heroic struggle against the dictatorship reduced the enthusiasm and membership of grassroots movements.

The Church of the Poor simply did not attract most of the poor, and the CEBs did not fulfill the heady goals of progressive leaders, some of whom held elitist attitudes toward the poor. Though perhaps not as few as some people estimate, the CEBs include but a fraction of the population.[14] Moreover, their ideology tends to be exclusionary toward such groups as women with domestic problems, youths, and Afro-Brazilians,[15] even though large numbers of the last do participate (Pierucci and Prandi 1996a). In addition, as CEBs came under tighter control by the clergy and were often torn asunder by internal strife produced by the democratic transition, they became less involved in politics and focused more on religious concerns (Vásquez 1997, 1998; Hewitt 1995; Perani 1987). They are no longer a major priority of the Church and have lost some of their capacity to strengthen citizenship.[16] Finally, the rapid growth and political ascendancy of Pentecostal Protestant religions in the 1980s posed a threat to the Church's centuries-old politico-religious hegemony and caused it to change its behavior to a more traditional pattern.[17]

A clear sign of this change has been a focus on institutional needs and religious activities using strategies reminiscent of the pre-1964 moral concordat. Riding a wave of political prestige at the start of the New Republic, the Church assumed this stance with public support from Tancredo Neves and then President José Sarney (Freston 1993a). The bishops have lobbied the government and politicians to resolve the Church's problems, and one bishop, the progressive Dom Mauro Morelli of Duque de Caxias, served in the government of President Itamar Franco (1992–1994) as head of a poverty relief effort. In 1989, the Vatican and the Brazilian armed forces signed an agreement reactivating the military chaplaincy.

Representatives of the CNBB and the governments of Fernando Collor de Mello (1990–1992) and Franco tried unsuccessfully to negotiate a Church-state protocol. The Church hoped to reinforce the legal validity of religious marriage, reestablish religious instruction in the public schools and religious assistance in public hospitals, and create a legal distinction between the Catholic Church and other religions. Furthermore, the Church worked to influence the state to safeguard financial assets and its philanthropic organizations' privileges. These needs became more urgent as previously generous European Catholic funding agencies reduced donations. Continued high levels of poverty maintained the demand for Church social assistance activities such as the Children's Pastoral, which received backing from the Franco government (Serbin 1995a).[18]

The Catholic Church as "Moral Watchdog"

Progressivism, however, did not die, and many aspects of the Popular Church survived to create a substantial progressive Catholic legacy. The great paradox of the post-1985 period was that a more conservative Church used that legacy to attempt to shape Brazilian democracy. Conservatism and traditional institutional interests commingled with the struggle for social justice.[19] The paradox is resolved by viewing the Church's approach as a coalescence of historical patterns, divergent political actors, and contemporary challenges in which spirituality and ecclesiastical conservatism are not necessarily inconsistent with social justice.

First, the conservative reaction had limits. It focused mainly on ecclesiastical structures and did not seek to interfere directly in Brazilian politics. Moreover, the Vatican could not—nor did it want to—completely wipe out the efforts of the Popular Church. John Paul II found much that was good in liberation theology, and he has praised the Brazilian Church for its social consciousness. Liberation theology received inspiration from the traditional social doctrine of the popes, and rooted in the nineteenth century, the social doctrine governs all internal ecclesial factions.[20] Moreover, though modified, the CNBB's progressive legacy has become part of Brazil's historical mosaic.

The Church is not just an ecclesial institution, but a Brazilian one as well, and the Vatican's moves are shaped by local history and conditions.

Second, pluralism exists not only in the larger religious arena but within the Catholic Church itself. This church has a far higher degree of internal complexity than the Pentecostal denominations, with groups ranging from radical liberationists to conservative, quasi-Pentecostal charismatics. But unlike the highly schismatic Pentecostals, the Catholic Church remains whole. Thus, liberation theologians could openly support the left in 1989 and 1994 while moderates gravitated toward centrist parties, such as the PSDB, and conservatives to the right.

Pluralism was also mirrored in ecclesiastical politics, including the bishops' efforts to save progressive programs. By electing Dom Lucas, the bishops placated the Vatican. However, they also chose a vice president (Dom Jayme Chemello) and the governing council of the CNBB from the Popular Church. Tensions arose between Dom Lucas and this group, but the balance of power preserved the CNBB's basic structure.

Finally, the bishops' political engagement in the 1980s and 1990s reflected their customary role in politics and a remarkable ability to adapt to the postauthoritarian era,[21] and their incentive for such involvement increased with the Pentecostal threat. The Catholic Church helped consolidate Brazilian democracy but also sought to keep its politico-religious hegemony, which had regularly served as a political surrogate for the people. Thus, a new version of the moral concordat emerged with the Church now acting as the "moral watchdog" of Brazilian society. Officially avoiding the partisan fray, it pronounced its moral and ethical outline for the country, denounced social injustice, and criticized the government's inability to solve the country's socioeconomic problems.

The values, ideals, and personnel of the Popular Church penetrated political structures and social movements[22]—a prime example being the CNBB. The bishops urged the writing of the constitution of 1988 and helped set its agenda. Most of the Church's statements echoed the liberationist "preferential option for the poor" and the union of faith and politics. Six months before the Constituent Assembly elections of 1986 the CNBB had issued "For a New Constitutional Order," a document emphasizing the rights and responsibilities of citizenship. It advocated protection of human rights and minority groups, greater economic equality, active political participation by the populace, a deconcentration of power in the highly oligopolistic media sector, and agrarian reform (CNBB 1990).

This effort recalled the Church's earlier campaigns to shape the constitutions of 1934 and 1946, but in 1986, the Church abstained from endorsing candidates for the Constituent Assembly. It instead urged voters to select individuals who fit a profile described by the Church, especially those dedicated to grassroots movements, social justice, and the struggle against authoritarianism. It warned against candidates who were in politics for personal gain, had ties to privileged groups, or were involved in corruption (CNBB 1990). Moreover, the Church deemphasized traditional, behind-the-scenes lobbying in favor of so-called popular amendments (eligible for consideration with 30,000 or more signatures) and public meetings with Constituent Assembly members that focused on the issues. The CNBB also set up a special commission to record, analyze, and publicize the work of the Constituent Assembly (CNBB 1990; Doimo 1995).

This campaign revealed a vision of Brazilian democracy that often seemed utopian, but it must be seen in the context of the Church's historical struggle against unequal social and political structures that predated the military regime. The Church had no illusions. It recognized that the new constitution had many shortcomings—agrarian structures, for example, were left largely intact—and the Church also understood that the even more important task of drafting enabling legislation still lay ahead. Most of this legislation has yet to be proposed.

The legacy of the Popular Church survived in other forms. Thanks to the Church's campaigns of the military era, the concept of human rights is today part of the common discourse of Brazilian democracy.[23] Many grassroots and nongovernment organizations and also the PT include people who began in groups such as the CEBs. Started in the 1960s, the CNBB's annual Lenten campaigns have maintained their focus on social issues such as hunger, agrarian reform, abandoned children, racial discrimination, women's position in society, housing, and the subhuman conditions of Brazil's jails (CNBB 1997), and a new Children's Pastoral has become highly successful in the battle against infant mortality (Serbin 1995a). The Church continued to demand a more just economic order, and it pushed agrarian reform through its support of the highly radical Movimento dos Sem-Terra (Movement of the Landless) and the continued sponsorship of *romarias da terra* ("land pilgrimages"). In 1996, the CNBB intensified focus on the land question by vigorously protesting a police massacre of more than twenty *sem-terra* at Eldorado dos Carajás (Beozzo 1997; CNBB 1996).[24] The Church has also been highly critical of the neoliberal economic policies of Collor and Fernando Henrique Cardoso (1995–). In 1997, for example, the CNBB opposed the controversial sale of the Companhia Vale do Rio Doce, a large and profitable state mining company. Cardoso, in turn, has criticized the progressive Church and liberation theology (Uchao 1998).[25]

The Church also maintained a number of traditional planks in its platform. It advocated the protection of the family; opposed artificial birth control, the sterilization of women, and abortion; and successfully fought to keep religious instruction permissible in the public schools. In effect, the

Church remained one of the major determinants of the Brazilian moral code. However, the Church's commitment to universal moral laws grates against pluralism and is not always compatible with tenets and requirements of liberal democracy.[26] Abortion was a major issue during the Constituent Assembly, and it pitted feminists against the bishops. In the mid-1990s, the topic emerged again as an important political issue, and there were congressional initiatives both to restrict and to expand access to it. Abortion and related themes created Church-state friction in 1997 when First Lady Ruth Cardoso expressed doubt about John Paul II's ability to influence congressional debate—speaking just as the pontiff arrived for his third visit to Brazil for an international conference on the family.

The Church and Elections

The Catholic Church viewed voter education as one of its primary contributions to democracy. It continued to use the type of profiles developed for the 1986 election, which favored the center-left because of an emphasis on social transformation and criticized traditional patronage politics—the venue of the conservative, rural-based parties. Profiles rather than endorsements allowed the Church to remain officially impartial in terms of party politics but still supportive of social change. Thus, the Church could still seek relations with successful candidates who did not fit the Catholic profile.[27] However, the line between electoral pedagogy and actual involvement was often fine.

The most visible engagement occurred among the progressive clergy. These priests and CEB members frequently backed PT candidates such as Catholic activist Luiza Erundina in her surprise victory in the 1988 São Paulo mayoral election. In the 1989 presidential election, the CNBB appealed once again for deep transformations in Brazilian society in its document "Ethical Demands for the Democratic Order" (CNBB 1989). Although the CNBB was officially impartial, progressive priests openly supported the PT's Luiz Inácio Lula da Silva against the conservative Collor. For example, the progressive leader Frei Betto issued a biography of Lula (Betto 1989).[28] Individual bishops kept their preferences private. Many Catholics were said to have supported the centrist Mário Covas of the Partido da Social Democracia Brasileira (PSDB, or Brazilian Social Democratic Party) during the first part of the two-stage election.

In the less-polarized 1994 contest between Lula and PSDB intellectual Cardoso, the CNBB distanced itself from radicalism and carried the fight for social justice into the political mainstream. For example, the CNBB held a Semana Social (Social Week) during which the term *excluídos* replaced the liberationist "oppressed."[29] This event gathered hundreds of leaders of local pastoral organizations to propose grassroots alternatives to national development schemes. They also debated some of the dominant themes of Brazilian democracy: the state and society, citizenship, corruption, ethics, the environment, and ethnicity.[30] Thus, the Church sought, not to transform, but to reform an unequal democratic-capitalist society into whose structures it hoped to integrate "the excluded." The Social Week ended with a CNBB-sponsored nationally televised presidential debate. Instead of journalists, grassroots leaders questioned the candidates—a historical first in Brazil.

With an estimated 36 million people watching, the Church attained its largest press coverage in recent years and reinforced its moral status (CNBB 1994a). The progressive Church again voted heavily for Lula (Pierucci and Prandi 1996a), and even though he lost, the Social Week had helped the *movimento popular* move into the media limelight and the formal democratic forum.[31] This transition reflected the movement's shift from an emphasis on grassroots organization to working through political institutions and organized civil society as a publicly recognized interest group (Doimo 1995).

The Pentecostal Challenge

The Catholic Church's concern with institutional and religious interests must be seen against a background of increasing social and religious pluralism and competition from Protestant Pentecostals. Democratic freedom, the growth of the media, and the growing complexity of an ever more urban society have increased pluralism and Pentecostal growth. Like the CEBs, Pentecostalism has offered a way for the poor to seek economic betterment, social dignity, and political participation, though in a conservative manner.

Pentecostal Growth

Protestant Pentecostal missionaries first came to Brazil at the turn of the twentieth century. They were distinguished from more traditional, so-called mainline Protestants (such as Lutherans) by their emphasis on the gifts of the Holy Spirit—for example, speaking in tongues.[32] In the 1950s, a second wave of Pentecostals increased membership through faith healing and revivals. Led by the Igreja Universal do Reino de Deus (IURD, or Universal Church of the Kingdom of God), yet a third wave of new denominations in the 1980s added to Pentecostal growth.[33] In 1950, more than 90 percent of Brazilians still adhered to Catholicism; today, the Catholic Church itself admits that as few as 75 percent of Brazil's 160 million people now belong to this faith (Cipriani 1994; Pierucci and Prandi 1996a). The Protestants' share of the population has grown from 2 percent in the 1930s to 4 percent in 1960 to approximately 13 percent in 1992.[34] In 1996, the figure was estimated at 15 percent (Berryman 1996). One study states that a new Pentecostal temple opens daily in the greater metropolitan area of Rio de Janeiro (R. Fernandes 1992).

Brazil's recent political history furnishes a partial explanation for this increasing pluralism. Catholic-military conflict during the authoritarian era provided an opportunity for other religions to expand through accommodation with the state, and although most of the armed forces remained Catholic, some sectors promoted Afro-Brazilian religion and Pentecostalism as ways to offset progressive Catholicism.[35] But Protestants were not especially strong supporters of the dictatorship.[36] Moreover, while some denominations expanded with aid from North American sponsors, causing Catholics to allege an imperialist conspiracy (Assmann 1986; Lima 1987), most have become "Brazilianized" and autonomous and have gained a momentum of their own. The new churches are uniquely Brazilian and entirely independent;[37] they are also part of a more dynamic, syncretistic neo-Pentecostalism.

The prime example is the IURD. It combines elements of Pentecostalism and Catholicism, and its use of exorcism indirectly confirms the existence and power of the spirits of Umbanda, a syncretistic Afro-Brazilian religion that is widely practiced. The IURD embraces an economically oriented, individualistic "prosperity theology," relies on the media to propagate its message, and is heavily involved in politics.[38] Started in 1977, by the mid-1990s the IURD had temples across Brazil and several million members; collected as much as $1 billion per year in tithes; and owned Brazil's third-largest television network, thirty radio stations, two newspapers, a bank, and other interests. The IURD rapidly spread to other parts of Latin America, the United States, Europe, and Africa.[39]

Social and cultural factors also help explain the growth of Pentecostalism. Pentecostals have largely built membership among the poor, uneducated, and politically excluded (Pierucci and Prandi 1996a), and the number of Protestant pastors, most of whom are poor, is double that of Catholic priests, most of whom achieve a middle-class lifestyle (Berryman 1996). In recent decades, Pentacostal denominations have raised thousands of temples in poor neighborhoods. In Belém, for instance, worshipers are typically migrants employed in low-paying service jobs, domestic service, or the informal sector. Many are jobless. Many hope to open a small business—a trend that is reinforced by "prosperity theology" (Chesnut 1997).

Pentecostal pastors utilize the most effective methods for attracting the disenfranchised and generating a feeling of welcome: greater lay participation; efficient mass communication; emphasis on the Bible; emotional spirituality and mysticism; revivals, miracles, exorcism, and faith healing; moralizing against drinking and adultery; creating a sense of belonging for migrants; personal attention to church members; and the acceptance of people with afflictions not addressed by Catholicism. Many Pentecostals are Afro-

Brazilians, whom the Catholic Church has had great difficulty in assimilating (Burdick 1993). In short, Pentecostals have had greater success because they have responded more effectively to people's suffering, immediate needs, and fears than either conservative or progressive Catholicism (Vasquez 1998; Chesnut 1997; Berryman 1996; Burdick 1993; Comblin 1993; *Revista Eclesiástica Brasileira* 1993a; Gomes 1992). During the economic crises of the 1980s, church membership burgeoned. In addition, in contrast with an uncompromising Catholic stance, the IURD has shown signs of greater flexibility on the issues of abortion and birth control (Machado n.d.).[40]

Persecution as both a mode of self-victimization and an attack on other religions has been another attention-winning strategy. The IURD, for example, disseminates the notion of persecution by Catholics and other groups in sermons and mass meetings (Fonseca 1996) and has gone on the offensive by encouraging a "holy war" against Afro-Brazilian religions (Berryman 1996), in some cases literally attacking their followers. Like all Protestant churches, the IURD rejects the sanctity of the Virgin Mary, and attacks on her are a part of its anti-Catholic repertoire. In 1995, an IURD pastor caused a national, media-generated scandal by kicking an image of Our Lady of Aparecida on television on October 12, the national holiday in honor of Brazil's patroness.[41]

Pentecostal expansion has produced "the first popular religiosity in Latin America that does not even implicitly recognize the institutional hegemony of the Catholic Church" (Freston 1993b, 94). Catholicism was always a public and civic religion into which all Brazilians were born and spent their lives. Now they choose a religion in an ever more varied religious arena. Conversion is commonplace, and the dissatisfied believer can switch (Prandi 1996; Pierucci 1996). Religion is no longer a unifying force, as the tendency is toward the separation of the populace into distinct religious groups (Prandi 1996).

Yet while Pentecostal growth is a watershed in Latin America, it must be acknowledged that the same forces of modernization that lie behind this phenomenon have also spurred the growth of the CEBs and the Catholic charismatics. All three categories stress *active participation* in contrast to the passive nature of traditional Catholicism. Pentecostalism is not necessarily an anti-Catholic phenomenon, but it is part of larger qualitative changes in Brazilian society and religion (Berryman 1996). CEBs and Pentecostalism acknowledge denominational tension but share some sociological roots—for example, helping the poor to cope with poverty (Mariz 1994; Berryman 1996)—although the CEBs have worked to transform structural conditions while Pentecostals have merely managed and may even legitimize them (Gaskill 1997). Thus, sociological reality does not necessarily inform political reality.

Pentecostals and Politics

To bolster their institutional bases, Pentecostal churches have sought formal political power, and one of their principal aims is to end the Catholic Church's status as Brazil's semiofficial religion. In the 1930s, progressive Protestants unsuccessfully sought to keep the Brazilian state religiously neutral; now the Pentecostals and in particular the IURD seek to become allies of the state. Edir Macedo, the founder and self-designated head bishop of the IURD, nearly achieved his goal of giving the invocation at Collor's inauguration (Freston 1993a). Such an act would have had enormous political impact—far more than Lutheran Ernesto Geisel's (indirect) election in 1973 as the first Protestant president to serve a full term and the (military-controlled) Congress's subsequent approval of a divorce law.[42] The IURD has subsequently used its influence with Collor and Cardoso administration officials to help build its business and religious strength. The Pentecostal churches have been especially successful in employing their new media might to reinforce their political power, and vice versa (Freston 1993a; R. Almeida 1996.) Because these churches are both a minority and newcomers, their efforts have been aggressive, whereas the CNBB has rested on its tradition of speaking for all Brazil.

In 1986, the Pentecostals performed impressively in the Constituent Assembly elections, electing eighteen candidates. Including other Protestants, the so-called *bancada evangélica* ("evangelical coalition") won a total of thirty-six seats. This number was comparable to an informal and very discrete *bancada católica* (Freston 1993a). The Pentecostal deputies were not members of the traditional political elite but new politicians elected on the basis of church connections. After the 1990 election, the *bancada evangélica* dropped to twenty-three members, but the IURD increased its share of the *bancada* from one to three members (in 1994, six). Protestant representatives have been twice as likely to win reelection as non-Protestants (Carneiro 1997). The *bancada evangélica* held thirty-five seats after the 1998 election, and the IURD elected fourteen members, including one of its top bishops, to become the largest Protestant contingent in the Congress.

The *bancada evangélica* is best described as part of the slightly rightist *centro fisiológico* ("clientelistic center"), which is more concerned with patronage than ideology. The *bancada* has openly defended the interests of its churches, sought government resources and privileges in competition with the Catholic Church, and obtained valuable television concessions in return for support of Sarney, in particular during his successful bid to extend his term. As a result, the *bancada* gained a reputation for practicing the sort of crass deal making for which the Brazilian Congress is famous. The *bancada* is *not* equivalent to the "new Christian right" of U.S. politics. In fact, the *bancada* voted slightly to the left of the Constituent Assembly as a whole. Its centrism, however, came into sharp relief during the Collor impeachment proceedings in 1992, when it remained ambiguous about its position until opting for removal at the end (Freston 1993b). In addition, *bancada* members are less supportive of the government than other conservative politicians, and within the *bancada*, denominational differences cause varying political behavior (L. Carneiro 1997).

The Pentecostals have used their media resources and direct appeals to the faithful to support conservative candidates in presidential and other elections. In 1989, they openly supported Collor and demonized Lula as a Communist, and they rejected Lula more than any other religious grouping in the 1994 presidential election (Pierucci and Prandi 1996a). In other elections, pastors urged their followers to vote for candidates who were sympathetic to IURD interests. Because of these churches' apparent ability to shape the vote, candidates from several parties have sought their support and tailored campaign rhetoric toward Pentecostal audiences (Fonseca 1996).

Although the *bancada evangélica* was one of the most prominent examples of Pentecostal political action, Pentecostal involvement has not led to any significant change in Brazilian politics from a top-down perspective. Pentecostals play along with the system, not against it. They run on existing parties' tickets but also engage more frequently than other politicians in the common practice of party switching. They do not embrace parties but view them as necessary evils that are subject to corruption (Freston 1993a, 1993b). Because they are a minority, they must rely on coalition building. Moreover, the schismatic tendency of Pentecostalism and its divisive effects on the *bancada* have cast doubt on the Pentecostals' ability to affect democratic consolidation (Gaskill 1997).

However, on the grassroots level, Pentecostal activity is incorporating the poor and illiterate into political structures (Pierucci and Prandi 1996a). Indeed, in a quest for votes and influence Pentecostal churches often act like political parties, and in terms of organization and discipline, they actually outdo much of the Brazilian political system, which is infamous for its ephemeral, baseless parties. In this sense, the Pentecostal churches stand in contrast to the *movimento popular*, which historically has channeled its energies more toward making specific demands on government and less on elections.[43] Only a small fraction of Pentecostals have participated in the *movimento* (Doimo 1995).

In the IURD, for instance, politics is an integral part of missionary work, and the church teaches the faithful to elect candidates who will attend to its needs. This link between faith and politics strongly resembles the position of liberation theologians and the CNBB, although the long-term goals and political style are far different. The IURD emphasizes the vote for a fellow

Pentecostal as support for a "brother" who truly understands persecution and acts as a bridge between the faithful and the outer world.

The IURD has developed a number of practices for organizing political activity. The leadership coordinates electoral strategy to ensure that its candidates do not compete with one another in legislative contests. In the IURD, the "'official candidate' exists as a function of the church; without the church he represents nothing and nobody" (Fonseca 1996, 79–80). The IURD publishes a newspaper with a political page that provides an alternative to the unfavorable coverage of the church in the mainstream press, and through the paper, the IURD's elected officials seek to offer accountability to their supporters. In addition, the church encourages voter registration. During campaigns members work as canvassers, and temples hold meetings at which candidates are introduced. Successful candidates try to maintain their electoral base by acting as "brokers" between members and government agencies. The IURD has also plugged into traditional patronage networks, once considered the domain of the Catholic Church. In Rio de Janeiro, for instance, the IURD Deputy Aldir Cabral became head of the state Secretariat for Work and Social Action and promptly filled top positions and other jobs with Pentecostals (Fonseca 1996).

Nevertheless, the Pentecostals' new political structures do not necessarily encourage democratic practice (Gaskill 1997; Carneiro 1997), and the candidates themselves are usually humble members of the church who have worked their way up the ranks. In the case of the Assemblies of God, a modified form of clientelism described as "participatory authoritarianism" has developed. The pastor-president of each church extends patronage and positions to loyal followers but retains the power to make political decisions and name candidates (Chesnut 1997). This and other examples suggest that Pentecostalism reinforces traditional patron-client relations (Gaskill 1997; Berryman 1996). Significantly, however, IURD members participate very little in political work such as community organizations, and they also express a high level of support for a (hypothetical) return to military rule (Carneiro 1997).

The Catholic Response

The Catholic response to Pentecostalism has been slow.[44] Criticisms and warnings about the so-called *seitas* ("sects") have long been common in the Catholic message, but only in the 1980s did the Church begin to study the Pentecostal phenomenon more carefully. It is important to recognize that the Brazilian Catholic Church, which established ecumenical relations with mainline Protestant denominations such as the Lutherans in the 1970s, has not viewed Pentecostalism through the prism of pure competition. The life of religious institutions, especially traditional ones such as the Catholic Church, is far more complex than a zero-sum battle over the faithful. The Catholic Church believes it is for *all* Brazilians. Moreover, the common view that Pentecostal growth results from Catholic flight is erroneous. Historically, most Brazilians have been only nominally Catholic and have had weak links to the clergy (Gomes 1992; De Groot 1996), and in recent decades, probably more people than ever have become active members of the Church (Gomes 1992). Nevertheless, Pentecostal success has moved the Church to go beyond denunciation to outlining specific, though tentative, strategies for increasing its followers.

Initiative came from the top. In the 1980s, Pope John Paul II called for a "new evangelization" in Latin America, and the 1992 Santo Domingo meeting worked to plan this campaign. Fundamental is the revival of pre–Vatican II spirituality and rituals. In the process the Church seeks its roots but also mimics the techniques and spectacles of the Pentecostals. Conservatives in particular have led this trend (Serbin 1993b; Oro 1996), and some clerics have even resorted to miracles and exorcism (R. Dias 1994). In effect, sectors of Brazilian religion have undergone a "pentecostalization," with Catholics and others taking ideas from one another (Machado 1996). The Church is also improving its media resources. Despite Pentecostal success, it still has Brazil's largest network of religious radio stations and publishing concerns (Della Cava and Montero 1991; Beozzo 1997), though it recognizes that it has used these tools less effectively than its competitors (Oro 1996).

At the core of the Catholic response is a group of transnational conservative movements, in particular the Catholic Charismatic Renewal, a "pentecostalized" movement born in the United States in the 1960s and exported to Brazil in the early 1970s. John Paul II has strongly encouraged these movements, which stress prayer and traditional spirituality, express loyalty to the pope, and enjoy the support of a number of bishops. In São Paulo, for example, the charismatics fill churches in both conservative and progressive areas, and charismatics make up approximately 3.8 percent of the population—more than double the number of CEB members (Pierucci and Prandi 1996a). Even liberationists praise the charismatics for revivifying faith and building a sense of community and participation within the Church. Charismatic support is mainly middle class, but the poor are also joining.[45] Although the charismatics emphasize personal salvation and shun liberation theology, they share the CEBs' interest in the Bible and charitable work.

Some participate in politics, and although they are generally thought of as conservative, their orientation varies. In 1994, the proportion of charismatics who voted for Cardoso was higher than that of any other religious group (Pierucci and Prandi 1996a). Some groups have become involved in progressive movements (Prandi and Souza 1996) and in at least one community surpassed the CEBs in this regard (Theije 1997).

Because of their conservatism, the CNBB waited until the mid-1990s to grant charismatics official status. By then, it was clear that they were the best option for stemming Pentecostalism. Even so, the CNBB set strict controls to keep the movement in line with official post–Vatican II beliefs and practices (Oro 1996; CNBB 1994b). The charismatics have also met resistance from liberationist clergy (Prandi and Souza 1996). Such tensions have kept the Catholic Church from building a united front against the Pentecostals, allowing different groups to emphasize their own strategies.

Conclusions

As Brazilian democracy proceeds, the Catholic Church will undoubtedly continue as a watchdog over the political process and governments' social and economic policies. It is clearly committed to democracy, though its approach and particular positions are sometimes antidemocratic.

Less predictable is the Church's reaction to Pentecostal growth and the new pluralism. The Church's historic religious monopoly and political dominance have saddled it with bureaucratic inertia and overconfidence about the Catholic nature of Brazilian culture, and the job of interpreting and reacting to pluralism will fall to a new generation of Catholic leaders who mature, not in the comfort of monopoly, but under the challenge of competition. That generation has yet to emerge. Religious pluralism has made Brazilian society and the church-state dialogue far more complex. People are increasingly active in their religious choices, and people's experience in church could ultimately strengthen democracy through a demonstration effect.

Seeking growth, respectability, and power, the Pentecostal churches have stepped into the breach in Brazil's highly fragile political system to offer alternatives to the poor, the disenfranchised, and frustrated aspirants to upward mobility. These churches are conservative, but like the CEBs, grassroots movements, and the country's many governmental organizations, they are helping to build civil society and are acting as intermediaries between the poor and the state. As Leandro Carneiro states, "Nobody goes to a church in order to join a political party but could maybe join a political party through going to church" (Carneiro 1997, 22). These churches are also teaching political consciousness by encouraging voting and attention to ecclesial demands on the state. The Pentecostals' electoral clout has helped their churches fill some traditionally Catholic spaces in the political system.

Because Pentecostalism has been politically active for only a short time, it is still too early to gauge its long-term impact on Brazilian democracy or whether that impact will be conservative or progressive.[46] In the words of Newton Gaskill, "There is no invariant relationship between Protestantism and authoritarianism or democracy" (Gaskill 1977, 85). The tendency for at least the larger and older churches is toward institutionalization, even to the point of acquiring some of the characteristics of the Catholic Church (Freston 1993a), which cast the historical mold for public religion through the moral concordat.

As the Pentecostals consolidate their religious and political bases, they will demand a role in the moral concordat (and with it increase their claims on the state), and Church-state issues will be a constant theme in Brazilian democracy. But Pentecostal churches will also gain a greater stake in maintaining the status quo. Moreover, Pentecostal leaders will have the added responsibility that accompanies institutionalization. Aggressive proselytization will diminish while an increased acceptance into society could increase the desire to win middle-class converts. The IURD has already cast its net toward the middle class. If the Pentecostals continue to win election to public office, church leaders will increasingly feel the need to please their constituencies. And because their followers are predominantly poor, they could also come under pressure to work for social transformation rather than for a short-term alleviation of poverty through alleged miracles or incremental measures such as abstinence from alcohol.

Although in the short run religious competition highlights the potential for conflict over believers and patronage, in the long run a convergence between the Catholic and the Pentecostal styles and interests could occur. As North American Catholics are strongly influenced by the dominant Protestant values and culture, so will Brazilian Pentecostals feel the weight of their country's much longer Catholic (and Afro-Brazilian) past. Brazil was never fully Catholic, and Pentecostal growth makes it even less so, but Catholicism will continue to be the defining matrix of Brazilian religious culture.

EIGHT

Democratizing Pressures from Below?

Social Movements in the New Brazilian Democracy

Kathryn Hochstetler

The stories told of Brazilian social movements have been intimately linked to the rise and fall of hopes about the quality of Brazilian democracy. In the 1970s and 1980s, accounts of Brazilian politics told of an unprecedented generation of social movements—of urban neighborhoods, women, environmentalists, the Catholic Church, lawyers, and many more groups—who joined in a sudden upsurge of mobilizations against the military. The new movements were hailed as harbingers of a potential new era of democratic participation and inclusion (Durham 1984; Mainwaring and Viola 1984; Scherer-Warren and Krischke 1987; Vigevani 1989; Assies 1993). This surge of grassroots mobilizations collapsed in 1984, however, along with hopes for Brazil's emerging civilian regime: "If it is true that the campaign for *diretas já* ["direct elections" of the civilian president in 1985] was the crowning moment of oppositional protests and expressed the generalized desire for democracy, it is also certain that it was their last year" (R. Cardoso 1990, 16).[1] One of the few quantitative studies of Brazilian social movements supports this account, counting a surge in archival documents about popular movements that began in 1981 and then dropped off sharply after 1984 (Doimo 1995, 120). After that point, more-traditional political actors regained control over the postmilitary agenda while the social movements faced "new dilemmas and internal conflicts" (Mainwaring 1989, 169).

A survey of articles on urban popular movements in Brazil shows them to be a harbinger of undemocratic woe. One by one, urban popular movements have succumbed to drug dealers (Leeds 1996), bureaucratization

(Fontes 1995), opportunities to participate in government (Sérgio Costa 1995), the unwillingness of people to participate (Fontes 1996), the new strength of Pentecostals in the favelas (Zaluar 1995), the influence of Catholics and leftists (Cunha 1993), and a host of other pitfalls. Along with the decline of the movements themselves, all these authors note the pathologies of the new Brazilian state, which calls itself democratic but cannot allow participation without cooptation, cannot protect its citizens from each other or from itself, and in every other way fails to provide the conditions of citizenship for many of its inhabitants. Thus, although hopes about Brazilian democracy and social movements are once again linked, now it is in a negative way.

In this chapter, I also explore the role of social movements in Brazil, the quality of political democracy there, and the relationship between the two since 1985. I conclude that a broader perspective on social movements belies the common claims of social movements' decline and even disappearance after the political transition in Brazil in the mid-1980s. Although the mid-1980s did see significant changes in social movements organizing in Brazil, popular and middle-class actors did not retreat from active mobilization then. In fact, they launched a new cycle of social movement protest that had important continuities with the previous period while also reflecting the changed political context. This new cycle shows social movements to be important and positive contributors to the effort to deepen Brazilian democracy and mend its obvious defects, but it also calls attention to some of the social movements' own ambiguities as democratic actors. My argument rests on two points of departure from many other analyses of social movements.

First, I focus on entire cycles of social movement protest and thus encompass a broad spectrum of social movements. This method is unlike that of most studies, which concentrate on a single issue network or even a single social movement organization. Such a narrow focus leads to a pessimistic view of social movements, for because of precarious resource and personnel bases, individual social movement organizations are notoriously ephemeral and specific issues also move on and off the political agenda. The fate of one or several movements can be falsely attributed to the social movement sector as a whole, and in the case of Brazil, observers of urban popular movements have tended to reach very negative conclusions about the social movements there. Some movements in Brazil have indeed succumbed to a range of causes that have caused their decline since 1984,[2] yet other social movements have tended to be more enduring, and new movements and coalitions even draw some of their supporters from previous participants in the urban popular movements.

In analyzing cycles, the focus is on the overall patterns of political contention rather than on the fate of particular organizing efforts,[3] and the overall cycle is more persistent than most of its constituent mobilizing efforts. At the same time, the concept of a cycle of protest assumes a classic dynamic of rise and fall. Protest cycles have a beginning, when some social actors recognize and exploit new opportunities for challenging elites; a middle, when the example and challenges of the first mobilizers promote a much broader social mobilization; and an end, when state elites respond to heightened contention with either reforms or repression, which close the opportunities that began the cycle and thus end the mobilization itself (Tarrow 1994, 153–55).

In addition to the process of emergence and decline, cycles are also characterized by several qualitative measures: "a quickened pace of innovation in the forms of contention [and] new or transformed collective action frames" (Tarrow 1994, 154). The studies of recent Brazilian social movements suggest that such a cycle of social movement protest was ended by the partial democratizing reforms of the mid-1980s—an outcome that could have been *expected* and not a failure of the social movements from the perspective of cycles of protest. As might also be expected from the perspective of social movement cycles, the new political system opened new opportunities for social movements to challenge elites, which resulted in a new cycle of social movement mobilization.

My second point of departure from other analyses of social movements lies in addressing the relationship of social movements and institutional democracy in the abstract. When political scientists first analyzed the emergence of large numbers of social movements in the 1960s, they often interpreted social movements as a sign of the breakdown of democracy (J. Nelson 1987). In this view, social movements were inherently undemocratic because they refused to limit their political participation to institutionalized channels and rejected existing mechanisms of accountability and compromise. The holders of this view presumed the state to be democratic and required social movements to prove their democratic credentials by adhering to the established practices of representative governments.

Recent scholars of social movements have tended to reverse the burden of proof by assuming the inherently democratic nature of social movements while being deeply suspicious of the state. Even the state's claim that it is a representative democracy falls far short of the participatory or direct democracy that these scholars attribute to social movements. They emphasize the mass base of social movements, temporarily and even spontaneously arrayed in protest against the dominant elites of state and society (Eckstein 1989). The holders of this view posit a fundamental opposition of state and society, which at its extreme becomes a kind of fetishization of social movements' autonomy (Hellman 1992). This second view of the state and social movements gained plausibility from the repression and exclusion of the Brazilian military government, which sharply opposed the military state and civil(ian) society. In this opposition, social movements were unequivocally democratizing pressures from below. They challenged the continuation of the authoritarian state, seeking to replace it with a democratic regime, and many of these scholars have concluded that the social movements also functioned as incubators of democracy, introducing participants to democratic practices within the movements that could be exercised later in new arenas (Mainwaring and Viola 1984).

Transferring this perspective on social movements and the state to the post-1985 period does result in a very negative view of the recent social movements in Brazil. The mass base of the pre-1985 movements has largely disappeared, and new citizens' groups have stepped closer to the state—lobbying it, accepting contracts from it, participating in its processes, and consequently trading off some of their hard-won autonomy. A closer view of the practices of these social movements shows that many of them operate in ways closer to traditional Brazilian clientelism or corporatism than to the ideal of internal democracy.

I agree with the second school that social movements are generally democratic actors; however, I argue that social movements' democratizing impact since 1985 cannot be understood if the second school's opposition of social movements and the state is transferred intact to the post-1985 period. The sharp division between social movements and the state is simply untenable given the many changes of the last decade in Brazil.

Social movements may oppose the state, but they cannot be wholly separated from it as it is still necessarily the focus of many of their demands. This is true partly because the state is still the most resource-dense of all actors in Brazil. More philosophically, a state that calls itself democratic *should* be the locus of a public sphere for broad public debate and collective decision making. As social movements engage the state and force it to be that locus, they are, indeed, democratizing pressures from below. This fact will require them to use new strategies that may not be strategies of pure opposition, nor fully institutionalized, but strategies that pull them into extended interrelationships with the state. From the point of view of social movements, these relationships carry the serious risk of subverting their agendas and logic to the state's agenda; the opposite risk still represents one of the best hopes for deepening Brazilian democracy.

Framing Collective Action: From Demilitarization to Citizenship

The development of shared collective action frames is one of the clearest indicators of an interactive cycle of social movement protest. In general, the concept of these frames draws attention to the role of ideas and understandings in social movement mobilizations. Frames are "the specific metaphors, symbolic representations, and cognitive cues used to render or cast behavior and events in an evaluative mode and to suggest alternative modes of action" (Zald 1996, 262). Master frames are generally at a higher level of abstraction and allow related movements to see themselves as part of a common struggle. As cultural products, frames tend to change quite slowly, but they can also change more rapidly through concerted efforts to use education, communications media, and dialogue to reframe existing understandings.

I believe that the protest cycle of 1978–1984 was held together by exactly such a master frame of "opposition to the military" while the cycle of social movements after 1985 have spoken collectively of "citizenship" as being the master frame. The second frame shares important continuities with the first, but it also reflects the changing political context. In both cases, the master frames gave the constituent movements a shared language to critique the existing state, and helped them work with other social actors toward democratizing the state.

During the military regime, the master frame of "opposition to the military" brought a certain degree of unity to a highly disparate set of social movements by granting them all a sense of being united under the same (military) oppression (R. Cardoso 1983). Women drew parallels between the authoritarian government and the authoritarian home, challenging the violence of each (Jaquette 1989; S. Nelson 1996). The shared frame gave political content to neighborhood movements clamoring for paved roads or electricity because of their implicit rebuke of the military government and its social and economic exclusionary practices (Soler 1994).

The language of inclusion and exclusion was central to this frame. The military regime, the ARENA party, and their allies were automatically mistrusted because of their political inclusion, and they were excluded in turn from the network of the antimilitary coalition. Alternative parties like the Workers' Party (PT) and the PMDB, on the other hand, were welcomed by the social movements because they shared the same master frame. The ultimate aim of the opposition coalition was not to participate in politics under the military regime but to use participation to replace it. This aim was expressed through the cognitive cue of "democratization." When the military government adopted the language of participation and responded to the opposition's mobilizations with increased political openings for some Brazilians (Assies 1993), this change in tactics became one of the most contested elements of the collective action frame.

One reason this cycle seems to have ended with the campaign for *diretas já!* was that the different reactions to the defeat of that campaign signaled substantially different understandings within the antimilitary coalition about what constituted democratization. The PMDB, sometime ally of the social movements, accepted an indirect presidential campaign in 1985 as its best route to democratic leadership and even allied with former military partisans to win the election. The PT, on the other hand, refused to participate in that indirect vote, saying that doing so would legitimate a grossly incomplete democratization process—the party even expelled three members who wanted to participate (Sader and Silverstein 1991). The social movements were divided between these two points of view, some siding with one interpretation of democratization and some with the other.

Once civilian control returned formally at every level of government level in 1985, social movements sought a more precise rendering of the political changes that were still necessary for democratization. Among the public as a whole, "democracy" had become a word with little content,[4] and this fact was reflected in the new frame. Social movements and other political critics developed the new frame in the 1990s, one based on citizenship *(cidadania)* (Menezes 1995). This frame of citizenship draws heavily on the language of inclusion and exclusion of the earlier frame, with social, political, and economic exclusion defining the absence of citizenship. According to this frame, citizenship extends far beyond the legal and political definition that is often used. Social and economic indicators of citizenship are central to the frame, with hunger (Müller 1986; CEAS 1993), violence (Yúdice forthcoming), and the lack of land (D'Incão 1991; J. Santos 1992; Comissão Pastoral da Terra 1993; Bergamasco and Norder 1995) often being singled out as signs of noncitizenship.

As Teresa Sales notes, the call for citizenship in Brazil is a social justice rights claim, not a liberal one—"Among us, citizenship begins with the social sphere" (Sales 1993, 56). The social movements themselves often use such language, as in the cross-sectoral movement that called itself Citizens' Action Against Hunger, Misery, and for Life (CEAS 1993). Also, the Instituto Brasileiro de Análises Sociais e Econômicos (IBASE), a Rio-based nongovernmental organization (NGO) that supports popular movements and communication, calls its newsletter the *Jornal da Cidadania (Citizenship Bulletin)*.[5] These names indicate a second use of this frame, in which organized social movement participants claim citizenship as a description of their own activities and seek to extend active citizenship to unorganized, excluded sectors (A. Silva 1993). In this use, the presence of citizenship is seen in active political and economic participation, which makes inclusion more positively valued in this frame, although not without contradictions.

The contradictions arise from the fact that the processes of inclusion and exclusion became much more complex after the political opening of the 1980s. The state (as formal governing actors and institutions) occupies an ambiguous position. On the one hand, new civilian governments at all levels have promised and sometimes delivered all kinds of inclusion. Every civilian government since 1985 has promised and delivered at least some land distribution (R. Tavares 1995a), governments at all levels have provided new political participatory opportunities (Alvarez 1990; Costa 1995), and civilian constitutional democracy generally provides opportunities for citizens to promote other kinds of inclusion.

At the same time, the state is at best tolerant of and at worst the perpetrator of many of the most violent kinds of exclusion (Dimenstein 1996). A total of 3,374 land conflicts between 1985 and 1990 left 563 dead, and from 1964 to 1991, only twenty-nine cases out of 1,630 rural killings went to trial, and there were only thirteen convictions (J. Santos 1992, 6–7). The Pastoral Land Commission of the Catholic Church, which compiled those figures, concluded in 1993 that the state has in essence granted impunity for rural violence (Comissão Pastoral da Terra 1993). Police forces themselves are major violators of urban rights and lives, with the complicity of political leaders (Human Rights Watch/Americas 1996; Pinheiro 1996a). From December 1995 to August 1996, 300 police officers were indicted for torture, but none were actually punished (*Folha de São Paulo*, January 1, 1997). President Cardoso announced a National Plan of Human Rights and a new human rights training course for police in November of that year, but few concrete results are evident so far. In one survey, Brazilians selected politicians, business leaders, and bankers as the most responsible for violating or blocking the expansion of rights (Cardia 1995, 360). It is small wonder that political inclusion is a contradictory value in this context.

Many of the social movements that have emerged since 1985 are mobilized around exactly these failings of the post-1985 state. They use the language of citizenship to evaluate the current political system and find it wanting. They themselves are citizens and they promote citizenship for others, but the new state is unprepared to receive their rightful claims. Since these claims rest on the assertion that the social movements themselves are unheard but democratic actors, it is necessary to investigate the processes of inclusion and exclusion within them as well.

In the survey cited above, Brazilians most often credited teachers, churches, and unions for expanding rights (Cardia 1995, 360). As this second group of actors has often worked with social movements on campaigns for citizenship, this survey result supports the social movements' claims to be democratizers of society. Yet beneath the general approbation, social movements also sometimes find each other blocking full citizenship. In the more benign cases, the errors are those of omission. For example, Sueli Carneiro, writing for the Movement of Black Women, explains their struggle as one that always moves in the direction of constructing full citizenship for black Brazilian women, which in addition to the defense of rights constitutionally won by the women's movement also means the struggle against the mechanisms of racial discrimination in the labor market, such as the euphemism "good appearance" (Carneiro 1990, 218). The divisions here could be resolved with a further elaboration of a (mostly) shared frame.

The divisions within the antiviolence movement, on the other hand, show just how deep the problem can be. One of the best-known antiviolence movements is the Viva Rio coalition, which began in 1993 to unite the divided city of Rio de Janeiro in the wake of extremely high levels of violence (Ventura 1994). In coordinator Rubem César Fernandes's words, "Viva Rio is dedicated exclusively to public service, of two kinds at present: to establish a bridge between slum dwellers and middle classes at the neighborhood level, and to bridge human rights and public security issues" (Yúdice forthcoming). Many individuals joined Viva Rio not only to demonstrate against police and drug-related violence but also to participate in innovative strategies like a citywide two minutes of silence on December 17, 1993, and to build a House of Peace where police shot and killed twenty-one favela (slum) dwellers in Vigário Geral. Despite the support of thousands of Rio residents, the two groups bridged by this coalition still view each other with suspicion. The middle-class sectors waver between seeing favela dwellers as common victims of urban violence or as the perpetrators of it. Favela dwellers recognize this ambiguity and sometimes resent the economic inclusion of their coalition partners. Caio Ferraz, of Vigário Geral, derisively renamed one mobilization from *Reage Rio* ("Rio react") to *Reage Rico* ("Rich react") (Yúdice forthcoming).

In the Viva Rio coalition, and in many similar movements concerned with violence and human rights in particular, social movements find limits to their shared language of citizenship. Nearly all use the language, but some are more included than others.[6] On the other hand, social movements find these limits to their commonality precisely because they are trying to stretch across social divides that are not often bridged in Brazil except through more hierarchical relations. The tensions between a Caio Ferraz and a Rubem César Fernandes, for example, are the tensions of two people from radically different experiences who have met face to face in dozens of meetings and who have thought creatively together about how to improve their communities and political institutions. They are not the tensions of the patron and the client or the mugger and the victim or any of the more common representations of cross-class relations. Similarly, black women in Brazil want to build on what they have learned and gained from mobilizing with white women, even if those mobilizations did not, finally, take them as far as they hoped. In the "social apartheid" that characterizes Brazil, the efforts social movements make to share and extend citizenship do make them, perhaps, incubators of new social and political relations.

Strategic Repertoires: Change and Continuity

A second qualitative characteristic of a cycle of social movement protest is a rapid innovation of new strategies of contention. In this regard, the perspective of cycles again differs from that of many social movement analysts who seek to limit the definition of social movements to only those that engage in particular forms of direct action and protest. As new political openings emerge, social movements should develop new forms of contention—and they do. Collectively, such sets of strategies are called repertoires of collective action. These are "not only what people *do* when they make a claim; it is what they *know how to do* and what society has come to expect them to choose to do" (Tarrow 1995, 91; emphasis in original). Thus, the innovation is based on a foundation of existing strategies.

Although the mobilizing frames showed substantial continuity from 1978 to 1997, Brazilian social movements' strategic repertoires have been considerably refurbished since 1985. New movements with new strategies have emerged while existing movements have tried a whole new range of participatory options. Some push the limits of many conventional definitions and expectations of social movements, and these largely lead to the conclusion of some observers that social movements have declined in Brazil since the formal transition to constitutional democracy. At the same time, many of the earlier strategies still persist. In this section, I first discuss the continuities and then briefly explore four new participatory strategies: nonprotest networking, participation on government councils, international networking, and land occupations. I conclude with a section on nongovernmental organizations (NGOs) as an alternative form of social organization and analyze their relationship with social movements.

Strategic Continuities

During their opposition to the military regime, Brazilian social movements learned to protest in large cross-sectoral coalitions. Especially during the early part of the cycle when the military reaction to the mobilization of certain sectors (e.g., students and labor) was often violent, opponents of the military joined safer mobilizations "to ventilate criticisms of the military regime without incurring more repression" (Ramos 1995, 6). Broad coalitions took up safer issues like indigenous rights (Ramos 1995), women's rights (Alvarez 1989b), and protecting the Amazon to express their opposition.[7] The same opposition coalition also put together more directly oppositional mobilizations on political issues, like the amnesty demonstrations in 1978–1979. The crowning moment of this strategy was the *diretas já* campaign, which pulled literally millions of people into the streets for festive rallies for direct elections of the president in 1985. Finally, such participation was buttressed by an underlying foundation of new organized connections among the social movement organizations. During the 1970s and 1980s, they built unprecedented networks and more formal federations both within and across their sectoral issues. The broad "antimilitary" frame discussed held together and justified all of these coalitions.

Since 1985, the "shared citizenship" frame has served as a similar bond for new cross-sectoral protests. The *diretas já* campaign had a direct equivalent in August and September of 1992 when millions of people again marched in the streets of the large cities calling this time for impeachment—ironically, of the first president to actually be directly elected (Sérgio Costa 1994). Eight hundred organizations—unions, church groups, professional associations, and social movements—joined in the Movement for Ethics in Politics, which coordinated these mobilizations (Garrison 1993, 7). As citizens, they challenged state actors to live up to their democratic claims. The campaign was successful in forcing the National Congress to play its assigned role in democratic accountability and to openly consider and vote for Collor's removal from office later that year. Later campaigns also used similar strategies, such as Viva Rio, which used a "network of networks" to bring tens of thousands of people out to protest against urban violence (Yúdice, forthcoming; *Isto É,* December 6, 1995, 40–42).

The acceptance of the strategy as part of the social repertoire can be seen in the way it is invoked by actors outside the social movement sector. Former president Itamar Franco suggested "resuscitating the *diretas já* and impeachment campaign models" to block privatization of the parastatal Companhia da Vale do Rio Doce (*Jornal do Brasil,* November 24, 1996), and a member of the Fluminense soccer team proposed a Flu React movement to retain the team's classification in Division I of the soccer rankings (*Jornal do Brasil,* November 26, 1996). Social movements themselves have also used the mass protest model for smaller and more specific mobilizations.

New Strategies: Nonprotest Networking

Mass street protests exemplified the sharp division of state and society in the earlier cycle, and the impeachment and antiviolence campaigns underlined the social movements' continuing harsh criticisms of the new semidemocratic state and its violations of citizenship in all forms. Most cross-sectoral networking since 1985, on the other hand, has more directly engaged the state and followed at least some of its rules for participation, and nonprotest networking within and across social movements has greatly expanded in the post-1985 years.

During the two years that were spent writing the 1988 constitution, women (Pinto 1994), environmentalists (Hochstetler 1997), and other social movements were brought together in issue-networks to influence the new document. These mobilizations were the last ones to involve significant numbers of the urban popular groups that were so active in the earlier cycle. Many of these groups achieved significant advances concerning the constitution itself, although there has been less progress in translating the constitutional text into actual laws and policies. In addition, social movements put together a cross-sectoral coalition, the Pro-Popular Participation Plenary, which mobilized to establish general language favoring citizen participation in both the constitution-writing process and the constitution itself (Hochstetler 1997). Another large coalition, the Union of Housing Movements of São Paulo, later became the first to use one of the constitutional provisions that allowed popular initiatives to introduce laws. In November 1991, the forty-five movements and associations involved presented their proposal for popular housing with 850,000 signatures from all over the country (A. Silva 1993).

Although street protests accompanied many of these efforts, most achievements came through using the new formal mechanisms for participation that were included in the constitution. Some networks of social movements, like the environmentalists, tried to elect representatives of their own movements to the new assembly while others worked to elect PT, PMDB, and other party candidates who were sympathetic to their concerns. Social movements gathered literally millions of signatures on the popular initiative amendments they were allowed to submit to the Constituent Assembly. At least 30,000 signatures were required to submit an amendment to the assembly, and organizations presented 168 amendments. Social movements then lobbied for these amendments as well as for and against language that came from the assembly itself. The Catholic Church set up an office in Brasília during this time to monitor the debates, and the plenary also had an office and issued regular newsletters. Around the country, social movements also participated in official consultations and town meetings on issues that concerned them. Success meant accepting extended relations with at least some state actors and following at least some rules for institutionalized participation.

Social movements were most willing to make such accommodations for the issues that were most central to their frame of citizenship. The largest number of amendment signatures (6,081,248) was gathered by unions and others seeking economic inclusion, and the second-largest number (4,857,041 signatures) was gathered for rights of various kinds (Doimo 1995, 195). Agrarian reform received 1,188,469 signatures for two related amendments (*Intercarta Cidadão 30,000*, January/February 1998, 1). Participation in the process as a whole was also justified on citizenship grounds by activists like the late Herbert de Souza ("Betinho"), a veritable symbol of citizenship in Brazil.[8]

After Brazil was chosen to host the 1992 United Nations Conference on Environment and Development (UNCED, or Earth Summit), an even more extensive cross-sectoral mobilization took place. A total of 935 social movements and NGOs of all kinds gathered in eight national encounters from June 1990 to the June 1992 conference, and there have been sporadic gatherings of the coalition since (Herculano 1995; Hochstetler 1997). Calling themselves simply the Brazilian Forum, these groups forged a dense set of linkages between organizations and issues that extended well beyond the earlier, more temporary linkages. The Earth Summit network later became the foundation for social movement networks built around hunger and violence issues, as well as more specific issues like protecting the Atlantic forest.

The Brazilian Forum considered its most important obligation to be organizing a parallel conference for NGOs and social movements to be held at the same time as the United Nations conference. As the citizen groups became steadily more disillusioned with the government's preparations, they increasingly turned to forging links with other national citizens groups (Hochstetler 1997). Yet the coalition also worked closely with government actors throughout the two-year preparation. Representatives of the forum sat on most preparatory committees, including the government's delegation to the official UN conference, and they worked closely with the city and state of Rio de Janeiro to plan what became a huge festival of NGOs and social movements from all over the world. They also monitored the substantive preparations and positions of their own government and lobbied for language and positions they preferred. During the preparatory meetings, the government delegations held formal briefing sessions for the forum representatives and listened to their suggestions.

The forum was also held together by the citizenship frame of this cycle. After several rancorous national meetings to define who could participate in the forum, participants approved a statement inviting "all NGOs and organizations of civil society which have practices oriented toward recuperating, protecting, and improving the environment and quality of life and which are recognizably independent in relation to the current model of development" to join them.[9] The final clause was meant to echo the language of economic inclusion and exclusion that is central to the citizenship frame. In fact, some environmentalists were dismayed at the extent to which the resonance between the citizenship frame and the development half of the conference agenda overwhelmed the environmental half of the agenda for many Brazilian social movement participants.

The dismay of the environmentalists in that case raises one of the ambiguities of this strategic innovation and, indeed, of the cross-sectoral protests as well. Cross-sectoral coalitions bring strength to social movement mobilizations because they inherently increase the numbers of participants and more participants means that the movements are more likely to capture the attention of the media, decision makers, and other potential supporters (and opponents). Basing the coalitions on shared master frames means that certain broadly defined values of the social movement participants are promoted through such mobilizations. At the same time, more-specific values are often sidelined during the broader mobilizations and thus go unrepresented and unmet. Ana Maria Doimo (1995, 194) cites the Constituent Assembly mobilizations as one such reason for the decline of local urban popular movements, and a group of environmentalists wanted to leave the Brazilian Forum during the UNCED preparations for exactly the same reason.[10] Given the voluntary nature of cross-sectoral coalitions, such value and strategic tradeoffs are not undemocratic. They do, however, point to some of the strategic complexity and frustrations of particular organizations or issue networks within the broader cycles of mobilization.

New Strategies: Participation on Government Councils

The original antimilitary coalition of the late 1970s and early 1980s included many politicians who gradually formed a number of parties on the left and center-left as the military regime loosened party and electoral rules. The 1982 state and local elections brought a number of these politicians to power, and still more were successful in subsequent elections. Some of these new politicians were actually members of social movements themselves, and many of them retained a commitment to the frame of grassroots participation and activism. These politicians, mostly from the PMDB and PT, converged on the idea of the government council as a site for citizen participation.

During the 1980s, social movements were invited to sit on councils at all levels of government to discuss and advise government officials on policy. At the national level, for example, environmentalists were allowed to select five representatives for a National Council on the Environment (CONAMA), and women gained a National Council on Women's Rights headed by feminist politicians and activists from the women's movement. Many of these organizations did initiate significant policy changes. In 1986, for example, the CONAMA passed a regulation requiring environmental impact assessments, and later, the National Council on Women's Rights asked President Cardoso to propose a law legalizing abortion, a permanent demand of the feminist movement (*Folha de São Paulo*, March 7, 1997). The most active councils and those with the broadest participation were established at local levels, where local citizens were invited to comment on urban development plans and other issues. Some of the councils were set up to actually allow decision making while many were only consultative (Assies 1993).

Some observers worry about the potential of such councils to coopt and dilute the demands of social movements. With an institutionalized channel for demands, Sonia Alvarez warned that women's movements might begin to censor their own more radical demands, weakening them as a source of change (Alvarez 1989b). Partisan politics also dominates many of the councils and conflicts with the social movements' agendas (Alvarez 1990). Even when aims do not actually conflict, different priorities might again sideline some of the more specific values of social movements. Finally, some of these councils and their paid advisory positions have been used quite openly to coopt especially vocal and talented movement leaders, bringing them into clientelist webs and silencing their criticisms (Sérgio Costa 1995).

In fact, the more prosaic fate of many of these councils is that they are largely ignored or underfunded and then often eliminated altogether, especially at the higher levels of government. Under the Sarney administration, CONAMA rarely met, and environmentalists received late invitations and information; under Collor, it briefly disappeared as a decision-making body.[11] More councils have persisted at local and state levels, especially because of the ideological commitment PT administrations have to social movement participation. Even among these efforts, local governments have had a hard time finding the balance between asking for more participation than social movements want (such participation competes with other activities) and allowing meaningful influence on policy decisions (Assies 1993; Abers 1996).

Citizenship in its more conventional political definition is clearly at stake in this new participatory opportunity offered by the state and often demanded by social movements. Many social movements believe that their routine presence and oversight will lead to more substantive achievements of citizenship through the councils as well, be it in area of the protection of human rights or in the better provision of government services. How much such achievements occur in fact depends on the integrity of the social movements themselves as well as on the integrity of the state actors. Neighborhood movement leaders have been especially susceptible to cooptation efforts.

New Strategies: International Networking

Since the late 1980s, Brazilian social movements have become a part of citizens' networks that span the world. These are not the first contacts between Brazilian social movements and international activists, but it is the first time that such contacts have been so routine and widespread. Like the networks social movements have built inside the country, the international networks also link both same-issue and cross-sectoral social movements (Clark, Friedman, and Hochstetler, 1998). This international networking has taken two forms so far.

First, Brazilian and international social movements and NGOs have formed instrumental coalitions to influence government decisions. Most often these coalitions have worked to develop new ways to pressure government decision makers. In one of the best-known examples, international environmentalists joined with associations of Brazilian forest peoples to influence the multilateral development banks to bring pressure to bear on Brazilian national and Amazonian development policies (Keck 1995). International human rights groups have also been a critical support for national human rights groups in Brazil, both during and after the military regime. International NGOs generally have supported the work of Brazilian NGOs and social movements by donating money and promoting global communications networks. One hazard of such coalitions is that they are vulnerable to nationalist criticisms, which have materialized with respect to the environmental mobilizations (Hurrell 1992) and recent foreign criticisms of Brazil's policies toward the landless movement (*Estado de São Paulo,* February 15, 1997).

Second, these international networks have also served as forums for the exchange of ideas and support beyond specific mobilizations. Many Brazilians attended the Earth Summit in Rio precisely for such international connections and community building rather than to try to influence the conference (Hochstetler 1997), and women's organizations have found new energy and inspiration in more than a decade of meetings of Latin American feminists (Sternbach, Navarro-Aranguren, Chuchryk, and Alvarez 1992). Meetings like these are fertile ground for affirming solidarities and identities, and such international experiences also teach new strategies and analyses.

New Strategies: Land Occupations

The new and old strategies discussed so far have mostly been used by social movements that were active in the early part of the mobilization cycle. No discussion of Brazilian social movements in the 1990s can be complete, however, without reference to the Landless Movement (Movimento dos Trabalhadores Rurais Sem-Terra, or MST). Although the MST has existed since 1984, its appearance as a major national actor is much more recent. As recently as 1994, agrarian reform seemed to have moved off the national agenda, and agrarian reform's strongest opponent, the União Democratica Ruralista (UDR), had closed its doors, saying it had completed its work (R. Tavares 1995a). Shortly afterward, however, the MST emerged in full force.

The MST conducts a two-pronged strategy that is nicely summarized by its slogan, Agrarian reform—by law or by disorder.[12] The MST strategy includes the ambiguity about the state that is typical of post-1985 movements. On the one hand, the MST tries to use new institutional channels to press its claims, especially the judicial system where it seeks legal title to land. The MST also keeps agrarian reform on the agenda of elected officials, including through a two-month march to Brasília where MST leaders met with President Cardoso in April 1997. On the other hand, the MST uses the direct action of land occupation to pursue its goals as well. The basic MST strategy is to move a cluster of families onto government-owned or unproductive private land to occupy it and farm it until they are granted title to the land. To support this aim, the movement has also engaged in occupying government buildings, especially those of the Institute for Agrarian Reform (INCRA). Occupation is a classic social movement strategy, and it depends primarily on sheer numbers of participants and direct action. It has also been a violent strategy, with much of the violence perpetrated against the MST by the hired guards of landowners and the military police. Elite resistance to land redistribution has remained one of the most persistent exclusions of the Brazilian political system.

The demand for land clearly fits within the citizenship frame of recent social movements, and the MST has underscored this connection since the mid-1990s, "seeking to situate the agrarian-reform issue within the broader movement to consolidate and further the democratic regime" (Tavares 1995a, 24). Before then, agrarian reform activists had remained quite focused on their own land concerns, although other social movement sectors had supported those claims, e.g., in the popular initiative that proposed a constitutional amendment for land reform. The new MST strategy has included adopting the language of "democratization of the land" and joining other coalitions of social movements like the Citizens' Action Against Hunger, Misery, and for Life. Polls show that 85 percent of the population supports the invasion of land as a legitimate tactic for such purposes as long as it is done without violence (*O Globo,* March 21, 1997). The combativeness of the MST has also become a model for new social movements. In Rio Grande do Sul, for instance, 1,500 families formed an urban version of the MST to demand housing, the Movimento dos Trabalhadores Sem Teto Urbano (Homeless Urban Workers' Movement) (*Zero Hora,* March 23, 1997).

As a model for social movement organizing, however, the MST displays some ambiguities. Although the organization maintains the public profile of a grassroots social movement, INCRA (which has an interest in passing on negative information about its most persistent critics) calculates that the MST worked with a budget of almost US$ 20 million in 1996. This money, from governmental and international sources, paid the salaries of 800 professional militants, making the MST's organizational profile more like that of an NGO than a social movement (*Folha de São Paulo,* March 9, 1997). This reliance on outside funding leaves the MST vulnerable to hazards similar to those faced by NGOs.

Sharing Citizens' Space: Nongovernmental Organizations

Scholars all over the globe and in many disciplines have turned to studying citizens' groups in recent years. One continuing debate is how to distinguish among the growing variety of nongovernmental, nonprofit organizations and how to analyze their interrelationships. The term nongovernmental organization, or NGO, is often used to label these actors at the broadest levels (Fisher 1998). Within Brazilian civil society, however, activists commonly distinguish between organizations they call NGOs and others they call social movements.[12] The dividing line differentiates between two sets of resources and two related kinds of action. NGOs generally have more financial and thus more institutional resources, which allow them to initiate longer-term projects through institutionalized kinds of action. Social movements generally have only the resource of volunteer labor, which tends to restrict them to shorter-term, mass-based protest activities.

NGOs, as defined, have existed in Brazil as far back as the colonial period (Landim 1993), but in recent years, they have appeared in virtually every issue area that concerns social movements. Most often, their longer-term institutionalized projects have involved *assessoria* (support), for popular social movements like neighborhood groups, rural workers, and women's organizations. Traditionally, they have remained in the background, providing education, information, and material resources to other organizations.

The NGOs have also innovated new strategies since 1985. In particular, they have begun to assert themselves as actors in their own right rather than simply as advisers to other social actors. Rubem César Fernandes, of the NGO Institute for Studies of Religion (ISER), has justified this new role through his depiction of NGOs as "private with public functions" (Fernandes 1994). This depiction rests on the assertion that NGOs have the resources and connections to articulate a more plural (in comparison to social movements) and more active (in comparison to the state) conception of citizenship in posttransition Latin America.

The new role began to develop during the Constituent Assembly mobilizations when NGOs were uniquely able to monitor the entire two-year process in faraway Brasília. Their organizational form is in many ways compatible with the post-1985 political opportunities, which encourage more institutionalized participation than protest. The UNCED preparations solidified the NGOs' new role, being, again, an extended process that required substantial infrastructure. Perhaps more important, the constant media coverage of the Earth Summit "gave the Brazilian population the opportunity to inform themselves about the vital role that NGOs were performing in their own society and a means to measure how much they had grown during the brief spaces that encompassed their existence" (Garrison 1993, 3). After the UNCED conferences, the most active NGOs joined together in a more-permanent forum, the Association of Brazilian NGOs (ABONG), which continues to meet regularly and to coordinate activities among its members. The label NGO (ONG in Brazil) has passed into the vernacular for many Brazilians, and most newspapers use the initials without spelling out the acronym. Individual NGO leaders like Betinho and Fernandes have become political figures in their own right and are regularly consulted by political leaders who have noted their influence.

Social movements have also observed the growing role of NGOs, with mixed responses. On the one hand, NGOs are important collaborators of social movements. In their traditional role as supporters of social movements, NGOs obviously increase the resources and possibilities of some social movement organizations and sectors. In their newer, more public role, they have also proved to be critical allies. In every one of the post-1985 mobilizations discussed here, social movements and NGOs have worked side by side to mobilize less-organized sectors. Social movements have seen firsthand how the greater institutional resources of NGOs allow them to overcome some of their characteristic problems. NGO activists never have to choose between going to work and going to mobilize in Brasília, for example. They have telephone budgets that are not part of their personal budgets, secretaries to take messages when they are out, and a continuous presence. Many social movement organizations have considered trying to change the form of their organization to share in some of these advantages, and some have done so. Others point to some of the quandaries NGOs face.

First, NGOs are predicated on higher levels of regular funding than volunteer social movements, and in Brazil, the tradition of paid membership in advocacy groups is weak—the *Folha de São Paulo* called the SOS Atlantic Forest Foundation's 4,000 national members a "rare case" (June 5, 1990). NGO resources largely come from governmental and international sources—nearly 5,500 Brazilian NGOs receive US$ 400 million annually from international sources—and when the dollar weakened against the Real after the *Plano Real* sharply lowered inflation, 86 percent of the NGOs in Brazil reported they were cutting employees and programs (*Veja*, May 31, 1995). Since then, many NGOs have turned to governmental funding sources, with an astounding 70 percent of Brazilian NGOs reporting some kind of partnership with government agencies in 1996.

NGOs influence or control R$ 1.4 billion (close to US$ 1.2 billion in 1996) in funds administered by the Ministry of the Environment, the Ministry of Social Security and Welfare, and international banks (*Folha de São Paulo*, June 9, 1996). Some ostensibly grassroots mobilizations have turned out to be substantially coordinated by for-profit and/or governmental actors. The Citizens' Action Against Hunger, Misery, and for Life, for example, in fact depends on thirty large state companies and public institutions for its multi-year campaigns (Miranda 1994). Such large sums of money inevitably raise issues of the autonomy of the NGOs from the organizations and agencies that fund them. One analysis concludes that many NGOs end up giving most of their time and effort to projects that were conceived by governments (Menezes 1995). Others see similar dangers in accepting international funds, although Fernandes of Viva Rio and ISER argues that the plurality of sources allows each NGO to petition an international NGO donor that best suits its agenda (Fernandes 1994, 80).

A second potential dilemma of NGOs concerns their relationship to other parts of the social movement spectrum. Many NGOs were specifically established to support and act as intermediaries for community groups, especially those of the favelas. Originally a shield for such movements against the military regime, NGOs are equally critical to guide social movements through the complex institutions and channels of democracy. The dilemma is that popular groups can become just as dependent on their own leaders and NGOs as they would otherwise be on the state (Ottmann 1995). One analysis by an NGO leader traces the pressures from both sides that NGOs link. Grassroots groups want NGOs to be their lawyers, helpers, and patrons, and the danger is that the NGOs will replace the grassroots groups as political participants. The state also wants the NGOs to participate as they are a more familiar kind of social actor, well-educated, and closer to the state in culture, and the danger here is that the NGOs will substitute for the state, doing things the state should do for its citizens (J. Neto 1996). This second dilemma plays out differently for middle-class social movements, for in some issue networks, like the environmental movement, NGOs and middle-class social movements sometimes see themselves as directly competing for scarce resources and media attention.

Finally, the lack of membership base of many NGOs causes some observers to raise questions about their accountability. Corruption and general ineffectiveness are only two of the potential dangers (Edwards and Hulme 1996). A variation of this concern is that employees of NGOs themselves might be opportunistically employment-motivated in a country where university graduates are often underemployed. One reporter noted as the Viva Rio coalition fractured that all the jobs associated with it went to the middle class (Yúdice forthcoming). NGOs claim that they can be as private individuals speaking for public interests (Fernandes 1994), and the current flow of resources to them suggests some confidence in this claim. Nonetheless, this is an important area for future research.

For these reasons, the social movement form of organization continues despite the advantages of NGOs in the new setting. The final critique of NGOs, however, also needs to be applied to Brazilian society movements of both cycles. At the peak of their breadth—the 1 million to 2 million people behind the biggest demonstrations or the most-supported popular amendments for the constitution—social movements aggregated about 1 percent of the Brazilian population. The organizations themselves and most of their mobilizations are much, much smaller and often not very representative of the population as a whole (Herculano 1995).

Observers in the 1990s acknowledge—as observers in the 1970s and 1980s often did not—that at least some social movement organizations are plagued with the same failings as other Brazilian actors. These include a tendency to clientelism, paternalistic leadership, and self-interested behavior. The MST enforces its strategies with sometimes harsh discipline (*O Globo*, March 9, 1997), and other organizations can suffer from bureaucratization and careerism. The processes of inclusion and exclusion exist within social movements as well, as in the example of black women within the women's movement who find only a part of their agenda addressed or the divisions within the antiviolence coalitions. Understanding that social movements are not immune from general patterns of political and social interactions—and why should they be?—prompts both analysts and activists to be more rigorous in questioning the actual democratic foundations of social movements. Both should be demanding greater accountability and representativity from these organizations rather than granting them democratic certification from the outset, both before and after 1984. At their worst, such internal characteristics demobilize participants and discredit social movements. At their best, they can spur a movementwide self-examination and growth and a more profound internal democracy.

Conclusion

Social movements have often been important forces and indicators of democracy in Brazil since 1985. Social groups that are excluded even by the new political system find political representation in their collective mobilization and protest, and social groups that have greater access under the new political system find broad coalition building across social movements a way to increase their impact on policymakers and help include new groups. In their solidarity, in their endless debates, in their capacity to shape the values and self-conceptions of participants, the internal workings of social movements still have the potential to shape a political culture that is more compatible with democratic ideals. At the same time, some organizations or movements of citizens do none of these things, and they should be acknowledged as well. A scholar of social movements in Brazil after 1985 could not do better than to follow the lead of Ana Maria Doimo: "I am neither looking for a [new collective] subject nor in search of fragments, because there is so much more at play, between one pole and the other, than one could possibly imagine" (Doimo 1995, 31).

In this chapter, I map some of that area between the two poles for Brazilian social movements since 1985. As self-identified citizens, they have explored new relations with the new state, sometimes working with it and sometimes spotlighting the ways it continues to violate its democratic claims and procedures. The image of the new Brazilian state that eventually emerges through the lens of recent social movement organizing is also between two poles: neither wholly democratic nor wholly authoritarian, it is a partial and uneven democracy. Social movements mean to deepen that democracy and often do so.

PART III

Emerging Processes in the New Democracy

NINE

Muddling Through Gridlock

Economic Policy Performance, Business Responses, and Democratic Sustainability

Peter R. Kingstone

cholars have noted frequently that poor economic performance and erratic policy making are key causes of regime breakdown. Regimes, democratic or otherwise, can and have survived economic instability (Remmer 1996; Feng 1997), but that has not been the case in Brazil. In the past, Brazil achieved high rates of growth under both democratic (1946–1964) and authoritarian (1967–1979) rule, yet both regimes collapsed in a context of significant economic problems and erratic policy performance. Thus, Brazil's history is marked by a persistent failure to preserve regime legitimacy through hard economic times. This issue has been particularly salient under the New Republic as successive presidents have attempted to heal the military's legacy of economic crisis through sweeping economic reforms. A set of market-enhancing reforms, labeled "neoliberalism," has profoundly challenged the organization of the economy and the state, and all Latin American nations have had difficulty implementing those reforms. In Brazil, the process has been even more delayed and more uneven than in most other nations.

Observers of Brazilian politics have been particularly skeptical about the ability of executives to implement neoliberal reforms. Scholars have focused specifically on the design of Brazil's political institutions, notably the character of the presidency, the party system, and the electoral system (discussed at length in Chapter 1). These analyses have described the political system with terms such "hyperactive paralysis" (Lamounier 1996), "feckless democracy" (Mainwaring 1995a, 394), and "inchoate" (Mainwaring and Scully 1995). Scholars have noted that the perverse features of Brazilian executive-legislative elections have complicated coalition building and made it hard to achieve social policy reform, stabilization, and a long-term resolution of the fiscal crisis of the state (Weyland 1996d; Kingstone 1998a; Bresser Pereira 1996, 23). Thus, the design of Brazilian political institutions raises sharp doubts about the durability of democracy.

Yet successive presidents have defied scholarly expectations by passing a broad array of reforms. Since 1994, Brazil has achieved effective stabilization with some of the lowest inflation rates in the region (IDB 1997). The country has effected a profound trade and financial liberalization as well as extensive commercial deregulation. Successive presidents have maintained a gradual, but successful, privatization program, and finally, the federal government has made considerable progress in rebuilding state capacity and improving federal control over government finances (discussed at greater length in Chapters 2 and 3).

The central argument of this chapter is that Brazil's reform has exceeded observers' expectations through incremental extensions of the program. In essence, each of the New Republic's presidents has been able to pass some small portion of the overall program. In turn, each successor has been able to use those reforms as a base on which to build further. The occurrence of regular elections has helped by allowing Brazil's leaders to rebuild proreform coalitions repeatedly, which has permitted the continuation of the process and has consequently kept Brazil "muddling through gridlock." As a result, the New Republic has managed to avoid the loss of credibility and legitimacy that helped bring down both earlier democratic rule (in 1964) and military rule (in 1985).

This preservation of credibility has been particularly important as it has helped maintain business support for democracy, thereby strengthening democratic sustainability. Business elites were critical in bringing an end to both democracy (Dreifuss 1981; Wallerstein 1980) and military rule (Bresser Pereira 1978; Frieden 1991). Business discontent alone is not a sufficient explanation for democratic breakdown, but business discontent and antiregime mobilization are crucial factors that link poor performance with democratic breakdown. The incremental, muddled reform process has weakened the likelihood of antiregime behavior in the business community in two key ways: First, slow moving reforms have led gradually to a much more stable policy environment and direction that has mitigated lingering business concerns about policy performance. Second, slow moving reforms have effected a rapid restructuring within the economy, displacing those business people who might seek military intervention as a response to their losing in the marketplace.

Nevertheless, as of 1998, the gridlock over fiscal issues continued to challenge Brazilian democracy in two important ways. First, persistent fiscal problems continued to undermine or dilute growth-oriented policies. Most critically, fiscal problems hurt export promotion and slowed growth and investment below their potential (FIESP 1997, 54–56; Fishlow 1997, 54–61). This set of fiscal concerns remained a source of concern for business. Second, the country remained vulnerable to a financial shock. Brazil had managed to weather three shocks—in 1995 in the wake of the Peso Crisis, in late 1997 as part of the Asian Flu, and again in late 1998 as the Asian crisis provoked a new round of rapid outflows of capital—and weathering those shocks has required austere policy measures with painful consequences for the population. However, a deeper shock could produce significant economic disorder or a significant change in policy orientation. Either one could test the depth of the business community's commitment to democracy.

Stabilization and Economic Reform

Brazil's myriad institutional obstacles (discussed in detail in Chapter 1) forced successive presidents to muddle their way through a virtually paralyzed legislature. As a consequence, they found it hard to implement coherent economic plans, and instead, each successive president spent much of his time addressing immediate financial concerns in a constant struggle against inflation and/or fiscal deficits. Nevertheless, each one was able to advance the economic reform agenda in some small, incremental way. In turn, these changes became a base upon which the next president was able to build. Thus, Brazilian economic reforms have advanced further than most scholars would have thought possible as successive presidents muddled incrementally through the gridlock. Unfortunately, these successes have come with a price of continuing high debt and deficits, policy contradictions, vulnerability to financial shocks, and lingering questions about democratic sustainability.

The Sarney Presidency: Brazil on the Verge of a Nervous Breakdown

José Sarney began his presidency facing a wide array of challenging issues but with few effective political mechanisms for addressing them. His central task was overseeing the writing of a constitution for the New Republic, but he also had to find a formula for stabilizing chronic inflation and renewing growth while satisfying popular longings for increased political participation and economic benefits. His tasks were complicated by a set of extraordinary constraints: a party system that had begun fragmenting almost immediately (expanding rapidly from five to nineteen parties); a state policy-making structure that could achieve little interministerial coordination; a bureaucracy thoroughly captured by private interests; and substantial foreign pressure for meeting debt obligations and implementing neoliberal reform (Sola 1988,

1995). Not surprisingly, the Sarney presidency seemed to confirm the worst fears that democratic governance was not consistent with sound economic performance.

Sarney's most visible economic policy initiatives all came in the area of stabilization. His first, and boldest, effort was the Cruzado Plan announced in February 1986. The plan included a new currency (the Cruzado), a temporary wage and price freeze, and the temporary prohibition of indexation of contracts. The plan also incorporated by fiat an across-the-board 8 percent wage hike. The results appeared instantly. Inflation declined from over 20 percent per month in February to less than 1 percent per month in March. In addition, the wage increase given to workers led to a sharp increase in purchasing power, and the combination produced a euphoric consumption boom. The public euphoria was an anticipated result, and Sarney successfully converted it into electoral support in the 1986 legislative elections for his party (the Party of the Brazilian Democratic Movement, PMDB).

Unfortunately, his decision to grant a wage increase was inspired by political considerations and violated technical considerations (Sola 1988), and this political manipulation of the plan contributed to its flaws and thereby guaranteed its collapse (Sola 1988; Kaufman 1988; Singer 1989; W. Smith 1987). One of the central problems of the plan was that the price freeze had widely varying effects. Firms that had adjusted prices upward relatively soon before the time of the freeze profited while those that hadn't lost significantly. The wage increase added to the problem by generating inflationary pressure that could not be expressed in official prices and sharpened the inequality of the freeze's effects across firms. The result was a sharp conflict along supply chains and a descent into illegality as firms sought to escape price controls in a variety of ways: refusing to produce goods unless buyers (either consumers or firms) paid premiums *(ágios);* withholding supplies and thereby creating artificial shortages; and a host of ways to cheat on official price tables (Baer 1995).

For many business observers, the government's political manipulation of the plan highlighted a central hypocrisy. Politicians were willing to impose sacrifices on businesses through highly invasive practices, but the government was unwilling to make the painful political decisions that would contribute to financial stability. As a consequence, the Sarney administration (and politicians generally) rapidly lost credibility with respect to economic management.

The problem for the Sarney government was that it had neither the political will nor the political capacity to reduce its budget deficit. For one, Sarney made it a priority to extend his presidential term to five years and consequently was locked in expensive bargaining with the Congress. A second crucial problem was that Sarney's party, the PMDB, was splintering continuously as it no longer represented the unified opposition to military rule. The result was that the Sarney government could function only by paying out patronage resources and by preserving congressional access to those resources.

Finally, the drafting of the new constitution, completed in 1988, exacerbated the state's bad fiscal condition because of a range of controversial measures. In addition to protecting the civil service and the national social security system, the constitution also mandated the transfer of over 20 percent of the federal government's revenues to the states and municipalities without accompanying spending obligations (see Chapter 3). Although it took several years for the full effect to appear, the 1988 constitution helped push Brazil into serious financial disorder by 1989. Moreover, the government's diminishing credibility forced it to offer ever higher interest rates with ever shorter terms of maturity to attract creditors. This dynamic fed on itself and helped Brazil move closer and closer to hyperinflation by the end of Sarney's term in office.

All of these problems manifested themselves in Sarney's subsequent efforts at stabilization. From 1987 to 1989, Sarney's economy ministers implemented several less ambitious plans, most of which contained some combination of more traditional orthodox elements along with wage and price freezes, and in one instance a new currency (the Cruzado Novo in the Summer Plan of 1989). Ultimately, all of these plans failed, primarily because of the government's inability to make its own fiscal adjustments and because of growing social (especially business) resistance to successive and ineffective wage and price freezes. As inflation rose up toward 80 percent per month in the wake of the Summer Plan's failure, Sarney's last finance minister, Maílson da Nóbrega, observed that Brazil needed surgery but kept getting just the anesthetic (quoted in Gall 1991, 41).

This chaotic policy performance helped spur Brazil's highly erratic economic performance in this period. Growth rates swung from over 7 percent in 1985 and 1986 to an actual contraction of the economy in 1988 followed by 3.2 percent growth in 1989. Subsector performance particularly reveals the erratic quality of growth in the period. For example, agriculture grew close to 10 percent in 1985, contracted over 8 percent in 1986, and grew over 15 percent in 1987. Industry averaged roughly 10 percent growth in 1985–1986, then fell to 1 percent growth in 1987 before contracting almost 3 percent in 1988 (Baer 1995, 385–86). Export growth helped protect Brazilian dollar reserves; however, gross debt grew from US$ 95 billion in 1985 to US$ 114 billion in 1989. The capital accounts also suffered as foreign investment slowed down, firms increasingly remitted profits, and debt servicing sent dollars out of the country. As a result, Brazil suffered net capital outflows almost continuously throughout the period (Baer 1995, 391).

The principal reason for the exit of both domestic and foreign capital was inflation. Inflation in 1985 was 235 percent per year. It dropped to 65 percent in 1986 in response to the Cruzado Plan, but by 1987 it was on the rise again, hitting 416 percent before climbing to 1,783 percent in 1989. By March 1990, the month the new president, Fernando Collor de Mello, took office, inflation was at 84 percent per month, and the currency was on the brink of collapse.

Although Sarney's economic reforms led to little progress, their failure helped push business and policy leaders into a relative consensus on the necessary policy direction. By the late 1980s, both business leaders and top policy leaders had come to see a pragmatic form of neoliberalism as the necessary direction for Brazil. Policymakers in the National Bank for Economic and Social Development (BNDES) referred to this pragmatic, neoliberalizing path as "competitive integration" (BNDES 1989a, 1989b). Like neoliberal reform, competitive integration entailed privatization and commercial liberalization but with an eye toward increasing domestic competitiveness. Sarney had made several tentative and limited moves in this direction, including some privatizations and limited commercial liberalization, but this policy orientation ultimately found ample expression in the 1989 presidential elections.

The Collor Presidency: The Assault on Brazil

As the 1989 presidential elections approached, several candidates articulated a "modernizing" agenda consistent with competitive integration. Initially, Brazilian business leaders preferred more-moderate candidates, such as Guilherme Afif (Liberal Front Party) and Mário Covas (Brazilian Social Democratic Party). However, business eventually mobilized support behind Fernando Collor de Mello—a brash "outsider" who promised to convert Brazil into a modern, competitive "Brazil, Inc." As Collor's fiery rhetoric caught the attention of the poorest, least-educated voters, he became the candidate to beat and the most likely candidate to defeat Luiz Inácio Lula da Silva—the Workers' Party left-wing alternative.

Although Collor threatened to make elites pay the costs of modernizing the country, his campaign proposals were largely pragmatic and consistent with the competitive integration vision. Although his rhetoric was antibusiness, his policy proposals were aimed at improving the competitiveness of the domestic economy, not gutting it. True to his platform, Collor pursued a modernizing, largely neoliberal program. His eventual impeachment in December 1992 on corruption charges clouded his record as president, but Collor accomplished a great deal in his two years in office. Moving very rapidly after his inauguration in 1990, Collor implemented a commercial liberalization, a substantial deregulation, a more aggressive privatization program, and a partial fiscal adjustment. Aside from the corruption that brought down his government, Collor's most serious problem was his inability to decisively address Brazil's fiscal crisis, and through it, inflation. That inability rested on congressional resistance to constitutional reforms and the weakness of Brazil's political institutions, not corruption (see Chapters 1 and 2).

To counter the inflationary crisis in early 1990, Collor implemented by decree the most interventionist and draconian stabilization plan in Brazil's history. The plan included the freezing of 80 percent of the nation's savings, the introduction of a new currency, temporary wage and price freezes, a substantial tax increase and a one-time tax levy on all financial transactions, and a series of measures designed to rein in government expenditures. Those measures included the intention of firing up to 360,000 federal government employees, ending free housing for government employees, and rounding up and auctioning the sizable fleet of cars made available to politicians in Brasília. Along with his drastic antiinflation plan, Collor also set in motion a sweeping process of deregulation (especially in the areas affecting foreign commerce), significantly streamlined the administration, initiated a privatization program, and introduced a schedule for a graduated reduction of import tariffs.

As dramatic as Collor's reforms were, they left unresolved the fundamental fiscal problems enshrined in the constitution. The fiscal deficit declined from 8 percent of GDP in 1989 to a surplus of 1 percent in 1990 based on Collor's set of reforms and the suspension of monetary correction of the debt. Yet Collor still faced the difficult task of mobilizing support for reform in Congress. Congressional resistance lay in members' strong connections to well-organized groups with vested interests in preserving aspects of the constitution that institutionalized fiscal chaos (Kingstone 1998a).

Collor hoped to build a proreform coalition in Congress by using limited patronage spending to influence the outcome of the October 1990 legislative elections. However, the elections returned traditional, patronage-dependent political elites rather than either Collor supporters or foes, and this defeat coupled with resurgent inflation forced Collor to shift his tack on stabilization. From early 1991 on, Collor moved steadily toward a conventional monetarist, tight-money solution. His new economy minister, Marcílio Marques Moreira, brought a significant measure of credibility to the position, but his International Monetary Fund (IMF) orthodox style imposed a deep recession on the country even though inflation remained at 25 percent per month.

Collor made one last effort to combat inflation at the end of 1991. With his popular support diminishing, he tried to push through Congress a massive constitutional reform package, labeled the *emendão* (literally, "giant amendment"). This amendment addressed several areas of fiscal concern, notably administrative reform, civil service reform, and fiscal reform. However, Collor's efforts became bogged down in complex negotiations involving demands for cabinet posts, support for a plebiscite on parliamentarism, rolling over state-level debt, business demands for tax relief, labor demands for wage increases, and congressional demands for more patronage spending. Despite his corruption, Collor's administration was marked by a singular refusal to play traditional patronage politics. Thus, Collor stood back as Congress scuttled his package rather than make compromises that had severe fiscal implications.[1] He did manage to secure a tax increase that helped him arrange an IMF standby agreement in 1991, but that tax increase fell on a set of taxpayers who were already paying too much, namely, salaried workers and formal sector firms (legally registered firms). On the business side, the 1991 tax increase helped break Collor's political support in the industrial community (Kingstone 1999a.).

Collor took office in 1990 promising to kill inflation with a single bullet, yet by 1991, it was clear that his bullet had missed. His various stabilization policies effectively choked off economic activity as Brazil declined into a brutal recession. The GDP contracted almost 6 percent in 1990, further contracted in 1991, and again in 1992 (−1.3 percent and −2.3 percent, respectively). Investments (fixed capital formation) began declining steadily in 1980 and reached a new low in 1992 at a paltry 14.5 percent of GDP. Employment declined markedly in virtually every area of the economy from December 1989 to December 1992. Meanwhile, real wages contracted over 13 percent in 1990, a further 20 percent in 1991, and only recovered a very little ground in 1992 (Baer 1995, 393). Unfortunately, the deep recession did little to defeat inflation, which declined rapidly from March 1990 into the middle of the year but from then on rose steadily. Accumulated inflation for 1990 (including the disastrous first three months) hit 1,477 percent. It fell to 480 percent in 1991 before climbing again to 1,158 percent in 1992. The combination of recession and high inflation imposed a tremendous burden on the economy.

Despite his failings, Collor's government did produce a coherent vision for renewing economic growth and did much to advance economic reforms. Much like Sarney, any efforts at promoting growth took a distant back seat to the problems of stabilization. Yet some of Collor's measures had a rapid effect. First, Collor's introduction of a schedule for the gradual reduction of tariffs over the period 1990–1994 genuinely opened the economy to foreign competition. Second, Collor's deregulation process effectively and dramatically removed a host of legal and bureaucratic controls of foreign commerce. Thus, by the end of 1990, not only was it cheaper to import products, but the logistics of importing products had become radically simplified. These changes extended to a series of administrative reforms that sharply weakened bureaucratic oversight of the process. For example, Collor's replacement of CACEX (the Foreign Commerce Commission) with the new Department of Foreign Commerce (DECEX) included a significant streamlining of the import-export process.

Moreover, Fernando Collor was far from being a strict neoliberal (see Chapter 2), and Collor's administration perceived the need for a continued state role in the economy and for a continued promotion of industry. This policy was reflected in several areas. First, Collor's first secretary of economic policy, Antônio Kandir, issued an industrial policy built explicitly on the BNDES idea of competitive integration. The plan laid out a framework, although not specific measures, for identifying and promoting sectors critical to Brazil's continued growth. Second, the government inaugurated a program to promote quality and productivity, the Brazilian Program for Quality and Productivity (PBQP), and called on industry's associations to help develop and disseminate quality standards.

The Collor administration also saw measures such as privatization and de-indexation of the economy as key parts of the effort to stimulate competitiveness in the private sector. One striking illustration of this fact was the Collor government's privatization of firms to renew investments in the economy and to encourage competitive adjustments—not to ease the state's fiscal problems. As a result, the privatization process moved much slower than in countries like Argentina and Mexico, yet, after privatization, some of the firms became significantly more competitive. For example, Usiminas, the first major privatization in 1991, reported record profits for 1997, and business people voted its head, Rinaldo Campos Soares, the business person of the year (Gazeta Mercantil, Balanço Anual 1997).

Finally, the Collor government produced some positive results on the fiscal side. Freezing the nation's savings also froze monetary correction (adjustment for inflation) on government debt. That saving combined with cuts in government spending significantly improved the country's operational deficit (including interest payments on the public debt). The operational deficit had reached almost 8 percent of GDP in 1989, but Collor produced a 1.4 percent surplus in 1990, which gradually decayed to a 2 percent deficit in 1992. Meanwhile, exports continued to grow while import growth remained relatively flat. As a result, debt servicing as a percent of export revenues fell from a high of over 40 percent in 1986 to only 20 percent in 1992 (IDB 1997, 273).

Unfortunately, Collor's impeachment cut short the possibility of making his program more consistent. With Collor's suspension and subsequent impeachment in December 1992, the presidency fell to Vice President Itamar Franco, and he permitted a reflation of the economy in line with his more populist instincts. As a result, GDP growth resumed, reaching 6 percent in

1994, and imports began to rise sharply as consumers took advantage of newly lowered tariff rates. Exports continued to outpace imports, and the newly liberalized stock market also drew in large sums of foreign capital. Yet the uncertainty encouraged so much capital outflow that Brazil lost close to US$ 16 billion in dollar reserves in fiscal year 1993/1994 alone. Meanwhile, inflation rose to roughly 50 percent per month in early 1994. The PBQP did set in motion a significant effort among sectoral associations to promote quality, and Brazilian productivity improved markedly between 1990 and 1997 (Brazilian Central Bank Bulletin, March 1998, Table 1-1). Still, the uncertainty of the Franco interregnum led business people to put most of their competitive adjustments and investments on hold and wait to see what would come next.

The Cardoso Period: Portrait of a Savior?

The reform process lagged badly until the emergence of Fernando Henrique Cardoso as the logical candidate for the 1994 presidential elections. Franco's presidency had accomplished little. Franco was deeply ambivalent about the reform process and, as a consequence, abandoned orthodoxy, slowed privatization, and ultimately made little effort to actively pursue any strategy (Baer 1995, 191). In that context, the economy began to grow again as both inflation and indexation returned. Brazilian actors knew how to take advantage of the short-term opportunities that the situation offered despite the widely recognized need to do away with inflation and indexation. Finally, in early 1993, with inflation again rising precipitously, Franco appointed Fernando Henrique Cardoso as finance minister and essentially turned over the reins of government to him.

As finance minister, Cardoso made a concerted effort to resolve the country's fiscal problems through constitutional revision. The writers of the 1988 constitution had stipulated that a review should take place five years after promulgation. However, few members of Congress were prepared to alter the distribution of benefits that the constitution had conferred on groups like public sector employees, labor unions, the patronage dependent elites in states and municipalities, and the large array of very narrow, special interests that benefited from the distribution of patronage. This reluctance was particularly strong because the review occurred in the context of a serious corruption scandal with elections only months away. Opponents effectively undermined the process by proposing 17,000 amendments and 12,000 subamendments to the constitution. Ultimately, only 32 amendments were ever read out of committee, of which only 6 passed (Aragão 1995).

Of the six amendments that were passed, one was crucial for economic reform: the creation of a special fund called the Social Emergency Fund (FSE). This fund recovered roughly $10 billion from transfer payments to the states and municipalities for a period of two years. Thus, rather than being a reform to the fiscal system generally, the FSE performed an ad hoc fiscal adjustment and left the real reform for later. Nevertheless, it was a crucial short-term measure that helped contain fiscal deficits and gave the government breathing room to begin efforts to stabilize the economy. Cardoso lobbied intensely for the measure, even appealing directly to the public and threatening to quit if Congress didn't approve it. The measure set the stage for Cardoso's introduction of Brazil's most successful stabilization plan in its history, the Real Plan. The almost immediate success of this plan translated into a landslide victory for Cardoso in the October 1994 presidential elections.

The Real Plan's success hinged on several critical differences between it and previous plans (G. Oliveira 1995; Sachs and Zini 1995; Fishlow 1997). First and foremost, the Cardoso team made credible commitments to keep the plan transparent, predictable, and gradual. The Immediate Action Plan (its formal name) was presented in Congress in December 1993, nearly three months before its actual implementation. Then, in February 1994, the Cardoso team introduced a new index of inflation, the unit of real value (URV), which was pegged to the exchange rate and adjusted daily. The government began adjusting its own contracts according to the URV and encouraged private actors to do the same.

The Cardoso team continued to promote its stabilization plan with important differences from previous efforts. The next step of the plan was to convert the URV into a new currency, the Real, on July 1, 1994. By then, most actors in the economy were quoting their prices with reference to the URV, and the adjustment to the Real happened relatively easily. This process stands in stark contrast to the invasiveness of previous stabilization plans and the sharp and unpredictable effect they had on contracts (Bresser Pereira, Maravall, and Przeworski 1993). The Cardoso team also benefited from the fact that the import reduction schedule had reached its conclusion as the plan went into effect. Thus, even if Brazilian producers felt tempted to raise their prices speculatively, they faced strict pricing discipline from imports. Finally, the plan also benefited from comparatively healthier federal finances than previous plans as a result of Collor's earlier fiscal adjustment and the impact of the FSE.[2]

The Real Plan was both an economic and a political success. The October 1994 presidential elections took place when inflation was below 2 percent per month, and inflation continued to fall—to 15 percent in 1995, 10 percent in 1996, and 7.5 percent in 1997, with projections for 1998 even lower (Brazilian Central Bank Bulletin, March 1998, Table 1-11). With inflation's retreat, capital resumed its flow back into the significantly liberalized economy. Direct foreign investment rose from under US$ 1 billion in 1993 to over

US$ 16 billion in 1997. Portfolio investment rose to US$ 24 billion by 1996. In total, Brazil had drawn in nearly US$ 80 billion in foreign investment and commercial loans by the end of 1996. With the substantial increase in capital inflows, the GDP grew 6 percent in 1994, 4.2 percent in 1995, 2.8 percent in 1996, and 3 percent in 1997 (Brazilian Central Bank Bulletin, March 1998, Table 1-2).

Politically, the success of the Real Plan made possible the continuation of the reform process. Lula (PT) led all polls in the months leading up to the final conversion of the currency in July 1994. At the time, the PT opposed virtually all the constitutional reforms that were widely believed to be nec-essary to restore fiscal order. The party also opposed the moderate neoliberal direction of the economy. Cardoso's success in implementing the Real Plan allowed him to step down in April 1994 and campaign as the plan's sponsor (J. Figueiredo 1995). In a historic victory, he secured the election in the first round of voting on October 3, 1994, and Cardoso rapidly converted his sweeping electoral mandate into a majority legislative coalition. With significant political support, Cardoso began 1995 focused on constitutional reforms to permit lasting fiscal adjustments.

The constitutional amendments were necessary to secure the long-term survival of the Real (Martone 1996; Fishlow 1997). The drawback of the Real Plan was that without lasting fiscal adjustments, the stability of the currency depended on a combination of an overvalued exchange rate and high real interest rates. Both of these factors lured in foreign investment at very high levels, but that meant the government was not free to devalue the Real by any significant measure, nor was it free to reduce interest rates sub-stantially. As a consequence, importers were sharply favored by policy over exporters and local producers, and domestic borrowers were largely shut out of the financial markets. Furthermore, the inflow of foreign capital, the rise of government borrowing, and the high real level of interest rates all increased debt and debt servicing costs.

As of 1998, those problems had not undermined the plan, although ob-servers had begun to sound warnings that danger to the plan was increasing, and events in 1997 and 1998 seemed to bear them out.[3] Nevertheless, Brazil maintained strong reserves owing to capital inflows, even after the Asian crisis of October 1997 and to a lesser extent after September 1998. More-over, over the period 1994–1997, capital inflows changed in composition, with private debt and foreign direct investment rising relative to portfolio investment. The former inflows posed far less of a threat to the country's balance of payments than portfolio investment (Kingstone 1999b), and the surge of imports also helped maintain price discipline. Thus, as of 1998, Brazilian stabilization remained safe.

This discussion points to the need for a resolution of the country's fiscal problems, however, and on that score, the Cardoso government has fared less well. During 1995 and 1996, Cardoso repeatedly failed to get congressional support for crucial reforms of the social welfare system, civil service, and the tax system (Weyland 1996d; Kingstone 1998a). The social welfare system alone already faced a $5 billion deficit as of 1996. In 1996 and 1997, Cardoso was able to make very limited inroads into the civil service, social welfare, and the fiscal system through incremental, small measures that could pass as ordinary law (Kingstone 1999a). He finally secured his first real legislative successes on social welfare and civil service only after the Asian financial crisis hit Brazil in October 1997. As of the 1998 elections, however, the reforms had yet to pass all stages of congressional voting and were still far more limited than observers believed were necessary.

One critical consequence of Cardoso's legislative difficulties was that like Collor and Sarney, he had to sacrifice a well-defined growth strategy to the imperative of stabilization-related reforms. However, Cardoso made a number of growth policy adjustments that tried to preserve a constructive role for the state and to protect local production. Cardoso's policies rested on three planks: an industrial policy for the automobile industry, an export promotion policy, and a series of measures that protected and/or promoted a wide variety of sectors.

The automobile industrial policy emerged in response to the very rapid increase in auto imports in late 1994 to early 1995. With imports rising, the Cardoso administration first raised tariffs on automobiles to 20 percent and then in May 1995 to 70 percent. In turn, it lowered tariffs on parts and machinery to 2 percent. Firms could then import finished autos at reduced tariffs at dollar values proportionate to the dollar values they exported. The reduced tariffs, naturally, only applied to firms producing domestically. The policy created sharp conflict, particularly with the Japanese and Koreans, but the government's insistence on maintaining the policy helped drive the Brazilian auto industry to record levels of production.

Export promotion, on the other hand, proved less effective. By 1996, it became clear that the Cardoso government would not be able to reform the tax system, and thereby remove the uncompetitive tax component from Brazilian production (what business people referred to as the "Brazil cost"). Consequently, Cardoso turned to smaller, nonconstitutional measures, the most important of which were the abolition of the tax on goods and services (ICMS) for exports and the lowering of the tax on capital goods imports. The Cardoso government predicted that the measures would sharply increase exports, but, instead, the policy helped to deepen the fiscal deficit while revealing that Brazil's success, contrary to the prescriptions of the neoliberal model, continued to rest on the attractiveness of the domestic market. Brazil attracted $9 billion in foreign direct investment in 1996, with projections of $16 billion in 1997 and over $200 billion by 2002. However, much of that investment was explicitly targeted to serving the domestic market. As positive as abolition of the ICMS on exports was, it did not sufficiently reduce the Brazil cost to encourage even the most competitive multinational corporation (MNC) producers to view Brazil as an export platform. As a result, the trade deficit exceeded US$ 5 billion in 1996 after months of government predicted surpluses, and it reached a US$ 9 billion deficit in 1997 (the deficit would have been even higher but the Asian crisis and its effects slowed imports drastically).

Finally, the government increasingly turned to special credit lines from the National Bank for Economic and Social Development (BNDES) and selective protection as mechanisms to compensate hard-hit sectors and promote competitive adjustments. Thus, early in 1995, the government raised import tariffs on 109 products in the automobile, consumer electronics, and electrical appliances sectors. In 1996, the government accused Asian competitors of dumping toys, textiles, and apparel in Brazil and sharply raised tariffs in all three areas. The quid pro quo was that the protected sectors then had to make competitive adjustments in anticipation of a later lowering of the tariffs.

On the credit side, the government finally responded to business complaints of poor conditions for competitive adjustments and aggressively reasserted the BNDES role in promoting development. Between late 1996 and early 1997, the BNDES announced several billion dollars worth of new credit lines for microenterprises, hard-hit sectors (such as consumer electronics, auto parts, furniture, and textiles), and pulp and paper. In late 1997, new lines were extended to large producers (since the earlier, much smaller credit lines did not offer sufficient resources for large firms) of capital goods, machinery, auto parts, and parts and equipment for the soon-to-be-privatized telecommunications sector.

Business Adjustments, Economic Performance, and Democratic Sustainability

Scholars have long argued that regimes in capitalist societies, democratic or otherwise, cannot survive protracted business hostility, and Brazil's history has certainly tended to confirm that view. Business resistance to and mobilization against the regime helped bring down democracy in 1964 and military rule in 1985. In the former case, it was "ungovernability" and a sense of chaos that led business elites to see antiregime choices as the solution. In the 1980s, the cause was the military government's imposition of unacceptable costs on business while failing to restore growth or control inflation.

It is important to note, however, that bad economic performance is not sufficient by itself to push businesses into antiregime activity. As Leigh Payne has argued (1995), business people prefer to adapt to their circumstances rather than call on the military for intervention. Yet they will shift into antiregime behavior if they believe that the policy environment has become dangerously unstable or uncertain and if they believe that policymakers have denied them access. In the New Republic, business anger has expressed itself over both of these issues; however, over time, both issues have been at least partially resolved.

Although business leaders expressed dismay over the degree of economic uncertainty throughout the Sarney regime, they invested a great deal of hope for improvement in the 1989 presidential elections. Thus, for the business community, the 1989 election was a critical event. Business leaders had expressed growing concerns over a wide range of issues: the incoherence of the new constitution, the erratic performance of the government, the growing gap in competitiveness between Brazil and the developed world, and even the performance of their own associations (Kingstone 1999a). Business leaders had become quite vocal about the need for a change of policy direction,[4] and they increasingly called for a "modernization" of the country's economic policy.

The term "modernization" was used with varied meanings, but at the core of all the various meanings lay a desire to decrease the role of the state but still promote a competitive restructuring of the economy. Thus, "competitive integration" defined a highly consensual policy path, and as a consequence, business people initially responded quite positively to Collor's substantial reform measures. Large majorities of business people in various surveys and research projects expressed the belief that the country was moving in the right direction (G. Oliveira 1991; Kingstone 1999a). Nevertheless, business leaders insisted that they still needed a stable, well-defined policy direction to orient their adjustment decisions. Liberalization and stabilization were important first steps—necessary but not sufficient.

It was only with Cardoso's election in 1994 that the business community would get the policy stability it sought. Cardoso's team was clearly committed to defense of the Real and the maintenance of low inflation, and the government brushed aside complaints about the level of real interest rates or the exchange rate in order to maintain its policy priorities. That, combined with low inflation, produced a much more stable and predictable environment for businesses to orient their own investment decisions.

Unfortunately, the story was not all positive. In the same period, real wages increased, but so did unemployment, with open unemployment rising from 4.5 percent in December 1992 to close to 6 percent by late 1997. However, open unemployment measures only those workers actively seeking jobs in the formal economy, so it significantly understates the real unemployment level. The Departamento Intersindical de Estudos Econômicos, Sociais e Estatísticos (DIEESE, a labor think tank) estimated unemployment in São Paulo at close to 16 percent in 1996. Meanwhile, the Federation of Industry of the State of São Paulo (FIESP), the most important business association, reported very large increases in the number of bankruptcies over 1996 and 1997 (FIESP Notícias On-Line, http://www.fiesp.org.br), and the central bank noted that bad credit reports had more than doubled between 1992 and 1997 (Brazilian Central Bank Bulletin, March 1998, Table 1-1).

The country also recorded sharply increasing levels of debt and deficits. Despite the Cardoso government's efforts to stimulate exports, the country registered rapid import growth that soon substantially outpaced exports. As a result, the trade deficit for 1996 exceeded US$ 5 billion and continued to deteriorate through 1997. Operational deficits climbed as well. The operational deficit in 1995 and 1996 hovered around 4 percent of GDP; at the same time, Brazil's total external debt rose sharply as well from US$ 124 billion in 1992 to over US$ 160 billion by 1996. Public sector internal debt rose even more sharply. By 1997, the Brazilian public sector domestic debt surpassed US$ 233 billion—double the level of 1994. Finally, a group of economists and business leaders persuasively argued that the country's fiscal imbalances made growth levels much more modest than they could and should be (FIESP 1997).

Cardoso's continued reform efforts went a long way toward providing policy stability for the business community. However, business leaders continued to argue, even as they supported Cardoso's reelection, that the government still needed to produce a strategic vision of development to renew economic growth, which, they insisted, required good communication between business and the state (IEDI 1992; Kingstone 1998b). In that area, Cardoso made greater progress.

Business leaders had complained throughout the 1980s and early 1990s about their inability to actively discuss the national policy direction with key policymakers (Payne 1994). In the case of Sarney, the problem was that the debate never took place. In the case of Collor, it was because the government actively shut the business leaders out. Thus, by 1993, business unrest was quite noticeable, and there was some speculation that segments of the business community had requested military intervention.

However, after 1994, Cardoso worked to solve the problem. Business leaders continued voicing criticism of Cardoso's specific policies and his tactical choices in pursuing those policies, but Cardoso's policies had restored a measure of order and predictability to the economic environment. Perhaps just as important, Cardoso was remarkably careful to meet regularly with business leaders and to send his ministers to meet with them as well. His first two ministers of planning, José Serra and Antônio Kandir, as well as his second head of the Ministry of Industry, Commerce, and Tourism (MICT), Francisco Dornelles, met with FIESP officials repeatedly to explain government priorities and to listen to business concerns. In private interviews, business people reported that the Cardoso government also met frequently with key leaders of the industrial community (Kingstone 1999a).

One crucial consequence of such communication was that the Cardoso government effectively modified its policy in response to industrialists' growing concerns. The Cardoso administration's first priority remained protection of the Real, and as a result, it maintained high, real interest rates and an overvalued exchange rate. However, spurred by the efforts of MICT Minister Dornelles and Planning Minister Kandir, the government attempted to alleviate the intense competitive and financial pressure on firms. Throughout 1996 and 1997, the Cardoso administration implemented small, incremental changes in the tax law, offered new lines of government credit, and extended tariff and nontariff protection.

These measures clearly helped the government from a political perspective, regardless of their impact from an economic perspective. Business pressure and criticism had been mounting throughout late 1995 and 1996, and business associations had begun courting Antônio Delfim Netto (the architect of the "Brazilian miracle," a prominent deputy, and the economic adviser to one of Cardoso's principal political rivals in 1996, Paulo Maluf). Quietly, a significant number of industrial associations began lobbying for relief from the competitive pressure from rapidly entering imports, and these associations—such as those related to auto parts, machine tools and equipment, toys, and textiles—correctly pointed out that the measures to protect the Real also sharply favored imports over domestic production. Business frustration publicly revealed itself in a massive campaign called the "march to Brasília," in which close to 3,000 business people descended on the capital in May 1996 in a coordinated lobbying campaign in favor of constitutional reforms (Kingstone 1999a).

Cardoso's deft policy quieted business criticism. Few business respondents I interviewed believed that the measures would resolve the microlevel problems facing industry (confidential author interviews, São Paulo, June 1996), but the Cardoso government got high marks for responding to the best of its ability to the set of business concerns. By late 1996, business opposition had quieted substantially.

By 1998, the incremental "muddling through gridlock" and Cardoso's efforts to improve business access had helped strengthen democracy against business opposition. Meanwhile, a second process was at work to stop another potential source of business agitation. Collor's neoliberal reforms had little direct impact on the business community between 1990 and 1993 because of the general chaos in the economy. However, after 1994, commercial liberalization led to both a surge of imports and new foreign direct investment. Both sources of competition significantly challenged domestic producers.

One could imagine the "losers" in this reform process making appeals to the military for intervention to stop a process threatening domestic industry. Clearly, the military might not help. Nevertheless, the concern became moot as industrialists rapidly responded to their changing circumstances. After 1994, industrialists largely fell into three camps: those that could survive intact, those that could not survive intact, and those that could survive through some form of association with foreign capital. The larger number of adjustment and association opportunities meant that the actual number of "losers" was small between 1994 and 1998 (at least among large firms). Furthermore, the process occurred so quickly that losers became economically and politically irrelevant too quickly to pose a threat. By contrast, the winners (or at least survivors) locked themselves into specific adjustment strategies, making them more dependent on continuation of the reform process. Thus, rapid restructuring, economic order, and good communication between business and the state served to hinder antiregime efforts.

Lingering Challenges

Unfortunately, the institutional problems discussed in detail by Timothy Power in Chapter 1 have not disappeared, and as of 1998, they posed three particular problems. First, they still represented an obstacle to formulating clear policy. Executive-legislative relations remained awkward. Executives remained dependent on ad hoc political strategies (such as repeatedly issuing provisional measures), and legislators remained dependent on patronage resources and tightly linked to narrow, special interests. Policy remained highly reactive to short-term problems as opposed to actively defining a coherent, long-term development path for the nation. Thus, future presidents are likely to continue facing obstacles to defining solutions for critical development problems, including redistribution, education, and competitive integration.

A second concern that rises out of this situation is that Brazil is likely to continue facing real risks to the long-term stability of the country's currency and economy. Stability as of 1998 depended on large-scale capital inflows that supported the Real, and these inflows depended on the over-valued exchange rate and high real interest rates. Only long-term resolution of the state's fiscal imbalances can ease the country's dependence on foreign capital, but long-term resolution is likely to come, if at all, only with slow, incremental reforms. Eventually, they may add up to one big one. However, the Asian Flu was a critical reminder that as long as Brazil remains dependent on outside capital, it is vulnerable.

Third, should foreign capital leave, as it left Mexico during the Peso Crisis, that could prove a substantial shock for Brazil. In that event, it is conceivable that inflation might return. It is also conceivable that balance of payment problems might force the government to significantly alter its policy orientation. Alternatively, they might open up the possibility of antireform or populist coalitions. Either one of these contingencies could threaten the interests of businesses that have become dependent on the continuation of the market-oriented reform process.

Interview and documentary evidence seemed to suggest that business support for democracy was relatively robust (Payne 1994; author interviews, São Paulo, September–October 1991 and June 1996).[5] Certainly, rapid restructuring coupled with Cardoso's efforts to consult with business leaders reinforced business support for democracy. However, if that support was simply instrumental, rather than normative, it could shift quickly.[6] Interviews with business people suggested that they often look to future events for hope when they lose faith in the present (Kingstone 1998c). Thus, as Sarney failed to contain inflation, business elites pointed to the 1989 election. As Collor failed to reform the constitution, business leaders pointed to the 1993 constitutional review and the 1994 elections. With Cardoso's limited reforms, business leaders looked to the 1998 elections. After winning those elections, if Cardoso fails to continue the reform process, it is not clear where business leaders would look for future relief. In any event, such an occurrence may well test the depth of the business community's commitment to democracy.

TEN

Democracy Looks South
Mercosul and the Politics
of Brazilian Trade Strategy

Jeffrey Cason

razil has traditionally been viewed as an extraordinarily protectionist
country, the last holdout against a neoliberal tide sweeping the Latin
American region, and it has only recently come around to more market-
oriented policies. The protectionist impulse has been present in both democratic and authoritarian periods, the current democratic period included.
Although this general characterization is true, it is also the case that in the
period since the inauguration of the first nonmilitary president in 1985,
Brazilian trade strategy has undergone a qualitative change in orientation.
At first tentatively, and with much greater force after 1990, Brazil has become part of a regional trading bloc, the Mercado Comum do Sul (Mercosul),
a bloc that is attracting a great deal of attention from foreign investors and,
increasingly, powerful nations or blocs in the North.

Although there is a correlation between the new and robust integration
scheme and political democracy in Brazil, it is not necessarily the case that
the two go together naturally. Indeed, because of the inherently technical
nature of integration, as well as the fact that it of necessity imposes substantial costs on particular segments of society, one might conclude that in fact
less democratic participation in trade policy might go hand in hand with the
integration process. After all, one of the concerns of many political actors in
and analysts of the integration process in the European Union (EU) is precisely a fear that as integration proceeds, democracy will suffer as more and
more decisions are made by "faceless bureaucrats" who do not need to respond to any particular political constituency.

This fear is compounded in the Brazilian context by the fact that trade policy has hardly been a topic of democratic discussion in either democratic or authoritarian regimes. The Foreign Ministry has never much enjoyed outside political meddling in its own decision-making process and has instead maintained an insulated bureaucracy of, indeed, "faceless bureaucrats." It may then be that the integration process that has taken root and prospered in Brazil is one that is hardly "democratic" at all and instead reflects strategic decisions made by the people who are charged with guarding Brazil's interests on the international stage.

In this chapter I argue that such a conclusion would be overly simplistic. Rather, there has indeed been a reciprocal relationship between democracy and economic integration in the Mercosul process. In general, this reciprocal relationship is as follows: The existence of democracy helped to lead to substantial change in Brazilian trade strategy, in particular, a change toward regional integration. The political leadership in Brazil (and Argentina) saw regional integration as a way to play down their traditional rivalries, and thus integration was an attempt to weaken their respective militaries and consolidate democracy. In this sense, the goal of democratic consolidation in the creation of Mercosul was analogous to the goal of avoiding future wars that played an important role in European integration. To be sure, the integration process built upon previous efforts already endorsed by both militaries to further cooperation, but by making the integration more institutionalized and solidifying cooperation between civil societies in Brazil and Argentina, the leadership of the new democracies hoped to make it more and more difficult to go back to rivalry and military competition. And, as recent political events have made clear—particularly the attempted coup in Paraguay in 1996—regional integration continues to act as a prodemocratic force.

At the same time, there is an important "democratic deficit" in Brazil's new foreign trade policy. Despite its "democratizing" genesis, this new cooperative relationship in the Southern Cone has actually had very little effect on democracy itself. It has generally *not* opened up foreign trade policy to democratic participation, despite occasional attempts to include more of civil society in the integration process. Indeed, many actors in civil society complain of a lack of access to policymakers. There have been some recent changes that attempt to address this "deficit" in trade policy by, for example, including more business and labor representatives in the official delegations that go to regional summits, and certainly, opinions are solicited from important economic actors. But trade policy—unlike, for example, domestic economic policy (see Chapters 2 and 9)—has not been changed much by the participation of actors in civil society. These actors might be heard, but with regard to foreign trade policy, they are heard largely to further the goals of policymakers.

In the first section I consider the genesis of the Mercosul trading bloc—

before it was called Mercosul—and its fundamentally political character. As will become apparent, increased economic cooperation between Brazil and Argentina in the mid-1980s had a political logic, one in which the cooperation was used to reinforce the new democratic regimes in both countries. In the second section I look at the actual creation of Mercosul and show that as integration deepened, it acquired an increasingly "technocratic" character, in part because of the way in which liberalization was implemented. The treaty that set out the economic agreement, the Treaty of Asunción, mandated scheduled and regular tariff reductions, and this automatic schedule made the actual liberalization much less susceptible to political pressures in any of the member countries. In other words, trade liberalization in Brazil has continued a long tradition of keeping a key aspect of economic policy making—foreign economic policy—away from democratic discussion.[1]

The third and fourth sections address two ways in which democracy has or has not been affected by the general change in trade policy, based on the empirical information presented and other theoretical propositions about the relationship between foreign economic policy and democratization. In the third section I ask if Mercosul really did consolidate democracy, as it set out to do. The answer is a qualified yes. In the fourth section I discuss the effect of Mercosul on the *quality* of democracy, and generally conclude that it has not affected it much, even though recent developments make this conclusion less categoric.

Laying the Groundwork for Integration

Despite many previously frustrated efforts at integration in Latin America, Argentina and Brazil embarked on an economic integration project in July 1986[2] after a period of sharp contraction in trade between the two countries that was brought on mostly by the debt crisis in Latin America. To illustrate the degree to which trade had collapsed, it is sufficient to note that whereas Brazilian exports to Argentina peaked in 1979 at US$ 1.1 billion, during the first half of the 1980s exports never topped US$ 880 million and reached a dismal low of US$ 612 million in 1985 (Manzetti 1990, 113).

The integration process marked a renewed attempt to spur growth and competitiveness by at least tentatively liberalizing foreign trade policies. This project began with a set of protocols signed by presidents José Sarney of Brazil and Raúl Alfonsín of Argentina that lowered tariff barriers in specific industries. The original agreements, the Argentine Brazilian Economic Integration Program (ABEIP), called for meetings between the presidents of both countries every six months at which they would sign additional protocols that had been negotiated by their representatives.

The ABEIP marked a break with previous integration efforts, primarily because the motivations for integration were more political than economic. Whereas Argentina and Brazil had traditionally been economic and military rivals in South America, the ABEIP agreements signaled a new push toward cooperation and an attempt to downplay past differences. The initiative for the ABEIP came from Argentine President Alfonsín, who made economic integration a top priority of his administration (Manzetti 1990, 114). The ABEIP also was begun as both countries were emerging from periods of military rule, and both saw the agreement as a way to strengthen their fledgling democracies.[3] Both new governments thought that if they tied themselves more closely to the other's economy, a renewal of traditional conflicts and rivalries would be less likely. Indeed, in this sense, democracy clearly had an effect on the integration process, as it gave political leaders an additional incentive to see the process through to conclusion, quite apart from any economic advantage that some sectors could enjoy.[4]

Although the program sprang from democratic motives, it was hardly the case that integration was a "democratic process." From the beginning, the ABEIP initiative was clearly state led. The private sector was generally not involved in the early negotiations, and only when its economic sectors were put on the agenda by trade negotiators did the private sector become involved. Luigi Manzetti argues that "the main drive behind the integration process was not so much pressure from industrial and agricultural groups as the converging political interests of the Sarney and Alfonsín administrations" (Manzetti 1990, 115). Needless to say, union representatives were also not consulted in the early stages of integration. In fact, many of these leaders in both countries were taken by surprise by the new initiatives.[5]

This limited political base led to substantial problems in the late 1980s when the integration effort stalled. Manzetti attributes this stall in part to the fact that the ABEIP was "not reinforced by supportive economic and social groups, which were not organized either spontaneously or by the governments" (Manzetti 1990, 133). Supporters of integration were in the state, not society. Given the fact that economic policy was by this time being buffeted even more by political considerations in newly democratic Brazil, one might very well have concluded that democracy might *prevent* further integration. After all, when viewed in the context of the massive economic and political instability of the late 1980s, any effort that carried high political risks (because of the economic upheaval it would cause) would seem to be dead in the water.

These political problems were reflected in the negotiations between Argentina and Brazil as the process seemed to be going nowhere. In observing this process, former Finance Minister Luiz Carlos Bresser Pereira complained of the "overnegotiation" of the ABEIP:[6]

The only reason to carry out economic integration is to create a market between Brazil and Argentina. But if it is necessary to manage such a market so much, it will never be created. Here the problem is both with Argentines and Brazilians. Both are *protocoleros*.[7] Perhaps the Brazilians are even more so than the Argentines. If we want to integrate, of course we have to negotiate; we cannot simply open up the market. But we must negotiate less. If we insist on negotiating everything, in such a way that no sector is driven out of the market by the other country, we are not really negotiating seriously. We are only simulating integration. (Bresser Pereira 1990, 224–25)

In fact, the integration process initiated in 1986 did stall later, because of both the continued economic instability in both countries and the lack of widespread political support for integration, especially in Brazil. The ABEIP was begun at a propitious moment, when both Argentina and Brazil were experiencing the fleeting success of their heterodox antiinflation plans, the Austral and Cruzado Plans, respectively. However, neither Brazil nor Argentina was able to control accelerating inflation for long, and wide fluctuations in exchange rates made coherent foreign trade planning exceedingly difficult. It appeared that the ABEIP might go the way of other Latin American integration initiatives—to the cluttered dustbin of ambitious plans that inevitably ran into political and economic obstacles.[8]

Mercosul Takes Off

Indeed, given the economic turmoil in both Argentina and Brazil in the late 1980s, and the failure of some of the protocols signed under the auspices of the ABEIP, there was good reason to be pessimistic. Nevertheless, the program was given new life by two factors originating in the international political economy: the end of the Cold War and the triumph of market-oriented ideology throughout the Americas.[9]

The end of the Cold War dramatically changed the international context, which had important implications for regional and international trade. Brazil and Argentina now saw themselves facing what appeared to be strengthening regional trading blocs, and with the fall of communism in Eastern Europe, they saw that Latin America might be ignored by the more industrialized countries. Mexico was in the process of striking a separate deal by entering into the North American Free Trade Agreement (NAFTA) negotiations with the United States and Canada, and it appeared that the future was one of regional economic groupings. Many people in both Argentina and Brazil saw economic integration as a way to strengthen their hand in dealing with the world's larger trading blocs.[10]

In other words, state strategies changed when global political and economic changes demanded it. New and attractive markets in Eastern Europe— markets that were keen on seeing their economies become part of the capitalist world economy—threatened to draw investment away from Latin

America. Just as this threat prompted Mexican president Carlos Salinas de Gortari to propose the NAFTA, this globalization prompted state elites in South America to embark on a strategy that would integrate their countries' economies in the world market. It became clear to leaders in both Argentina and Brazil that they were in danger of being left behind in an increasingly integrated world economy. Above all, investments from multinational corporations were much more likely to go to countries where these corporations had a free hand to integrate their strategies within a larger, global arena.[11]

These changed international circumstances coincided with domestic political changes in both Brazil and Argentina that led to the election of leaders convinced of the need to modernize and open their economies (for Brazil, see Chapters 2 and 9). Fernando Collor de Mello and Carlos Menem, both elected in 1989, viewed regional integration as a way to maintain themselves as players in the world economy. They were also much more ideologically committed to a neoliberal strategy, the so-called Washington consensus.[12] They sought to cut state spending, privatize state-owned industries, deregulate their economies, and generally pursue free-market reforms.

One of these free-market reforms, which were meant to ease both countries into a more competitive international environment, was Mercosul, created in March 1991. The main actors in this integration process were Argentina and Brazil, although Paraguay and Uruguay were also included in the agreement. Mercosul set forth a timetable that would establish a free market for goods between the member countries (in most products) by the end of 1994. Not only was this an extremely fast timetable for integration, but the specificity of the measures that were adopted to encourage integration was unprecedented.[13] In addition, as J. A. Guilhon Albuquerque (1992) points out, democracy had an interesting effect on the speed of the integration process: given that at the time the constitutions of Argentina and Brazil prevented reelection of the president in either country, Collor and Menem both hoped to accomplish a key transition in the process before the end of their terms.

The accelerated timetable did not always proceed smoothly, and one of the main obstacles to integration was the disparity in macroeconomic policies between the two main partners, Argentina and Brazil. Whereas Argentina had embarked on a stringent economic stabilization policy in April 1991, Brazil continued to avoid one until July 1994. The main consequence of this disparity for the integration process was an overvaluation of the Argentine peso, which led to a flood of Brazilian imports in Argentina.

As a consequence, in November 1992, Argentina imposed a "statistical tax" on imports ranging from 3 percent to 10 percent.[14] One of the main targets of this new levy was the Brazilian exports that were flooding the Argentine market. To encourage Argentina to moderate its protectionist behavior, the Brazilians agreed to address the trade imbalance with Argentina by purchasing more Argentine wheat and oil (Manzetti 1994, 124). Consequently, the Argentines agreed to phase out the import levy.

Other conflicts were resolved in a similar way: give and take on the main issues with the overall goal of integration in the forefront of the minds of policymakers. Whereas in previous integration efforts such small conflicts had led to a stagnation of the integration process, Mercosul was a different animal, and it had the strong support of the political leadership in both countries. In addition, substantial portions of the business community actively supported the integration process, which made it more difficult for policymakers to turn back. Furthermore, as Table 10.1 indicates, both Brazil and Argentina experienced an explosion in regional exports, and most of this trade has been with one another. Between 1989 and 1996, the percentage of all of foreign trade with the country's principal Mercosul partner more than doubled in Argentina and more than tripled in Brazil, and this increasing integration made the process itself nearly irreversible. The economic facts of life have changed in the region, and this change is qualitative—with the increasing interdependence of key sectors such as automobiles and processed food products—as much as it is quantitative.

Democratic Consolidation and Mercosul

If the economic facts of life have changed, we might ask, Have the political facts of life changed as well? Did Mercosul really consolidate democracy, as

TABLE 10.1
Argentine and Brazilian Exports to Mercosul, 1985–1997
(in millions of U.S. dollars)

Year	Argentine Exports to Mercosul Countries	Brazilian Exports to Mercosul Countries
1985	668	990
1986	895	1,176
1987	769	1,388
1988	875	1,637
1989	1,428	1,367
1990	1,833	1,249
1991	1,978	2,309
1992	2,327	4,097
1993	3,684	5,397
1994	4,803	5,922
1995	6,522	6,154
1996	7,802	7,388
1997	8,996	9,567

Source: International Monetary Fund (1992, 83, 112; 1997, 103, 136–37).

it was supposed to? Did it make it more difficult to go back to an authoritarian regime, as its originators envisioned? The answer is a qualified yes.

There are good reasons to be skeptical of the ability of international institutions or agreements to guarantee democracy, since national sovereignty remains a key principle in the international system. Indeed, history is replete with pronouncements of commitments to "democratic values" by countries that are far from democratic; as Laurence Whitehead points out, the signatories of the Organization of American States (OAS) Final Act of Bogotá in 1948 declared their defense of "the free and sovereign rights of their peoples to govern themselves in accordance with their democratic aspirations" (Whitehead 1986, 5), and they included Nicaragua's Anastasio Somoza as a signatory, among other tyrants. In other words, nations can avow a commitment to democracy in their international agreements, but they do not necessarily have to do anything to live up to that commitment.

Nevertheless, it appears that Mercosul is different in its ability to promote democracy for several reasons. First of all, as already noted, it emerged with a democratic motivation, which itself has an important legacy. Second, it emerged just as the Cold War ended, which made the world much "safer for democracy." The United States no longer bases its foreign policy on anticommunist principles, principles that had frequently led the United States to support regimes that were hardly democratic, even if they were friendly. Finally, globalization—interpreted here as increased economic interdependence, which leads to greater reliance on foreign economic linkages—has meant that nations are at greater risk if they engage in "inappropriate" internal political behavior, since much more of their economies are vulnerable to international sanctions, whether formally or informally applied.

What these factors have led to is an increased importance for what Whitehead refers to as "political and economic inducements" by the international community in favor of democratization (Whitehead 1986, 12). Whitehead notes that unlike the United States, which has tended to rely on its projection of military power, the European Community used such inducements to encourage democracy in southern European countries that hoped to join its ranks. With the end of the Cold War, these inducements have become much more salient than military power in encouraging democracy, and in the case of Mercosul, they have actually been tested.

Although the New Republic in Brazil has not been threatened—in terms of its democratic consolidation—the regional bloc itself has been tested. In April 1996, one of the members, Paraguay, was threatened by a military coup led by General Lino César Oviedo, who attempted to overthrow the elected government of Juan Carlos Wasmosy.[15] Wasmosy clearly wavered when his government was threatened, but interestingly, it appears that international forces were crucial in leading him to stand up for democracy in the face of military threat. When Wasmosy decided to dismiss Oviedo as commander of the army and was confronted with a severe military crisis as a result, he was willing to take a "leave of absence" to defuse the crisis. Nevertheless, both the United States and Brazil—speaking for Mercosul—encouraged him to stand up to the military and remain in office. Apparently Brazil's ambassador in Paraguay, Márcio de Oliveira Dias (who had joined President Wasmosy in the U.S. ambassador's residence), first helped draft the gambit of a "leave of absence" (which Oviedo scorned) and then later encouraged the Paraguayan president to stand up to the military threat. In addition, Brazil's army minister, Zenildo de Lucena, called Oviedo to urge him to desist from his plans to unseat Wasmosy's constitutional government (Valenzuela 1997, 49–50).

Although it cannot be argued that the intervention of Mercosul definitively stopped the attempted coup against Wasmosy, the Brazilians viewed their intervention as crucial. As Paulo Bornhausen, the president of Mercosul's Combined Parliamentary Commission, noted, "Mercosul demonstrated that it represents a security against democratic instability and that it has an important political component."[16] Indeed this fact was demonstrated, and it is symbolically important that Mercosul nations were more than willing to interfere in the internal affairs of a member country when democracy was threatened.

That willingness of Mercosul countries to support democracy also illustrates the importance of internal democracy for commercial relations with the outside world; after all, if the coup had succeeded in Paraguay and the other Mercosul nations had kept Paraguay in the economic group, the bloc could very well have found its other international negotiations jeopardized. This possibility led the Brazilian Foreign Ministry to declare that "any actions that imply a break in the constitutional and democratic order would gravely affect cooperation between Brazil and Paraguay,"[17] not simply because Brazil (or other Mercosul countries) disapproved of authoritarian governments, though of course they might, but because they realized that any disruption of the democratic processes would affect their ability to negotiate with key trading partners.

The Quality of Democracy in Foreign Trade Policy

If an authoritarian reversal is less likely because of the existence of Mercosul, that situation is certainly to be applauded by people who value democracy. But at the same time, has it made democracy in any way more participatory? Or is it the case that a "democratic deficit" has been opened quite wide when it comes to economic integration? Though the answer is not unqualified, largely it is the case that the quality of democracy has hardly been enhanced by the Mercosul process.

The "democratic deficit" that is commonly referred to in the European Union (Featherstone 1994; Neunreither 1994; M. Smith 1996) is quite different from the one in Mercosul. In the European case, the deficit arises from problems associated with transferring too much authority to supranational institutions such as the European Commission, for the fear of many Europeans is that as integration proceeds, more decisions of national import will be taken by a faraway bureaucracy in Brussels, with only minimal participation by national parliaments or other representative institutions in the member states.

The same is clearly not a problem in Mercosul; indeed, one of the defining features of the process is its lack of such supranational institutions. In effect, the Brazilians, as the dominant players in the Mercosul process, are unwilling to relinquish sovereignty to a supranational institution. Although there is a Mercosul headquarters in Montevideo (the Mercosul Administrative Secretariat), it does little more than collect statistical information and has no independent decision-making power. In other words, Mercosul is an intergovernmental integration process par excellence.

The "democratic deficit" critics of the EU might, then, consider the Mercosul process more democratic, since there is little fear that unaccountable supranational bureaucrats could take control of the process without being checked by elected politicians. There is no need to create a democratic legitimacy for supranational institutions; as Mitchell Smith points out, "It is useful to think of the EU as a recently established democratic regime trying to accumulate sufficient legitimacy to remove the possibility of alternative regimes from the political agenda" (M. Smith 1996, 296). Mercosul does not have to concern itself with creating such legitimacy, for control of the process is firmly in the hands of elected national governments.

In the case of Mercosul, however, there is another kind of democratic deficit, one that is related more to the degree to which decisions about the evolution of the trading group are the subject of democratic discussion. This issue relates to the problem that Atul Kohli (1998) identifies as "too much and not enough democracy" in recently democratized countries; there is both pressure for changes in economic policy in these countries—often expressed during electoral periods—and a concomitant concentration of executive authority in these states, which makes leaders less responsive to demands from social groups that have a keen interest in economic policy making.

In Brazil, this concentration of authority regarding Mercosul is centered in the Foreign Ministry, Itamaraty. Traditionally, Itamaraty has had wide discretion in setting Brazil's foreign economic policy, and whether the political regime was democratic or not did not greatly affect its diplomacy or geopolitical goals.[18] With Mercosul, Itamaraty saw an opportunity to expand Brazil's influence in South America and, in particular, once it was established, to act as a counterweight to the United States in the hemisphere. Indeed, as Manzetti points out, one of the principal reasons that Brazil began integration in the first place was not to promote democracy but to carry out Itamaraty's decision "to pursue a more active commercial policy in the region via bilateral accords" (Manzetti 1990, 115). In other words, Brazil's policymakers have viewed Mercosul as a way to expand their economic influence.

To illustrate the point, one can compare the Brazilian and Argentine attitudes toward hemispheric free trade: whereas many Argentine policymakers have hoped to find a way to enter into NAFTA, the Brazilians are much more cautious about a strategy that would link them irrevocably with the North American market and view an American free trade association with much more suspicion than their southern counterparts. Indeed, the Brazilians are much more interested in a South American free trade association than one that would include both South and North America.

Given this strategic thrust to policy, it is not surprising that Itamaraty has preferred to limit debate about the Mercosul process. Nevertheless, the ministry has not been completely autonomous (especially with regard to business) and has sometimes acted to include people from civil society in hemispheric trade negotiations—for instance, at the ministerial meeting of all the countries party to negotiations over a potential free trade area of the Americas held in Belo Horizonte, Brazil, in May 1997. In these negotiations, there was participation of large segments of civil society at the meeting and at the parallel business forum. Different groups in civil society, including business and labor unions, were also consulted prior to the meeting.[19]

It would appear, then, that with the maturation of the economic bloc, politics is beginning to catch up, but that would be a misleading conclusion. One must consider that the goal of Brazilian policymakers at the Belo Horizonte meeting was to slow down the negotiations concerning the free trade area. Therefore, consulting widely played into the hands of Itamaraty: since many actors in civil society are reluctant to rapidly open the Brazilian economy to foreign competition, increasing "the voice" of civil society meant that the process would necessarily slow down. As Senator Fernando Bezerra, the president of the Confederação Nacional da Indústria, put it: "The United States wants to accelerate integration, so that it begins in 2005. For our part, we want to slow it down."[20] Such a comment was music to Itamaraty's ears.

Thus, making negotiations over the free trade area more "democratic" removed the process from a "fast track." One of the reasons that the U.S. executive branch needs a "fast track" authority to negotiate trade accords (where a trade agreement has to be voted up or down by Congress, with no amendments) is to make it possible to impose unpopular decisions on constituencies that might be harmed by trade agreements reached by the executive. Since trade liberalization necessarily imposes costs on different economic sectors, increasing the voice of groups who might be harmed by such liberalization tends to militate against agreement. In the case of Mercosul, little voice was provided in its negotiation, which increased the possibility of achieving an agreement. As Mercosul confronts the possibility of hemispheric integration—and since one of the goals of the Brazilians is to slow this process down—it is relying on democratic procedures to strengthen Mercosul and weaken the prospects for broader trade liberalization.

Conclusion: Democratization and Integration

This description of the development of Mercosul demonstrates that there has been a reciprocal relationship—not always direct—between democracy and economic integration for Brazil and other countries of the Southern Cone. This relationship was quite explicit in the beginning of the integration process, but it has existed throughout.

First, integration was initially carried out for explicitly political reasons: to consolidate the newly minted democratic regimes in both Argentina and Brazil. Because of this political logic, the integration project received high-level attention from the political leaders throughout the process. It was given the extra push any integration effort needs—because of its complexity and the virtual necessity of economic losers in the process—by the aim of achieving democratic sustainability.

Second, the process of integration has in fact accomplished some of what it was meant to. One could reasonably make the argument that Mercosul has made it more difficult for any of the countries in the region to introduce military rule again. Certainly it is unlikely that if the Brazilian military decided to assume power again that the country's integration colleagues would actually be able to reverse the process. Mercosul did adopt this more political character on one occasion, when its intervention helped thwart the military coup in Paraguay, and this demonstrated political function has in itself strengthened the democratic nature of the Mercosul region. In this sense Mercosul parallels the European Union, in which membership is open only to democratic states.

Third, despite its "democratizing" nature, the Mercosul process clearly has only marginally affected the "quality" of democracy in Brazil. Although it has stimulated the organizations of certain sectors in civil society—both business and labor—to press their claims in the process, integration is still largely a state-run process. Some elite sectors of business are heard when they feel pain as a consequence of economic policy, but this situation is not terribly different from the circumstances during the military regime.

Finally, Mercosul demonstrates how difficult it is to make trade policy "democratically," if by that we mean with substantial participation by civil society. In trade policy, substantial democratic participation usually leads to a continuation of the status quo. After all, trade liberalization implies "adjustment," which is a nice way of saying "economic pain." In this sense, the Mercosul process confirms what we already know: it is difficult to impose political and economic costs in an open political environment without well-established institutions (Haggard and Kaufman 1992). We should therefore not be surprised that Brazil's trade policy has not been carried out democratically.

ELEVEN

An Ugly Democracy?
State Violence and the Rule of Law in Postauthoritarian Brazil

Anthony W. Pereira

A major claim on behalf of democracies is that they more closely approximate the rule of law than do most authoritarian regimes[1] and, consequently, they offer citizens more protection from arbitrary state abuse and violence (Dahl 1971, 27–29; Przeworski 1991, 16, 31; Tilly 1995, 370). This democratic promise has not yet been realized in Brazil. While under military rule, lethal violence perpetrated by state agents in Brazil was comparatively low compared to what occurred in Argentina, Chile, and Uruguay (Stepan 1988, 70; Drake 1996, 29–30); under democracy, Brazil's state violence increased to become the highest in the region (Chevigny 1995; Pastoriza 1996, 16–17).[2] Thus, while the defense of human rights was part of the moral basis of opposition to Brazil's military regime, in fact, both relative and absolute levels of state violence seem to have increased under democracy.

In the first section of this chapter I show how Brazil's arbitrary state violence poses a problem for democracy and how it might be reduced. In the second section I argue that state violence is especially problematic in Brazil because of two features of the country's political culture and recent history. The first is the wide gap between formal legality and political and social practice (producing what I call "elitist liberalism"), and the second is the military regime's prior use of complex forms of legalism to claim legitimacy for its rule. I then look at two attempts at political reform in the post-1985 period: the struggle to investigate the cases of the people who were killed or disappeared during the military regime of 1964–1985 and the attempt to curb contemporary police violence. I argue that the first reform, while advancing democratic consolidation in important ways, did not challenge elitist liberalism while the second reform has at least the potential to do so.

The Problem of State Violence

Illegal state violence poses a problem for democratic consolidation for at least two reasons.[3] First, such violence negates a fundamental democratic liberty, the freedom of individuals and groups to pursue their interests and to make political claims without fear of repression (Sklar 1989). Second, widespread unconstitutional state violence is a negation of the democratic accountability of coercive institutions to the legal order and the judicial apparatus entrusted with its enforcement. In many instances, such violence also vitiates the accountability of coercive institutions to elected officials.

The first point can be elaborated with reference to the concept of polyarchy developed by political theorist Robert Dahl (1971). In polyarchic societies, citizens have an equal right to participate in politics (Dahl conceives of this right primarily as voting, but we can widen the scope of participation to include popular forms of claim making such as marches, petitions, demonstrations, rallies, strikes, boycotts, and so on). If police forces systematically intimidate, repress, and kill people who engage in such claim making, then the right of those people to express themselves politically without fear and to participate in politics on an equal basis is diminished. The more widespread and unchallenged this kind of state repression is, the further away from polyarchy one moves and the closer one approaches what Dahl calls a competitive oligarchy (Dahl 1971, 7), in which contestation between elites exists but in which rights to mass participation are restricted.

In post-1985 Brazil, most state violence has not been directed against groups and individuals making political claims. Instead, much of it has targeted the poor, the socially marginal, and the nonwhite, from whose ranks the "criminally suspect" are disproportionately drawn. This violence is also corrosive of democracy, because it represents unchecked violations of the constitution by state agents that rob the legal order of substance and, in some cases, diminish the impact of electoral choices, if elected officials oppose such violence. When the repressive apparatus within the executive branch of government (including the military, police, intelligence agencies, and prison services) is effectively insulated from external control, a coercive "state within the state" coexists with another state that is more responsive to electoral mandates and judicial restraint.

On that level, the shooting of street children or prisoners is as "political" as the repression of the left was in the 1960s and 1970s, because both types of violence reduce the broad extension of citizenship rights and the democratic control of the state's means of violence. In actual democracies, neither full equality of citizenship nor total freedom from arbitrary state violence exists, but some polities approach the ideal to a greater degree than others. The magnitude of Brazil's state violence indicates that the country falls much further short of the ideal than do its neighbors Argentina, Chile, and Uruguay.

How can state violence in a democracy be kept in check? Under some circumstances, citizens may protest the state's abuse of others' human rights out of self-interest. Acting on the belief that in an unconstitutional order nobody is safe, citizens will protest even if present state transgressions against others benefit them, because by doing so, they are protecting themselves from state abuses in the future (Przeworski 1996, 6–9). In such a society, all citizens have a common interest in preventing the state from abusing their rights.

This argument is suggestive, but it does not fully capture the logic of public responses to state violence. It assumes that citizens view their relationship with the coercive apparatus as essentially the same—that they see themselves as equally vulnerable to state transgressions, or equally endowed with citizenship rights so that the victims of state violence share a common status with nonvictims. To the extent that state coercion is applied predictably and selectively to particular, readily identifiable groups, citizens' calculations of their interests will change. Certain segments of the population will conclude that they are indeed safe despite widespread human rights abuses by the state, especially if they can afford private security, which frees them from reliance on the police. These segments of the population will not have an interest in protesting state transgressions, and democratic rights will be fragile.

Historically, this has been the situation in Brazil. For example, according to one study, the first armed and uniformed police force was created in Rio de Janeiro in 1831 to reinforce the coercive power of slaveowners by disciplining slaves who might otherwise have remained unsupervised in the impersonal environment of the city. This discipline was applied more against "offenses against public order" than conventional crime and had more to do with the control of "the dangerous classes" than enforcing liberal norms of legal equality (Holloway 1993, 5, 9, 283, 291). Under such circumstances, upper-class and high-status individuals saw themselves as immune to police violence, which created a relatively low degree of consensus about the legitimacy of police intervention in society.

In contemporary Brazil, two kinds of change might lead to the development of such a consensus. First, an increase in the perceived intensity and randomness of state (and societal) violence could induce higher-status individuals to believe that they are not safe and that they share a common interest with the rest of society in restraining state violence (and creating more effective police forces to combat societal violence). Second, an increased normative commitment to human rights throughout society, including within the state's repressive institutions, could persuade state actors to obey the law and citizens to protest state transgressions regardless of their individual calculation of self-interest. The first kind of change seems to have occurred in Brazil since the transition to civilian rule in 1985, and some political reforms have attempted to induce the second type of change. However, certain features of Brazil's political culture and recent history pose barriers to such changes; those features are the ideology and practice of elitist liberalism and the legalism of the military regime.

The Ambiguity of Law in Brazil

Brazil has experienced a profound tension between the formal constitutional and legal frameworks of its political regimes and the informal political practices that take place within them. In part, this tension derives from the social distance between elites, with an Ibero-Catholic or at least mainly European heritage, on the one hand, and the mulatto, Afro-Brazilian, and Amerindian populations that form the mass base of society, on the other. The Brazilian expression *para o inglês ver* ("for the English to see") captures the ambiguity of law in this context. Legal change in a society in which many laws are merely decorative, *para o inglês ver*, implies that how new laws will be enforced is especially ambiguous. Brazilian legality thus contains strong elements of fantasy and desire.

The law in Brazil is also inconstant and voluminous. The country has had eight constitutions in the 175 years of its independent existence,[4] and it has had at least six extraconstitutional changes of government since independence. The present constitution, promulgated in 1988, is one of the longest and most detailed in the world, but many of its provisions exist only on paper because the legislation to implement their enactment has not been passed (Rosenn 1990, 778). The judiciary, one of the most beleaguered in Latin America, is still overloaded, understaffed, and lacking in independence from the legislative and executive branches.[5]

Furthermore, the gap between the universalism of formal legality and the actual extension of citizenship rights is exacerbated by the country's hugely inegalitarian economy. Inequalities in the distribution of income in Brazil are some of the most extreme in the world. Brazil's Gini coefficient (a measure of income inequality according to which the closer it approximates 1.0, the more concentration of income exists) is one of the highest in the world at 0.63. This figure is higher, for example, than the comparable figures for South Africa and India.[6] Brazil's inequalities also have a racial and regional dimension, as in the Northeast, which has a much larger percentage of blacks and mulattoes than other areas, the average life expectancy is seventeen years shorter, adult literacy 33 percent lower, and GDP per capita 40 percent lower than in the South (United Nations Development Programme 1994, 99).

Brazil's inequalities are reflected in other statistics as well. In 1996, the Brazilian government announced that 30 percent of the population, or almost 50 million people, did not have birth certificates and thus lacked a legal existence. The chief reason for not having the document was lack of money—the certificates cost an average of 15 reais (then about US$ 15). José Gregori, then the national secretary for human rights, called the birth certificate "the inaugural act of citizenship" and declared that the existence of such a large number of "noncitizens" was "unacceptable in a serious country at the end of the twentieth century."[7]

The prospects for the rule of law and democracy under such conditions have been characterized as quite limited by some of Brazil's leading social theorists. Brazilian philosopher Marilena Chauí writes that Brazil's is a "verticalized and hierarchized" society "in which social relations are always realized either in the form of complicity (when the social subjects recognize each other as equals) or in the form of orders and obedience between a superior and an inferior." Thus, the idea of "equality of rights and the juridical equality of citizens" does not exist (Chauí 1994, 27).[8]

The analysis of Brazilian anthropologist Roberto Da Matta leads to a similar conclusion. He asserts that the same cordiality and conviviality that delight foreign visitors to Brazil, and that are often more muted in societies such as the United States, produce personal exceptions to every rule. Brazilian sociability in all its various manifestations, the agglutinative material that frequently enables society to function despite the breakdown of formal institutions, is based on a corporative and personalistic rationality that defies the application of a cold, blind justice. Laws are so abundant, changeable, and complex that to actually survive, one cannot obey them—one must have recourse to the *jeitinho,* the trick or maneuver, the drawing on personal favors or exceptions. At the same time, Brazilians have an exaggerated hope that law can produce social change—if one day the laws are obeyed (Da Matta 1978, 184–85).

Analysts of Brazil's criminal justice system note the same asymmetries and dilemmas in its functioning as do Chauí and Da Matta in their observations of Brazilian society as a whole. Scholars note that criminal law in Brazil creates special conditions of imprisonment for a large number of citizens, such as state officials, university graduates, the military, members of the clergy, and trade union leaders (Skidmore 1988, 302; Kant de Lima 1995, 245). Roberto Kant de Lima argues that Brazilian legal culture has its roots in pre-Republican, hierarchical conceptions of society, which has created an inquisitorial style of treatment of criminal suspects. He argues that Brazil has no universal system of applying laws; different rules are expected for distinct layers of citizens and laws are not enforced between distinct classes but only internally, among peers (Kant de Lima 1995, 244–46).

The nonuniversal application of law gives rise to what might be called "elitist liberalism," a policy that justifies the granting of rights on a particularistic basis.[9] This policy contrasts with the policies of other political cultures, such as that of Argentina discussed in Guillermo O'Donnell (1984), where belief in and expressions of social equality are more widespread and deeply rooted. Elitist liberalism renders attempts to control the state's application of violence particularly problematic: If some people "deserve" more protection of their rights than others, how do societal actors know when the state has gone too far? If the state's application of law has always been nonuniversal, how can its agents be controlled and held accountable to the electorate?

Historically, elitist liberalism has been reinforced by the application of state coercion in a stable and predictable manner. State violence against the poor or "torturable" classes did not generally evoke widespread condemnation from more privileged members of society because it was not seen as a potential threat to their own persons and property; indeed, it was often done in defense of the latter. State coercion, then, reflected and reinforced deep divisions within the population and generally did not evoke reactions of solidarity on the part of "civil society" against the state. Such a pattern seemed to hold sway in Brazil until the early 1970s, when popular mobilizations against the military regime installed in 1964 appeared to change the relationship of state coercion to civil society.

The Struggle for the Collective Memory of Those Killed and Disappeared

The military regime created after a coup d'etat in 1964 changed the rules surrounding the application of state coercion in Brazil. Although the Brazilian state had long repressed the poor, the socially marginal, and selected political opponents (Pinheiro 1991), the military regime oversaw an enormous increase in the coercive capabilities of the state. This increase took the form of a centrally coordinated security apparatus, with expanded intelligence and repressive powers, accompanied by a national security ideology that broadened the definition of political opposition.

By the early 1970s, the regime had subjected thousands of political activists to brutal treatment on its military bases and in its police stations and prisons. After this experience, many activists placed new value on human rights. A variety of groups came together to press for amnesty for political prisoners and the exiled, and the movement, which made use of extensive transnational linkages, gathered momentum in the second half of the 1970s. The key umbrella organization that protected and fostered this movement was the Catholic Church, and specific organizations included the Church's commissions for peace and justice *(comissões de justiça e paz)*, the National Bishops' Commission (Conferência Nacional dos Bispos do Brasil, CNBB), and the Brazilian Commission for Amnesty (Comissão Brasileira de Anistia).

Perhaps the most important of these organizations was the São Paulo Commission for Peace and Justice (Comissão de Justiça e Paz, CJP), founded in 1972 and headed by Archbishop Dom Paulo Evaristo Arns (Pope 1985, 431). The São Paulo CJP became the spearhead of the Church's human rights campaign in Brazil and one of the few associations with the resources, will, and moral authority to challenge the military regime on particular cases of human rights abuse. Its directors were mostly prominent, middle-class members of the liberal professions, but the CJP also included representatives of the student and trade union movements, both prime targets of regime repression at that time. Many of these original members went on to play important roles in the debates over human rights and the problem of state violence in the 1980s and 1990s. They included Hélio Bicudo, who became a congressman for the Workers' Party (Partido dos Trabalhadores, PT) and was active on the issue of police reform; José Gregori, secretary for human rights in the government of Fernando Henrique Cardoso; and Dalmo Dallari, a law professor and advocate of judicial reform (Pope 1985, 433).

In the mid-1970s, for a number of reasons, which included the pressure of human rights groups, the military regime embarked on a policy of gradual and controlled political liberalization, known in its later stages as the *abertura* ("opening"). A significant step in this process was the 1979 amnesty law (Law Number 6,683 of August, 28, 1979) that set the parameters for subsequent debates about retroactive justice.[10] The amnesty applied to both sides of the political conflicts of the 1960s and 1970s: to political prisoners and exiles, whose release and return caused celebrations among opponents of the regime, and to members of the security forces who had engaged in killing and torture. By granting immunity from prosecution to the latter, the 1979 law helped secure the adherence of the majority of the armed forces and police to the *abertura*.

Like the Chilean self-amnesty and unlike the Argentine, Brazil's amnesty was not subsequently overturned. Nor did the return to a civilian regime in 1985 result in the swift establishment of a truth commission to delve into human rights abuses, as occurred with the Sábato commission in Argentina and the Rettig commission in Chile. In the words of Congressman Bicudo, "The great error of the amnesty was to place a smokescreen in front of the repression."[11] Equally important, the amnesty diminished the strength of the cross-class alliance against state violence represented by the São Paulo CJP. The 1979 law restored the human rights of political opponents of the military regime but did not offer protection to those in the lower classes still suffering from police violence and predation. In the words of the president of the São Paulo CJP in 1981–1982, José Gregori, in post-1979 Brazil there was an urgent need for the "verticalization of the abertura, in the sense of extending its gains to the marginalized sectors also" (Pope 1985, 444). This process of verticalization is still incomplete.

Brazil witnessed no movement for truth about the killed and disappeared comparable in influence to the *madres de la plaza* ("mothers of the plaza") in Argentina and Chile. In those two countries, the *madres* publicly protested the silence that surrounded the disappearance of their family members under military rule, even before the democratic transitions had been completed in 1983 and 1990, respectively, and came to symbolize the desire of many people in their nations for justice after years of arbitrary state terror and repression. The fact that there was no such movement in Brazil may be owing in part to the fact that the Brazilian military regime had retained a much more extensive legal façade and made a much stronger claim for the "normalcy" of its repression than had its Argentine and Chilean counterparts.[12] Most of the repression in Brazil had come, furthermore, not at the moment of the founding of the regime (as in the other two cases), but after a four-year period of authoritarian consolidation that included the creation of a new legal structure.

The military regime's legalistic rationalization of much of its repression may ultimately have failed to gain it widespread legitimacy, but it did contribute to the maintenance of the passive acquiescence of much of the population for a long time and the cloaking of state violence with a mantle of due process. Paradoxically, this legalism made the struggle for the rule of law after the democratic transition more difficult in that it contributed to a lack of urgency about the need for changes in the legal system.[13]

It might be thought that the fact that people had disappeared was simply not a major issue in Brazil,[14] but this conclusion would be somewhat misleading. Many of their relatives were unsatisfied by the blanket amnesty for the security forces, which they felt encouraged impunity and amnesia. A network of groups established on a statewide basis—such as Torture Never Again (Tortura Nunca Mais) and the Commissions of the Relatives of the Dead and Disappeared (Comissões de Familiares dos Mortos e Desaparecidos), supported by international NGOs such as Americas Watch and Amnesty International—kept the issue alive in the 1980s. In addition, some of the families of the disappeared initiated legal actions against the federal government to discover the whereabouts of their family members. Their demands were that the government locate the bodies of the disappeared, supply death certificates, make the deaths official, and pay compensation to the families of the victims.[15]

Progress on the issue was slow owing to the polarization of positions on both sides. Relatives and friends of the disappeared, some of whom had themselves engaged in guerrilla operations against the regime, claimed to represent the best traditions of the nation, an idealistic and courageous resistance to a tyrannical regime. The military, for its part, argued that it had defeated a ruthless and subversive enemy of order in a patriotic and selfless struggle to defend the majority of Brazilians.

For reformers, the advantages of doing something rather than nothing about the disappeared were threefold. First, the issue was the initial test of a legal system and a judiciary that had been seriously compromised by authoritarian rule, one that was unwilling to investigate or protest massive and systematic human rights violations. Some retroactive justice, if only to atone for past wrongdoing and to restore the possibility of the rule of law, was necessary (B. Santos, Marques, and Pedroso 1996, 46). Second, some human rights advocates stressed the strategic dimension of the struggle: that a thorough investigation into past human rights abuses could lead to the dissemination of information about what happened and increase the probability that such atrocities would not happen again.[16] Third, and probably most important, the issue was of great symbolic value. What was at stake in this debate was the Brazilians' collective memory of the military regime, and the human rights groups were trying to construct a critical memory that could serve as the basis for a new kind of society that genuinely respected human rights.

It has been argued that the Brazilian military won the battle against its armed and unarmed opponents in the 1960s and 1970s but lost the war of the nation's collective memory. This, at least, is the view frequently expressed by members of the military themselves (D'Araújo, Soares, and Castro 1994, 13). However, judging by the time it took to investigate the disappeared after the transition, it would seem that the Brazilian military regime has done better in the battle for collective memory than its counterparts in Argentina and perhaps even Chile.

Demands for an accounting did occur after the military withdrew to the barracks. The first salvo was fired immediately after the transition in 1985 with the publication of the book *Brasil: Nunca mais* (Brazil: Never again). The book, which became a best-seller,[17] was the result of a secret, five-year investigation of human rights abuses under the military conducted by researchers operating out of the Catholic Church in São Paulo. The book contained an appendix listing the names of 125 people who had allegedly been disappeared by the security forces (Arquidiocese de São Paulo 1985, 291–93). The book's publication in the first year of the new democratic regime served as a reminder that certain segments of the population would not forget the military regime's repression and desired to use that memory to demand some sort of accounting and atonement from the state.

The demand for justice for the victims of state violence was strongly rejected in some quarters, and two books by members of the military quickly followed the publication of *Brasil: Nunca mais.* Marco Pollo Giordani's 1986 volume *Brasil: Sempre* (Brazil: Forever) is an explicit attack on the human rights book that begins with a chapter on the treachery of the Brazilian Communist Party's failed 1935 uprising in Brazil. It denies that torture was routinely used by the military regime and contains a list of military and civilians killed by the forces of "subversion" between 1964 and 1985. Carlos Alberto Brilhante Ustra's 1987 work *Rompendo o silencio* (Breaking the Silence) contains a chapter entitled "Terrorism: Never Again," an explicit rebuttal of *Nunca mais,* and an introduction by a former minister of the army extolling those members of the military who had fought against "agitators and terrorists."[18]

Despite the counterattacks against it, *Nunca mais's* meticulously documented main point—that the military regime had systematically tortured and killed opponents, most of them unarmed civilians—gained widespread exposure in the mainstream media. Nonetheless, no action was taken to initiate an official investigation of these crimes under the first civilian government of José Sarney, who himself had been an enthusiastic supporter of the military regime. The 1988 constitution did include a legal innovation called *habeas data,* which established the right of Brazilian citizens to request copies of all information on them kept in government files.[19] However, because of concerns about privacy, the framers of the constitution restricted the language of this provision to cover only those persons wanting information about themselves. The barrier to investigation of the cases of the disappeared—the noncooperation of the military, police, and intelligence authorities who retained records that might reveal their fates—thus remained untouched by this provision (Rosenn 1990, 795).

Some efforts to facilitate investigations were made at the state and municipal levels. In the late 1980s, the Workers' Party administration in the city of São Paulo, and that of the Partido Democrático Trabalhista (PDT) in the city and state of Rio de Janeiro, allowed organizations representing families of the disappeared increased access to archives of the *Institutos Médicos Legais,* state institutions that, among other things, issue death certificates. This access gave these organizations more information and, in São Paulo, resulted in the 1990 uncovering of a mass grave for indigents that contained the remains of six of those who had disappeared.[20]

Action at the federal level was slow as the presidency passed from Sarney to another politician who had supported military rule, Fernando Collor de Mello. Nonetheless, under Collor, a small step toward truth telling was taken in 1991 when the federal government sent the archives of the political police, or Departamento de Ordem Política e Social (Department of Political and Social Order, DOPS), back to the states of Rio and São Paulo. These archives, which had been held in Brasília by the federal police since the

DOPS was disbanded in 1982, provided some additional information to families of the disappeared. DOPS archives were opened to the public in the states of Minas Gerais, Paraná, Pernambuco, Rio de Janeiro, and São Paulo.

The real breakthrough came after the inauguration of President Fernando Henrique Cardoso in January 1995. Cardoso was the first elected Brazilian president since the transition who had been an opponent of the military regime—he had lost his professorship at the University of São Paulo for political reasons and had spent several years in exile. Several of his closest advisers and ministers had also been considered politically suspect by the security forces, as the newly opened DOPS archives revealed.[21] Symbolically, the inauguration of the Cardoso administration represented a reconciliation of the forces that had opposed one another during the years of repression: Cardoso's vice president, Marco Maciel, had his start in politics in the 1964 coup and had remained a staunch supporter of the military regime until its end.

By the end of Cardoso's first year in office, a law had been passed that enacted the recommendations of the earlier congressional committee (Law Number 9,140 of December 4, 1995). The law established the Special Commission on the Political Killed and Disappeared (Comissão Especial dos Mortos e Desaparecidos Políticos) to investigate the disappeared, recognized that 136 people had been killed by the security forces, and invited relatives of others believed to have disappeared to present their evidence to the commission. The affected families were required to supply the commission with a letter that claimed, or documents that showed (one) that the person had died a nonnatural death; (two) that the death had occurred in a state facility or similar environment between the years covered by the 1979 amnesty (September 2, 1961–August 15, 1979); and (three) that the person had a history of involvement with a political organization. A publicity campaign advertised the existence of the commission and the opportunity that it represented to the families of those who had been killed or had disappeared.

The seven-person commission—which included a representative of the relatives of the disappeared, a deputy from Congress's human rights committee,[22] and a member of the armed forces—was instructed to (one) study the cases of disappearance and killing brought before it and to vote on whether or not the state was responsible; (two) recommend the issuance of official death certificates for those people proved to be dead; (three) compensate victims' families for the disappearances and killings for which the state was responsible; and (four) try to locate the remains of victims in those cases where some evidence of possible burial sites existed. The commission made substantial progress on the first two points in 1996–1998, replacing official lies with more accurate histories in many cases. By August 1998, the commission had examined 366 cases (including the original 136 listed in the bill that created the commission), recognized 280 individuals as having been killed or disappeared under the military regime, and indemnified family members in 265 of those cases.[23]

A number of factors are relevant in explaining why the commission was created when it was. The passage of time after 1985 had probably weakened the credibility of the military's intransigent opposition to an investigation of the disappeared and favored the arguments of the international and domestic groups advocating some kind of accounting.[24] President Cardoso, for his part, had a political history that indicated some sympathy for the reformers, and his strong electoral mandate gave him the needed political leverage to sponsor the law that created the commission. Finally, the advocates of reform were aided both by the development of earlier, nongovernmental truth investigations, the most important of which was *Brasil: Nunca mais* and by the powerful demonstration effect of foreign truth commissions. Beginning in the early 1970s, the truth commission had become part of an internationally recognized repertoire for dealing with state crimes, and such commissions had been established in about twenty countries (Garton Ash 1998, 35). Established in Argentina, Chile, South Africa, and El Salvador before its creation in Brazil, the truth commission offered the catharsis of revelation and the satisfaction of seeing atonement even when prosecution of the people responsible for the crimes was impossible.

In Brazil, the commission's work in investigating the cases of those killed and disappeared under the military regime was a step forward toward democratic consolidation. For the first time, the state recognized responsibility for the crimes of the past, and that recognition made the future realization of the rule of law more likely by clearing away the smokescreen of silence and impunity that shrouded the past acts of state violence.

For most ordinary Brazilians, however, the violence of the past is of far less pressing concern than the violence of the present. The police force in one Brazilian state, São Paulo, was officially reported to have killed 1,470 people in a single year, 1992 (Chevigny 1995, 148)—more than three times the highest estimate of the number of politically killed and disappeared in the whole country during twenty-one years of military rule.[25] Clearly, police violence casts a long shadow on the promise of democracy in Brazil.

Restraining Police Violence

> *Em cada morro uma história diferente*
> *Que a polícia mata gente inocente*
> *E quem era inocente hoje já virou bandido*
> *Pra poder comer um pedaço de pão todo fodido.*
> *(On each hill a different story*
> *That the police kill innocent people*

And who was innocent is a bandit today
So he can eat a fucked-up piece of bread.)

—Chico Science, "Banditismo por uma questão de classe"
(Banditry for Reasons of Class)

Control of those state institutions that wield coercive power, both by other state institutions and by civil society, affects the exercise of citizenship. The literature on democratic consolidation has devoted considerable attention to civil-military relations at the elite level as well as such matters as the prevention of military coup attempts and the reduction of military autonomy. In general, however, there is insufficient attention in the literature to the issue of the democratic control of everyday forms of state coercion, by which I mean routine policing, intelligence work, and military operations that do not involve the seizure of the executive or the shutting down of other branches of government. Over time, changes in practices in these realms have the potential for "hollowing out" democratic regimes from within through the gradual expansion of the budgets, functions, and autonomy of the coercive institutions that engage in them. The recent heavy increase in the role of the Mexican and Colombian militaries in the interdiction of drug trafficking is an example of this process.

The killings involving the police in Brazil pose the threat of just such a hollowing out of democracy. When levels of societal violence are high, it is likely that the police will kill in the line of duty. But in Brazil, the failure of the courts to fairly and efficiently discriminate between legitimate self-defense and summary execution—and to punish the latter—has created a situation of widespread impunity. This impunity has enabled the wielders of everyday coercion to make subjects of citizens on a regular basis.

There are two main types of police forces engaged in the application of everyday coercion in the country. These are the plainclothes civilian police, in charge of criminal investigation, and the uniformed military police (*polícia militar*, or PMs), who share some similarities with French gendarmes, Italian carabinieri, and Spanish civil guards and are responsible for patrolling the streets. It is the violence of the military police that I shall concentrate on. The PMs are state forces under the nominal control of the state governors but integrated, as the name implies, into the armed forces. The result is a system of dual control in which important decisions about police training, equipment, and policies toward civilians are made by the military.

The PMs' violence became a major public issue as the result of a series of brutal massacres that have occurred since 1990. In October 1992, 111 prisoners were killed by military police in the São Paulo prison of Carandiru. In July 1993, seven street children were gunned down by PMs outside the Candelária Cathedral in Rio de Janeiro. In August of the same year, twenty-three residents of the Rio de Janeiro favela Vigário Geral were shot and killed by military police. Massacres have also taken place in rural areas. Eleven landless people were killed by military police in Corumbiara, Rondônia, in August 1995, and in Eldorado de Carajás, Pará, nineteen landless demonstrators were massacred by military police in April 1996. These incidents, reported around the world by the global media, are the visible manifestations of social conflicts that take place daily in Brazil's urban peripheries and rural areas.

It is important to put the killings in context. Both the victims and the perpetrators, the lower rank and file (*soldados* or *praças*) of the police, often share the same lower-class background and nonwhite identity. The terrain on which they meet is likely to resemble a zone of low-intensity warfare. In the peripheries of large cities, bands of drug traffickers provide well-armed young men with lucrative but often short careers. They engage in conflict with competing bands and the PMs, who are formally responsible for the daunting task of suppressing the traffic. In the countryside, a powerful and growing movement of the landless—with the slogan, "Occupy, Resist, Produce"—organizes land occupations on the part of the rural poor that often meet with violent resistance on the part of the affected landowners. It is the military police who are sent in to enforce "order" in those situations. Urban drug trafficking and rural land occupations are not the only social situations to which police violence has been a response, but they form the backdrop of many of the most egregious instances of that violence.

Interpretations of contemporary police violence vary. Some people think it reflects an overall increase in the level of violence in Brazilian society. By 1992, Brazil had a murder rate about twice that of the United States, itself no stranger to violence,[26] and by 1998, the state had lost any pretense of possessing a monopoly on legitimate force—it was estimated that private security guards greatly outnumber the almost 400,000 military police in the country.[27] As the country urbanized in the 1960s and 1970s, traditional forms of social control, such as patron-client relations, unraveled. The lack of proper jobs for the urban poor, the pervasiveness of consumerism, and the illegitimacy and corruption of political institutions influenced a generation of bandits "for reasons of class," young men ready to use violence to gain access to the goods denied them by the market economy. The police, charged by the upper and middle classes with the task of protecting them from the bandits, have responded with violence of their own.

Other analysts recognize these developments but correctly insist that much of the police brutality can be traced back to the military regime. After 1967, the state police forces were placed under the command of army generals and brought into the war against "subversion," and civilian police forces, who engaged in noninvestigatory policing, were made a part of the PMs.[28] The PM operations were reorganized to fit a militarized conception of public security (Pinheiro 1996b, 27; Mesquita Neto 1997, 9), and the investigatory capacities of the plainclothes civilian police were relatively neglected.[29] The PMs' view of the citizenry was essentially repressive, and civilian suspects were often viewed as enemies—with U.S. training and influence playing a role in the development of this attitude.[30]

Furthermore, a rigid hierarchy within the military police results in a treatment of enlisted men by officers that some critics characterize as brutal and demeaning. Officers, who in most states earn ten to twenty times more than their subordinates,[31] can punish the enlisted men for a variety of offenses in the barracks. In the words of one analyst, "The inequality and authoritarianism within the police has reproduced and reinforced . . . the inequality and authoritarianism within Brazilian society" (Mesquita Neto 1997, 6). However, this strict internal control is not maintained on the streets, where patrols are usually commanded by sergeants, and the sense of humiliation and subjugation that some of the enlisted members of the police feel is often channeled into aggressive displays of power in the subduing of civilians. In the words of a São Paulo prosecutor, "The internal violence of the corporation comes out when the PMs deal with the public."[32]

Just as the boundaries of the political conflict over the investigation of the disappeared were shaped by the 1979 amnesty, the struggle to curb police violence was constrained by another act of the military regime. In 1977–1978, the government of Ernesto Geisel conducted a maneuver to protect the military police from civilian control. As part of a more general reform, jurisdiction for military police crimes against civilians (committed in the course of their duties or with police equipment) was transferred from civilian courts to state military police courts (Mesquita Neto 1997, 8).[33] These latter courts consisted of one civilian judge and four members of the military police.

As the issue of police violence gained in public visibility in the 1990s, human rights activists began to criticize the operation of the state military courts and to demand that civilian courts once again be granted jurisdiction over police abuses of civilians. The state military courts were found to be adequate mechanisms for the punishment of internal infractions by the police—such as insubordination, neglect of duty, and corruption—but in cases in which PMs had killed or beaten civilians, impunity was common, for the military police who judged these cases tended to give the benefit of the doubt to their fellow policemen. One study of a court in Pernambuco, for example, shows that the higher the rank of the military police officer, the less likely he was to be convicted (Zaverucha 1996). The courts were also very slow, with some cases taking up to ten years to resolve while the accused member of the PM continued his regular duties. Finally, in those relatively rare cases of PM violence against civilians in which the police were convicted, some violation of the complex procedural requirements was often invoked by the courts in order to suspend the sentences.[34]

The debate over the state military justice system and its apparent inability to constrain police violence heated up in the wake of massacres at Carandiru, Candelária, Eldorado de Carajás, and elsewhere. Defenders of the status quo accused the human rights reformers of having a hidden agenda. In demanding that cases of police human rights abuses against civilians be transferred to civilian courts in the short-term, the defenders alleged that what the reformers really wanted was to civilianize the military police for political purposes.

As members of the military, military police cannot form unions; civilian police can, and the latter could form a support base for the leftist parties to which most of the human rights activists belong. Furthermore, argued the traditionalists, civilian courts would not necessarily be more capable of punishing police violence than the state military courts because the civilian court system is overburdened and because Brazilian juries might be reluctant to convict policemen accused of killing people with criminal records.[35] Finally, it was argued that the civilian Ministério Público (Attorney General's Office) already had the constitutional right to monitor any investigation carried out within the military police and that in most states, the court of appeals above state military justice was civilian. Civilian oversight of state military justice was therefore already adequate.

For their part, many of the reformers agreed that their eventual goal was to civilianize the police force, but they asserted that they wanted to do so, not for party political reasons, but to promote human rights. They saw the reduction of military control over the police force as important for the consolidation of democracy (for this argument, see Stepan 1988, 96). Furthermore, some of them argued that the main issue was not that the civilian courts would be more punitive than the state military courts but that the civilian courts would be more legitimate because they would end what amounted to self-policing by the PMs and subject the police to a more rigorous form of external control. In addition, the reformers doubted that the civilian courts would allow as much impunity as the state military justice system.

The first round of this debate was ended in August 1996 when a compromise bill amending the jurisdiction of the state military courts was signed by President Cardoso. At the same time that the special commission was studying cases of the killed and disappeared, the government passed a law that took all cases of intentional homicide *(homicídio doloso)* by the military police against civilians out of the jurisdiction of the state military courts and put them into the purview of their civilian counterparts.[36] Policemen accused of killing in the line of duty would no longer be tried in their own PM courts but would have to face civilian judges and juries. Reformers hailed the decision as small but significant progress toward the rule of law. They also recognized that the step was incomplete, and a bill to remove cases alleging bodily injury *(lesões corporais)* of civilians by police from the state military justice system was soon introduced in Congress.

Because state coercion has generally been predictable and selective, wide social inequalities have separated citizens, and the ideology and practice of elitist liberalism has been pervasive; the assumption that citizens will protest the abuse of others' rights for fear they might be victimized themselves has not held in Brazil. However, certain recent changes may be altering this situation. Well-publicized incidents in which the police abused "ordinary citizens" have increased, suggesting to many people that police violence has become increasingly out of control and is spreading beyond the confines of the urban and rural periphery.[37] This concern may have given higher-status individuals an incentive to push for greater controls over the police in their own self-interest.[38] In addition, police strikes in June and July 1997, which were marked by armed confrontations between the police and the military in some cities, stimulated the search for viable reforms of the public security system in Congress and the executive branch.[39] Such incidents have also apparently persuaded much of the public that carrots as well as sticks are necessary for improved police performance and that the police should be paid more if they are to adequately protect society.[40]

The sense of a police crisis in Brazil could also help harmonize different views of the problem. Middle-class human rights activists have often pointed to the violations of the rights of criminal suspects, leading some people to charge that the activists defend "bandits." Other people, especially lower-class victims of criminals, are often principally concerned with the absence, inefficiency, or predation of the police, which can lead them to feel abandoned by the state and to participate in acts of vigilantism. Both police failures—to respect the procedural rights of suspects and to respect and defend poor communities—can be attributed to the same problem, an inadequate police force.

The dynamics of self-interested strategic action are unlikely, on their own, to lead to successful reforms in the way police forces are managed. Attempting to control the police through legal sanctions alone would also reflect something of the exaggerated hope in law observed by Da Matta because many middle- and upper-class individuals are likely to continue to pursue privatized security strategies—to hire their own security services and opt out of the debate about the performance of the state sector. Furthermore, police on the streets have wide discretion in their use of force, and reforms that rely exclusively on their fear of being caught and punished are unlikely to be sufficient. Finally, because not all citizens see police violence as harmful to society—many would prefer a "hard line" to deter criminals—an increased willingness on their part to protest police transgressions must come primarily from a change in values.

For this reason, state efforts to inculcate normative adherence to human rights among the police and citizens are important and likely to have an impact. The discussions surrounding the 1988 constitution, which amply recognizes human rights (see especially Title II, Chapter 1, Article 5), may have increased societal awareness of the importance of human rights and lowered public tolerance of police abuses. The 1996 promulgation of the National Program for Human Rights under President Cardoso, which was supposed to have a similar effect (Brazil, Presidência da República 1996b),[41] mandated the creation of specific educational programs within police forces and communities.

Some evidence suggests that training and educational programs can be effective in curbing police transgressions.[42] The state of São Paulo, for example, officially reported that military police killings fell from 1,450 in 1992 to 402 in 1993, 519 in 1994, 618 in 1995, 398 in 1996, 435 in 1997, and 204 in the first five months of 1998 (Mesquita Neto 1998, 32) without any legal change having been made. The continuing drop was attributed to new training in human rights and community policing (Chevigny 1995, 178).[43] Grassroots programs of legal education have also been created, although the awareness of legal rights on the part of many among the marginalized population is still very low and it is probably too early to gauge the impact of these programs.[44] What these various approaches indicate is that the 1996 law changing the jurisdiction of military police courts is likely to represent one encounter in a much larger struggle, one involving a variety of proposed institutional reforms, to make the police in Brazil more accountable.

Conclusion

The concept of the rule of law contains within it the ideal of full equality of citizenship. This ideal has not been fully realized in any actually existing democratic polity, but some polities come closer to it than others. Despite the creation of a formally democratic regime and two broadly inclusive and competitive presidential elections in 1989 and 1994, Brazil's political practices fall shorter of the ideal than those of Argentina, Chile, and Uruguay. The Brazilian transition took place in the context of extreme socioeconomic inequality, state coercive institutions that were either not effectively controlled by the state and/or were in alliance with private forces (landowners, merchants), the existence of a high degree of coercive force in private hands, and pervasive practices of elitist liberalism. Thus, especially in rural, frontier, and peripheral urban areas, a fundamental attribute of democracy—the protection of citizens from arbitrary acts by the state—is often missing, and a vital public good—security—is not provided to all people (Przeworski 1995, 39). The situation has led some observes to characterize Brazil as a democracy with "low intensity citizenship" (O'Donnell 1993, 1361) or even "without citizenship" (Pinheiro 1996a, 17).

Reducing state violence has been made difficult by various aspects of Brazil's past. Brazil's social structure and political practices contain many elements that mitigate against the universal application of laws and rules. Also, the Brazilian military regime made particularly strenuous efforts to cloak its repression in the mantle of normalcy and legality, so that a sense of urgency in dealing with the question of state coercion was lacking after the transition to civilian rule. However, neither of these legacies is necessarily an insurmountable barrier to political reform.

In this chapter I have focused on two such reforms, one involving the investigation of the disappeared under military rule and the other the legal prosecution of alleged human rights violations by the police. The first reform was made easier by the existence of an internationally recognized institution, the truth commission, to deal with past crimes by the state. Through this commission, the state for the first time acknowledged responsibility for killings carried out by agents of the military regime. However, because the measure's mandate restricts compensation to the families of a small number of mostly middle-class political activists, it does not challenge the elitist liberalism that has traditionally characterized the provision of justice in Brazil.

The 1996 measure subjecting military police accused of killing civilians to civilian courts and jury trials, on the other hand, represents a first step in what could be a far broader change. Although on its own the measure is unlikely to have a major impact on the problem of uncontrolled police violence in the country, it does begin to dismantle the corporate protections that have insulated the police from democratic accountability. Further reforms currently being discussed in Brazil, including eliminating special courts for the military police altogether, merging the civilian and military police into one civilian force, and paying the police higher salaries, might also contribute to the creation of a more egalitarian administration of justice.

For a long time, analyses of new democracies have been dominated by a preoccupation with their stability. One scholar writes that many democracies coexist with high levels of arbitrary state violence and then adds that although democracy "will not be as pretty as constitution writers have wished it to be . . . at least, under some conditions, it can last" (Przeworski 1996, 20). It may be, however, that an increasing number of Brazilians are unsatisfied with this type of democracy and are considering the quality, and not just the stability, of their democracy. They are hoping that their "ugly" democracy can be made more beautiful.

TWELVE

A New Brazil?
The Changing Sociodemographic Context of Brazilian Democracy

Timothy J. Power and J. Timmons Roberts

nderstanding politics requires attention to social structure. As simple and intuitive as this observation may be, it has too often been overlooked in recent analyses of democratization.[1] Single-country studies of political change—of which this volume is an example—have an understandable tendency to become wrapped up in actors, institutions, and political processes and to disregard social and demographic factors altogether. This tendency appears premised on the assumption that one can always treat political factors as variables while holding social-structural factors constant. This assumption, more often than not, is erroneous—particularly so in the case of Brazil, a nation of extraordinary diversity and dynamism.

To appreciate this point, a brief comparison of political and social change is in order. Since World War II, Brazil has had three distinct political regimes: the democratic regime of 1946–1964, the military-authoritarian regime of 1964–1985, and the regime that is the subject of this volume, the democratic New Republic that began in 1985. Each has spawned a major literature, and studies of Brazilian politics are replete with comparisons, both explicit and implicit, among the three regimes. What these comparisons often fail to note is that these three political regimes existed in three fundamentally different social contexts. Table 1.1 documents these contexts with a broad brush, comparing 1955, 1975, and 1995. These dates were not chosen arbitrarily but, rather, represent convenient measurement points in recent political history. The years 1955 and 1975 represent the precise midpoints of the first democratic republic and the military regime, respectively. The year

1995 represents the tenth anniversary of the New Republic. Coincidentally, these dates also correspond rather closely to the rise to power of the dominant president in each of the three regimes: Juscelino Kubitschek (elected 1955), General Ernesto Geisel (inaugurated 1974), and Fernando Henrique Cardoso (inaugurated 1995).

Looking at the data in Table 12.1, a social scientist from Mars might reasonably wonder whether presidents Kubitschek, Geisel, and Cardoso governed the same country. Comparing only the two democratic regimes, one sees that the first, initiated in 1946, governed a nation that was predominantly rural, where a majority of workers labored in agriculture or mining, in which only a quarter of the citizens could vote, which depended on one product for more than half of its export earnings, and where television was accessible only to the wealthiest of families in large cities. The current democratic regime, initiated in 1985, operates in a country that is nearly 80 percent urbanized, where more than half of workers are in the service sector, in which three-fifths of the population is enfranchised, which has an extraordinarily diversified economy, and in which four-fifths of the households have television. The two democratic regimes were bridged by a military dictatorship that suspended political freedoms while presiding over revolutionary changes in the social and productive structures of Brazil.

The data in Table 12.1 provide only a rudimentary sketch of postwar social change, and we return to many of these same variables later in the chapter, but nevertheless, the data are sufficient to demonstrate that the three postwar political regimes existed in three different social contexts. It is

Table 12.1

Selected Indicators of Social Change in Brazil, 1955, 1975, 1995

Indicator	1955	1975	1995
Population	61 million	105 million	155 million
Percent Urban	41	62	79
Percent Illiterate (>5 years old)	52	37	22
Life Expectancy at Birth (in years)	50	62	67
Voters as Percentage of Population	24	35	62
Workers in Agriculture, Mining (%)	56	37	26
Workers in Services (%)	29	42	54
Coffee as Percent of			
Merchandise Exports	55	17	6
Households with Television (%)	1	40	81

Note: Figures are approximations; 1955 and 1975 values are mostly linear interpolations from decennial censuses.
Sources: Faria (1983, 120); IBGE (1993, 1995–1996, 1996); W. Santos, Monteiro, Caillaux (1990); Wood and Carvalho (1988, 87).

evident that no analysis of the conditions for democratic sustainability in Brazil can be complete without an adequate exploration of the sociodemographic changes since 1985.

This chapter conducts such an exploration, for three primary reasons. First, while other chapters in this volume analyze the "actors" in late twentieth-century Brazilian democracy, we must not neglect the "stage" on which politics is played out: social structure. A comprehensive appraisal of any regime requires attention to actors, institutions, processes, and structure. Second, we examine sociodemographic change to caution against inappropriate comparisons between the New Republic and the regimes that preceded it. When one is abstractly debating the social underpinnings of politics or the prospects for democratic consolidation in Brazil, it is reasonable to ask, Which Brazil? The Brazil of 1998 is very different from the one that witnessed the first steps toward liberalization and meaningful political competition at the end of the 1970s. Third, and most important, in sketching certain social and demographic features of contemporary Brazil, we propose to evaluate their positive or negative implications for the sustainability of political democracy.

It was not easy to choose which specific sociodemographic variables should be included in this democracy-centered review. Choosing only areas in which significant change has occurred might bias our results in a "positive" direction, portraying Brazil as increasingly hospitable to sustainable democracy. Likewise, choosing only areas in which little change has occurred (e.g., poverty and inequality) might promote the opposite bias, perhaps even veer into a sociological determinism that would predict a future democratic breakdown. Thus, we ultimately opted for a set of selection criteria that direct attention to both continuity and change and that have undisputed macropolitical significance.

The criteria led us to isolate seven core issue-areas for sociodemographic analysis, with some selected because of their novelty in the postauthoritarian era and some because they represent perennial problem areas for Brazil in which (relatively) little change has taken place since 1985. These core areas are the expansion of the electorate, the acceleration of urbanization, the rise of the informal labor market, the persistence of social inequality, the ongoing challenges of education and literacy, the rapidly increasing density of civil society, and the rise and oligopolization of television. Though the variables encompass both change and continuity, what links all of them together is that they have all impacted the kind of political system that has taken shape in Brazil since 1985. After reviewing these important sociodemographic issue-areas, we conclude with some cautiously optimistic reflections on the possibilities for democratic sustainability in Brazil.

Electoral Demographics: Population and Enfranchisement

Brazil has undergone tremendous demographic change since World War II. In the 1950s, high fertility boosted the population at a rate of nearly 3 percent a year, which meant the population was doubling every twenty-three years—with the urban population doubling at a rate of once every fourteen years through the 1970s. However, the situation has changed dramatically in the New Republic. Figures for 1996 from the Instituto Brasileiro de Geografia e Estatística (IBGE), the Brazilian census bureau, show that by that time, the overall population growth rate had plummeted to just 1.3 percent per year, a rate at which Brazil would double in size in fifty-four years (IBGE *Anuário* 1997; Bernardes 1997; *Folha de São Paulo* 1997c). Brazil is now therefore close to the U.S. population growth rate of 1.1 percent per year, and the Brazilian rate is expected to fall further in coming years.

Currently, Brazil's population stands at slightly over 160 million, and the IBGE is projecting that the population will stabilize at around 230 million in the year 2030. The post-1980 drop-off in population growth occurred rapidly and somewhat unexpectedly. Therefore, in coming years, the nation will have relatively little time in which to shift its social policy priorities from those of a typical Third World country—in which the population is overwhelmingly young—to those of a First World nation, which must handle the twin challenges of an aging population and a shrinking labor force. These considerations are already finding their way into the public policy debate, particularly as they regard the solvency of the social security and pension systems.

Since 1945, Brazilians have tripled in number, but the electorate has multiplied by more than twelvefold. The most rapid and far-reaching changes in enfranchisement have taken place since the end of the military regime: the national electorate expanded by more than 40 percent in the 1980s alone. Only two months into the New Republic in 1985, the National Congress granted the suffrage to illiterates for the first time in the twentieth century. With the adoption of the constitution of 1988, the voting age was lowered to sixteen, which added 2 million potential voters. The tradition of compulsory voting has been maintained: voting is mandatory except for sixteen- and seventeen-year-olds, for citizens older than seventy, and for illiterates. In sum, the expansion of the electorate has been nothing short of revolutionary both in absolute and in proportional terms: while only 16 percent of the entire population had the right to vote in 1945, over 60 percent of Brazilians were enfranchised in the mid-1990s (Fig. 12.1). The electorate is now over 100 million voters, making Brazil the world's third-largest democracy.

In terms of geographic distribution, Brazil's five distinct regions have

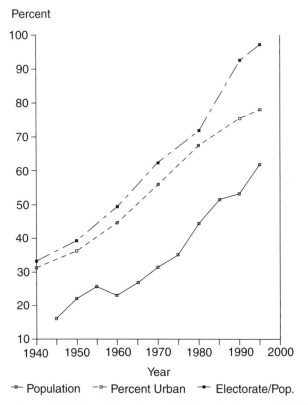

Percent

100
90
80
70
60
50
40
30
20
10

1940 1950 1960 1970 1980 1990 2000

Year

-■- Population   -□- Percent Urban   -▪- Electorate/Pop.

FIGURE 12.1 Population Growth, Urbanization, and the Expansion of the Electorate as a Percent of the Population in Brazil, 1940–1995. *Sources:* IBGE 1986, 1995, 1997

experienced dramatically different population shifts since 1945. The drought-prone and still semifeudal Northeast region had tremendously high birthrates but during much of the period was the source of out-migration to the industrial cities of the Southeast and to the Center-West and Amazon regions. Although birthrates were significantly lower in the more developed South and Southeast regions, these regions are the most populous today. In 1994, the South and Southeast together had about 61 percent of the national electorate. Among the three less-developed regions, the Northeast had about 27 percent of the voters, and the North and Center-West about 6 percent each (IBGE *Anuário* 1995).

The skewing of the national population toward the South and Southeast is not reflected in the allocation of political power. The more modern regions of the country have an advantage in presidential elections, which are national and direct, but in the distribution of legislative power, the situation is quite different. Because of a constitutional cap on the number of elected deputies per state (currently seventy) as well as the gross overrepresentation of small states in Congress, the developed regions are deprived of the political power that would be theirs in a truly proportional system. São Paulo, which contains 22 percent of the national population and produces more than 35 percent of the GDP, is restricted to 12 percent of the seats in the National Congress. In contrast, the less developed North, Northeast, and Center-West regions, which together have 41 percent of the national population and only 38 percent of the electorate, control 53.4 percent of the seats in Congress. This malapportionment has actually worsened since the end of military rule, primarily because of the creation of new states in the North.

The explosion of electoral participation in the New Republic quickly revealed some of democracy's growing pains. In the 1986, 1990, and 1994 legislative elections, the percentage of blank and spoiled ballots averaged 40 percent of all votes cast. In previous research on this phenomenon, we found that the rapid extension of suffrage combined with the maintenance of compulsory-voting legislation and the open-list variant of proportional representation combined in ways that inhibited the effective incorporation of new voters and thus facilitated an increase in invalid votes (Power and Roberts 1995).

The perception of growing voter alienation caused elite opinion to begin to swing against mandatory voting in the late 1990s. Its abolition would likely have immediate political consequences, as the effective electorate could potentially shrink by as much as a third and the new, reduced electorate would afford greater relative influence to the more urban, educated, literate, and middle-class voters. With this in mind, the record of opinion polling and election returns throughout the New Republic (e.g., J. Almeida 1996; *Folha de São Paulo* 1990; A. Singer 1990) suggests that voluntary voting would boost the performance of left and center-left parties while reducing the electoral space of populist and clientelistic candidates. Thus, the question of compulsory voting has ethical implications for future democratic development: maintaining mandatory voting is in many ways dissatisfying but abolishing it would likely privilege in electoral terms precisely those Brazilians who are already more privileged in economic and social terms (Elkins 1997).

Urbanization and "Favelization"

Brazil is now predominantly an urban nation, and it became so rapidly by global standards: Brazil was nearly 70 percent rural in 1940 but is now nearly 80 percent urban (Fig. 12.1; IBGE *Anuário* 1995). From 1950 to 1980, the number of cities over 20,000 in population skyrocketed from 96 to 482 (Faria 1983, 140), and in 1991, a quarter of the nation's people lived in their states' capitals (IBGE *Anuário* 1994). Urbanization is occurring in all regions of Brazil, but the most dynamic industrial activities are being con-

centrated in the Southeast of the nation, especially the greater São Paulo area, which has about 20 million residents and about one-third of the nation's economy (Faria 1983; IBGE *Anuário* 1996).

The urban structure of Brazil is changing, and there is a flowering in all regions of mid-sized cities with populations between 100,000 and 500,000 residents (Faria 1983; IBGE *Anuário* 1993). The growth of these cities appears to be linked to the shift of Brazil's economy from production for internal markets to a new emphasis on exports as well as to cumulative improvements in the transportation infrastructure. Likewise, improvement of living conditions in Brazil has been tied to the growth of these cities and the lessening of pressure on the older megacities (São Paulo and Rio) and the state capitals (Portes 1989).

A substantial proportion of residents in Brazil's cities live in favelas, or squatter-settled self-constructed neighborhoods that are often on the margins or at the interstices of the cities. Living conditions in the favelas are perilous. Recent figures indicate that there are over 3,500 favelas in Brazil ranging in size from a few hundred residents to the Favela da Roçinha in southern Rio de Janeiro, which has over 400,000 people. Favela conditions can be identified in the 1991 census, which uncovered the facts that a quarter of all households in the nation still lack an inside water supply and 66 percent lack sewage treatment facilities (IBGE PNAD 1994, 175). There were favelas in the large metropolises and in the smaller interior cities in the 1980s, and it is now likely that 3.3 million new houses and the upgrading of 3.1 million more are needed to meet Brazil's housing and sanitation needs (Krahenbuhl 1996).

What does an overwhelmingly urban Brazil portend for democracy? Recent history offers some clues. In Brazil's first democratic experiment of 1946–1964, when the urban population was growing at the fantastic rate of 5 percent annually, urbanization had palpable political effects. The shift in population away from the interior meant a decline in traditional methods of political control, such as *coronelismo* (Leal 1977), and the exposure of voters to new sources of political information and mobilization in the cities. In electoral terms, urbanization was associated with a secular trend away from traditional conservative parties and toward working-class movements (Soares 1973).

The coup of 1964 only underlined the urban-rural cleavage. In the 1964–1985 period, urbanization was positively associated with resistance to the military government (Kinzo 1988), and as the military recognized this fact it banned direct elections for mayor in the state capitals and in nearly 200 other "national security" cities. Likewise, in the New Republic, the "oppositionist" tendencies of the highly urbanized regions (especially the state capitals) are still visible—other things being equal, rural voters are more likely to support the national government while big-city voters are more likely to be critical.

Generalizing broadly, the larger urban centers are clearly the most politically pluralistic areas of Brazil, and they bring leftist and opposition parties, new social movements and NGOs, unions and professional associations, and diverse media outlets together into islands of vigorous debate. In this most abstract sense, urbanization is a positive democratic trend in the long term, as a more dynamic civil society, greater pluralism of political information sources, and heightened electoral competitiveness continue to make extensional gains throughout the national territory.

But moving from this abstract appraisal of urbanization to a more immediate assessment generates a very different picture. Inordinate pressures have mounted on the larger urban centers and state capitals, especially the twin megacities of São Paulo and Rio de Janeiro. Overcrowding, "favelization," pollution, transportation problems, spiraling crime rates, and a declining ability to deliver basic services have meant a downturn in the quality of life for many big-city residents. A declining quality of life in the larger, older, and predominantly coastal cities is not necessarily a threat to democracy, especially with the emergence of the economically dynamic and increasingly attractive mid-sized cities of the interior.

But it is the gradual loss of citizenship and "stateness" in the megacities that poses the most immediate challenge to democratic sustainability.[2] The growth of the favelas and other "irregular" settlements means a decline in the ability of state authorities to deliver basic services to the population, thus depriving urban marginal residents of social, economic, and political citizenship. And where government agencies do not successfully penetrate, the "state" in the Weberian sense is often constituted by organized crime, particularly drug traffickers who control important favelas in Rio and São Paulo. These are important areas of urban Brazil that effectively escape state control, and in recent years, they have become battlegrounds pitting unaccountable state coercion, in the form of corrupt police forces, against equally unaccountable private coercion, in the form of heavily armed drug lords and their agents. As Anthony Pereira demonstrates in Chapter 11, these conflicts impede the rule of law in democratic Brazil.

Arguments about the absence of "stateness" and the rule of law are also relevant to rural areas (Maybury-Lewis 1994; Pereira 1996), but they are especially relevant in urban Brazil. First, in the absence of concerted state action, urbanization and "favelization" appear to be secular tendencies. Second, state authority and capacity are tested in precisely the areas that are political and administrative centers of Brazil. Third, the crime issue provides one of the easiest justifications for reactionary coercive elements to claim a breakdown in law and order under the democratic regime. Fourth, the large cities contain a significant portion of Brazil's middle class, whose support is crucial for democratic legitimation. And finally, urban marginals themselves are a constituency numbering in the millions whose basic needs have not yet been addressed by any regime, whether authoritarian or democratic. Only when they are convinced that the state can solve their problems, extending to them the true rights of citizenship, will they shift their loyalties from private to public authorities. Democratic sustainability is therefore intertwined with the resolution of Brazil's pressing urban problems.

Economic Growth, Jobs, and the Rise of the Informal Sector

Although growing rapidly since 1945 (though sporadically after 1980), the Brazilian economy was broadly restructured in the course of five decades. In 1940, two-thirds of the economically active population (EAP) worked in the "primary" sector: in agriculture, mining, rubber tapping, Brazil nut extraction, and lumbering; in the mid-1990s the number stood at just above 20 percent (Figure 12.2). Moreover, agriculture went from 25 percent of the country's economic output to just 10 percent, and Brazil's historical export mainstay, coffee, was displaced by manufactured goods. Industry contributed over 35 percent of Brazil's gross national product (GNP) in 1990 while employing just 20 percent of its workers (Fig. 12.2). Industrialization Brazil-style has therefore been described as unable to "absorb" significant portions of Brazil's labor force. Employment in industry doubled from 1950 to 1980 but has since decreased as a share of the workforce, supplanted by the boom in the service sector.

Employment in the service sector—a category of extraordinary diversity, ranging from hairdressers and street vendors to bankers, doctors, and real estate executives—now accounts for nearly half of the jobs in Brazil. Less discussed has been the growth of government employment in Brazil. The

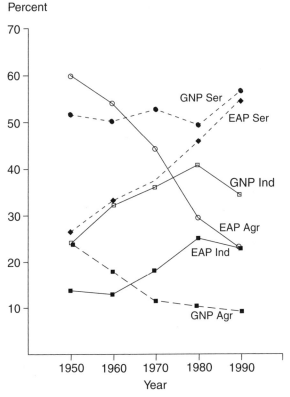

FIGURE 12.2 The Shifting Economy and Jobs: Gross National Product (GNP) and Employment (Economically Active Population [EAP]) by Sector, Brazil, 1950–1990. *Source:* Oliveira 1993, 9.

data on this are lacking, but when nurses, teachers, military, and state employees were considered in the 1990 count, the government sector accounted for more than 10 percent of all Brazilian workers. The growth of the Brazilian middle class, and especially women's career mobility, appear to have been closely linked to the expansion of public employment.

The recent boom in service sector employment was not matched by a commensurate increase in that sector's contribution to the country's GNP (Fig. 12.2), which indicates the role that both urban and rural "informal" sector jobs played in absorbing the nation's unemployed during the economic crisis years of the 1980s and early 1990s. Informal-sector workers are usually defined as lacking a legal job contract, which in Brazil is popularly referred to as a *carteira assinada* ("signed work card"). Many of these "informals" work for themselves or for small firms, most are paid "under the table" in cash, and they have no legal recourse if they fall sick, are underpaid, mistreated, or laid off.

The size of Brazil's informal sector has been debated, but it is probably between half and two-thirds of the nation's workforce. Surveys in the early 1990s found over half of all Brazilian workers did not have a signed work card, and a 1995 household survey found that 57 percent did not contribute to the national social security system known as *previdência social* (IBGE PNAD 1993, 61; 1996, 41; 1997; IDB 1996). There were substantial differences within these overall trends: three of every four northeasterners did not have employment that contributed to social security in 1995, and the same was true of four out of five domestic servants nationwide (IBGE PNAD 1996, 42). Finally, despite frequent popular and journalistic assertions to the contrary, most informal workers were not in these jobs by choice—one of the IBGE surveys showed that a majority would have liked to switch to a job with a signed work card (IBGE 1993, 61).

The implications of the informal sector are legion, but here we focus on those that are strictly political in nature. First, the expansion of the informal sector alters the traditional state-society relationship. From the perspective of the Brazilian state, the informal sector represents not only lost tax revenue but also an increasing portion of the economy and population outside the direct influence of policy. From the perspective of the informal workers, the social safety net does not normally encompass them, a fact that often renders meaningless both the discourses and the actions of politicians and state elites. For example, the worker protections innovated by the 1988 constitution, often described as *conquistas* by formal-sector labor activists, are devoid of meaning for half of the EAP. The arguments cited earlier about a decline in "stateness" and the lack of citizenship for nonelites are again relevant.

A second political implication of the informal sector is that a huge potential constituency of workers is lost to Brazil's labor unions, which not only weakens the ability of the unions to amass political clout through a majoritarian movement but also creates a gulf between formal and informal workers that politicians are all too willing to exploit. Kurt Weyland's elegant concept of "neopopulism" attaches theoretical significance to this phenomenon (Weyland 1996c). According to him, there is a new wave of populists in Latin America who recognize that formal-sector workers are now less available for political mobilization, given that they were mostly incorporated in the earlier wave of "classical" populism and its promotion of import-substitution industrialization (ISI). But these same neopopulists also recognize that informal-sector workers are ripe for political mobilization, which is most easily achieved by pitting them against the entrenched "elites" who were the "winners" of the ISI era. For Weyland, neopopulists are also economic neoliberals. Thus, in the neopopulist vernacular, the term "elites" is also applied to established trade unions and their leaders, who are viewed as a "labor aristocracy" no less privileged and no less rent seeking than the middle class, the protected industrialists, the state bourgeoisie, and the other usual (ISI-bred) suspects that dominated from the 1930s to the 1970s.

Neopopulists, of whom the best Brazilian example is President Fernando Collor, mobilize informal workers against the "privileges" of organized labor, given that both neoliberal politicians and informal-sector workers have a common interest in the deregulation of the labor market (Weyland 1996c, 10–13). If Weyland's argument is correct and the politics of neoliberal adjustment works in this way to drive a wedge between formal-sector and informal-sector workers in Brazil and elsewhere, then the prospects for a broad, inclusive, and popular coalition building are bleak in the medium term.

This argument extends to macropolitical trends. Informal-sector workers appear easy to *mobilize* on a *temporary* basis (as voters) but difficult to *organize* on a *permanent* basis (into complex associations). Thus, these workers may contribute to the election of populist politicians but subsequently (in the absence of organizational clout and intermediating leaders) be unable to hold those same politicians accountable. This lack of any mediating structure is a key difference between classical populism and the current wave of neopopulism, and the problem is clearly rooted in the changing social structure of Brazil.

The Persistence of Poverty and Social Inequality

Observers of Brazil are well aware that the tremendous postwar economic expansion did not bring benefits equally to the majority of Brazilians. Brazil's already skewed inequality of income worsened significantly after 1960, and by the end of the 1980s, Brazil was, as journalists pointed out, the "world champion of inequality" (E. Cardoso 1995; World Bank 1995; Suplicy and Buarque 1996; Barros and Mendonça 1996a, 1996b). Bolivar Lamounier summed up the legacy of inequality that was bequeathed to the New Republic:

[Income] concentration was still going on in the 1970s. The lowest 20% of the economically active population had gone from 3.9% of total income in 1960 to 3.4% in 1970, to 2.8% in 1980; the top 10% from 39.6% to 46.7%, to 50.9%. This means that the governmental policies practiced throughout this period, at best, did not counteract structural forces making for greater inequality; at worst they aggravated their effect. Combined with the massive character of absolute poverty that prevails in the Northeast and in the outskirts of all major cities, this degree of income concentration is undoubtedly one of the steepest challenges to democratic consolidation. (Lamounier 1989b, 134)

In 1990, five years into the democratic regime, the combined income of the richest 1 percent of Brazilians—about 1.5 million people—was two-thirds more than that of the poorest half of the country—about 75 million people (Faria 1983, 160; J. Oliveira 1993, 32). Another way to look at Brazilian inequality is that the richest 20 percent of the population earned thirty-two times more income than did the poorest 20 percent. Inequality in wealth (assets like property, vehicles, and stocks and bonds) and power are probably much greater but more difficult to measure and rarely discussed. Brazil's extremely high inequality is frequently cited as a prime cause of the country's phenomenal rates of violent crime, which are many times higher than those of similar nations (Amaral 1995).

Statistics, though important, do not express the devastating intensity of relative and absolute deprivation of the Brazilian poor. We do know that for three and a half decades, about 40 percent of the population was classified as "in poverty" (E. Cardoso 1994). The poverty line in Brazil is not consistently defined, but it often is directly or indirectly based on the basic food basket *(cesta básica)* needed to survive for a month, so families at or below the poverty line were often scarcely able to feed themselves, let alone clothe, house, and transport themselves to work. Many people were far below the poverty line. Though there is poverty in all regions of Brazil, the Northeast is still by far the poorest region, and the Southeast and South have the highest average incomes (Coes 1995; IBGE PNAD 1996; Wood and Carvalho 1988).

Inequality in Brazil cannot be understood without exploring its racial and ethnic dimensions. The nation was forged from the combination of Iberian colonists, indigenous peoples of the region, and slaves brought from Africa. Racial mixing occurred far more frequently than in most other nations, and recognition of skin color today represents more of a continuum than one of discrete categories. The legacy of miscegenation helped inspire the myth of a "racial democracy" of equal opportunity in Brazil, a thesis that has been thoroughly discredited by modern empirical research on race (Motta 1997).

There was some change in the official statistics on the racial composition of Brazil over the period considered in this chapter, but it appears to have been less the result of racial mixing than of a shift from categorical assignment by census takers (in the 1950, 1960, and 1970 censuses) to the option of respondent self-identification since 1980. The ranks of people calling themselves mixed *(pardos)* have grown substantially from about 28 percent in the mid-1950s to around 40 percent since the 1980 census (IBGE censuses and IBGE PNAD 1995). These figures suggest that movements to create black pride and self-identification have not been entirely successful: the percentage identified by census takers as "black" in the 1950s was about 10 percent, twice the rate who identified themselves as such in 1995. Beliefs about the racial inferiority of blacks remain deeply entrenched in Brazilians of all races. An influential 1995 book reported that black and *pardo* Brazilians were as likely as whites to agree with prejudicial survey statements about black Brazilians (Turra and Venturi 1995, 96–156).

The myth of a "racial democracy" of a color-blind Brazil remains alive for many Brazilians, but there is substantial evidence that race continues to be a strong determinant of marginalization and poverty. Simply put, although not formally excluded from economic and political participation,[3] Brazil's poor tend to be of darker skin than the wealthy and more powerful classes. In 1990, Afro-Brazilians were twice as likely as whites to live on less than one minimum monthly salary; *pardos* were far closer to blacks in this regard than to whites (IBGE *Censo* 1991). At the other end of the spectrum, white privilege continues: whites were five times as likely as blacks and three and a half times as likely as *pardos* to earn ten or more minimum salaries a month. It has been widely noted that blacks are nearly completely absent from the top ranks of corporate ownership and military and government bureaucracies. Racial inequality in Brazil cannot be reduced to class: even controlling for education and other elements of "social capital," race continues to explain substantial portions of income and wealth inequality (Lovell and Dwyer 1988). Many of these observations about racial inequality are also true of gender inequality, which social change in Brazil has been slow to erase. There are also interaction effects of racial and gender discrimination: the combination of female and nonwhite status is a strong predictor of poverty (Lovell 1998).

The intense regional, racial, and income disparities in Brazil are well documented, but what do they imply for democracy? The political implications of inequality have been exhaustively anticipated in the social science literature (e.g., Burkhart 1997, 149–52), and from Aristotle to Seymour Martin Lipset, social theorists have remarked that unequal societies constitute a daunting obstacle to democratic governance. In his classic work on the conditions for democracy, Robert Dahl noted that inequality tends to affect the chances for democratic consolidation in two major ways: in terms of the distribution of political skills among the population and in terms of the generation of social frustration that the regime is then hard-pressed to address (Dahl 1971, chap. 6). More recently, quantitative cross-national studies have tended to confirm an inverse relationship between inequality and democratization (e.g., Muller 1988, 1995).

The case of Brazil presents a stark test of these insights. If the persistence of poverty and inequality has not yet threatened the *survival* of Brazilian democracy, it has clear implications for the *quality* of democracy. Dahl's two intervening variables are clearly important here. First, the skewed distribution of economic power in Brazil clearly translates into inequality in the distribution of political skills and resources. It is true that this phenomenon has been partially offset by the astounding expansion of the franchise and by the proliferation of popular organizations, both of which are good news for democrats. But periodic voting does not come close to equalizing the entrenched power disparities caused by abysmal income distribution, nor does organized civil society yet encompass the majority of Brazil's poor and excluded. Second, social frustration may actually be aggravated by the combination of "inertial" inequality with democratic freedoms. For the vast majority of Brazilians, the only political resource is the vote. If, after repeated use, the vote has no apparent effect on the problems of poverty and inequality, the result is apathy, cynicism, and the delegitimation of parties and politicians. This phenomenon has been linked to the plebiscitarian voting patterns and to the weak legitimacy of democracy generally during the first decade of the New Republic (Moisés 1995).

With the brief exception of the Cruzado Plan in 1986, the persistence of inflation in the 1985–1994 period effectively prevented Brazil from making any headway on the twin issues of poverty and inequality. Inflation is an excellent though depressing example of how inequality often begets greater inequality. Prior to the onset of the inflationary spiral, the protective assets that afford a partial hedge against inflation were unevenly distributed among the population, being generally available only to the middle class and above. (Such assets include bank accounts, specialized financial instruments, access to dollars, ownership of real estate, and investment in consumer durables such as vehicles and telephone lines that hold value and are easily resold, not to mention the intellectual skills that are required to understand and cope with the economics of inflation.) When inflation hit, it effectively functioned as a punishing "tax" on the individuals who did not possess the protective assets. The poor were hit the hardest because their sole income was wages—which even with frequent adjustments could not keep pace with inflation—and because what little wealth they had was mostly held in cash. (Under hyperinflation, "cash kills.") The wealthy persevered.

The fact that inflation had a different impact on the rich and poor was no secret, and thus economists long suspected that the fastest-acting social policy in Brazil might simply be price stabilization. Initial data from President Cardoso's *Plano Real*, which began in July 1994, indicate it has indeed reduced the number of Brazilians living in poverty, initially by about a quarter (Rocha 1996). According to IBGE figures, the first year of the *Plano Real* markedly improved the Gini index of income inequality, from 0.600 in 1993 to 0.565 in 1995. When compared to cross-national data from the World Bank, the new Gini index would strip Brazil of the world championship in income inequality, moving it into sixth place behind Guatemala, South Africa, Kenya, Zimbabwe, and Panama (cited in Suplicy and Buarque 1996, 1). Still, comparisons such as these do little to comfort the majority of Brazilians: desperate poverty is widespread in Brazil, and the gap between the rich and poor is immense (Neri, Considera, and Pinto 1996).

However salutary, Cardoso's inflation control was a necessary emergency measure, not a sufficient social policy. By 1998, the redistributive effects of the *Plano Real* had apparently run their course, and unemployment was at its highest point since 1984.[4] The *Plano Real* needs to be supplemented by long-term and far-reaching social, educational, and employment policies, which amounts to a difficult balancing act, for although these social policies need to be implemented yesterday, their adoption must not adversely affect macroeconomic stability. We know that inflation punished the poor for the first ten years of democracy, and we know that if inflation returns it will do so again—thanks to entrenched inequalities that democracy has yet to solve.

Education and Illiteracy

Education is directly tied to Brazil's poverty and inequality (Haddad 1995; IDB 1996; Rosetti 1996b; R. Barros and Mendonça 1996a),[5] and officially reported rates of illiteracy dropped substantially, from around 60 percent of Brazilians over age fourteen in 1950 to about 20 percent in 1995 (IBGE *Censo, Anuário,* PNAD, various years). The official definitions have varied over the years, but usually respondents are considered illiterate only if they cannot sign their names. This definition has been harshly criticized, and estimates of "functional illiteracy" run as high as a third of adult Brazilians (Rosetti 1996b). These people cannot read newspapers or books, can barely do basic mathematics, and therefore tend to look for manual labor jobs. Half of Brazilian adults never completed more than four years of elementary school—six years is considered the minimum to participate in modern life in Latin America and to keep learning (Haddad 1995)—and Brazil's rate of primary school completion is among the worst in Latin America (IDB 1996, 278).

Within Brazil, education and literacy—and the opportunities they bring—are unevenly distributed. Until 1980, females were less likely to be able to read and write than males, but that situation reversed slightly in the 1990s. Rural residents are nearly three times as likely as urban residents to be illiterate, and people with little or no income are nearly twenty times more likely to be illiterate as those with over two minimum salaries—27 percent versus 1.3 percent (IBGE PNAD 1990). Around 30 percent of black and mulatto Brazilians are illiterate, but only 12 percent of whites and 2 percent of Asian-Brazilians are. Finally, nearly a third of the people in the Northeast (32 percent) are officially classified as illiterate, nearly three times the rates in Brazil's wealthier South and Southeast regions (11.6 percent and 12.4 percent, respectively).

Public universities in Brazil are free, and the federal institutions are the best in the country. But access to them is highly unequal: often, it is effectively only the upper-middle and wealthy classes that can afford the preparation in private secondary schools that is necessary for students to pass the competitive entrance exams, called the *vestibular.* Of the students in the federal universities, 44 percent come from the top 10 percent of the income distribution (Birdsall, Bruns, and Sabot 1996, 40). The federal government spends over $5 billion a year on public universities, providing free tuition to many students who could afford to pay. Thus, at the university level, the children of wealthier families often receive a quality education at no cost while students from more humble backgrounds are forced to pay tuition at lower-quality, for-profit private institutions (Paul and Wolff 1996).

Meanwhile, primary schooling languishes (J. Toledo 1996). Public primary schools, especially in rural areas and small towns, are reported to be "so bad that students drop out. If they stay, they learn little or almost nothing" (Haddad 1995). Somewhere between 3 million and 6 million Brazilian children between the ages of seven and fourteen are not attending school (Haddad 1995; Rossetti 1996b)—the dropout rate can be inferred from the astonishing differential between the 1994 enrollments in primary school (31.1 million students) and secondary school (4.4 million students). In the same year, the number of students enrolled in institutions of higher education was about 1.7 million (IBGE 1995–1996, 82).

We draw attention to this disjuncture between university and basic education because it offers an additional insight into the maintenance of social inequality. Higher education policy has long directed resources disproportionately toward the relatively small number of students enrolled in the free federal universities (currently about 300,000, or one in six college students) rather than toward an alternative goal of boosting overall university enrollment rates, which would probably require charging tuition to those who can afford to pay.[6] Thus, in 1989, Brazil's higher education enrollment rate, measured as the percentage of twenty–twenty-four-year-olds studying in all types of postsecondary institutions, was a meager 11 percent. This figure compared to about 16 percent in Thailand, 32 percent in Spain, and 38 percent in South Korea (IBGE 1995–1996, 83).

One might object that in spite of Brazil's comparatively low enrollments, the federal universities have served the country extremely well and that the goal of providing a free college education is a worthy one. We agree. But although the free federal university system may have been inspired by universalistic principles, in practice it tends to reinforce basic social inequalities via the erection of class-based barriers to university admission and the concentration of scarce budgetary resources in relatively few hands. Somewhat paradoxically, left-wing parties are the most vocal opponents of charging tuition for federal universities, despite persuasive evidence that free higher education serves to reproduce the national elite.

Turning to basic education, Brazil's shortcomings on this score have been magnified by recent changes in both local and global economic structures. In terms of the Brazilian economy, the immense dropout rate and the generally poor quality of primary education guarantee continued poverty and inequality, as well as hinder the increases in productivity that will be necessary to sustain economic vitality in the long term. In terms of the global economy, Brazil's educational system weakens its competitiveness vis-à-vis other industrializing nations. When the "Asian Tigers" burst onto the scene in the 1980s, for example, it was widely noted that countries such as Taiwan, South Korea, and Singapore had secondary education enrollment rates two to three times that of Brazil (Haggard 1990, 238–41). Even taking into account the generally weaker commitment to education in Latin America, Brazil still fares poorly: of the cohort of Latin American children that began primary school in 1991, only 72 percent of Brazilian children reached grade five, compared to 84 percent of the children in Mexico and 95 percent of those in Chile and Uruguay (UNESCO 1995).

Issues of education and literacy, then, affect Brazil in two fundamental ways: internally, in terms of income equality and social justice, and externally, in light of an increasingly globalized economy in which human capital is more important than ever before. Policymakers increasingly recognize these facts. In the 1990s, forward-looking local governments—particularly those of PT mayor Luiza Erundina in São Paulo, PT governor Cristovam Buarque in the Federal District, and PSDB governors Tasso Jereissati and Ciro Gomes in Ceará—have placed a renewed emphasis on primary education, especially teacher recruitment and student retention.[7] To its credit, the Cardoso administration also emphasized basic-level education after 1995, with Education

Minister Paulo Renato de Souza pushing to reverse the spending priorities that have favored elite universities for so long. These policies are necessary to ensure that Cardoso's economic reforms, which have stimulated renewed (albeit uneven) growth in the second half of the 1990s, do not aggravate poor income distribution owing to the very low educational baseline. Reviewing a decade of neoliberal reforms in Latin America, the Inter-American Development Bank warned in 1997:

High inequality in education . . . has conditioned the impact of accumulation on income distribution. Greater inequality in education has brought with it greater income concentration. But there has also been an indirect effect. Educational inequity has limited the distributive effect of the accumulation of physical capital. In those countries with greater concentration of education, increased investment has *worsened* income distribution, possibly because it has increased the benefit of education, which is scarce, and reduced the need for unskilled labor. (IDB 1997, 72; italics added)

These are sobering insights from an organization that has supported structural adjustment, and they point to some daunting challenges to future social development in a liberalized Brazil. Concentrations of education, income, and political power seem to go hand in hand, and Lamounier (1989b) aptly characterized the Brazilian political economy as a case of "inequality against democracy." If Dahl (1971) is correct that inequalities in income and education translate directly into the distribution of political resources and skills, then persistent problems of illiteracy and inferior public education constitute a major challenge to democratic sustainability in Brazil.

Civic Participation: The Rise of Churches, Social Movements, and NGOs

Since 1985 Brazil has seen an explosion of participation in voluntary associations such as labor unions, professional groups, churches, environmental and women's social movements, and other nongovernmental organizations (NGOs). Because of the very dispersed and grassroots nature of these groups, their numbers are difficult to obtain or even estimate. However, trade union membership has increased by over tenfold since 1960, mostly since the political opening began to accelerate around 1980 (W. Santos 1985; IBGE *Anuário* 1995). Both rural and urban workers' unions reported memberships over 7.5 million each in 1992, and a 1995 household survey estimated that 11.3 million Brazilians were members of unions, equivalent to 16.2 percent of the labor force (IBGE PNAD 1996, 35). Although fewer in number, professional white-collar workers have unionized at an even faster rate: only 40,491 were union members in 1960, but 549,680 were in 1992, a thirteenfold increase. Because salaries did not keep pace with inflation during military rule, unions of professionals were responsible for some of the most visible strikes during the democratic transition (W. Santos 1985). Many of the newly unionized workers were government employees (*funcionários públicos*) in the direct or indirect federal administration.

Another important development in Brazilian labor is the growth of linkages between and among these various categories of workers. Many rural, urban manual, and professional workers in Brazil have been brought together in the first labor confederation to be truly independent of the Brazilian state, the Central Única dos Trabalhadores (CUT), which is closely tied to the Worker's Party (PT), both groups having had their origins in the labor unrest in greater São Paulo in the late 1970s (French 1993; Keck 1995). These two groups have attracted significant scholarly attention. But despite the considerable secondary literature on working-class militance in Brazilian politics, we still know surprisingly little about middle-class labor unions—especially the *funcionários públicos*, even though they occupy a central place in the battles over state reform (see Chapter 2).

Religious groups have also become increasingly diverse and independent of the state (see Chapter 7), and looking at religious identification, it is clear that the dominance of the Catholic Church has weakened considerably in recent decades. Historically, over 95 percent of the Brazilian population was Catholic, but the 122.4 million self-declared Catholics in the 1991 census would represent a considerable drop to around 83 percent, and most analysts believe that the true figure is now closer to 75 percent—possibly even lower. Whatever the correct percentage, these affiliation statistics often overstate religious commitment, because for many Catholics membership in the church is nominal at best.

Conversely, Protestant churches, which boast more cohesive and participatory congregations, are gaining considerable ground. From 1.7 million members in 1950, most of them in traditional, mainline denominations, the number of Brazilian Protestants rose to 13.2 million in the 1991 census, with almost all of the growth occurring in the burgeoning Pentecostal movement. A 1997 report estimated the figure at 16 million, which would mean that one in ten Brazilians is now a Protestant (A. Barros and Capriglione 1997). Spiritualists and other religionists increased from 0.8 million and 0.4 million in the 1950 census to 2.3 million and 1.4 million in 1991, respectively.

Other civic groups grew rapidly during the period as well. The environmental movement exploded during the run-up to the Earth Summit in Rio de Janeiro in 1992 but has tapered off somewhat since then (Chadwick 1997; Landim, ed. 1988; Roberts 1996). Other NGOs are active in the areas of human rights, citizenship, racial justice, women's issues, and health, to name only a few, and many are becoming semigovernmental organs (see also Chapter 8). Their total memberships remain uncertain, but their political power is substantial as they control over $1.4 billion of resources, of which about $400 million is from abroad. Many of these groups grew with the support of the Christian-based communities of the progressive wing of the Catholic Church during the 1970s and 1980s. The Movimento dos Sem-Terra (Movement of the Landless) is just such a group. Exploding in the mid-1990s, it has flexed substantial political muscle by occupying ranches and sparking a national debate on the injustices of land tenure patterns in Brazil (McNee 1997; see also Chapter 7). Other groups, such as soccer clubs, neighborhood groups, and political and business interest groups, are more difficult to track, but many of them have increased substantially in number and membership.

This rapidly increasing density of Brazilian civil society is transforming the nation's politics, economy, and culture, and these transformations "from below" constitute what is arguably the most striking difference between the political landscape in the 1990s and that of the previous democratic experiment in 1946–1964. Today, a vibrant and diverse network of fully autonomous secondary associations provides a countervailing force against state power. In this volume, Kathryn Hochstetler provides a detailed analysis of social movements and NGOs, Kenneth Serbin documents the new religious marketplace in Brazil, and, to varying degrees, the other authors introduce a rich panoply of nonstate actors that have recently emerged to the forefront of political life (e.g., Peter Kingstone on business lobbies, Anthony Pereira on human rights groups, and William Nylen on PT-affiliated movements such as CUT).

As social theorists from Alexis de Tocqueville to Robert Putnam have argued, a vigorous civil society provides fertile ground for democratic government. An enormous amount of literature has suggested that as membership in secondary associations increases within a given society, then (one) "private" forms of political interaction, such as clientelism, are eroded; (two) "public" or "civic" styles of politics, based on republican notions of citizenship, are more likely to take root; (three) virtually all forms of political participation increase across the board; (four) values of equality and solidarity tend to become more diffused; (five) norms of interpersonal trust—critical not only to political democracy but also to economic development—become more ingrained; (six) the ideal of self-government becomes more highly valued; and (seven) citizens are empowered in a way that allows them to hold their leaders more accountable (Putnam, Leonardi, and Nanetti 1993, 86–91; see also Putnam 1995a, 1995b).

Thus, it is not surprising that in Latin America, Eastern Europe, and elsewhere in recent years, the growth of civil society has weakened the long-term basis for authoritarian domination, facilitating transitions to democracy (Huntington 1984, 1991; Linz and Stepan 1996). Also, in their justly famous study of Italy, Robert Putnam and the others found that the growth of a civic community—or what the authors termed "social capital"—was causally linked to more effective government institutions at the local level (Putnam, Leonardi, and Nanetti 1993). Although a longitudinal Putnam-like study has yet to be conducted in Brazil, impressionistic evidence indicates a similar pattern, with social movements and NGOs engendering innovative policies, greater accountability, and a gradual devolution of the policy debate to the level of ordinary people. These organizations are also a potent antidote to clientelism and corruption. Although such practices will never be wiped out, the presence of civic associations deters them by promoting transparency and accountability. For all of these reasons and more, the new vibrancy of civil society and the popular organizations is likely to contribute positively to the quality of democracy in Brazil.

The Diffusion and Control of Electronic Media

Because of Brazil's high levels of illiteracy and poverty, the electronic media cast a far wider shadow than any other source of information. Radios spread earliest, reaching over half of Brazil's households by the late 1960s (IBGE PNAD 1993). The first television stations began to broadcast in Rio and São Paulo in 1950, and the medium began to spread slowly until its reach became nearly universal: while in 1970 just under one quarter of households had a television set, by 1995 some 81 percent did (IBGE *Anuário* 1975, 1996, 61). Since 1980, the number of Brazilian households with a television set has been greater than the number with a refrigerator, a pointed irony in a tropical country (74.8 percent in 1995 according to IBGE PNAD 1996). The remote regions of Brazil's interior gained television transmitters just since the 1970s, and now in even the remotest Amazon there is access to national Brazilian television (Roberts 1995). Sales of television sets have again been skyrocketing since the *Plano Real* was introduced in 1994 (Conjuntura Econômica 1997).

Statistics on the penetration of television are impressive, but they are meaningless without reference to the status of the other media. In 1994, there was one television set for every four Brazilians, a level similar to many neighboring countries, but only 1 newspaper for every 20 inhabitants, about one-third the level of developing nations overall (*Folha de São Paulo* 1997d). This disparity is best understood by comparing the circulation of print media in Brazil to that of neighboring countries at a similar level of economic development. In 1992, for example, the circulation of daily newspapers in Brazil was a paltry 55 per 1,000 inhabitants compared to 143 in Argentina, 147 in Chile, 205 in Venezuela, and 240 in Uruguay (UNESCO 1995). Television dwarfs the print media, but within the television industry itself one player dominates. Despite the proliferation of cable and satellite dishes, many areas of Brazil still receive only the dominant Globo network, which regularly commands wide majorities of the viewership across the nation (Roberts 1995). It is only when one takes all factors into account—low literacy, the preeminence of television over newspapers, and a dominant player in network broadcasting—that one can truly appreciate the political salience of television's Globo network.

Far from being the result of a process of a natural "diffusion" of technology, the ownership, spread, and content of television stations in Brazil are the result of varied and widespread political manipulation. Two decades of policies by the military regime (1964–1985) subsidized television purchasing and infrastructure while helping TV Globo build a virtual monopoly in exchange for favorable coverage (Straubhaar, Olsen, and Nunes 1993, 121). Since then, positive coverage by Globo has proved a precious commodity for politicians.

In mid-1984, during the campaign for *Diretas Já!* ("Direct Elections Now!"), TV Globo abandoned its longtime military allies to support the opposition candidate, Tancredo Neves, for president. Tancredo then named to the Ministry of Communications a longtime Bahia governor, the indescribable Antônio Carlos Magalhães (known ubiquitously as ACM), owner of Globo affiliates in his home state and a close friend of Globo magnate Roberto Marinho. After Tancredo's death, Globo provided strong support for José Sarney, who maintained ACM at the ministry through the end of his term. In the 1989 elections, Globo provided none-too-subtle support for the campaign of Fernando Collor de Mello (V. Lima 1993) and backed him as president until the corruption scandals of 1992. Globo also gave favorable coverage to Fernando Henrique Cardoso in the campaign of 1994, once again illustrating the network's impressive impulse to support the government of the day. Although Globo's influence is often exaggerated in opposition discourse, there is no denying that presidents have cultivated Globo's support and vice versa.

Begun by the military regime, the politicization of media policy continues under the New Republic. Since 1985, licenses to operate television and radio stations ("concessions") have routinely been awarded to federal legislators in return for political support (AESP 1992; Lobato 1995; Lobato et al. 1995a; Sylvio Costa and Brener 1997). Efforts to alter licensing policy in a more transparent direction have been thwarted by legislators and by the centralization of authority in the Ministry of Communications (Aufderheide 1997). Politicians who have won concessions from the ministry have developed media empires in their home states, which they then use to subtly or overtly influence their coverage on local television and radio news and in major newspapers they own or control (Lobato et al. 1995b; Lobato 1995,

6). In some states, more than half of the local congressional delegation owns a television station, a radio station, or both. The electoral effect of this media manipulation is uncertain and much debated, but it is clear that Brazil's move to democracy has not been matched with a democratization (in this case, deconcentration of ownership and market share) of its most powerful communication medium, television (V. A. Lima 1993; C. E. L. Silva 1993).

Television has undoubtedly made some positive contributions to Brazilian democracy, notably by covering the mass mobilizations in favor of direct elections and Collor's impeachment. But the ongoing inequality in access to the electronic media weakens the quality of Brazilian democracy in several ways. First, the closed nature of the concessions-awarding process means that politicians grant most television and radio licenses to themselves, restricting entry to other actors and freezing the political elite in place. Second, oligopolization of television is an incentive to political personalism— this trend is actually most obvious, not at the federal level, but in subnational politics. Third, the political manipulation of the electronic media restricts the free flow of information and hampers true political pluralism. This factor is partially offset by the free television time that is awarded to all parties for sixty days prior to an election, but owner/politicians still have the upper hand when it comes to the day-to-day reporting of the news.

Two examples of political manipulation include the biased manner in which TV Globo reported on the final presidential debate in 1989, which is thought to have swayed some undecided voters away from Lula and toward Collor in the last days of the campaign, and the case of Lídice da Mata, a left-wing candidate who surprisingly won the mayoralty of Salvador da Bahia in 1992 and against whom the Magalhães clan used its local newspaper and Globo affiliate television station in a smear campaign that undermined her ability to govern. Of course, in a free market economy, owners of the means of communication are free to behave as they wish—but when public airwaves are consistently used for private ends, the quality of political debate suffers. Nonelite actors, especially popular organizations and progressive movements, find it difficult to express alternative viewpoints.

Historically, greater informational equality is a key requisite for successful democratization (Simpson 1997), and three reforms could alter the current Brazilian equation of inequality. Over time, improved literacy and education could reduce the dominance of electronic media over other forms of political information; the state could depoliticize communications policy by moving forward on current plans to create an independent regulatory agency, which would presumably remove licensing from the direct control of politicians; and various public interest groups, such as the National Forum for the Democratization of Communication, could succeed in forcing reforms that would grant greater media access to societal organizations (Aufderheide

1997). Until and unless such reforms are adopted, Brazilian democracy will enter the Age of Information with a decidedly unlevel playing field.

Summary and Conclusions

We began this chapter with an implicit question. In terms of conduciveness to democratic sustainability, how does the Brazil of the late 1990s compare to earlier time periods? The evidence indicates that, increasingly, this is a *new* Brazil: the shifting social context appears less and less like that of military rule and bears little resemblance to that which existed under the first democratic regime in 1946–1964. But as our analysis has shown, what is new is not necessarily positive for lasting democracy. For some of the "change" areas, the evidence seems quite unsettling. Unconstrained urbanization, for example, has contributed to crime, social exclusion, and a decline in stateness and governability in the largest cities. The rise of the informal sector fragments the working class, fosters "outsider" politics, weakens political accountability, and presents numerous challenges to public policy. And even though the Brazilian press is freer than ever before, the rise of television may have exacerbated informational inequality and contributed to a hitherto unimaginable form of machine politics—what Sylvio Costa and Jayme Brener (1997), updating the classic 1948 work by Victor Nunes Leal (1977), have termed *coronelismo eletrônico*.

The areas of "continuity" that we discussed—persistent poverty, inequality, and poor educational levels—constitute ongoing threats to democratic sustainability. Antedating 1985, 1964, and 1946, these are problems that seem impervious to political change in Brazil. However, long-term democratic legitimation (not to mention economic development and competitiveness) depends on the state's making some headway against these perennial problems. One of the most noteworthy aspects of Brazilian political discourse is that all parties and politicians, from left to right, give priority to these very same issues, offering "solutions" and pledging immediate redistribution should they be elected to power. But when real change is imperceptible at best, as it has been throughout the New Republic, the contrast between discourse and action is painfully obvious. In the 1990s, the addressing of social inequalities took a backseat first to inflation control and later to constitutional reform; this sequencing forces us to wonder whether the political willpower to bring about real change will materialize when neoliberal reforms are finally "complete," if they ever are (see Portes 1997).

But these problem areas should not distract our attention from some of the more positive trends we have identified. Rapid urbanization has created undeniable social problems, but the smaller proportion of Brazilians living in rural areas means that there is less space for traditional forms of political domination such as clientelism and *coronelismo*. At the midpoint of the previous democratic regime, 1955, only 41 percent of Brazilians lived in urban areas compared to 79 percent today. Moreover, basic literacy has increased from 48 percent in 1955 to about 78 percent today, meaning that the country is much better prepared for a sustained investment in secondary education than it was during the first democratic experiment. The expansion of the suffrage has also made for a vastly more inclusive polity. It is difficult to imagine that in 1945, when Brazil's first democracy commenced, only 16 percent of Brazilians were voters; today, that figure stands at 62 percent. Finally, at the level of organized civil society, the Brazil of the turn of the millenium would have been utterly unrecognizable a generation ago. The explosion of interest groups, professional associations, churches, social movements, and NGOs since 1980 has changed the political landscape forever.

Given these extraordinary changes, we *suspect* that Brazilian civil society has now become too complex to govern by authoritarian means—although some actors would still be happy to test our hypothesis. Granted, the evidence for this assertion is suggestive, not conclusive, but in advancing it we draw attention to several factors. The first is that the twin concepts of suffrage and popular mobilization to make suffrage effective are now firmly inscribed in the repertoire of collective action in the New Republic. In 1984, the unprecedented *Diretas Já!* campaign helped bring about the transition to democracy; in 1989, the first presidential elections in twenty-nine years stimulated an impressive degree of mobilization within the electorate; and in 1992, the youthful *carapintadas* ("painted faces") spearheaded the popular campaign that helped drive Fernando Collor from office. These were three milestones of popular empowerment, and—thanks mostly to unforgettable television images—they are burned into the national consciousness. Mobilization is now always on the agenda. We note that an enfranchisement rate of more than 60 percent, and an electorate approaching 100 million, would presumably make it very difficult for a future authoritarian coalition to suspend direct elections or civil liberties, as the military did with relative ease in 1964.

The second factor, which we have briefly sketched but which is amply documented elsewhere in this volume, is the phenomenal growth of civil society. The accumulation of nonstate organizational power in Brazil, when added to universal enfranchisement and to secular background changes such as urbanization and increasing literacy, would make it very difficult indeed to "turn back the clock" on Brazilian democratization at the end of the century. This is not to argue that democracy cannot be brought down, for it certainly could be. It is simply to suggest that any attempt to do so would have to reckon with an overwhelmingly urban nation, an empowered civil society, and the demonstration effect of periodic mass mobilization in Brazil since the early 1980s. Any one of these factors alone would be difficult enough for a coup to suppress, but taken together, they are quite formidable. We suspect that any authoritarian closure would likely be unsustainable and short-lived.

This points to our central, though still tentative, conclusion about the social context for democratic sustainability in Brazil. Sustainability refers both to survival and to the quality, i.e., the capacity for continuous self-improvement, of political democracy. As regards the quality of democracy, we have identified many problems that inhibit—and will inhibit well into the twenty-first century—the full inclusion of Brazilians into the polity, economy, and society. On many issues, especially poverty and inequality, prospects for the short and medium terms remain grim. But as regards the potential for *survival* of the post-1985 democracy, we have identified a number of trends that have solidified a social basis conducive to democracy, or perhaps to put it more accurately, *a social basis inimical to authoritarian retrogression.*

This tentative conclusion leads us to surmise that from a sociopolitical perspective, Brazil may now have entered a transitional phase of "low intensity democracy" that is likely to last for some time. With the polity having crossed the threshold into polyarchy, is it possible that sociodemographic factors now preclude a move backward into authoritarianism while simultaneously impeding the move forward into a regime of fully participatory, more egalitarian, higher-quality democracy? Is Brazil condemned to sociopolitical immobilism within a nominally democratic framework? Only time will tell whether democracy can be intensified, from above or from below.

We might conclude by saying that the glass is half empty, for in a cross-national, comparative perspective, the Brazilian social context for democracy remains relatively unattractive. But from our intranational, historical perspective, we prefer to see the glass as half full. Compared to the Brazil of a generation or two ago, the conditions for sustained democracy are better now than ever before.

NOTES ⊞

Introduction

1. The literature on the Brazilian military regime is vast. We cannot hope to provide a fair bibliographical overview in this space, so we restrict ourselves to a few representative citations. The best single-volume history of the regime is provided by Skidmore (1988), who methodically draws on the voluminous literature in both Portuguese and English. Another excellent overview, written from the viewpoint of the Brazilian opposition, is M. Alves (1985). The classic collection of theoretical essays on the regime is Stepan (1973). Other valuable works are Bresser Pereira (1984), F. Cardoso and Lamounier (1978), Kinzo (1988), and McDonough (1981); dozens more are cited in the Bibliography.

2. On the period of the transition to democracy (1974–1985), see especially Lamounier (1984, 1989a), Martins (1986), Share and Mainwaring (1986), Mainwaring (1986b), and the essays in Selcher (1986). The richest theoretical appraisal of the transition period, with some attention to the early New Republic, is provided by the various essays in Stepan, ed. (1989). For early (and often pessimistic) appraisals of the New Republic, see Hagopian (1990, 1992), Hagopian and Mainwaring (1987), Pang (1989), W. Smith (1987), and especially M. Souza (1989). The best collection of essays on the early years of the new democracy is F. Reis and O'Donnell (1988).

Chapter 1

Thanks go to Douglas Chalmers, Frances Hagopian, Scott Mainwaring, William C. Smith, and Kurt Weyland for their helpful comments on an earlier draft of this chapter. The author is solely responsible for any shortcomings that remain.

1. For Venezuela, see Levine (1973) and Karl (1986); for Spain, see Share (1986) and Maravall and Santamaría (1986). For an alternative, sixfold typology of constitution-making environments in new democracies, see Linz and Stepan (1996), pp. 81–83.

2. For a brief introduction to the institutional debate in Brazil, see Sadek (1995).

3. For a detailed overview of the process, see Martínez-Lara (1996).

4. Since the proclamation of the Republic in 1889, Brazil has always had a presidential system except for a brief parliamentary interlude in 1961–1963. During that period, President João Goulart had his powers severely curtailed, but he won them back in a plebisicite in January 1963.

5. The constitution originally scheduled the plebiscite for September 7, 1993. After the governmental crises of 1992, Congress decided to move up the date to April 21, 1993.

6. The only qualification is that the revision could not touch certain *claúsulas pétreas* ("bedrock clauses"), the intentionally nonamendable constitutional provisions that enshrine basic political and civil rights, the federal form of government, and other such fundamentals of the polity.

7. During the revision, journalistic observers commented that one motivation for

reducing the presidential term was concern within the center and right majority of the assembly that Luiz Inácio Lula da Silva of the PT—who enjoyed a seemingly insurmountable lead in the early 1993–1994 opinion polls—was on his way to becoming the next president.

8. The translations from the Portuguese are mine.

9. Among academics and political scientists, there appeared to be strong support for parliamentarism, but presidentialism also had prominent defenders. For an excellent introduction to the academic debate in Brazil, see the exchange between Maria Hermínia Tavares de Almeida and Luiz Felipe de Alencastro published in CEBRAP's journal, *Novos Estudos,* in March 1993 (M. Almeida 1993; Alencastro 1993).

10. For a study of partisan voting under these conditions, see Samuels (1999).

11. See, among others, Lamounier (1990, 1991), O. Lima (1990), O. Lima, ed. (1991), Nicolau (1993), and Pedone (1993). The best introduction in English is Mainwaring (1991).

12. From a survey conducted by the author among 162 federal legislators in the Fiftieth Legislature during May and June 1997. In the Forty-ninth Legislature in 1993, the same survey question found that 58.2 percent of the federal legislators supported the mixed system, 39.7 percent supported PR, and 2.2 percent supported SMDP (N=185). In the Forty-eighth Legislature in 1990, the results were 49.2 percent mixed, 39.5 percent PR, and 11.3 percent SMDP (N=249).

13. In 1990, the equivalent figure was 72 percent in favor of the open-list variant; in 1993, it was 68.2 percent.

14. Germany, by way of contrast, uses party lists. For an illustration of how the German system might be adapted to Brazil, see Nicolau (1993).

15. In a little-known episode in the ANC, a coalition of small-state legislators almost succeeded in adopting the *voto federativo ponderado* (weighted federal rule), a method of presidential election copied directly from the U.S. Electoral College. This method would have weakened the larger, more developed states and imparted a decidedly conservative bias to future presidential elections. The amendment received 246 votes for and 225 against but fell short of the needed absolute majority of 280 voters (ANC vote 316, March 22, 1988).

16. When the issue was put to a vote in the *Congresso Revisor,* compulsory voting was maintained by a margin of 236 to 193 votes (*Folha de São Paulo,* March 15, 1994).

17. In a thoughtful objection to voluntary voting, José Antônio Giusti Tavares raises the opposite hypothesis—that the abolition of compulsory voting would strengthen traditional conservatives in Brazil (J. Tavares 1998, 178–83).

18. An excellent introduction to recent literature on parties and elections is O. Lima, Schmitt, and Nicolau (1992). For historical background on the party system see M. Souza (1976) and Lamounier and Meneguello (1986). For parties and elections under authoritarian rule, see Jenks (1979), Lamounier (1984, 1989a), Kinzo (1988), E. Diniz (1990), and Von Mettenheim (1995). On the New Republic, see Kinzo (1993), Nicolau (1996b), and especially Mainwaring (1995a, 1999). Other useful studies include Lamounier (1990) and O. Lima (1993). Behavioral studies of parties include Kinzo (1989), A. Figueiredo and Limongi (1995a, 1996), and Ames (1994). The uniqueness of the PT is amply documented by Keck (1992).

19. On Congress, see Abreu and Mattos Dias (1995), Ames (1995a, 1995b), Baaklini (1992), CEBRAP (1994), A. Figueiredo and Limongi (1994a, 1994b, 1995a, 1995b, 1996), Fleischer (1994), Krieger, Rodrigues, and Bonassa (1994), Novaes (1994), and Power (1996). For introductions to legislative procedure, see Coelho (1989) and A. Barros (1995).

Chapter 2

I would like to thank Frances Hagopian, Wendy Hunter, Peter Kingstone, Gabriella Montinola, William Nylen, Anthony Pereira, and Timothy Power for many useful comments and the University Research Council of Vanderbilt University for its generous support. An earlier version of this chapter appeared in *Journal of Interamerican Studies and World Affairs* 39, no. 3 (Winter 1997). I am grateful to Eleanor Lahn and the North-South Center for permitting the reproduction of large parts of this article.

1. Following Weber (1976, 29), I define the state as the territorially based institution that "successfully claims the monopoly of legitimate physical coercion for the execution of its orders." The core of the state—and the focus of my analysis—is the complex bureaucratic apparatus dedicated to administration, coercion, and fiscal extraction. To the extent that the state "formulate[s] and pursue[s] goals that are not simply reflective of the demands or interests of social groups, classes, or society" (Skocpol 1985, 9), state autonomy prevails. State capacity, in turn, denotes the state's ability to attain these goals and implement its decisions; the more institutionalized the state structures are, the more the state can sustain this ability. Finally, state strength is the combination of state autonomy and state capacity.

2. This argument is reflected both in modernization theory (LaPalombara 1967, 51–55) and in neo-Marxism (Carnoy 1984, chaps. 5, 6, 8).

3. This argument diverges from the linear logic that predominates in the social sciences. Rather than postulating persistent decline or linear progress, I argue that initial failure can trigger reform. And rather than assuming that democratization always has the same effect, I argue that it furthers reform in the context of a deep crisis even though it helped bring about the crisis in the first place. For a "micro foundation" of these nonlinear arguments, see Weyland (1996e).

4. On this distinction, see Skocpol (1985).

5. Confidential author interviews with numerous social security officials in Brasília and Rio de Janeiro, 1988–1990, 1992, 1994–1996.

6. President Sarney reformulated this rule in 1987, turning appointments from rewards for past behavior (voting for Tancredo Neves on January 15, 1985) into blackmail for guaranteeing future compliance, namely, supporting Sarney's personal goals in the Constituent Assembly of 1987–1988. Confidential author interview with the ministerial official administering this patronage in Brasília, March 1990.

7. SEPLAN (1989) provides a fascinating inside account of the problems caused by rampant clientelism.

8. Varsano (1996, 4). Personnel spending by state and municipal governments rose by a whopping 44 percent in real terms between 1985 and 1990 (MARE 1996, 55).

9. Rio Branco (1989); Solimeo (1989); "Banco Mundial revela que BNDES favorece 'panelinha'," *Jornal do Brasil*, January 2, 1990, 13.

10. For instance, the Sindicato de Hospitais de São Paulo used to have an INAMPS director on its payroll. Confidential author interview, São Paulo, December 1989.

11. IBGE *Anuário* (1989, 948) and (1992, 948). The share of cash in M1 is a commonly used indicator of tax evasion (Peters 1991, 209–16). Since exploding inflation created a strong disincentive to using cash in Brazil during the late 1980s, the increase reported in the text is particularly noteworthy and suspicious.

12. Computed from IBGE *Anuário* (1986, 467) and (1992, 941, 1022).

13. Tanner (1994) shows how the increased importance that Brazil's new democratic government attributed to its current political support undermined budget balance.

14. Brazil's economic problems helped weaken the state as skyrocketing inflation eroded tax revenues and as the debt crisis created a fiscal drain. But economic problems were not responsible for many other aspects of state deterioration, such as deeper clientelistic penetration.

15. For a similar argument, derived from a comparison of Spain, the ex-USSR, and Yugoslavia, see Linz and Stepan (1996, 381–85).

16. Confidential author interview with a military contractor, Rio de Janeiro, February 1990.

17. Given military hierarchy, coups bring outsiders to power only under exceptional circumstances, such as after Bolivia's defeat in the Chaco War.

18. The same is true for Peru under Fujimori (Mauceri 1995), Mexico under Salinas (Elizondo 1994), and Argentina under Menem (Palermo and Novaro 1996, 143–48, 273–75).

19. The resulting discontent is vividly described in Bornhausen (1991).

20. Confidential author interview with a businessman, São Paulo, June 1995.

21. Computed from IBGE *Anuário* (1992, 941, 1022).

22. Collor (1995) claimed that powerful business sectors also opposed privatization.

23. Pimenta (1995). Nevertheless, Collor succeeded in reducing the number of public servants (*estatutários*) from 712,740 in 1989 to 620,870 in 1992 and the number of all state employees from 1.489 million in 1989 to 1.284 million in 1992 (MARE 1996, 33).

24. For instance, four top *técnicos* quit the Secretaria da Receita Federal and opened their own private consulting firm, which helped business people exploit loopholes in tax legislation that they themselves had helped create ("Ex-fiscais da Receita assessoram empresas," *Jornal do Brasil, Negócios e Finanças,* May 24, 1992, 2).

25. Computed from IBGE *Anuário* (1992, 941, 1022).

26. F. Cardoso (1994, chaps. 1, 2, 4). In chapter 3, Cardoso put considerable emphasis on social goals—as Collor had done (*Diretrizes* 1989, chap. 4). And like Collor, Cardoso has been criticized for not carrying out these promises. On Cardoso's plans for state reform, see Presidência de República. Câmara (1996a).

27. Cardoso's efforts to limit clientelism have of course been hindered by his electoral and governing alliance with the clientelistic PFL and PMDB and by the influx of ever more clientelistic politicians into his own PSDB.

28. "Crise no Funcionalismo Piora em 98," *Folha de São Paulo,* August 3, 1997, 1.

29. Banco Central (1996) describes the bailout program for banks, but—interestingly—does not quantify its enormous cost. Selective protection, for instance, for the automobile industry, was motivated partly by the difficulties that the *Plano Real* caused for Brazil's balance of trade, but it was also the result of forceful lobbying and political connections, such as the close links between former Planning Minister José Serra and São Paulo industrialists (confidential author interviews with representatives of São Paulo business associations, July 1997).

30. Lemgruber (1996); "Esquecida e Mal Lembrada," *Folha de São Paulo,* September 19, 1997, 1–2.

31. "Reeleição em campo," *Istoé,* November 8, 1995, 22–23.

32. "Deputados aprovam fim da estabilidade," *Folha de São Paulo,* July 10, 1997, 1–6; "Promulgada Reforma Administrativa en Brasil," *El Mercurio,* June 8, 1998, A6.

33. "Previdência passa em 1° turno," *Jornal do Brasil,* September 24, 1997, 3.

34. See, for instance, "Repasse de verbas beneficia fiéis ao governo," *Gazeta Mercantil,* July 10, 1996, A-10.

35. Varsano (1996, 9). This figure corrects for an accounting trick introduced during

1995, namely, the postponement of salary payments to the beginning of the subsequent month, which transferred salary payments due in December 1995 to January 1996.

36. In the U.S. case, similar economic self-interests made business people support state reform (Knott and Miller 1987, 36–37, 78–81).

37. I deliberately avoid the concept "consolidation," which suffers almost inevitably from lack of precision, the danger of tautology, and a mix-up of analytical and normative categories. Also, this concept directs attention to the risks of a sudden overthrow of democracy, which seems very low in contemporary Brazil, and deemphasizes much more important questions, namely, what actual impact the formal rules of democracy have and whether democratic principles are effectively realized.

38. This Argentine saying applies in principle to Brazil, although tax evasion there has never reached the astronomical levels prevailing in Argentina in the 1980s.

Chapter 3

1. For the purposes of this chapter, I define "democracy" as a system of rule guaranteeing the rights of elites to contest for state power, the rights of citizens to participate in and be represented in the polity, and the protection of the civil liberties of the ruled. "Democratization" refers to the process by which these guarantees are established and strengthened de jure and de facto. De facto democracy assumes a level of substantive democracy, that is, social equity and economic rights that, although not essential for establishing the existence of democracy, are crucial to the overall process of democratization.

2. Wherever subnational elections precede national elections in the democratization process, especially if those elections are the "founding" elections of a new democracy, local elites and not national rulers will design the federal structure. Invariably, they do so in ways that favor subnational government and weaken central states (see Linz and Stepan 1996, 34).

3. I assume that the existence of a weak, fragmented state is a danger to democracy as it favors the power of privileged social groups and debilitates political groups espousing more universalistic motives. For the argument, see Weyland (1996a) and Chapter 2.

4. Public goods that must address specific local preferences (e.g., infrastructure, local industrial policy, and housing) are handled more efficiently at the subnational level. The greater the diversity of local preferences across jurisdictions, the larger the benefits from decentralization (see Oates 1972).

5. How this process contrasts with "the old federalism" in Brazilian history is intellectually interesting but only of secondary importance to the arguments explored in this chapter.

6. Most of the historical detail of political decentralization in Brazil before, during, and after the transition to democracy cannot be discussed here. For more thorough accounts, see L. Graham (1987), Selcher (1990), Abrucio (1994), Sallum (1996), and Souza (1997).

7. The ICM improved on the state sales taxes it replaced by charging only on the added value in each stage of production. The reforms also allowed the cities to manage their own taxes, primarily the Imposto sobre Serviços de Qualquer Natureza (Tax on Services, ISS), which did not apply to the services already taxed by the ICM.

8. Although the state governments could set ICMS rates, these powers were governed by certain federal laws. For more on these rates, see Longo (1994).

9. The new fiscal structure of Brazil was not atypical of fiscal federalisms in the most advanced countries. The states and municipal governments in Brazil accounted for 49

percent of public sector expenditures in 1992, a figure comparable to the United States (50.5 percent) and Germany (45.7 percent). Like other fiscal federalisms, the Brazilian national state administered progressive taxes on income while subnational governments controlled taxes on property (Lagemann 1995, 330–31). Only the aforementioned distortion of having two value-added taxes administered by two different levels of government remained a particularity of the Brazilian case.

10. Although these figures suggest that de facto policy responsibilities were shifted to subnational governments along with resources, they do not specify whether the increase in spending was indicative of improvements to the quality of services. The figures also do not show whether increased spending did not simply fund unsustainable public payrolls and local rent seeking. In order for these increases in social and educational spending to have value they would have had to be accompanied by subnational fiscal reforms and a political dedication to improve public efficiency.

11. This patrimony included both finance and jobs in the upper echelons of bank management. Proof of the escalating politicization of the state banks under democratization is the fact that the deterioration of their liquidity commenced a few months before the first governors' election in 1982 and intensified with the elections of 1986 (see Sola 1995, 52; Loyola 1993, 9–10).

12. For an analysis of the legislation, see IPEA (1992) and Loyola (1993).

13. The administrative reform bill, passed by the Chamber of Deputies in April 1997, gave subnational governments the authority to dismiss civil employees in order to meet the *Lei Camata* standards.

14. Federal governments operating in the wake of the 1988 constitution had not been oblivious to the impending problem of the fiscal war. The constitution empowered the National Council of Fiscal Policy (Conselho Nacional de Política Fazendária, CONFAZ), an organization under the command of the Ministry of the Economy and composed of all the state secretaries of the economy, to regulate state fiscal incentives. By law, no new fiscal incentive scheme could be implemented unless the members of CONFAZ agreed to it *unanimously*. Central state managers thought that the unanimity requirement would discourage the proliferation of state incentive programs, but in practice, state governments often ignored CONFAZ guidelines. Some states even bartered their votes on the council to states proposing incentive schemes in exchange for approval of their own programs (Affonso 1995, 60).

15. *Diário do Comércio,* April 9, 1996. Some of the key governors in this movement include Cristovam Buarque (PT, Federal District), Jaime Lerner (PDT, Paraná), Dante de Oliveira (PDT, Mato Grosso do Sul), Antônio Britto (PMDB, Rio Grande do Sul), and Maguito Vilela (PMDB, Goiás).

16. This tendency is true of reforming coalitions as initial successes attenuate opposition to change. For the argument, see Berensztein (1996).

17. The provision allows the federal government to hold 20 percent of constitutionally mandated transfers to the states and municipalities until "all contingencies are covered." The final phrase gives Brasília extraordinary discretion over these funds.

18. For an analysis of these policies, see Cano (1994:, 232–33).

19. The full complexity of this still unfolding case cannot be treated here. For a more complete assessment, see *Veja,* March 5, 1997, 22–29.

20. Garcia had been governor of Minas Gerais briefly between 1984 and 1986 while Tancredo Neves, the elected governor, ran for the presidency.

21. The most important statement of this new policy in Minas Gerais can be found in Minas Gerais (1989).

Chapter 4

1. Brazil has three levels of government: federal, state, and municipal. A *município* in Brazil is equivalent to a county in the United States: it can comprise both rural and urban areas and can also comprise more than one urban area. The IBGE considers a municipality "urban" if it contains 20,000 people.

2. Although agrarian interests are still well-represented in the Brazilian Congress, many people now call the Chamber of Deputies a "national city council" because of its turn toward the expression of urban interests. Still, the Chamber of Deputies (and the Senate) continue to overrepresent the more rural states of Brazil's North and Northeast regions.

3. Except for mayors of capital cities in some states, whom the governor continued to appoint for several years.

4. Montero (Chapter 3, Table 3.1) and I use different sources, and thus our figures differ slightly.

5. Most automatic transfers come from the Fundo de Participação dos Municípios (FPM), which comes from the central government, or from municipalities' share of the value-added tax (ICMS), which state governments collect and distribute.

6. The federal government's use of budgetary funds as a political tool has declined and is likely to remain limited because of Brazil's ongoing fiscal crisis.

7. Bremaeker (1995) uses 4,974 as the total number of municipalities; the IBGE data I use include more.

8. São Paulo senator, vice-governor, and later governor, Orestes Quércia built his political machine around support for *municipalismo*. His disappearance from the political scene in the 1990s parallels the disappearance of the *municipalista* movement, which indicates the ephemeral nature of the movement and its dependence on politicians. The history of the *municipalista* movement is an unwritten aspect of Brazil's transition (but see Montoro 1974 and Castro 1987).

9. State governors appointed the mayors of state capitals. Elections were also not held in about 180 municipalities designated as important to national security, which included municipalities with a large military presence, some border municipalities, and municipalities with hydroelectric installations.

10. Interview with federal deputy Alberto Goldman (PMDB-SP), São Paulo, November 10, 1996.

11. Interview with Antônio Carlos Pojo do Rêgo, congressional liason to the minister of planning, Brasília, June 13, 1997.

12. I recognize that there is an endogeneity problem here; that is why I have attempted to separate out distal and proximal causes. Politicians in Brazil have always sought executive-level positions, but the distal factors pushed them to reconsider the place of municipal-level positions in relation to state- and national-level positions.

13. For an explanation of the "dip" in 1978, as well as a more detailed explanation of the trends, see Samuels (1998, chap. 3).

14. I discuss in greater detail the significance of deputies' taking state-level positions as well as municipal-level positions in Samuels (1998, chap. 3).

15. For purposes of revenue distribution, municipalities with 10,000 or fewer inhabitants are treated equally. For larger municipalties, the federal government employs a formula for provision of FPM funds.

16. Population figures for municipalities created after 1993 were unavailable.

17. Furthermore, the increase in automatic revenue transfers to municipalities has

acted as a disincentive for municipalities to collect revenue from taxes under their control.

18. Interview with Maria José de Macedo, coordinator of regional administration, secretary of planning, São Paulo state government, São Paulo, October 22, 1996.

Chapter 5

1. Stepan (1971) and R. Schneider (1971) examine the doctrine of national security and its influence on the military regime. The major military journals of the era, such as *Revista Militar Brasileira*, underscore the importance of this doctrine on officers' attitudes.

2. See Stepan (1988, 94–97) for a fuller list of the characteristics that mark civil-military relations in a democratic regime.

3. Military regimes whose policies were judged to be more controversial among the public tended more toward internal fragmentation and division.

4. See Hunter (1997, chaps. 2, 3) for a more extensive discussion of the military's strong position at the time of the transition to civilian rule in 1985.

5. See Chapter 11 for a more developed discussion of the compensation issue.

6. For a fuller explanation of this argument, see Hunter (1997, chap. 1).

7. This observation stems from a vast number of author interviews with active-duty and retired military officers.

8. See Hunter (1997, chap. 3) for a discussion of how military prerogatives fared in the Constituent Assembly.

9. See Hunter (1995, 431–39).

10. On the importance of coming up with appropriate missions for the armed forces, see Hunter (1996, 1–9).

11. There is an interesting discussion of this period in Linz and Stepan (1996, 177–78).

12. The figure is roughly $125,000 in damages for each family.

13. This section draws heavily from Hunter (1998).

14. The military justice system, with its whole parallel universe of courts and justices with separate jurisdictions, represents another important realm of institutional prerogatives and privileges (Zaverucha 1997, 38–40). On January 24, 1996, the Chamber of Deputies finally passed a bill, by a margin of 236 to 186 with 15 abstentions, that transferred intentional crimes (*crimes dolosos*) but not other human rights violations committed by PMs from the military justice system to the civilian justice system. Although this change represents an advance, it is telling that a watered-down bill was still contested quite vigorously eleven years after Brazil's transition to democracy.

15. The most recent Conference of American Armies recognized economic inequality, terrorism, drug trafficking, and ethnic conflict as the primary threats to security within the region (see Olson 1995, 205).

16. If anything like this has been done before, the results have not been made public. I inquired about the possibility of doing such a survey but encountered opposition to the idea.

17. The figure of 32.9 percent who answered "the military" in Brazil compares to 10.6 percent in Chile and 4.3 percent in Argentina (see *Latinobarómetro* 1995, question P61B).

18. Appearing in Linz and Stepan (1996, 174), the original source of this data is an Instituto Brasileiro de Opinião e Pesquisa (IBOPE) poll. It is cited also in Lamounier and Marques (1992, 149).

19. Cited by Linz and Stepan (1996, 173), this finding was reported originally by Muszynski and Mendes (1990, 71).

Chapter 6

The author wishes to thank the editors of this volume, Margaret Keck, Scott Martin, and William Smith for helpful comments and criticisms on previous drafts of this chapter.

1. A fourth argument suggests that the PT is a destabilizing presence because Brazil's powerful elites will sabotage its efforts to participate effectively and, in so doing, bring grief to the nation. I disregard this argument for two reasons. First, the PT's active participation in democratic politics at local, state, and congressional levels up to the time of this writing certainly encountered significant opposition from disaffected elites, but by no means has that opposition been destabilizing or otherwise threatening to democratic stability. Second, if such opposition were to occur (for example, in the event of a presidential victory by a PT candidate), the problem for analysis would be not the PT but those who oppose it.

2. Juan Linz's (1978, 29–31) definition of loyal (also disloyal and semiloyal) opposition remains the best in the literature. A loyal opposition can be seen, according to Linz, through the "public commitment to legal means for gaining power, and rejection of the use of force," "the rejection of any 'knocking at the barracks,'" the full acceptance "of legitimacy as participants in the political process to parties . . . that have the right to rule thanks to the support they received from the electorate," and the rejection of any "readiness to curtail the civil liberties of the leaders and supporters of parties attempting to exercise constitutionally guaranteed freedoms."

3. Marx and Engels, in their "Manifesto of the Communist Party," wrote that "the first step in the revolution by the working class, is to raise the proletariat to the position of ruling class, to win the battle of democracy" (Marx and Engels 1978, 490). A similar argument is made in Lenin (1969). Such a position is clearly visible in the party's origins. In the words of the PT's secretary of communications, Gilberto Carvalho:

> While critical of "Real Socialism," the founding generation of the PT developed a dream over thirty years of making revolution. Nicaragua and El Salvador were models in our minds. The weight of the Sandinista revolution was very big for us: we felt it could be done here too. We developed the Leninist thesis of accumulating forces in political institutions, then breaking with those institutions and making the revolution; power was not just taken, but constructed. Thus, the early ambiguity of the party regarding democracy. (Carvalho 1996)

For further evidence of such thinking in the early years of the PT, see Harnecker (1994), Baia (1996), C. Azevedo (1995), and Keck (1992).

4. The most recent case of such cooptation is the Brazilian Social Democratic Party (PSDB) during the PSDB presidency of Fernando Henrique Cardoso. See, for example, Puls (1997); also *Folha de São Paulo* (1997a). The PT's integrity on this score, however, is not unquestioned; see, for example, *Folha de São Paulo* (1997f). Throughout the party's history, however, evidence of wrongdoing on the part of members in public office or in positions of public confidence has been punished by expulsion from the party.

5. Most theorists of democratization would agree with Susan Stokes that "citizens must be presented with at least the outlines of alternative policies, outlines that serve as credible maps of real government action, if elections are to support popular sovereignty" (Stokes 1995, 76).

6. The fact that Brazilian party politics is dominated by conservative and exclusionary elites is a conclusion amply supported in the literature, including this volume. See

Ames (1995a), Hagopian (1992, 1993), Mainwaring (1992–1993, 1995b), and O'Donnell (1992).

7. Eliza Reis and Zairo Cheibub provide an exemplary argument in this regard: "The combined effect of acute poverty and accentuated inequality is to engender such dissimilar life chances and cognitive experiences that split political cultures result [between "haves" and "have nots"]. Under these circumstances one is led to conclude that the chances for democratic consolidation in Brazil, as in other Third World societies, will be greatly affected by the prospects for socially and politically incorporating the worse-off" (Reis and Cheibub 1997, 224).

8. See Mainwaring (1992–1993, 1995b); also Baaklini (1992). Providing a clear example of the norm, in the fourteen months spanning 1995 and the first third of 1996, ninety-two federal deputies changed their party affiliations. Such *trasformismo* accelerated as the 1998 elections drew closer.

9. PT founder, two-time presidential candidate, and "honorary president" Lula gives an example: "Time passes and you evolve, learning all the way. . . . Fifteen years ago [1981], I never would have imagined letting a businessman into the PT, and yesterday I went to Brasília to sign the party registration cards of fifty businessmen who applied for party membership. Back then, I didn't accept them, but they didn't accept me either. They too have evolved" (Silva 1996).

10. For this transformation of the Latin American left's goals and strategies, see Castañeda (1993), Cavarozzi (1992), Harris (1992), Sader (1995), and M. Garcia (1994).

11. Much of this historical overview is drawn from Keck's (1992) excellent account of the PT's first decade and from Harnecker's (1994) collection of interviews with PT founders and early activists; also useful were Keck (1989), Rodrigues (1990, 7–33), Guidry and Probst (1997), and Branford and Kucinski (1995).

12. This latter "Leninist" idea was expressed most notably by the party's intellectual "leftists" (rather than by the "unionists" or "popular organizations"). See Harnecker (1994, especially101–10); Keck (1992); and Moisés (1985, 19). Also see note 3 above.

13. In 1997, citing irreconcilable differences with local party militants and leaders, Espirito Santo's governor, Victor Buaiz, withdrew from the PT and, later, affiliated with the Green Party.

14. Other dimensions of the magnitude and diversity of experience in local governance were equally impressive and telling. Following 1996, the PT administered municipal governments in twenty-two states, as opposed to eighteen in 1992–1996 and ten in 1988–1992. And while 16 (or 62 percent) of its 1988–1992 administrations were located outside of São Paulo (the PT's home state, so to speak), the corresponding figures for 1992–1996 were 45 (or 80 percent) and 102 (or 89 percent) for 1996. Minas Gerais was the state with the largest number of PT-led administrations in 1996 (30), followed by Rio Grande do Sul (26) and São Paulo (13). In addition, while only ten (or 42 percent) of the cities administered by the PT from 1988 to 1992 had a primarily nonindustrial economic base, thirty-three (or 59 percent) of those picked up in 1992 were nonindustrial (information is from Keck 1992, 157, 277; Bittar 1992, 301–24; PT n.d., 1993).

15. Membership data from PT (1996a). Party preferences from Instituto Gallup (1995).

16. Elsewhere I labeled this process "institutional learning" (Nylen 1997a). See Guidry and Probst (1997) for a "neo-institutionalist" explanation for the PT's moderation.

17. Keck (1992), Cavarozzi (1992), and C. Couto and Abrucio (1993) each argue that the operative logic of playing by the rules of "institutional politics" (i.e., the negotiating, compromising, and interest-aggregating logic of *políticos*) contradicted the vi-

sion of the party's bases (organized labor and existing social movements) that the party should represent the needs and interests of its constituent grassroots social movements and support those movements' efforts outside the institutional arena of politics, even if doing so meant compromising electoral prospects. According to this argument, these competing "logics" lie at the root of much of the PT's party infighting.

18. For case studies of PT municipal administration, see Nylen (1997a, 1997b, 1998), Couto (1995), Kowarick and Singer (1994), Branford and Kucinski (1995, 76–91), Somarriba and Dulci (1995), Jacobi and Teixeira (1996), and Abers (1996). Also see issues of the São Paulo-based journal *Pólis* (Instituto de Estudos, Formação e Assessoria em Política Sociais), which regularly publishes articles on "popular democratic" (i.e., PT-administered) municipal governments and policies. Similarly, the PT's own trimesterly magazine, *Teoria e Debate,* often runs articles describing and analyzing PT administrations.

19. Somarriba and Dulci (1995, 25–29) carry out such a comparison for the case of Belo Horizonte, capital of Minas Gerais, focusing on the PT administration's (1993–1996) construction of low-cost housing and sanitation works in previously unserved areas of the city. Jacobi (1995a) and Cohn (n.d.) carry out similar comparisons in the issue-areas, respectively, of education and health for the PT's administration of São Paulo (1989–1993).

20. It is instructive to note that when Brazil's federal government in 1995 sought out the country's most successful experiences in "innovative local government" for inclusion in an exposition at the United Nations 1996 Habitat 2 Conference in Istanbul, Turkey, eight of the eighteen projects selected came from PT-administered cities. One poster in the party's national office bragged, "The party administers less than 1% of our cities, but it contributes 44% of the projects that officially represent Brazil." The eight cities were Angra dos Reis (R.J.), Betim (M.G.), Belo Horizonte (M.G.), Diadema (S.P.), Londrina (P.R.), Pôrto Alegre (R.S.), Santo André (S.P.), and São Paulo (S.P.) (see PT 1996b). Similarly, when UNICEF sponsored the publication of a fifteen-volume series of exemplary educational programs in Brazil, five of the fifteen cases came from PT-administered cities (see MED/UNICEF/CENPEC 1993).

21. In 1998, my ongoing research directly addressed this question as well as others related to the consciousness-raising and politicizing impact on participants of the PT's institutional innovations promoting greater *participação popular* such as the Participatory Budget. For suggestive preliminary findings, see Nylen (1998).

22. See M. Dias (1996) regarding a national poll of 2,680 respondents administered in mid-May of 1996 by the Vox Populi opinion research firm.

23. PT president José Dirceu has argued that media zeal in reporting unsubstantiated accusations of corruption against PT administrations in mid-1997 belies their partisan biases (Dirceu 1997).

24. "The data on total participation in the regional meetings demonstrate that while 250 organizations and a total of 403 individuals participated in 1989, these numbers grew to 650 organizations and 10,735 individuals in 1993"–Jacobi and Teixeira (1996, 23).

25. For a detailed case study of how the OP process functioned in the city of Betim, Minas Gerais, see Nylen (1997a); for Belo Horizonte, see Somarriba and Dulci (1995); for Pôrto Alegre, see Abers (1997).

26. Data for Pôrto Alegre and Belo Horizonte from Jacobi and Teixeira (1996) and Somarriba and Dulci (1995).

27. Other typical complaints from participants have included a sense that the process

involves too many tedious meetings, that not enough money is actually controlled by the OP process, and that administration officials do not keep participants abreast of the status of ongoing negotiations and implementation.

28. Personal interview with Marco Aurélio Garcia, São Paulo, June 14, 1996.

29. Because the PT has always been an opposition party in Congress, and because its commitment to "ethical politics" prohibits its delegation from trading votes for patronage, clientelistic benefits have not been made available to PT constituents. Some people have argued that the extent to which such benefits are seen by many Brazilians is the primary function of politics, which may have had a negative effect on the PT's capacity to gain and hold office.

30. There were nine national *encontros* between 1980 and 1994. In addition to debating "party line," these conferences also served to elect the party leadership from among candidates representing the "*tendências*" or factions within the party, all of whom are given time and space to present their ideas and lobby for their candidacies. The PT presents this process as a "school of democracy" for its members and as the source of an "organic" conceptualization of party goals and strategy that effectively respond "from the bottom up" to changing circumstances and changing perception. Sometimes even the leadership loses out and is compelled by party rules to abide by majoritarian decisions attained in secret balloting (see the interview with Francisco Weffort in Harnecker 1994, 91–94; also see M. Alves 1993, 235–37).

31. Party unity is further preserved by rejecting the very notion of an internally hegemonic position (i.e,. maintaining the "umbrella organization" image of the party), and party goals and strategies are said to emerge organically from the day-to-day grassroots struggles of all Brazilians and from the ongoing program debates among *petistas* who are fully engaged in those struggles.

32. Gazzola (1993); also C. Alves (1994) and Felix and Suassuna (1994).

33. This discussion would seem to confirm Otto Kirchheimer's classic observation that "mass integration parties" like the PT eventually turn into more moderate catchall parties as candidates' and officeholders' learning-by-doing combines with a general "de-ideologization" in the interests of greater electoral viability (Kirchheimer 1966, 184–95). Foundational commitments to grassroots constituents and radical structural transformations are abandoned, according to Kirchheimer, in order to attract a broader variety of voters.

Far from "de-ideologizing," however, I would argue that the PT actually became more clearly ideologized as heterodox groups succeeded in elevating or prioritizing certain longstanding basic principles (and deemphasizing others) from the ideological grab bag that reflected the PT's founding alliance of heterogenous social and political forces. The ideas that stand out most clearly are the embracing of "internal democracy" within the party, the critique of peripheral capitalism's tendency to produce inequality, the assertion that the state remains the best instrument by which to counteract this inequality, and the belief that partisan activism combined with greater citizen participation in governance can transform formal democracy and state policy making from essentially elitist games to increasingly popular ones.

Chapter 7

I wish to thank Philip Berryman, Ralph Della Cava, and Carol Drogus for their insightful comments on an earlier draft of this chapter. Thanks go also to Father Alberto Antoniazzi and David Dixon for their reading of yet an earlier version. I, of course, am responsible for any shortcomings. Rogério Alves de Barros provided valuable research assistance, and my wife, Regina Barros Serbin, provided love and support throughout this project.

1. This trend is evident in the abandonment of studies on the Church and the plethora of works on Pentecostal Protestantism. For overviews of Protestant growth, see Berryman (1996), Stoll (1990), and Martin (1990). A corollary of this change is the shift of scholarly attention from religion and *politics* to religion and *culture,* although the emphasis on culture may not be giving way to church-state studies (see note 3). For a statistical analysis of pluralism, see Pierucci and Prandi (1996a).

2. Quotation and observation from Berryman (1996); also see Prandi and Souza (1996).

3. Long out of vogue in Brazil as sociological and anthropological studies of religion dominated the field, studies of church-state relations are once again becoming necessary as Pentecostals attain power (see Freston 1993a; Pierucci 1996; Prandi 1996; Giumbelli 1996; Gill 1998). Although church-state relations before 1985 revolved around ideological conflict, under democracy they have shifted to the more traditional issues of religious freedom, church-state collaboration, and electoral bargaining. For example, the neglected financial angle of church-state relations is now an important focus (see Serbin 1995b, 1996b; Pierucci 1996; Prandi 1996; Gill 1998).

4. By and large, writes Peter McDonough, the members of the Brazilian elite "have not been acculturated to the cut-and-thrust of doctrinal debate; a lack of metaphysical certitude does not appear to bother them" (McDonough 1981, xxiv).

5. This point is also made by Prandi and Souza (1996).

6. For an alternative view that discusses the long-range sociopolitical implications of Pentecostalism, see Petersen (1996).

7. Fleet and Smith (1997) point out that the positions of the present-day Latin American church still contain antidemocratic vestiges.

8. For a discussion of these secret meetings, see Serbin (1996c, 1997, 1997b, 1998c).

9. For a detailed discussion of the moral concordat, see Serbin (1995a, 1996b).

10. This phrase is suggested by Lowden (1996).

11. An avalanche of literature that was mainly sympathetic to the transformation of the Catholic Church's role in Latin American politics appeared beginning in the 1960s; for more recent major examples in the Brazilian case, see M. Azevedo (1987), Burdick (1993), Casanova (1994), Della Cava (1985, 1989, 1992a), Della Cava and Montero (1991), Doimo (1992, 1995), Ireland (1991), Mainwaring (1986a), Mainwaring and Krischke (1986), Mainwaring and Wilde (1989), Paiva (1985), Pierucci, Souza, and Camargo (1986), Pope (1985), Sanchis (1992), and Teixeira (1988). For critical reinterpretations of the church's role, see Serbin (1996c, 1997, 1998a, 1998b, 1998c). There is a vast literature on liberation theology; for analyses, see Berryman (1987), Libânio (1987), Sigmund (1990), and C. Smith (1991).

12. A somewhat similar analysis of the Chilean church is employed by Michael Fleet and Brian H. Smith, who employ the term "overarching moral framework" (Fleet and Smith 1997).

13. Dom Lucas spent more than a decade in the Roman bureaucracy before becoming Brazil's archbishop-primate in 1987. In 1998 he returned to the Vatican bureaucracy. For background on him, see CNBB (1984, 1991) and Serbin (1991a). There are a variety of interpretations of the conservative reaction—for a comprehensive overview, see Beozzo (1994, chap. 4); also see Libânio (1983), Mainwaring (1986a), Cox (1988), Della Cava (1989, 1992a, 1992b, 1993), Lernoux (1989), Pressburger and Araújo (1989), Martin (1990), ISER (1990), P. Montero (1992), Ghio (1992), Cleary and Stewart-

Gambino (1992), Daudelin and Hewitt (1995), P. Oliveira (1992), Serbin (1993c), Doimo (1995), Comblin (1996), Berryman (1996), Bernstein and Politi (1996), Löwy (1996), and Vázquez (1997). For the Chilean and Peruvian cases, see Fleet and Smith (1997); for Santo Domingo, see Serbin (1994). Although I employ the terms "progressive" and "conservative" in this analysis, I recognize their diminishing utility. For further discussion, see Serbin (1998c).

14. Pierucci and Prandi (1996a) estimate CEB membership at 1.8 percent of the population. Also see the important (and optimistic) statistical study by Valle and Pitta (1994), and for an appraisal of Valle and Pitta's research, see P. Oliveira (1994). For skeptical views of previous large CEB estimates, see Hewitt (1991, 1995), Daudelin and Hewitt (1995), Burdick (1993), and Drogus (1992).

16. See Burdick (1993) for a critical evaluation of the CEBs' unattractiveness to the poor and for a perceptive essay on the Catholic Church (Burdick 1994); also see Berryman (1996) and Perani (1987). For a rigorous critique of Burdick's postmodernist, microsocial approach, see Vásquez (1998), which presents a detailed overview of the crisis over the progressive church from the perspective of the "macrodynamics" of the capitalist world-system.

16. This is the argument of Hewitt (1995). However, if political and economic conditions in Brazil became decidedly worse, it is possible that the CEBs could once again become politically important. Furthermore, the emphasis on the devotional observed in the CEBs should not be seen as diametrically opposed to the political, for the devotional can *feed into* the political at particular junctures. Also see my discussion of the Semana Social below. Drogus (1997) points out that CEBs help raise the political consciousness of poor women but also notes that they have brought about little social change because of women's continued subordinate position in both Brazilian society and the church.

17. The church's specific religious response to Protestant growth is discussed in the section on Pentecostalism. Gill (1998) has observed that this pattern affects the Latin American church everywhere.

18. The Brazilian example paralleled the spectacular turn of events in Mexico, where church and state renewed relations in 1992 after more than a century of estrangement and violent conflicts. For an overview, see Gill (1995). Doimo (1995) suggests a certain bureaucratization of Brazilian nongovernmental organizations as they have become more dependent on funding from the Brazilian government, North American agencies, and the World Bank.

19. Doimo (1995) notes that the church is experiencing another paradox: the attempt to reproduce the notion of community in an urban-industrial society in which it must try to appeal to the masses.

20. On the continued importance of papal social doctrine, see Casanova (1997).

21. The church went through a similar process during the democratic-populist period from 1946 to 1964 (see, for example, Serbin 1992b; Casanova 1997).

22. A similar argument is developed by Cleary (1997), who describes the church's contemporary role as "nation building"; also see Pressburger and Araújo (1989), and Altemeyer (1996).

23. To achieve this concept meant an ecumenical effort that involved mainline Protestant denominations and the World Council of Churches.

24. On the church and the land question, also see Iokoi (1996).

25. As nation-states became weaker because of privatization schemes and economic globalization, the transnational-oriented church stepped into areas neglected by the states. It perhaps could even "assume a proactive role in shaping some aspects" of the

new globalized system. "In a sense the papacy has been trying to re-create the universalistic system of medieval Christendom, but now on a truly global scale" (Casanova 1997, 122–23).

26. For a detailed analysis of the church's influence on issues related to the family and reproduction, see I. Ribeiro and Ribeiro (1994); on abortion, see Serbin (1995b), Jarschel (1991), Blay (1993), and L. Ribeiro (1994).

27. This point is suggested by Gill (1998). However, led by Dom Eugenio Araujo Sales, the cardinal-archbishop of Rio de Janeiro, some bishops issued explicit recommendations against certain candidates in the 1998 elections, but apparently with little success.

28. Frei Betto had a long history of involvement with the Workers' Pastoral of São Paulo and as an adviser to Lula.

29. The *excluídos* were also the focus of the CNBB's 1995 annual fraternity campaign (see *Revista Eclesiástica Brasileira* 1995). "Exclusion" is not new; it originated in discrimination against social groups such as African slaves during Brazil's colonial era. In contemporary Brazil, the concept denotes a lingering political inequality that not only prevents social and economic integration of the poor into society but often demonizes them as "bandits" requiring elimination (see Nascimento 1994; also see D. Almeida and Tavares 1995; Andrade 1993; and Ventura 1994). Exclusion worsens as Brazil absorbs new technologies that further widen the gap between people inside and those outside the new "technical culture" (Valle 1995).

30. See CNBB (1993, 1994a, 1994b), *Zero Hora* (1994), Archdiocese of Belo Horizonte (1994), and Poletto (1995). The theme of ethnicity gained prominence at the Catholic grassroots as the progressives' focus turned from economic to cultural oppression, a shift powerfully evident in the protests by Afro-Brazilians and Brazil-Indians against discrimination by "white Catholicism" during the seventh national gathering of CEBs at Santa Maria, Rio Grande do Sul, in 1992 (Libânio 1992).

31. Contrast this trend with earlier progressive fears that traditional political channels could harm the popular movement (see, for example, Perani 1987).

32. In Brazil, all Protestants, mainline and otherwise, are sometimes referred to as *evangélicos*. This term should not be confused with the subgroup of North American Protestantism known as "evangelicals."

33. On Protestant growth, see Freston (1993a) and Mendonça and Velasques (1990).

34. Statistics on the number of Protestants are precarious (see the discussion in Freston 1993a).

35. Chesnut (1997). On Afro-Brazilian religion, see Negrao (1996), Brown (1994), and Della Cava (1985).

36. Freston (1993a). As Freston points out, the history of Protestant-military relations has yet to be written.

37. The principal churches that have been founded in Brazil are Brasil para Cristo, Casa da Benção, Nova Vida, Deus Amor, IURD, Internacional da Graça Divina, and Renascer em Cristo.

38. The definition of neo-Pentecostalism is an unsettled issue among scholars, but the criteria listed in the text provide a good working definition. The class base of neo-Pentecostalism may vary across the region. It is mainly a lower-class phenomenon in Brazil, but in Guatemala, for instance, neo-Pentecostalism has grown among the middle and upper classes. On Guatemala, see Steigenga (1997); on prosperity theology, see Mariano (1995); on individualism, see Freston (1993a).

39. For an overview of the IURD, see Serbin (1996a); also see numerous articles since the mid-1980s in such Brazilian dailies as *Folha de São Paulo, Jornal do Brasil,* and

O Estado de São Paulo; R. Almeida (1996); Berryman (1996); M. Barros (1995); and Giumbelli (1996). On the universal church and for an overview of neo-Pentecostalism, see Mariano (1995); on Brazilian religious expansionism, see Oro (1994).

40. At the same time, it should be remembered that the Pentecostal churches rely on a great reservoir of popular religiosity built by Catholicism and Afro-Brazilian religions over five centuries. There are a number of similarities between Catholicism and the neo-Pentecostal religions, for example, the IURD's highly hierarchical structure. Though the search for the new tempts some people to speak of the "decatholization" of Latin America, continuities should also be studied, and they will become more evident as time passes.

41. The incident prompted the police and federal authorities to look into IURD activities and finances, although the investigation dragged on for years without apparent results (see Serbin 1996a; Pierucci 1996). Aparecida was recognized as Brazil's patroness by the pope in 1931. The government designated October 12 as a national holiday in 1980.

42. President João Café Filho (1954) was also Protestant. He was elected vice president in 1951 and served out only part of the remainder of Vargas's term after the latter committed suicide in August 1954.

43. The *movimento,* however, may be shifting toward greater electoral involvement (see Beozzo 1997); also see the discussion of the Semana Social earlier in this chapter.

44. Berryman (1996) discusses Catholic lethargy in this respect. Gill (1998) argues that the Latin American bishops have long had a vigorous and explicit strategy to compete with Protestantism, but his evidence is not highly convincing.

45. On the charismatics, see Theije (1997), Prandi and Souza (1996), Oro (1996), Machado (1996), Berryman (1996), Della Cava and Montero (1991), Lernoux (1989), and Bernardes (1995). For a critical appraisal, see Wanderley and Boff (1992); on the charismatics' relative lack of strength, see Comblin (1993).

46. Observers of the Pentecostal phenomenon disagree about its long-term impact. Some see it as a clearly conservative force (see Chesnut 1997). The opposite view holds that it has potential for progressive political action (see Burdick 1993; Freston 1993a; Berryman 1996). From the latter's perspective, the left and labor unions have much to learn from Pentecostalism because of its community-based action (see Berryman 1996). I concur with Gaskill (1997), Freston (1993a), and Fonseca (1996) that because of the recentness of its appearance in politics, the long-term political consequences of Pentecostalism are unpredictable. Gaskill further argues a very obvious point—unfortunately lost on many social scientists—that the assertion about an "incipient" or "latent" Pentecostal contribution to democracy is tantamount to foretelling the future. Finally, as Gill (1998) points out, survey evidence demonstrates that political views among Protestants in other Latin American countries do not vary greatly from those of the general populace.

Chapter 8

I would like to thank the editors, Jack Hammond, Mimi Keck, Tony Pereira, and Bill Smith for their thoughtful and challenging comments on an earlier version of this chapter. Any remaining errors and failures of interpretation are, of course, my own.

1. Unless otherwise noted, all translations are mine.

2. Before their recent role of prominence in decline, urban popular movements also carried the distinction of having once been the most promising embodiment of hopes

for democratization, in both the political and the economic forms that the citizenship frame encompasses (Assies 1993). Their recent decline gains dimension from the height of those past hopes. What is striking in a closer investigation of this "decline" is that some of it began with the formation of the organizations in the 1970s. Ruth Cardoso was already warning in 1983 that the activities and demands of many of the urban popular movements bore little resemblance to the democratic role claimed for them (Cardoso 1983), and some of the stories of decline describe developments in the 1970s (Cunha 1993; Gondim 1989–1990).

3. In writing of cycles, I am not denying that individual social movement networks or organizations may have their own dynamics and reasons for mobilizing—or not—as well. For example, identity-based social actors like women (Paoli 1991) or Afro-Brazilians (Segato 1995) may need to overcome special internal and external barriers to their political participation. Within such special considerations, the dynamics of a cycle of protest can provide additional encouragement or discouragement for mobilization.

4. A 1989 Datafolha poll found that less than 20 percent of respondents actively favored dictatorship but that many also were not sure democracy mattered. This attitude was especially prevalent among Brazilian young people (cited in R. Cardoso 1990, 23–24).

5. Online at http://www.ibase.br/ibase/ibase.html

6. The gap is not a new one, as it also divided social movements during earlier mobilizations, as in the distance between middle-class feminists and neighborhood feminine groups within the women's movement (Alvarez 1990).

7. Interview with Renato Cunha of the Movimento em Defesa da Amazônia (now a member of the environmental group GAMBÁ), Salvador, Bahia, September 5, 1991.

8. Betinho was Herbert de Souza, a sociologist who founded IBASE after returning from political exile in 1979. Betinho died in August 1997 of AIDS contracted through blood transfusions for his hemophilia. The effusions in the presentation of one of Betinho's books are representative of his symbolic role: "Fighting for the right to life, Betinho became the citizen who expressed the pain and the hope of all who confront the covetousness and profit ethic of our capitalists of every species, who fail to prize fundamental human rights" (De Souza 1991, 9).

9. Participant observation, VI Encontro Nacional, Fórum Brasileiro, São Paulo, September 27–29, 1991.

10. Interviews with three NGO delegates to CONAMA, 1991.

11. In Portuguese, the slogan is *Reforma agrária—Na lei ou na marra*. The translation I give in the text is Jack Hammond's, who notes, "*Na marra* might best be rendered 'by any means necessary'; it suggests but does not necessarily imply violence" (Hammond 1997, note 1).

12. This definition is drawn from a year of participant observation of the Earth Summit preparations in 1990 and 1991. I attended three of the national gatherings and state and local meetings in five states and conducted more than fifty interviews with activists of all kinds. Although these definitions are based on the distinctions Brazilian activists themselves draw, they are more indicative of general orientations than wholly accurate descriptions. Two indisputable NGOs, IBASE and ISER—the "I" stands for Institute in both cases—have organized many of the mass protest mobilizations discussed in the text, but the social movement label stretches to cover organizations like the environmental group Agapan, which has existed for twenty-five years and has a secretary, a building, and a whole set of long-term projects.

Chapter 9

1. Most published accounts of the Collor administration are quite critical of him for understandable reasons. Nevertheless, it is also fair to say that that criticism has been overstated. In certain respects, Collor was quite reasonable. His political agenda was not outrageous given the extraordinary challenges his program confronted and the "ungovernability" of the Brazilian polity. His economic program was certainly not unreasonable, particularly if compared with those of other neoliberal reformers in Latin America. This view of the Collor administration can be found in both Kingstone (1999a) and Bresser (1996).

2. The basics of the plan are discussed by G. Oliveira (1995), Fishlow (1997), and in brief by Baer (1995).

3. These warnings have included Rudiger Dornbusch's claim that the Real was 40 percent overvalued in June 1996, which provoked a storm of controversy in Brazil and on Wall Street, but also includes more moderate positions from the Bank of International Settlements and prominent Brazilian economists such as Edmar Bacha, Andre Lara Resende, and Celso Martone. Ultimately, these warnings proved prophetic, as a speculative run on the Real in January 1999 forced the government to abandon the exchange rate anchor. This event is discussed at greater length in the foreword. As of July 1999, the basic dynamic described in this chapter remained true. The Real stabilized at a lower value and the Brazilian economy recovered much faster than expected. Nevertheless, the economic policies required to protect the Real exacted a high price, while politically Cardoso appeared more vulnerable than ever before. Thus, the process of reform is again in considerable doubt.

4. Many analysts have noted that the organization of Brazilian business interests is quite fragmented. Nevertheless, focusing on fragmentation obscures the extent to which leading business organizations across sectoral lines had come to accept that Brazil's economic model (import-substitution industrialization) was broken. The business community did lobby as individual firms or sectors for highly specific benefits, and as a community, business spoke with many voices. Yet, those voices called for roughly the same set of solutions. An important exception was that small business tended to have different perceptions than big business. This difference is captured in Nylen (1992).

5. Payne (1994) particularly reveals the wide array of views in the business community, including the presence of normatively committed democrats. Author interviews in São Paulo during 1991 and 1996 found similar expressions of normative commitment, although not the topic of research. These expressions ranged from opposition to Collor's *emendão* on the grounds that trying to shove a massive constitutional package through Congress was an abuse of authority, to expressions of support for impeachment as part of a healthy cleaning up of politics, to the confession of one Brazilian director of a multinational subsidiary that he had been ashamed to travel abroad when Brazil was a dictatorship. Nevertheless, it is not clear how robust this tendency would be in the face of an economic crisis. The business community has certainly invested heavily in learning how to participate in democratic politics, but as one business informant observed, it is not clear that many would protest a *Fujimorização* (self-coup, imitating Alberto Fujimori of Peru) in a context of crisis. Until business groups are tested in that way, the depth of democratic commitment will remain in question.

6. This point speaks to the central problem of Adam Przeworski's rejection of legitimacy as a critical concept and his purely instrumental definition of consolidation. For Przeworski, a democracy is consolidated when it becomes the decentralized equilibrium option for all politically relevant actors. This conception implies that democracy is

only a means and not an end in itself. Thus, the disappearance of Brazil's dollar reserves in a rapid panic could alter business elites' equilibrium option overnight. If Brazilian business elites did not value democracy for itself, then presumably they might turn to antiregime solutions. However, if democracy has any normative value, then business elites would not seek to undermine it. The difference emerges clearly if we think about American business elites and what it would take to make them turn to antidemocratic options. It is hard to imagine such circumstances. For that reason, I find the Linz and Stepan (1996) definition of consolidation much more convincing than that of Przeworski.

Chapter 10

I would like to thank the editors for their helpful comments on an earlier version of this chapter. I would also like to thank—for research grants supporting fieldwork—the American Philosophical Society and Middlebury College and—for their research assistance—Ana Kang, Laura Potter, and Kirby Salerno.

1. There has been some attempt to increase social participation in the integration process through the institutionalization of labor and business participation. Nevertheless, while business has been incorporated to some degree, labor is still largely marginal to the process. For more on the role of social groups, see Alimonda (1994), Hirst (1996) and Montenegro (1995).

2. Although the economic integration process got under way in the mid-1980s, analysts have traced the beginning of cooperation back to the late 1970s when Brazil, Argentina, and Paraguay agreed to jointly manage water resources in the Paraná River (Guilhon 1992). For more on the roots of the change in Brazilian foreign policy, see Fernandez (1992) and Hirst (1984).

3. As Manzetti notes, "Argentina and Brazil were no longer divided by any significant dispute, and Argentina had even acknowledged Brazil's prominent political and economical role in Latin America. Both administrations favored demilitarizing the South Atlantic to keep it free of East-West confrontations" (Manzetti 1990, 115).

4. Felix Peña, who has been a key actor in Mercosul negotiations, argues that there were three main motivations for closer cooperation: "consolidating democracy, transforming our economies by means of technical progress (with greater social equity, so as to consolidate democracy), and inserting ourselves competitively in international markets" (Peña 1992, 128).

5. As Chudnovsky and Porta point out, "The public formalization of the agreements came as a surprise, and their signature was not preceded by a broad debate in either country; on the contrary, it was the debate's starting point" (Chudnovsky and Porta 1989, 115).

6. Araújo (1990, 244) argues that the more pragmatic nature of the integration process may in fact make its success more likely.

7. The term refers to the idea that for integration to proceed, new "protocols" must be negotiated at every turn.

8. As Manzetti noted in an article published in 1990: "The ABEIP's future prospects are not rosy. At this point, it is hard to imagine the ABEIP going much further than it already has" (Manzetti 1990, 137). However, as Bouzas pointed out around the same time: "The modest results of the ABEIP in recent years . . . should not be considered negatively. On the contrary, [the ABEIP's] survival in such an unfavorable international context should be considered an important accomplishment" (Bouzas 1990, 37).

9. For more on the triumph of market-oriented ideas, see Stallings (1992), Bierstecker (1995), and Varas (1995).

10. For a discussion of the global and regional context confronting Mercosul, as well as an early view of the challenges facing the trading bloc, see de Almeida (1993).

11. For more on the end of the Cold War as a driving force behind the acceleration of the Mercosul process, see Guilhon (1992).

12. For a concise description of the "Washington Consensus" by the author who coined the term, see Williamson (1990).

13. The Mercosul agreement also abandoned the sector-by-sector approach to integration that had been the basis of the ABEIP. The Mercosul agreement called for across-the-board tariff reductions, since such general reductions were "judged to be more effective in overcoming domestic lobbies" (*North-South Focus,* December 1992, 1).

14. "Mercosur Presidents Push Forward," *Business Latin America,* January 11, 1993.

15. For a detailed account of the Paraguayan coup attempt, see Valenzuela (1997).

16. "Estabilidade não convence," *Gazeta Mercantil Latinoamericana,* April 29–May 5, 1996.

17. Ibid.

18. For a detailed record of Itamaraty's development, see Mendes de Oliveira Castro (1983).

19. "Indústria influirá na formação da ALCA," Revista da Indústria, February 17, 1997; "Integração das Américas exige muita cautela," *Revista da Indústria,* March 3, 1997.

20. "Brasileiros com o pé no freio," *Gazeta Mercantil Latinoamericana,* August 12–18, 1996.

Chapter 11

1. I write "most authoritarian regimes" because the rule of law is not necessarily democratic; the prototypical *rechstaat* (state based on the rule of law), in Prussia, was authoritarian. The position taken here is that the rule of law is necessary but not sufficient for democracy.

2. Data on posttransition state violence in these countries are fragmentary but consistently point to both an absolute and a relative increase in Brazil. This chapter does not offer a comprehensive explanation of the increase, but I find the nuanced theoretical perspectives of Della Porta (1995), Holden (1996), and Stanley (1996) promising places to begin to build one.

3. The theorist who has argued most convincingly and insistently that the existence of formally democratic institutions does not settle the question of democracy is Guillermo O'Donnell. His recent work persuasively asserts that democracy refers as much to the state's legal order as to the regime, and his work influences the following discussion (see O'Donnell 1997).

4. Brazil's history in this regard is common in Latin America; the twenty Latin American republics have averaged 12.6 constitutions each in their postindependence periods (Rosenn 1991, 57).

5. See Capriglione and Santa Cruz (1996) for a valuable survey of the state of the Brazilian judiciary. They report (p. 59) that with 5,895 lower court judges and 86,000 judges in total in the country, Brazil has a relatively low ratio of judges per 100,000 inhabitants: 5.4 compared to 17 for Columbia, 16 for Uruguay, 11 for Argentina, 11 for Costa Rica, 9 for El Salvador, 8 for Bolivia, 8 for Nicaragua, 5 for Ecuador, and 4 for Chile. The data for the other countries are from Neira (1996, 8–9).

6. World Bank (1996, 196–97). The Brazilian figure is derived from a 1989 survey. Brazil has the highest Gini coefficient of the sixty-five countries for which data are listed in this report. See also the article by the Brazilian economic journalist Joelmir Beting

cited in the Bibliography (Beting 1996). Beting attributes Brazil's high inequality, in part, to the differential application of monetary correction to salaries between 1964 and 1994. Although the incomes of the better-off were adjusted as prices rose, those of the poor were not, causing a widening of the gap between them. The implementation of the *Plano Real* since 1994 appears to have reversed this trend somewhat and increased the average real income of some of the poorest wage earners (Beting 1996, 164), although these gains have been partially offset by rising unemployment.

7. "Brasil tem 50 milhoes de 'clandestinos,'" *Folha de São Paulo,* November 17, 1996, 1–12. The announcement was probably an overestimate. In 1999, for example, the Federal government's IBGE (Instituto Brasileiro de Geografia e Estatistica) announced that only 1 million people lacked birth certificates. From *Veja,* November 17, 1999, 35.

8. All translations from the Portugese in this chapter are mine.

9. I develop this idea in greater depth in Pereira 1998. It might be objected that liberalism is always elitist because universalistic laws ignore inequalities of condition. Thus Anatole France mockingly praised "the majestic egalitarian of the law, which forbids rich and poor alike to sleep under bridges, to beg in the streets, and to steal bread" (in *Le Lys Rouge,* 1894). That, however, is an observation about the effects of the law. I am using elitist liberalism to connote something different and even more fundamentally corrosive of the rule of law—the nonuniversal application of law is not liberal at all, and what I am referring to is elitism plain and simple, reflecting Brazil's Catholic and corporatist heritage. Although I cannot fully counter such an argument here, my formulation recognizes the uneasy coexistence of illiberal and liberal ideologies in Brazilian political culture denying the enduring and growing appeal of the latter.

10. I use the terms "retroactive justice" and "corrective justice" interchangeably in the text. Both are imprecise, in that all justice is retroactive and corrective, and both refer to all measures enacted by posttransition regimes to make up for injustices committed by the previous regime, often a long time ago.

11. Interview with Hélio Bicudo, then a congressional deputy for São Paulo from the Workers' Party, in São Paulo, January 23, 1995. Bicudo did not run for reelection in 1998 and is no longer in the Congress.

12. A full explanation for the difference in repertoires of the human rights groups in each country is not possible here. Citing the lower numbers of deaths in Brazil does not in itself seem sufficient, as the families of the more than three hundred killed were potentially a large enough base from which could have arisen a few protesting *madres.* With regard to the comparison with Chile, Robert John Barros (1996) shows how the Pinochet regime did make extensive efforts to legalize and constitutionalize its rule, but only after the bloody coup of 1973.

13. In Argentina, in contrast, the sense of urgency regarding the need to restore the rule of law was astute. For a compelling account of the politics of retroactive justice there, see Nino (1996).

14. The argument that Brazil's relatively low number of killed and disappeared made the investigation of these cases irrelevant to the rule of law is not convincing. It seems to me that any pattern of systematic torture and killing by security forces is a major breach of the rule of law, no matter how many people were victims. Consequently, how the postauthoritarian regime addresses this issue is of major consequence for the legality of the new order.

15. Interview with Dona Helena Pereira dos Santos, Tortura Nunca Mais, São Paulo branch, October 7, 1994.

16. The argument of Ackerman (1992, 69–98) that posttransition societies should ignore issues of corrective justice in order not to divert attention from the essential task

of rewriting constitutions seems misguided in this regard. In some circumstances, the two tasks are linked—creating a rule of law for citizens in the future may rest on how past injustices are resolved because the latter reflects upon the credibility of the new order.

17. Weschler (1990, 72) reports that the book remained in the number-one position on the Brazilian best-seller list for twenty-five weeks after its publication in 1985 and that 200,000 copies of it were in circulation by the end of the 1980s. A revised English-language edition was published in the United States (see Dassin 1986).

18. The Ustra book is primarily a self-defense. The author, a member of the Destacamente de Operacões Internas-Comando Operacional de Defesa Interna (DOI-CODI) in the early 1970s, was publicly accused of torture in 1985. Similar debates about the collective memory of military rule and its repression have broken out more recently, as when the film *Lamarca* (1994), based on the true story of a captain who deserted the army to join the armed left, was released. The film *O Que É Isso, Companheiro?* (released in the U.S. as *Four Days in September* [1997]), about the 1969 kidnapping of the U.S. ambassador, was particularly controversial. The latter, based on a book of the same name by Fernando Gabeira, a participant in the kidnapping and now a member of Congress, seemed to generate more criticism from the left than from the right. For an interesting example of this criticism, see Reis Filho (1997).

19. The struggle for "the collective memory" of the military regime continues, with the founding of university archives and collections of the period, the trickling out of information from newly opened government archives, and pressure to open more archives. In February 1997, a new policy governing the classification and release of government documents promised to ensure that more information will be available to researchers in the coming years.

20. This story is skillfully told in Joao Godoy's 1994 documentary film *Vala comum* (Mass grave).

21. Members of the new government who had files in the São Paulo DOPS included First Lady Ruth Cardoso; Pérsio Arida, the first head of the central bank; Pedro Malan, minister of finance; Francisco Weffort, minister of culture; the late Sérgio Motta, general-secretary of the PSDB and later minister of communications; and José Serra, the first minister of planning and later minister of health. See "Arquivos do Deops Tem fichas até do papa," *Folha de São Paulo* December 12, 1994, A12, and "Equipe salta de ficha do Deops para o poder," *Folha de São Paulo,* December 3, 1994, 1–6.

22. This committee was created for the first time in 1995 and was first chaired by Hélio Bicudo (PT-SP).

23. Interview with Rodrigo Ribeiro and Helber Pereira, staff members of the commission, in Brasília on August 21, 1998. Ribeiro and Pereira supplied me with a commission report that confirmed these figures. There is a discrepancy between the number of victims and indemnifications, because five families did not want the latter and ten indemnifications were pending at the time of the interview. Compensation was calculated in this way: average life expectancy minus the age of the person at the time of the disappearance or killing multiplied by 3,000 reals (then roughly US$ 2,500 at the time).

24. The international actors favoring the creation of a commission included Amnesty International and Americas Watch, but not the U.S. government, which was conspicuous by its silence on the issue. U.S. Information Agency official John Dwyer told me that after Cardoso's election, his agency had considered issuing a statement urging the Brazilian government to investigate the killed and disappeared but that the suggestion was ultimately rejected as inappropriate (interview, Washington, D.C., July 8, 1996).

25. This information is well-known, but I repeat it here to place the violence of the two periods in perspective. The comparison excludes criminal suspects who were killed

under the military regime, data on which are unavailable and unlikely to ever become so. The startling nature of these kinds of statistics provoked Paulo Sérgio Pinheiro to entitle his brilliant essay "The Past Is Not Dead: Nor Is It Yet the Past" (Pinheiro 1996b), and it has also motivated important work such as that by Caldeira (1996).

26. Carlos Franco, "Brasil Supera EUA em Mortes Violentas," *O Estado de São Paulo,* September 26, 1994, C3. Brazil's murder rate more than doubled between the late 1970s and the late 1990s, and in 1996, it was 24.8 per 100,000 compared to 10.1 in the United States. This was one of the highest murder rates in Latin America—Colombia topped the list with 89.5 per 100,000 (data from Mesquita Neto 1998, 32; Blount and Otis 1997, 56).

27. Mesquita Neto (1998, 13) reports that in 1994, there were 385,600 soldiers in the military police. Although fewer than the number of private security guards, this figure surpasses the total number of troops in all three branches of the armed forces in the same year—336,800.

28. The PMs were placed back under the command of appointees of elected state governors in 1982.

29. Interview with then-Congressman Hélio Bicudo (PT-SP), January 23, 1995.

30. For a work on the U.S. role in training and advising the Brazilian police, see Huggins (1998). Between 1959 and 1969, 641 members of the Brazilian police received training in the United States or at the international American Police Academy in Panama. A public safety program managed by the United States Agency for International Development (USAID) supplied equipment, management consulting, and training to police in Brazil and assisted in the expansion of the Federal Police in 1965—from the 1971 congressional testimony of Theodore D. Brown, chief of the USAID public safety program in Brazil (U.S. Senate 1971, 1–6).

31. News from Brazil supplied by Serviço Brasileiro de Justiça e Paz (SEJUP), No. 280, July 17, 1997.

32. Interview with Franco Caneva, Jr., prosecutor in the state military justice system, São Paulo, October 17, 1996.

33. A 1977 reform issued by the executive reinterpreted the constitution so as to expand the concept of military crimes—judged in state military courts—to include crimes by military policeman against civilians. This reinterpretation was upheld by the Brazilian Supreme Court in 1978.

34. Interview with Franco Caneva, Jr., and Fernando Sérgio Barone Nucci, prosecutors in the state military justice system, São Paulo, October 17, 1996.

35. Interview with Dr. Getúlio Correa, president, Associaçao dos Magistrados das Polícias Militares Estaduais (Association of State Military Police Judges) and judge in the state military justice system, Florianópolis, Santa Catarina, September 25 and 30, 1996. Judge Correa's belief that Brazilian juries will be reluctant to convict policemen accused of killing people with criminal records might be well-founded. Summary executions by the police, far from being universally condemned, are often applauded by a population that feels threatened by crime and unprotected by the state. In Brazil in March 1995, for example, military police were filmed shooting to death a subdued, unarmed suspected criminal as they held him face down on the sidewalk; when the video was shown on a television news program, 86 percent of viewers surveyed said that the police had behaved correctly (*Veja,* March 15, 1995, 46).

36. The precise language was "crimes . . . quando dolosos contra a vida e cometidos contra civil"—"intentional crimes against life and committed upon a civilian" (Law Number 9,299 of August 7, 1996). The law also took the same crimes out of the jurisdiction of the federal military justice system, which handles crimes committed by members of the

armed forces. However, the highest court in federal military justice, the Superior Tribunal Militar (Superior Military Court), ruled that the law was unconstitutional and as of October 1998 had not enforced it.

37. The most notable of these incidents occurred in late March 1997, when nine police officers were arrested after a photographer videotaped officers physically abusing motorists and trying to extort money from them at a roadblock set up to apprehend drug traffickers in an industrial suburb of São Paulo. One policeman was shown shooting at a car that drove away from the roadblock; the passenger in the vehicle was killed. The video was shown throughout Brazil and provoked considerable outrage (*New York Times,* April 2, 1997, A3).

38. The squeezing of the middle class brought on by the Real Plan might have also contributed to this dynamic, to the extent that downwardly mobile members of the middle class could have felt they were losing their previous immunity from police violence, and thus had a greater stake in controlling the police.

39. The police strikes began in Minas Gerais in late June 1997, when the state governor awarded pay increases to military police officers but not enlisted men. Although forbidden by law, members of both the civilian police and the military police subsequently engaged in similar strikes in more than ten states, demanding increases in their pay, which averaged less than $500 a month. The strikes led to the use of the army for police patrolling in nine states, negotiations with strike leaders, and subsequent pay raises ("Armas Rebeladas," *Veja,* July 30, 1991, 28–35; Mesquita Neto 1997, 1998, 35).

40. A Datafolha survey of 4,601 people in ten state capitals conducted on July 24, 1997, revealed that 89 percent of the respondents thought the demands for salary increases by the police were just (News from Brazil supplied by the Serviço Brasileiro de Justica e Paz [SEJUP], No. 282, July 31, 1997).

41. The program includes many specific institutional measures to reduce police abuses of human rights and is not merely an exhortatory document. It is unclear at this point to what extent these measures have been implemented.

42. Some changes are slowly occurring in this area. For example, human rights training of military police officers has been initiated in São Paulo and Minas Gerais. It remains to be seen what the long-term affects of such programs will be—whether, for example, the principles imparted in such courses are integrated into the overall structure and practices of the military police organization.

43. Prosecutors argued that another reason for the drop in violence was a new policy in which PMs who killed in the line of duty were taken off regular beats, sent for psychological counseling, and given administrative jobs with daytime hours. The PMs saw this policy as punishment, because many of them had second jobs (*bicos*) that they were able to squeeze in between patrol shifts but would be unable to maintain if they had regular daytime administrative shifts (interview with Franco Caneva, Jr. and Fernando Sérgio Barone Nucci, prosecutors in the state military justice system, São Paulo, October 17, 1996). For more on the São Paulo police reforms, see Reddy and Pereira (1998, appendix D).

44. These programs are one element of the movement for "the popular dissemination of juridical knowledge" begun at the law school at the University of Brasília, known as "law found in the streets"—*direito achado na ruaa* (Sousa 1993, 9).

Chapter 12

The authors are grateful to Dr. Simon Schwartzman of IBGE and Dr. Claudio Considera of IPEA for facilitating access to data sources. They also wish to recognize the influence of three distinguished Brazilian scholars—Glaucio Ary Dillon Soares, Vilmar Faria, and Wanderley Guilherme dos Santos—whose important works on the politics of sociodemographic change during the Second Republic (Soares 1973) and the military regime (Faria 1983; W. Santos 1985) inspired this much more modest effort on the New Republic. Any errors of fact or interpretation are entirely the responsibility of the authors.

1. An important recent exception is the working paper by Schwartzman (1997), and we refer readers to that paper for coverage of several topics that we do not engage at length here, including race, agrarian reform, and industrial employment.

2. For a broader perspective on the unevenness of state penetration and the rule of law in Brazil, perpetuating what the authors call a "disjunctive democracy," see Holston and Caldeira (1998).

3. For a study of black political participation in the New Republic, see Berquó and Alencastro (1992).

4. The IBGE reported that for the month of February 1998, unemployment in the six largest metropolitan areas (Rio, São Paulo, Belo Horizonte, Salvador, Recife, and Pôrto Alegre) reached 7.42 percent of the economically active population (*Jornal do Brasil* 1998).

5. For an excellent, comprehensive overview of education in Brazil, see Birdsall and Sabot (1996).

6. According to 1995 data from the Organization for Economic Cooperation and Development's World Education Indicators project, Brazil spent 5 percent of its GDP on education, compared to an average of 4.7 percent for the forty-three countries studied. The reasons for Brazil's high ranking lay mostly in the higher education sector: Brazil's expenditure of $14,300 per student was 63 percent higher than the average for the same forty-three countries. The equivalent figure for developed countries only was $8,700 per student (*Jornal do Brasil,* November 24, 1998).

7. For a study of Erundina's Movimento de Alfabetização de Jovens e Adultos (MOVA), a literacy program in São Paulo between 1989 and 1993, see Stromquist (1997).

BIBLIOGRAPHY

Abers, Rebecca. 1996. "From Ideas to Practice: The Partido dos Trabalhadores and Participatory Governance in Brazil." *Latin American Perspectives* 23: 35–53.

———. 1997. "Inventing Local Democracy: Neighborhood Organizing and Participatory Policy-Making in Porto Alegre, Brazil." Ph.D diss., Department of Urban Planning, University of California at Los Angeles.

———. 1998. "From Clientelism to Cooperation: Local Government, Participatory Policy, and Civic Organizing in Porto Alegre, Brazil." *Politics and Society* 26(4): 511–537.

Abranches, Sérgio. 1978. "The Divided Leviathan: State and Economic Policy Formation in Authoritarian Brazil." Ph.D. diss., Department of Political Science, Cornell University, Ithaca, N.Y.

———. 1988. "Presidencialismo de coalizão: O dilema institucional brasileiro." *Dados* 31(1): 5–38.

Abreu, Alzira Alves de, and José Luciano de Mattos Dias, eds. 1995. *O futuro do Congresso brasileiro*. Rio de Janeiro: Editora Fundação Getúlio Vargas.

Abrucio, Fernando Luiz. 1994. "Os barões da federação: O poder dos governadores no Brasil pós-autoritário." Master's thesis, Department of Sociology, Universidade de São Paulo, São Paulo, S.P.

Abrucio, Fernando Luiz, and Cláudio Gonçalves Couto. 1996. "A redefinição do papel do estado no âmbito local." *São Paulo em Perspectiva* 10(3): 40–47.

Ackerman, Bruce. 1992. *The Future of Liberal Revolution*. New Haven: Yale University Press.

Acuña, Carlos H., and William C. Smith. 1995. "The Politics of 'Military Economics' in the Southern Cone: Comparative Perspectives on Democracy and Arms Production in Argentina, Brazil, and Chile." In *Political Power and Social Theory*, vol. 9, edited by D. E. Davis and H. Kimeldorf, pp. 121–57. Greenwich, Conn.: JAI Press.

Adler, Emanuel. 1987. *The Power of Ideology: The Quest for Technological Autonomy in Argentina and Brazil*. Berkeley and Los Angeles: University of California Press.

AESP (Associação de Emissoras de São Paulo). 1992. "Concessões e apoio politico: Tudo será como antes?" January: 24–25.

Affonso, Rui de Britto Alvares. 1988. "Federalismo tributário e crise econômica: Brasil 1975–1985." Master's thesis, Department of Economics, Universidade Estadual de Campinas, Campinas, S.P.

———. 1994. "A Crise da federação no Brasil." *Ensaios FEE* 15(2): 321–337.

———. 1995. "A federação no Brasil: Impasses e perspectivas." In *A federação em perspectiva: Ensaios selecionados*, edited by Rui de Britto Álvares Affonso and Pedro Luiz Barros Silva, pp. 57–75. São Paulo: FUNDAP.

———. 1996. "Os municípios e os desafios da federação no Brasil." *São Paulo em Perspectiva* 10(3): 3–10.

———. 1997. "Decentralização e crise federativa: A especificidade do Brasil." Paper presented at the Twentieth International Congress of the Latin American Studies Association, Guadalajara, Mexico, April 17–19.

Afonso, José Roberto Rodrigues. 1994. "Descentralização fiscal: Revendo idéias." *Ensaios FEE* 15: 353–89.

———. 1995. "A questão tributária e o financiamento dos diferentes níveis de governo." In *A federação em perspectiva: Ensaios selecionados,* edited by Rui de Britto Álvares Affonso and Pedro Luiz Barros Silva, pp. 315–328. São Paulo: FUNDAP.

Afonso, José Roberto Rodrigues, and Nelson de Castro Serra. 1994. "Despesa pública— competências, serviços locais, descentralização: O papel dos municípios." Texto para discussão No. 23. Rio de Janeiro: CEPP.

Agüero, Felipe. 1994. "The Latin American Military: Development, Reform, and 'Nation-Building'?" In *Security, Democracy, and Development in U.S.–Latin American Relations,* edited by L. Schoultz, W. C. Smith, and A. Varas, pp. 243–64. New Brunswick, N.J.: Transaction Publishers.

———. 1998. "Las fuerzas armadas en una época de transición: Perspectivas para el afianzamiento de la democracia en América Latina." In *Control civil y fuerzas armadas en las nuevas democracias Latinoamericas,* edited by Rut Diamint. Buenos Aires: Universidad Torcuato di Tella Nuevohacer–Grupo Editor Latinoamericana.

Alencastro, Luiz Felipe de. 1993. "Cultura democrática e presidencialismo no Brasil." *Novos Estudos* 35 (March): 21–30.

Alimonda, Hector. 1994. "Mercosur, Democracy, and Labor." *Latin American Perspectives* 21: 21–33.

Almeida, Dom Luciano Mendes de, and Maria da Conceição Tavares. 1995. *Os excluídos: Debate entre os autores.* Petrópolis: Vozes.

Almeida, Jorge. 1996. *Como vota o brasileiro.* São Paulo: Casa Amarela.

Almeida, Maria Hermínia Tavares de. 1993. "Em defesa da mudança." *Novos Estudos* 35 (March): 15–20.

———. 1994. "Redefinição de competências entre esferas de governo na prestação de serviços públicos na área social." Final Report, "Balanço e perspectivas do federalismo fiscal no Brasil." São Paulo: IESP/FUNDAP.

Almeida, Ronaldo. 1996. "A universalização do Reino de Deus." *Novos Estudos* 44 (March): 12–23.

Altemeyer, Fernando, Jr. 1996. "A pastoral católica no ano de 1995." *Tempo e Presença* 285 (January–February): 23–25.

Alvarez, Sonia E. 1989a. "Politicizing Gender and Engendering Democracy." In *Democratizing Brazil: Problems of Transition and Consolidation,* edited by A. Stepan, pp. 205–51. New York: Oxford University Press.

———. 1989b. "Women's Movements and Gender Politics in the Brazilian Transition." In *The Women's Movement in Latin America: Feminism and the Transition to Democracy,* edited by J. S. Jaquette, pp. 18–71. Boston: Unwin Hyman.

———. 1990. *Engendering Democracy in Brazil: Women's Movements in Transition Politics.* Princeton: Princeton University Press.

Alves, Carlos Eduardo. 1994. "Candidate Lula Disagrees With PT Government Program." *Folha de São Paulo,* February 10, p. 10 (from FBIS-LAT-94-031, February 15, p. 38).

Alves, María Helena Moreira. 1985. *State and Opposition in Military Brazil.* Austin: University of Texas Press.

———. 1993. "Something Old, Something New: Brazil's Partido dos Trabalhadores." In *The Latin American Left: From the Fall of Allende to Perestroika,* edited by B. Carr and S. Ellner, pp. 225–242. Boulder, Colo.: Westview.

Amaral, Luis Henrique. 1995. "Desigualdade entre ricos e pobres é causa maior da criminalidade." *Folha de São Paulo,* September 3, 1: 17.

Amato, Mário. 1992. Interview by the author with the president of Federação das Indústrias do Estado de São Paulo (FIESP), São Paulo, June 9.

Ames, Barry. N.d. "Disparately Seeking Politicians: Strategies and Outcomes in Brazilian Legislative Elections." Political Science Paper 126, Washington University (cited in Melo 1995, 38).

————. 1987. *Political Survival.* Berkeley: University of California Press.

————. 1994. "The Reverse Coattails Effect: Local Party Organization in the 1989 Brazilian Presidential Election." *American Political Science Review* 88, no. 1 (March): 95–111.

————. 1995a. "Electoral Strategy under Open-List Proportional Representation." *American Journal of Political Science* 39: 406–33.

————. 1995b. "Electoral Rules, Constituency Pressures, and Pork Barrel: Bases of Voting in the Brazilian Congress." *Journal of Politics* 57, no. 2: 324–43.

Amorim Neto, Octavio. 1995. "Cabinet Formation and Party Politics in Brazil." Paper prepared for the Nineteenth International Congress of the Latin American Studies Association, Washington, D.C., September 28–30.

Anderson, Charles W. 1967. *Politics and Economic Change in Latin America.* New York: Van Nostrand Reinhold.

Andrade, Paulo Fernando Carneiro de. 1993. "A condição pós-moderna como desafio à pastoral popular." *Revista Eclesiástica Brasileira* 53 (March): 110–11.

Antoniazzi, Alberto, and Cleto Caliman. 1994. *A presença da Igreja na cidade.* Petrópolis: Vozes.

Aragão, Murillo de. 1995. "Ação dos grupos de pressão nos processos constitucionais recentes no Brasil." Paper presented at the Latin American Studies Association, Washington D.C., September 28–30.

Araújo, José Tavares de, Jr. 1990. "El programa de integración Argentina-Brasil y las tendencias actuales de la economia mundial." In *Argentina-Brazil: Perspectivas comparativas y ejes de integración,* edited by Monica Hirst, pp. 239–48. Buenos Aires: Editorial Tésis.

Archdiocese of Belo Horizonte. 1994. *Ética: Pessoa e sociedade.* Subsídios para reflexão, Arquidiocese de Belo Horizonte, projeto Construir a Esperança. Belo Horizonte.

Arquidiocese de São Paulo. 1985. *Brasil: Nunca mais.* Petrópolis: Vozes.

Arretche, Marta T. S. 1996. "Mitos da descentralização: Mais democracia e eficiência nas políticas públicas?" *Revista Brasileira de Ciências Sociais* 11: 44–66.

————. 1998. "Políticas sociais no Brasil: Descentralização em um estado federativo." Paper prepared for the XXI meeting of the Latin American Studies Association, Chicago.

Assies, Willem. 1993. "Urban Social Movements and Local Democracy in Brazil." *European Review of Latin American and Caribbean Studies* 55:39–58.

Assmann, Hugo. 1986. *A Igreja eletrônica e seu impacto na América Latina.* Petrópolis: Vozes.

Associação de Emissoras de São Paulo. *See* AESP.

Aufderheide, Patricia. 1997. "The Role of the Brazilian Public in Cable Television Policymaking." *Comunicação e Política* 4, no. 2 (May–August): 55–80.

Azevedo, Clovis Bueno de. 1995. *A estrela partida ao meio: Ambigüidades do pensamento petista.* São Paulo: Entrelinhas.

Azevedo, Marcello de Carvalho. 1987. *Basic Ecclesial Communities in Brazil.* Translated by John Drury. Washington, D.C.: Georgetown University Press.

Baaklini, Abdo I. 1992. *The Brazilian Legislature and Political System.* Westport, Conn.: Greenwood.

Baer, Werner. 1995. *The Brazilian Economy: Growth and Development.* New York: Praeger Publishers.

Baia, Paulo Fernandes. 1996. "A economia política do Partido dos Trabalhadores: Um estudo sobre o discurso petista (1979–1994)." Master's thesis, Department of Political Economy, Pontifícia Universidade Católica de São Paulo, São Paulo, S.P.

Banco Central. 1996. *PROER: Programa de estímulo à reestruturação e ao fortalecimento do Sistema Financeiro Nacional.* Brasília.

Banco Nacional de Desenvolvimento Econômico e Social (BNDES). 1989a. "Integração competitiva: Uma estratégia para o desenvolvimento brasileiro." Área de Planejamento, Brasília. November.

———. 1989b. "Integração competitiva: Uma nova estratégia para a industrialização brasileira." Paper presented by Luiz Paulo Vellozo Lucas, chief of the Planning Department at the United Nations Industrial Development Organization Technical Meeting, Vienna, Austria, April 4–7.

Barrera, Aglas Watson, and Maria Liz de Medeiros Roarelli. 1995. "Relações fiscais intergovernamentais." In *Reforma tributária e federação,* edited by Rui de Britto Álvares Affonso and Pedro Luiz Barros Silva, pp. 129–160. São Paulo: FUNDAP.

Barros, Alexandre de Souza Costa. 1978. "The Brazilian Military: Professional Socialization, Political Performance, and State Building." Ph.D. diss., Department of Political Science, University of Chicago.

———. 1995. "How the Brazilian Congress Functions." In "Brazilian Congressional Guide 1995–1999," edited by Maria das Graças Rua, Working Paper WP95-3, Institute of Brazilian Business and Public Management Issues, George Washington University.

Barros, Andréa, and Laura Carpiglione. 1997. "Soldados da fé e da prosperidade." *Veja,* July 2. World Wide Web version.

Barros, Mônica do Nascimento. 1995. "A Batalha do Armagedon: Uma análise do repertório mágico-religioso proposto pela Igreja Universal do Reino de Deus." Master's thesis, Federal University of Minas Gerais, Belo Horizonte, M. G.

Barros, Ricardo Paes de, and Rosane Mendonça. 1996a. "O impacto do crescimento econômico e de reduções no grau de desigualdade sobre a pobreza." Série Seminários no. 25/96. Rio de Janeiro: IPEA.

———. 1996b. "Os determinantes da desigualdade no Brasil." In IPEA, *A Economia Brasileira em Perspectiva: 1996,* pp. 421–74. Rio de Janeiro: IPEA.

Barros, Robert John. 1996. "By Reason and Force: Military Constitutionalism in Chile, 1973–1989." Ph.D. diss., Department of Political Science, University of Chicago.

Beloch, Israel, and Alzira Abreu. 1983. *Dicionário histórico-biográfico brasileiro* (4 volumes). Rio de Janeiro: Fundação Getúlio Vargas.

Beozzo, José Oscar. 1994. *A Igreja do Brasil.* Petrópolis: Vozes.

———. 1997. "Sinais marcantes na pastoral católica." *Tempo e Presença* 291 (January–February): 20–23.

Berensztein, Sergio. 1996. "Rebuilding State Capacity in Contemporary Latin America: The Politics of Taxation in Argentina and Mexico." In *Latin America in the World Economy,* edited by Roberto Patricio Korzeniewicz and William C. Smith, pp. 229–248. Westport, Conn.: Greenwood Press.

Bergamasco, Sonia Maria Pessoa Pereira, and Luiz Antonio Cabello Norder. 1995. "A trajetória do estatuto da terra e o paradoxo agrário dos anos 90." *Reforma Agrária* 25: 169–84.

Bernardes, Ernesto. 1995. "Na linha de frente da guerra." *Veja.* September 20, 72–76.

———. 1997. "Menos é melhor." *Veja,* July 2. World Wide Web version.

Bernstein, Carl, and Marco Politi. 1996. *His Holiness: John Paul II and the Hidden History of Our Time.* New York: Doubleday.

Berquó, Elza, and Luiz Felipe Alencastro. 1992. "A emergência do voto negro." *Novos Estudos* 33 (July): 77–88.

Berryman, Philip. 1987. *Liberation Theology.* Philadelphia: Temple University Press.

———. 1996. *Religion in the Megacity: Catholic and Protestant Portraits from Latin America.* Maryknoll, N.Y.: Orbis Books.

Beting, Joelmir. 1996. "Os paraísos do quatrilhão." *Veja,* December 25, 154–64.

Betto, Frei. 1989. *Lula: A biografia política de um operário.* São Paulo: Estação Liberdade.

Bierstecker, Thomas J. 1995. "The 'Triumph' of Liberal Economic Ideas in the Developing World." In *Global Change, Regional Response: The New International Context of Development,* edited by Barbara Stallings, pp. 174–96. Cambridge: Cambridge University Press.

Bingemer, Maria Clara Lucchetti, and Roberto dos Santos Bartholo, Jr., eds. 1997. *Exemplaridade ética e santidade.* São Paulo: Edições Loyola.

Birdsall, Nancy, Barbara Bruns, and Richard H. Sabot. 1996. "Education in Brazil: Playing a Bad Hand Badly." In *Opportunity Foregone: Education in Brazil,* edited by Nancy Birdsall and Richard H. Sabot, pp. 7–48. Washington, D.C.: Interamerican Development Bank.

Bittar, Jorge. 1992. *O modo petista de governar.* São Paulo: Teoria e Debate.

Blay, Eva. 1993. "Em cinco anos, nada de novo." *Teoria e Debate* 22: 73–75.

Blount, Jeb, and John Otis. 1997. "Law and Order." *Latin Trade* (June): 48–57.

Blumenthal, Sidney. 1982. *The Permanent Campaign.* New York: Simon and Schuster.

Boito, Armando, Jr. 1991. "Reforma e persistência da estrutura sindical." In *O Sindicalismo Brasileiro nos Anos 80,* edited by Armando Boito, Jr., pp. 43–91. Rio de Janeiro: Paz e Terra.

Bomfim, Antúlio, and Anwar Shah. 1994. "Macroeconomic Management and the Division of Powers in Brazil." *World Development* 22: 535–42.

Bornhausen, Roberto Konder. 1991. *Reflexões sobre o Brasil.* Cadernos do IRS no. 18. São Paulo: FIESP.

Bouzas, Roberto. 1990. "La crisis de la déuda, la vulnerabilidad externa, y el programa de integración y cooperación Argentina-Brasil." In *Argentina-Brazil: Perspectivas comparativas y ejes de integración,* edited by Monica Hirst, pp. 31–37. Buenos Aires: Editorial Tesis.

Branford, Sue, and Kucinski, Bernardo. 1995. *Brazil: Carnival of the Oppressed; Lula and the Brazilian Workers' Party.* London: Latin America Bureau/Russell.

Brasileiro, Ana Maria. 1973. *O município como sistema político.* Rio de Janeiro: FGV.

Brazil. Grupo Interministerial de Política Industrial. 1986. "Política industrial." July.

———. Ministério da Economia, Fazenda, e Planejamento. 1990. "Diretrizes gerais para a política industrial e de comércio exterior." June 26.

———. Presidência da República. 1991a. "Brasil: Um projeto de reconstrução nacional."

———. Presidência da República. 1991b. "Desregulamentação, ano I."

Brazil. Secretaria de Assuntos Estratégicos, Centro de Estudos Estratégicos. 1996. "Documento sobre política de defesa nacional," 1, no. 2: 7–15.

Bremaeker, François E. J. de. 1995. "Perfil das receitas municípais." Série Estudos Especiais no. 6. Rio de Janeiro: Instituto Brasileiro de Administração Municipal.

Bresser Pereira, Luiz Carlos. 1978. *O colapso de um aliança de classes.* São Paulo: Brasiliense.

———. 1984. *Development and Crisis in Brazil, 1930–1983.* Translated by Marcia Van Dyke. Boulder, Colo.: Westview Press.

———. 1990. "Presupuestos y obstáculos de la integración Argentina-Brazil." In *Argentina-Brasil: Perspectivas comparativas y ejes de integración,* edited by Monica Hirst, pp. 223–26. Buenos Aires: Editorial Tesis.

———. 1996. *Economic Crisis and State Reform in Brazil: Toward a New Interpretation of Latin America.* Boulder, Colo.: Lynne Rienner Publishers.

Bresser Pereira, Luiz Carlos, José Maria Maravall, and Adam Przeworski, eds. 1993. *Economic Reforms in New Democracies: A Social Democratic Approach.* Cambridge: Cambridge University Press.

Brown, Diana DeG. 1994. *Umbanda: Religion and Politics in Urban Brazil.* New York: Columbia University Press.

Bruneau, Thomas C., and W. E. Hewitt. 1992. "Catholicism and Political Action in Brazil: Limitations and Prospects." In *Conflict and Competition: The Latin American Church in a Changing Environment,* edited by Edward L. Cleary and Hannah Stewart-Gambino, pp. 45–62. Boulder, Colo.: Lynne Rienner Publishers.

Bueno, Lauro. 1995. "The Paradox of Police Violence within Brazil's New Democracy: A Look at São Paulo's Military Police." Master's thesis, Department of Political Science, New School for Social Research, New York.

Burdick, John. 1993. *Looking for God in Brazil.* Berkeley and Los Angeles: University of California Press.

———. 1994. "The Progressive Catholic Church in Latin America: Giving Voice or Listening to Voices?" *Latin American Research Review* 29, no.1: 184–97.

Burkhart, Ross E. 1997. "Comparative Democracy and Income Distribution: Shape and Direction of the Causal Arrow." *Journal of Politics* 59 (February): 148–64.

Burns, Nancy. 1994. *The Formation of American Local Governments: Private Values in Public Institutions.* Oxford: Oxford University Press.

Caccia Bava, Silvio. 1995. "Participação popular e democracia representativa no fortalecimento do poder local." In *Subsidiariedade e fortalecimento do poder local* 6: 81–66, 95. São Paulo: Fundação Konrad-Adenauer-Stiftung.

Caldeira, Teresa. 1996. "Crime and Individual Rights: Reframing the Question of Violence in Latin America." In *Constructing Democracy: Human Rights, Citizenship, and Solidarity in Latin America,* edited by Elizabeth Jelin and Eric Hershberg, pp. 197–211. Boulder, Colo.: Westview Press.

Câmara dos Deputados. *See* CD

Cammack, Paul. 1982. "Clientelism and Military Government in Brazil." In *Private Patronage and Public Power: Clientelism in the Modern State,* edited by Christopher Clapham. London: Frances Pinter.

Campos, H. L. 1991. "Os interesses regionais na Assembléia Nacional Constituente." Masters' thesis, Department of Sociology, Universidade Estadual de Campinas (UNICAMP), Campinas, S.P.

Cano, Wilson. 1994. "Concentración, desconcentración, y descentralización en Brasil." In *Territorios en transformación: Análisis y propuestas,* edited by José Luis Curbelo, Francisco Alburquerque, Carlos A. de Mattos, and Juan Ramón Cuadrado, pp. 223–238. Madrid: Fondo Europeo de Desarrollo Regional.

Cantanhêde, Eliane. 1997. "Renda mínima: Programa aproxima governo e oposição." *Folha de São Paulo,* October 12.

Capriglione, Laura, and Angélica Santa Cruz. 1996. "Sem lei nem ordem" *Veja* 11 (December): 58–63.

Cardia, Nancy. 1995. "Direitos humanos e exclusão moral." *Sociedade e Estado* 10: 343–89.

Cardoso, Eliana A. 1994. *Economia brasileira ao alcance de todos*. 16th ed. São Paulo: Editora Brasiliense.

Cardoso, Fernando Henrique. 1975. *Autoritarismo e democratização*. São Paulo: Paz e Terra.

———. 1994. *Mãos à obra, Brasil*. Brasília: n.p.

Cardoso, Fernando Henrique, and Bolivar Lamounier, eds. 1978. *Os partidos e as eleições no Brasil*. Rio de Janeiro: Paz e Terra.

Cardoso, Ruth Correa Leite. 1983. "Movimentos sociais urbanos: Balanço crítico." In *Sociedade e política no Brasil pós-64*, edited by B. Sorj and M. H. T. D. Almeida, pp. 215–39. São Paulo: Editora Brasiliense.

———. 1990. "Participação política e democracia." *Novos Estudos* 26: 15–24.

———. 1992. "Popular Movements in the Context of the Consolidation of Democracy in Brazil." In *The Making of Social Movements in Latin America: Identity, Strategy, and Democracy*, edited by A. Escobar and S. E. Alvarez, pp. 291–302. Boulder, Colo.: Westview Press.

Carneiro, Leandro Piquet. 1997. "The Church as Political Context: Civic Culture and Political Participation Among Protestants." Paper delivered at Twentieth International Congress of the Latin American Studies Association, Guadalajara, Mexico, April 17–19.

Carneiro, Sueli. 1990. "Projeto nacional: A organização nacional das mulheres negras e as perspectivas políticas." *Revista de Cultura Vozes* 84: 211–19.

Carnoy, Martin. 1984. *The State and Political Theory*. Princeton: Princeton University Press.

Carvalho, Gilberto. 1996. Interview by William Nylen with the National Communications Director for the PT, São Paulo, June 12.

Casanova, José. 1994. *Public Religions in the Modern World*. Chicago: University of Chicago Press.

———. 1997. "Globalizing Catholicism and the Return to a 'Universal' Church." In *Transnational Religion and Fading States*, edited by Susanne Hoeber Rudolph and James Piscatori, pp. 121–43. Boulder, Colo.: Westview Press.

Castañeda, Jorge G. 1993. *Utopia Unarmed: The Latin American Left After the Cold War*. New York: Alfred A. Knopf.

Castro, Celso Corrêa Pinto de. 1990. *O espírito militar: Um estudo de antropologia social na Academia Militar das Agulhas Negras*. Rio de Janeiro: Zahar.

———. 1993. "A origem social dos militares: Novos dados para uma antiga discussão." *Novos Estudos* 37: 225–31.

Castro, Maria Helena Guimarães de. 1987. "Equipamentos sociais, política partidária e governos locais no Estado de São Paulo (1968–1982)." Unpublished M.A. thesis, UNICAMP.

Cavarozzi, Marcelo. 1992. "The Left in Latin America: The Decline of Socialism and the Rise of Political Democracy." In *The United States and Latin America in the 1990s: Beyond the Cold War*, edited by J. Hartlyn, L. Schoultz, and A. Varas, pp. 101–27. Chapel Hill: University of North Carolina Press.

CD (Câmara dos Deputados). 1995a. *Proposta de emenda à constituição*. No. 173-A, 1995. Brasília.

———. 1995b. *Proposta de emenda à constituição*. No. 175-A, 1995. Brasília.

———. 1996. *Proposta de emenda à constituição*. No. 33-D, 1995. Brasília.

CEAS. 1993. "O desafio da luta contra a fome." *Cadernos do CEAS* 146: 7–9.

CEBRAP (Centro Brasileiro de Análise e Planejamento). 1994. "O desafio do Congresso Nacional: Mudanças internas e consolidação institucional." *Cadernos de Pesquisa* 3 (November).

Chadwick, Bruce. 1997. "Non-Governmental Organization Growth: Brazil 1970–1995." Web site visited May 8. http://www.columbia.edu/~bpc1/QuickTime/ngos7095.html

Chalmers, Douglas. 1977. "The Politicized State in Latin America." In *Authoritarianism and Corporatism in Latin America,* edited by J. M. Malloy, pp. 23–45. Pittsburgh: University of Pittsburgh Press.

Chauí, Marilena de Souza. 1994. "Raízes teológicas do populismo no Brasil: Teocracia dos dominantes, messianismo dos dominados." In *Os anos 90: Política e sociedade no Brasil,* edited by Evelina Dagnino, pp. 19–30. São Paulo: Brasiliense.

Chesnut, Andrew. 1997. *Born Again in Brazil.* East Rutherford, N.J.: Rutgers University Press.

Chevigny, Paul. 1995. *Edge of the Knife: Police Violence in the Americas.* New York: New Press.

Chudnovsky, Daniel, and Fernando Porta. 1989. "On Argentine-Brazilian Economic Integration." *CEPAL Review* 39: 115–34.

Cidade, Carlos Alberto Macedo. 1995. Interview by the author with legislative director, National Confederation of Industry, Brasília, June 14.

Cipriani, Gabriel. 1994. "The Catholic Church and Religious Pluralism in Brazil." *Notícias CNBB* (International Edition) 6, no. 16 (January–March): 1–4.

Clark, Ann Marie, Elisabeth J. Friedman, and Kathryn Hochstetler. 1998. "The Sovereign Limits of Global Civil Society." *World Politics* 51: 1–35.

Cleary, Edward L. 1997. "The Brazilian Catholic Church and Church-State Relations: Nation Building." *Journal of Church and State* 39, no. 2 (spring): 253–72.

Cleary, Edward L, and Hannah Stewart-Gambino, eds. 1992. *Conflict and Competition: The Latin American Church in a Changing Environment.* Boulder, Colo.: Lynne Rienner Publishers.

CN (Congresso Nacional). 1994a. *Revisão da constituição federal.* No. 24, 1994. Brasília.

———. 1994b. *Relatório final da comissão parlamentar mista de inquérito criada através do requerimento.* Brasília.

CNBB (Conferência Nacional dos Bispos do Brasil). 1984. *Membros da conferência nacional dos bispos do Brasil.* São Paulo: Edições Paulinas.

———. 1989. *Exigências éticas da ordem democrática.* Documentos da CNBB No. 42. São Paulo: Edições Paulinas.

———. 1990. *Participação popular e cidadania: A igreja no processo constituinte.* Estudos da CNBB No. 60. São Paulo: Edições Paulinas.

———. 1991. *Membros da conferência nacional dos bispos do Brasil.* Brasília.

———. 1993. *Ética: Pessoa e sociedade.* Documentos da CNBB No. 50. São Paulo: Edições Paulinas.

———. 1994a. *Brasil: Alternativas e protagonistas—por uma sociedade democrática.* Petrópolis: Vozes.

———. 1994b. *Orientações pastorais sobre a renovação carismática católica.* Documentos da CNBB No. 53. São Paulo: Paulinas.

———. 1995. "Pronunciamento sobre a conjuntura nacional." May 18. Mimeograph.

———. 1996. "Nota da conferência nacional dos bispos do Brasil sobre o massacre de Eldorado dos Carajás, Estado do Pará." *Revista de Cultura Vozes* 3 (May–June): 3–5.

———. 1997. *A fraternidade e os encarcerados: Cristo liberta de todas as prisões.* São Paulo: Editora Salesiana Dom Bosco.

CNI (Confederação Nacional da Indústria). 1995. *Custo Brasil.* Rio de Janeiro.

————. 1996. *Custo Brasil: Agenda no Congresso Nacional.* Rio de Janeiro.

Coelho, João Gilberto Lucas. 1989. "O processo legislativo brasileiro após a constituinte: Reformulações regimentais." Brasília: INESC.

Coes, Donald V. 1995. *Macroeconomic Crises, Policies, and Growth in Brazil, 1964–90.* Washington, D.C.: World Bank.

Cohn, Amélia. N.d. "Descentralização, saúde e democracia: O caso do município de São Paulo." *Cadernos CEDEC,* no 44.

————. 1991. *Brasil: Um projeto de reconstrução nacional.* Brasília: Presidência.

Collier, David, and Steven Levitsky. 1997. "Democracy with Adjectives." *World Politics* 49(3): 430–51.

Collor de Mello, Fernando. 1995. Interview by Kurt Weyland, Brasília, June 9.

Comblin, José. 1993. "A nova evangelização." In Clodovis Boff et al., *Santo Domingo: Ensaios teológico-pastorais,* pp. 206–24. Petrópolis: SOTER.

————. 1996. *Cristãos rumo ao século XXI.* Petrópolis: Vozes.

Comissão de Familiares de Mortos e Desaparecidos Políticos. 1995. *Dossiê dos mortos e desaparecidos políticos a partir de 1964.* Recife: Companhia Editora de Pernambuco.

Comissão Pastoral da Terra. 1993. "O campo brasileiro em 1992." *Cadernos do CEAS* 148:76–84.

Comitê Brasileiro Pela Anistia. 1984. *Dossiê dos mortos e desaparecidos.* Pôrto Alegre: Assembléia Legislativa.

Conca, Ken. 1997. *Manufacturing Insecurity: The Rise and Fall of Brazil's Military-Industrial Complex.* Boulder, Colo.: Lynne Rienner Publishers.

Confederação Nacional da Indústria. *See* CNI

Conferência Nacional dos Bispos do Brasil. *See* CNBB

Congresso Nacional. *See* CN

Conjuntura Econômica. 1997. "Conjuntura estatística" (April).

Coppedge, Michael. 1995. "Freezing in the Tropics: Explaining Party-System Volatility in Latin America." Paper presented to the Midwest Political Science Association, Chicago, April 6–8.

Cordeiro, Hésio. 1984. *As empresas médicas.* Rio de Janeiro: Graal.

Costa, João Bosco Araújo da. 1996. "A ressignificação do local: O imaginário político brasileiro pós-80." *São Paulo em Perspectiva* 10(3): 113–18.

Costa, Sérgio. 1994. "Esfera pública, redescoberta da sociedade civil, e movimentos sociais no Brasil." *Novos Estudos* 38: 38–51.

————. 1995. "Atores da sociedade civil e participação política: Algumas restrições." *Cadernos do CEAS* 155: 61–75.

Costa, Sylvio, and Jayme Brener. 1997. "Coronelismo eletrônico: O governo Fernando Henrique e o novo capítulo de uma velha história." *Comunicação e Política* 4(2): 29–53.

Costa, Vera L. C. 1998. "Descentralização da educação no Brasil: As reformas recentes no ensino fundamental." Paper presented at the Latin American Studies Meeting, Chicago.

Couto, Cláudio Gonçalves. 1995. *O desafio de ser governo: O PT na prefeitura de São Paulo (1989–1992).* São Paulo: Paz e Terra.

Couto, Cláudio Gonçalves, and Fernando Luiz Abrucio. 1993. "A dialética da mudança: O PT confronta-se com a institucionalidade." *Cadernos CEDEC,* no. 31.

————. 1995. "Governando a cidade? A força e a fraqueza da câmara municipal." *São Paulo em Perspectiva* 9(2): 57–65.

Cox, Harvey. 1988. *The Silencing of Leonardo Boff.* Bloomington, Ind.: Meyer-Stone Books.

Cunha, Flávio S. 1993. "Movimentos sociais urbanos e redemocratização—A experiência do movimento favelado de Belo Horizonte." *Novos Estudos* 35: 133–43.

Dagnino, Evalina. 1994. *Anos 90: Política e sociedade no Brasil.* São Paulo: Brasiliense.

Dahl, Robert. 1971. *Polyarchy, Participation, and Opposition.* New Haven: Yale University Press.

Dain, Sulamis. 1995. "Conclusão." In *Reforma tributária e federação,* edited by Rui de Britto Álvares Affonso and Pedro Luiz Barros Silva, pp. 161–68. São Paulo: FUNDAP.

Da Matta, Roberto. 1978. "Você sabe com quem está falando? Um ensaio sobre a distinção entre indivíduo e pessoa no Brasil." In *Carnavais, Malandros e heróis: Para uma sociologia do dilemma brasileiro,* edited by Roberta da Matta, pp. 139–93. Rio de Janeiro: Zahar Editores.

D'Araújo, Maria Celina, Glaucio Ary Dillon Soares, and Celso Castro, eds. 1994. *Os anos de chumbo: A memória militar sobre a repressão.* Rio de Janeiro: Relume Dumará.

Dassin, Joan, ed. 1986. *Torture in Brazil.* New York: Vintage Books.

Daudelin, Jean, and W. E. Hewitt. 1995. "Latin American Politics: Exit the Catholic Church?" In *Organized Religion in the Political Transformation of Latin America,* edited by Satya Pattnayak, pp. 177–94. Lanham, Md.: University Press of America.

de Almeida, Paulo Roberto. 1993. "O Mercosul no contexto regional e internacional." *Política Externa* 2: 86–103.

De Groot, C. F. G. 1996. *Brazilian Catholicism and the Ultramontane Reform, 1850–1930.* Amsterdam: CEDLA.

Delfim Netto, Antônio. 1992. Interview by the author with federal deputy (PDS, São Paulo), Brasília, June 24.

Della Cava, Ralph. 1985. *A Igreja em flagrante: Catolicismo e sociedade na imprensa brasileira, 1964–1980.* Editora Marco Zero. Rio de Janeiro: ISER.

———. 1989. "The 'People's Church,' the Vatican, and Abertura." In *Democratizing Brazil,* edited by Alfred Stepan, pp. 177–94. New York: Oxford University Press.

———. 1992a. "Política do Vaticano 1978–1990: Uma visão geral." In *Catolicismo no Brasil atual,* vol. 3, *Unidade religiosa e pluralismo cultural,* edited by Pierre Sanchis, pp. 231–58. São Paulo: Edições Loyola.

———. 1992b. "Vatican Policy, 1978–90: An Updated Overview." *Social Research* 59(1): 171–99.

———. 1993. "Thinking about Current Vatican Policy in Central and East Europe and the Utility of the 'Brazilian Paradigm.'" *Journal of Latin American Studies* 25: 257–81.

Della Cava, Ralph, and Paula Montero. 1991. *E o verbo se faz imagem: Igreja católica e os meios de comunicação no Brasil, 1962–1989.* Petrópolis: Vozes.

Della Porta, Donatella 1995. *Social Movements, Political Violence, and the State: A Comparative Analysis of Italy and Germany.* Cambridge, Eng.: Cambridge University Press.

Departamento Intersindical de Assessoria Parlamentar. *See* DIAP (Departamento Intersindical de Assessoria Parlamentar).

(DIAP). 1992. *Boletim do DIAP* (August). Brasília.

———. 1996. *Os cabeças do Congresso Nacional: Uma pesquisa sobre os 100 parlamentares mais influentes no poder legislativo, ano III.* Brasília.

Dias, Maurício. 1996. "Informe JB." *Jornal do Brasil,* June 21.

Dias, Rosinha Borges. 1994. "Projeto pastoral 'Construir a Esperança.'" In *A presença da Igreja na cidade,* edited by Alberto Antoniazzi and Cleto Caliman, pp. 36–47. Petropólis: Vozes.

Dimenstein, Gilberto. 1996. *Democracia em pedaços: Direitos humanos no Brasil.* São Paulo: Companhia das Letras.

D'Incão, Maria Conceição. 1991. "A experiência dos assentamentos: Contribuição ao debate político da reforma agrária." *Lua Nova* 23: 83–106.

Diniz, Clélio Campolina. 1995. "Dinâmica regional recente e suas perspectivas." In *A federação em perspectiva: Ensaios selecionados,* edited by Rui de Britto Álvares Affonso and Pedro Luiz Barros Silva, pp. 417–429. São Paulo: FUNDAP.

Diniz, Eli. 1990. "O ciclo autoritário: A lógica partidário-eleitoral e a erosão do regime." In *O balanco do poder,* edited by Olavo Brasil de Lima Júnior, pp. 73–86. Rio de Janeiro: Rio Fundo Editora.

Dirceu, José. 1996. Interview by the author with the PT National Federal Secretary for International Relations, São Paulo, June 14.

———. 1997. "Marca do PT: A ética." *Folha de São Paulo,* June 8.

Diretrizes de Ação do Governo Fernando Collor de Mello. 1989. Brasília: n.p.

Doimo, Ana Maria. 1992. "Igreja e movimentos sociais pós-70 no Brasil." In *Catolicismo no Brasil atual,* vol. 2, *Cotidiano e movimentos,* edited by Pierre Sanchis, pp. 275–308. São Paulo: Edições Paulinas.

———. 1995. *A vez e a voz do popular: Movimentos sociais e participação política no Brasil pós-70.* Rio de Janeiro: Relume-Duman.

Drake, Paul. 1996. *Labor Movements and Dictatorships: The Southern Cone in Comparative Perspective.* Baltimore: Johns Hopkins University Press.

Dreifuss, Rene. 1981. *1964, a conquista do estado: Ação política, poder, e golpe de classe.* Petrópolis: Vozes.

———. 1986. "Nova república. Novo exército?" In *Nova república: Um balanço,* edited by F. Koutzii, pp. 168–93. Pôrto Alegre: L & PM Editores.

Drogus, Carol Ann. 1992. "Popular Movements and the Limits of Political Mobilization at the Grassroots in Brazil." In *Conflict and Competition: The Latin American Church in a Changing Environment,* edited by Edward L. Cleary and Hannah Stewart-Gambino, pp. 63–86. Boulder, Colo.: Lynne Rienner Publishers.

———. 1997. *Women, Religion, and Social Change in Brazil's Popular Church.* Notre Dame, Ind.: University of Notre Dame Press.

Durham, Eunice Ribeiro. 1984. "Movimentos sociais: A construção da cidadania." *Novos Estudos* 10: 24–30.

Eckstein, Susan, ed. 1989. *Power and Popular Protest: Latin American Social Movements.* Berkeley and Los Angeles: University of California Press.

Edwards, Michael, and David Hulme, eds. 1996. *Beyond the Magic Bullet: NGO Performance and Accountability in the Post–Cold War World.* West Hartford, Conn.: Kumarian Press.

Elizondo, Carlos. 1994. "Where Has the Developmental State Gone?" Paper for Eighteenth International Congress of the Latin American Studies Association, Atlanta, March 10–12.

Elkins, Zachary. 1997. "Who Would Vote? Understanding the Consequences of Mandatory Voting in Brazil." Paper presented at the Twentieth International Congress of the Latin American Studies Association, Guadalajara, Mexico, April 17–19.

Erickson, Kenneth Paul. 1977. *The Brazilian Corporative State and Working Class Politics.* Berkeley and Los Angeles: University of California Press.

Eris, Ibrahim. 1992. Interview by Kurt Weyland with former central bank president (1990–1991), São Paulo, May 27.

Falcão, Daniela. 1997. "Bolsa-escola diminui evasão no DF." *Folha de São Paulo,* July 8.

Faoro, Raymundo. 1958. *Os donos do poder: Formação do patronato político brasileiro.* Porto Alegre: Editora Globo.

Faria, Vilmar. 1983. "Desenvolvimento, urbanização, e mudanças na estrutura do emprego: A experiência brasileira do últimos trinta anos." In *Sociedade e política no Brasil pós-64*, edited by Bernardo Sorj and Maria Hermínia Tavares de Almeida, pp. 118–63. São Paulo: Editora Brasiliense.

Featherstone, Kevin. 1994. "Jean Monnet and the 'Democratic Deficit' in the European Union." *Journal of Common Market Studies* 32: 149–70.

Federação da Indústria do Estado de São Paulo. *See* FIESP

Felix, Jorgemar, and Luciano Suassuna. 1994. "PT vs. PT." *ISTOÉ*, February 16, 27–29 (from FBIS-LAT-94-045, March 8, pp. 34–36).

Feng, Yi. 1997. "Democracy, Political Stability, and Economic Growth." *British Journal of Political Science* 27: 3 (July): 391–418.

Fernandes, José Augusto Coelho. 1992. Interview by Kurt Weyland with executive secretary of the Confederação Nacional da Indústria, Rio de Janeiro, July 29.

Fernandes, Rubem César. 1992. *Censo institucional evangélico 1992: Primeiros comentários.* Rio de Janeiro: ISER.

———. 1994. *Privado porém Público: O terceiro setor na América Latina.* Rio de Janeiro: Relume Dumará and Civicus.

Fernandez, Wilson. 1991. "El pensamiento brasileño acerca de la integración." *Revista de Ciencias Sociales* 6: 44–62.

———. 1992. *Mercosur: Economia, política, y estrategia de integración.* Montevideo: Fundación de Cultura Universitaria.

Ferreira, Wolfgran Junqueira. 1965. "Aspectos negativos da reforma tributária." *Revista de Administração Municipal.* 73: 414–423.

FGV (Fundação Getúlio Vargas). 1996. *A economia brasileira em gráficos.* Rio de Janeiro.

FIESP (Federação da Indústria do Estado de São Paulo). 1997. *O custo do atraso,* June 23.

Figueiredo, Argelina, and Fernando Limongi. 1994a. "A Câmara por seus membros: Imagem e realidade." São Paulo, Centro Brasileiro de Análise e Planejamento (CEBRAP). Mimeograph.

———. 1994b. "Mudança constitucional, desempenho do legislativo, e consolidação institucional." Paper presented at the Eighteenth Conference of the Associação Nacional de Pós-Graduação e Pesquisa em Ciências Sociais (ANPOCS), Caxambu, Minas Gerais, October.

———. 1995a. "Partidos políticos na Câmara dos Deputados: 1989–1994." *Dados* 38(3): 497–525.

———. 1995b. "Poderes legislativos e o poder do Congresso." *Monitor Público* 2(5): 33–38.

———. 1996. "Presidencialismo e apoio partidário no Congresso." *Monitor Público* 3(8): 27–36.

Figueiredo, José Rubens de Lima, Jr. 1995. "Opinião pública, intencionalidade e voto." *Opinião Pública* 2(2): 73–82.

Figueiredo, R., and Bolivar Lamounier. 1996. *As cidades que dão certo: Experiências inovadoras na administração pública brasileira.* Brasília: MH Comunicação.

Fisher, Julie. 1998. *Non-Governments: NGOs and the Political Development of the Third World.* West Hartford, Conn.: Kumarian Press.

Fishlow, Albert. 1997. "Is the Real Plan for Real?" In *Brazil under Collor,* edited by Susan Kaufman Purcell and Riordan Roett, pp. 43–61. Boulder, Colo.: Lynne Rienner Publishers.

Fleet, Michael, and Brian H. Smith. 1997. *The Catholic Church and Democracy in Chile and Peru.* Notre Dame, Ind.: University of Notre Dame Press.

Fleischer, David V. 1994. "Political Corruption and Campaign Financing in Brazil: The Distraction Finesse of Impeachment, Congressional Inquests, Ceremonious Sackings, and Innocuous Legislation." Paper presented to the Sixteenth World Congress of the International Political Science Association, Berlin, August 21–25.

———. 1996. "Poder local e o sistema eleitoral brasileiro." In *Poder local face às eleições municipais de 1996.* São Paulo: Konrad Adenauer Stiftung.

Folha de São Paulo. 1990. "Maioria dos eleitores vota por obrigação." August 15, A-7.

———. 1997a. "Corrupção na reeleição." October 8.

———. 1997b. "Dilema do PT." May 12.

———. 1997c. *Folha* 97: Texto Integral 95/96. *Empresa Folha de Manhã* S/A. CD-Rom.

———. 1997d. "País tem 156 mi de pessoas, revela IBGE." June 26, 3: 13.

———. 1997e. "PT x PT." May 28.

———. 1997f. "Tendências/Debates." June 7.

———. 1998. "Eleitores participam cada vez menos." September 13, Especial-7.

Fonseca, Alexandre Brasil. 1996. "Uma igreja na política: Voto, clientelismo e mediação na Igreja Universal do Reino de Deus." *Cadernos do CEAS* 164 (June–August): 66–88.

Fontes, Breno Augusto Souto-Maior. 1995. "Clientelismo urbano e movimento popular: A construção das redes do poder." *Revista Brasileira de Estudos Políticos* 81: 119–57.

———. 1996. "Estrutura organizacional das associações políticas voluntárias." *Revista Brasileira de Ciências Sociais* 11: 41–59.

Foresta, Ronald. 1992. "Amazônia and the Politics of Geopolitics." *Geographical Review* 82: 128–42.

Forum Brasileiro de ONGs. 1991. *Documento Final do Encontro de Brasilia.* Brasília, Mimeograph.

French, John. 1993. *The Brazilian Workers' ABC: Class Conflict and Alliances in Modern São Paulo.* Chapel Hill: University of North Carolina Press.

Freston, Paulo. 1993a. "Brother Votes for Brother: The New Politics of Protestantism in Brazil." In *Rethinking Protestantism in Latin America,* edited by Virginia Garrard-Burnett and David Stoll, pp. 66–110. Philadelphia: Temple University Press.

———. 1993b. "Protestantes e política no Brasil: A constituinte ao impeachment." Ph.D. diss., Department of Social Sciences, Universidade Estadual de Campinas, Campinas, S.P.

Frieden, Jeffry. 1991. *Debt, Development, and Democracy: Modern Political Economy and Latin America, 1965–1985.* Princeton: Princeton University Press.

Friedmann, John. 1992. *Empowerment: The Politics of Alternative Development.* Cambridge: Blackwell.

Fundação Getúlio Vargas. *See* FGV

Galazi, Jô. 1996. "Real ainda ampliará benefícios, crê pesquisadora." *Estado de São Paulo* 12 (June): A7.

Gall, Norman. 1991. "The Floating World of Brazilian Inflation." Instituto Fernand Braudel, São Paulo, September. Mimeograph.

Garcia, Marco Aurélio. 1994. "Esquerdas: Rupturas e continuidades." In *Anos 90: Política e Sociedade no Brasil,* edited by E. Dagnino, pp. 119–26. São Paulo: Brasiliense.

———. 1996. Interview by William Nylen with PT National Secretary for International Relations, Brasília, June 14.

Garrison, J. W., II. 1993. "La Conferencia de Rio y el florecimiento de las ONGs brasileñas." *Desarrollo de Base* 17: 2–11.

Garton Ash, Timothy. 1998. "The Truth about Dictatorship." *New York Review of Books,* February 19, 35–40.

Gaskill, Newton J. 1997. "Rethinking Protestantism and Democratic Consolidation in Latin America." *Sociology of Religion* 58(1): 69–91.

Gay, Robert. 1994. *Popular Organizations and Democracy in Rio de Janeiro*. Philadelphia: Temple University Press.

Gazeta Mercantil. *Balanço anual*. Various years. São Paulo.

Gazzola, Luoia Helena. 1993. "Victories of Leftist Factions within Workers Party Viewed." *O Estado de São Paulo*, May 25 (from FBIS-LAT-93-101, May 27, p. 29).

Geddes, Barbara, and John Zaller. 1989. "Sources of Popular Support for Authoritarian Regimes." *American Journal of Political Science* 33: 319–47.

Ghio, José María. 1992. "The Latin American Church and the Papacy of Wojtyla." In *The Right and Democracy in Latin America*, edited by Douglas A. Chalmers, Maria do Carmo Campello de Souza, and Atilio A. Boron, pp. 183–201. New York: Praeger.

Gill, Anthony. 1995. "The Politics of Religious Regulation in Mexico: Preliminary Observations." Paper presented at the Nineteenth International Congress of the Latin American Studies Association, Washington, D.C., September 28–30.

———. 1998. *Rendering unto Caesar: The Catholic Church and the State in Latin America*. Chicago: University of Chicago Press.

Giordani, Marco Polo. 1986. *Brasil: Sempre*. Pôrto Alegre: Tchê Editora.

Giumbelli, Emerson. 1996. "Da religião como problema social: Secularização, retorno do sagrado, liberdade religiosa, espaço e comportamento religioso." Unpublished paper.

Gomes, Wilson. 1992. "Cinco teses equivocadas sobre as novas seitas populares." *Cadernos do CEAS* 139 (May–June): 39–53.

Gondim, Linda Maria. 1989–1990. "Os movimentos sociais urbanos, a questão de organização e a democracia interna." *Revista de Ciências Sociais* 20–21: 31–60.

Graham, Lawrence. 1987. "The Role of the States in the Brazilian Federation." In *Subnational Politics in the 1980s: Organization, Reorganization, and Economic Development*, edited by Louis A. Picard and Raphael Zariski, pp. 119–139. New York: Praeger.

———. 1990. *The State and Policy Outcomes in Latin America*. New York: Praeger.

Graham, Richard. 1990. *Patronage and Politics in Nineteenth-Century Brazil*. Stanford: Stanford University Press.

Guidry, John A., and Lothar Probst. 1997. "Consistencies of Democracy: Opposition Parties in Brazil and Germany." Paper prepared for the Twentieth International Congress of the Latin American Studies Association, Guadalajara, Mexico, April 17–19.

Guilhon Albuquerque, J. A. 1992. "Mercosul: Integração regional pós-guerra fria." *Política Externa* 1: 112–21.

Haddad, Sérgio. 1995. "Analfabetismo no Brasil: O que há de novo?" *Folha de São Paulo*, September 8, 1: 3.

Haggard, Stephan. 1990. *Pathways from the Periphery: The Politics of Growth in the Newly Industrializing Countries*. Ithaca: Cornell University Press.

Haggard, Stephan, and Robert Kaufman. 1992. "The Political Economy of Inflation and Stabilization in Middle-Income Countries." In *The Politics of Economic Adjustment*, edited by Stephan Haggard and Robert Kaufman, pp. 270–315. Princeton: Princeton University Press.

Hagopian, Frances. 1990. "'Democracy by Undemocratic Means?' Elites, Political Pacts, and Regime Transition in Brazil." *Comparative Political Studies* 23(2): 147–70.

———. 1992. "The Compromised Consolidation: The Political Class in the Brazilian Transition." In *Issues in Democratic Consolidation: The New South American Democracies in Comparative Perspective*, edited by S. Mainwaring, G. O'Donnell, and S. Valenzuela, pp. 243–93. Notre Dame, Ind.: University of Notre Dame.

———. 1993. "After Regime Change: Authoritarian Legacies, Political Representation, and the Democratic Future of South America." *World Politics* 45: 464–500.

———. 1996. *Traditional Politics and Regime Change in Brazil.* New York: Cambridge University Press.

Hagopian, Frances, and Scott Mainwaring. 1987. "Democracy in Brazil: Problems and Prospects." *World Policy Journal* (summer): 485–514.

Hammond, John L. 1997. "Law and Disorder: The Brazilian Landless Farmworkers' Movement." Paper prepared for Nineteenth International Congress of the Latin American Studies Association, Washington, D.C., September 28–30.

Harnecker, Marta. 1994. *O sonho era possível: A história do Partido dos Trabalhadores narrada por seus protagonistas.* Havana: MEPLA/Casa América Livre.

Harris, Richard L. 1992. *Marxism, Socialism, and Democracy in Latin America.* Boulder, Colo.: Westview Press.

Hellman, Judith A. 1992. "The Study of New Social Movements in Latin America and the Question of Autonomy." In *The Making of Social Movements in Latin America: Identity, Strategy, and Democracy,* edited by A. Escobar and S. E. Alvarez, pp. 52–61. Boulder, Colo.: Westview Press.

Herculano, Selene. 1995. "The Field of 'Ecologism' in Brazil: Between Citizenship and Heroism—Class, Educational, Biographic Backgrounds and Implications for the Movement." Paper prepared for the Nineteenth International Congress of the Latin American Studies Association, Washington, D.C., September 28–30.

Hewitt, W. E. 1991. *Basic Christian Communities and Social Change in Brazil.* Lincoln: University of Nebraska Press.

———. 1995. "Religion and the Consolidation of Democracy in Brazil: The Role of the Comunidades Eclesiais de Base." In *Religion and Democracy in Latin America,* edited by William H. Swatos, Jr., pp. 45–58. New Brunswick, N.J.: Transaction Publishers.

Hintze, Otto. 1981. *Beamtentum und Bürokratie.* Göttingen: Vandenhoeck and Ruprecht.

Hirst, Monica. 1984. "Política externa: A experiencia brasileira." *Dados* 27: 377–94.

———. 1996. "A dimensão política do Mercosul: Atores, politização, e ideologia." Unpublished paper.

Hochstetler, Kathryn. 1997. "The Evolution of the Brazilian Environmental Movement and its Political Roles." In *The New Politics of Inequality in Latin America: Rethinking Participation and Representation,* edited by D. Chalmers, C. Vilas, K. Hite, S. Martin, K. Piester, and M. Segarra, pp. 192–216. Oxford: Oxford University Press.

Holden, Robert. 1996. "Constructing the Limits of State Violence in Central America: Towards a New Research Agenda." *Journal of Latin American Studies* 2(2): 435–59.

Holloway, Thomas. 1993. *Policing Rio de Janeiro: Repression and Resistance in a 19th-Century City.* Stanford: Stanford University Press.

Holston, James, and Teresa P. R. Caldeira. 1998. "Democracy, Law, and Violence: Disjunctions of Brazilian Citizenship." In *Fault Lines of Democracy in Post-Transition Latin America,* edited by Felipe Agüero and Jeffrey Stark, pp. 263–96. Miami: North-South Center Press.

Huggins, Martha. 1998. *Political Policing: The United States and Latin America.* Durham, N.C.: Duke University Press.

Human Rights Watch/Americas. 1996. "Brazil: Fighting Violence with Violence—Human Rights Abuse and Criminality in Rio de Janeiro." *Human Rights Watch/Americas* 8: 1–29.

Hunter, Wendy. 1995. "Politicians against Soldiers: Contesting the Military in Post-Authoritarian Brazil." *Comparative Politics* 27: 425–43.

———. 1996. *State and Soldier in Latin America: Redefining the Military's Role in Argen-*

tina, Brazil, and Chile. Peaceworks no. 10. Washington, D.C.: United States Institute of Peace Press.

———. 1997. *Eroding Military Influence in Brazil: Politicians against Soldiers.* Chapel Hill: University of North Carolina Press.

———. 1998. "Civil-Military Relations in Argentina, Brazil, and Chile: Present Trends, Future Prospects." In *Fault Lines of Democracy in Post-Transition Latin America,* edited by F. Agüero and J. Stark, pp. 299–322. Coral Gables, Fla.: North-South Center Press at the University of Miami.

Huntington, Samuel P. 1957. *The Soldier and the State.* Cambridge: Harvard University Press.

———. 1984. "Will More Countries Become Democratic?" *Political Science Quarterly* 99(2): 193–218.

———. 1991. *The Third Wave: Democratization in the Late Twentieth Century.* Norman: University of Oklahoma Press.

Hurrell, Andrew. 1992. "Brazil and the International Politics of Amazonian Deforestation." In *The International Politics of the Environment,* edited by A. Hurrell and B. Kingsbury, pp. 398–429. Oxford: Clarendon Press.

Instituto Brasileiro de Administração Municipal (IBAM). 1976. *Relações Intergovernamentais União-Município.* Rio de Janeiro: IBAM.

IBGE (Instituto Brasileiro de Geografia e Estatística). Various years. *Anuário estatístico do Brasil.* Rio de Janeiro.

———. Various years. *Censo demográfico.* Rio de Janeiro.

———. Various years. Pesquisa nacional por amostra de domicílios–PNAD. *Síntese de indicadores.* Rio de Janeiro. 1995 is the Web version; 1996 is a print version of 1995 PNAD.

———. 1995–1996. *Brasil em números.* Vol. 4. Rio de Janeiro.

———. 1998a. "Cadastro de cidades e vilas do Brasil 1996." (Computer archive downloaded from the IBGE Web site, www.ibge.gov.br). Accessed on October 29, 1998.

———. 1998b. "Dados tabulados dos censos de 1996, resultados definitivos da contagem da população 1996." (Computer archives downloaded from the IBGE Web site, www.ibge.gov.br). Accessed on October 29, 1998.

IDB (Inter-American Development Bank). 1994. *Economic and Social Progress in Latin America, 1994 Report. Special Report, Fiscal Decentralization.* Washington, D.C.: IDB/ Johns Hopkins University Press.

———. 1996. *Economic and Social Progress in Latin America: 1996 Report. Special Section, Making Social Services Work.* Washington, D.C.

———. 1997. *Economic and Social Progress in Latin America: 1997 Report. Special Section, Latin America After a Decade of Reforms.* Washington, D.C.

IEDI (Instituto de Estudos para o Desenvolvimento Industrial). 1991. *Carga fiscal, competitividade industrial, e potencial de crescimento econômico.* São Paulo.

———. 1992. "Modernização competitiva, democracia, e justiça social." *Mudar para Competir* (June).

IESP (Instituto de Economia do Setor Publico). 1997. *Indicadores IESP* 59 (March–April). São Paulo.

———. 1998. *Indicadores IESP* 67 (July–August). São Paulo.

Instituto Brasileiro de Geografia e Estatística. *See* IBGE

Instituto de Economia do Setor Público. *See* IESP

Instituto de Estudos da Religião. *See* ISER

Instituto de Estudos para o Desenvolvimento Industrial. *See* IEDI

Instituto de Pesquisa Econômica Aplicada. *See* IPEA

Instituto Gallup de Opinião Pública (and Fundação Pedroso Horta). 1995. "Principais gráficos e tabelas da pesquisa de âmbito nacional sobre partidos políticos e problemas nacionais." Mimeograph.

Inter-American Development Bank. *See* IDB

International Monetary Fund. 1992. *Direction of Trade Statistics Yearbook.* Washington, D.C.

———. 1997. *Direction of Trade Statistics Yearbook.* Washington, D.C.

Iokoi, Zilda Márcia Grícoli. 1996. *Igreja e camponeses: Teologia da libertação e movimentos sociais no campo, Brazil e Peru, 1964–1986.* São Paulo: Editora HUCITEC.

IPEA (Instituto de Pesquisa Econômica Aplicada). 1992. "Analise econômico-financeira dos bancos estaduais." Working paper, January.

Ireland, Rowan. 1991. *Kingdoms Come: Religion and Politics in Brazil.* Pittsburgh: University of Pittsburgh Press.

ISER (Instituto de Estudos da Religião). 1990. "Estação de seca na Igreja." *Comunicações do ISER* 9: 39.

Jacobi, Pedro. 1995a. "Alcances y límites de los gobiernos locales progresistas en Brasil: Las alcaldías petistas." *Revista Mexicana de Sociología* 2: 143–62.

———. 1995b. "Descentralização, educação e democracia: O caso do município de São Paulo." *Cadernos Cedec,* no. 49.

Jacobi, Pedro, and Marco Antonio Carvalho Teixeira. 1996. "Orçamento Participativo: O caso de São Paulo (1989–1982) à luz das experiências de Pôrto Alegre e Belo Horizonte." Mimeograph.

Jaquette, Jane S. 1989. "Introduction." In *The Women's Movement in Latin America: Feminism and the Transition to Democracy,* edited by J. S. Jaquette, pp. 1–17. Boston: Unwin Hyman.

Jarschel, Heidi. 1991. "Aborto: Entre a fome e o desejo." *Tempo e Presença* 256 (March–April): 37–39.

Jenks, Margaret Sarles. 1979. "Political Parties in Authoritarian Brazil." Ph.D. diss., Department of Political Science, Duke University, Durham, N.C.

Jornal do Brasil. 1997. "D. Lucas quer a CVRD para brasileiros." March 21, p. 20.

———. 1998. "Desemprego recorde aflige país." April 7.

Kandir, Antônio. 1992. Interview by author with former Secretary for Economic Policy, Ministry of Economics, Finance, and Planning (1990–1991). São Paulo, June 8.

Kant de Lima, Roberto. 1995. "Bureaucratic Rationality in Brazil and the United States: Criminal Justice Systems in Comparative Perspective." In *The Brazilian Puzzle: Culture on the Borderlands of the Western World,* edited by David Hess and Roberto Da Matta, pp. 241–69. New York: Columbia University Press.

Karl, Terry Lynn. 1986. "Petroleum and Political Pacts: The Transition to Democracy in Venezuela." In *Transitions from Authoritarian Rule: Latin America,* edited by Guillermo O'Donnell, Philippe Schmitter, and Laurence Whitehead, pp. 196–219. Baltimore: Johns Hopkins University Press.

———. 1990. "Dilemmas of Democratization in Latin America." *Comparative Politics* 23: 1–21.

Kaufman, Robert. 1988. *The Politics of Debt in Argentina, Brazil, and Mexico: Economic Stabilization in the 1980's.* Berkeley, Calif.: Institute of International Studies.

Keck, Margaret. 1989. "The New Unionism in the Brazilian Transition." In *Democratizing Brazil: Problems of Transition and Consolidation,* edited by A. Stepan, pp. 252–96. New York: Oxford University.

———. 1992. *The Workers' Party and Democratization in Brazil.* New Haven: Yale University Press.

———. 1995. "Parks, People, and Power: The Shifting Terrain of Environmentalism." *NACLA Review* 28(5): 36–41.

Kingstone, Peter. 1998a. "Constitutional Reform and Macro-Economic Stability: Implications for Democratic Consolidation in Brazil." In *The Problematic Relationship between Economic and Political Liberalization*, edited by Phil Oxhorn and Pamela Starr, pp. 133–60. Boulder, Colo.: Lynne Rienner Publishers.

———. 1998b. "Corporatism, Neoliberalism, and the Failed Revolt of Big Business in Brazil: The Case of IEDI." *Journal of Interamerican Studies and World Affairs* 40(4): 73–95.

———. 1998c. "Political Continuity versus Social Change: The Sustainability of Neoliberal Reform in Brazil." *Nafta: Law and Business Review of the Americas* 4(2): 38–56.

———. 1999a. *Crafting Coalitions for Reform: Business Strategies, Political Institutions, and Neoliberal Reform in Brazil.* University Park: Penn State University Press.

———. 1999b. "Short Money and Long Cycles of Instability: Brazil and the Problem of Dependence on Foreign Finance in the 1990's." In *Financial Globalization and Democratization in Emerging Markets*, edited by Leslie Elliot Armijo and Thomas Bierstecker, pp. 151–76. London: Macmillan.

Kinzo, Maria D'Alva Gil. 1988. *Legal Opposition Politics under Authoritarian Rule in Brazil.* New York: St. Martin's.

———. 1989. "O quadro partidário e a constituinte." *Revista Brasileira de Ciência Política* 1, no. 1: 91–124.

———. 1993. *Radiografia do quadro partidário brasileiro.* São Paulo: Fundação Konrad-Adenauer-Stiftung.

Kirchheimer, Otto. 1966. "The Transformation of the Western European Party Systems." In *Political Parties and Political Development*, edited by J. LaPalombara and M. Weiner, pp.177–200. Princeton: Princeton University Press.

Knott, Jack, and Gary Miller. 1987. *Reforming Bureaucracy: The Politics of Institutional Choice.* Englewood Cliffs, N.J.: Prentice-Hall.

Kohli, Atul. 1998. "Democracy amidst Economic Orthodoxy: Trends in Developing Countries." In *Development at a Crossroads: Uncertain Paths to Sustainability after the Neoliberal Revolution*, edited by Michael Carter, Jeffrey Cason, and Frederic Zimmerman, pp. 153–77. Madison, Wis.: Global Studies Program.

Kowarick, Lúcio, and André Singer. 1994. "The Workers' Party in São Paulo." In *Social Struggles and the City: The Case of São Paulo*, edited by L. Kowarick, pp. 225–56. New York: Monthly Review Press.

Krahenbuhl, Lair. 1996. "A crise habitacional é a crise do Brasil." *Folha de São Paulo*, March 11, 2: 2.

Krieger, Gustavo, Fernando Rodrigues, and Elvis Cesar Bonassa. 1994. *Os donos do Congresso: A farsa na CPI do orçamento.* São Paulo: Editora Ática.

Kritz, Neil J., ed. 1995. *Transitional Justice: How Emerging Democracies Reckon with Former Regimes.* Vol. 2. Washington, D.C.: United States Institute of Peace Press.

Kugelmas, Eduardo, Brasílio Sallum, Jr., and Eduardo Graeff. 1989. "Conflito federativo e transição política." *São Paulo em Perspectiva* 3: 95–102.

Lagemann, Eugênio. 1995. "O federalismo fiscal brasileiro em questão." In *A federação em perspectiva: Ensaios selecionados*, edited by Rui de Britto Álvares Affonso and Pedro Luiz Barros Silva, pp. 329–53. São Paulo: FUNDAP.

Lamounier, Bolivar. 1984. "Opening through Elections: Will the Brazilian Case Become a Paradigm?" *Government and Opposition* 19(2): 167–77.

———. 1989a. "Authoritarian Brazil Revisited: The Impact of Elections on the Abertura."

In *Democratizing Brazil,* edited by Alfred Stepan, pp. 43–79. New York: Oxford University Press.

———. 1989b. "Brazil: Inequality against Democracy." In *Democracy in Developing Countries,* vol. 4, *Latin America,* edited by Larry Diamond, Juan J. Linz, and Seymour Martin Lipset, pp. 111–58. Boulder, Colo.: Lynne Rienner Publishers.

———. 1990. *Partidos e utopias: O Brasil no limiar dos anos 90.* São Paulo: Edições Loyola.

———. 1991. "Parlamentarismo, sistema eleitoral, e governabilidade." *Nova Economia* 2(2): 9–25.

———. 1994. "Brazil: Towards Parliamentarism?" In *The Failure of Presidential Democracy,* edited by Juan J. Linz and Arturo Valenzuela, pp. 179–219. Baltimore: Johns Hopkins University Press.

———. 1996. "Brazil: The Hyperactive Paralysis Syndrome." In *Constructing Democratic Governance: Latin America and the Caribbean in the 1990's,* edited by Jorge J. Domínguez and Abraham F. Lowenthal, pp. 166–88. Baltimore: Johns Hopkins University Press.

Lamounier, Bolívar, and Alexandre H. Marques. 1992. "A democracia brasileira no final da década perdida." In *Ouvindo o Brasil: Uma análise da opinião pública brasileira hoje,* edited by B. Lamounier, pp. 137–58. São Paulo: Editora Sumaré.

Lamounier, Bolivar, and Rachel Meneguello. 1986. *Partidos políticos e consolidação democrática.* São Paulo: Brasiliense.

Landim, Leilah. 1993. *Para além do mercado e do estado? Filantropia e cidadania no Brasil.* Rio de Janeiro: ISER.

———, ed. 1988. *Sem fins lucrativos: As organizações não-governamentais no Brasil.* Rio de Janeiro: Instituto de Estudos da Religião.

LaPalombara, Joseph. 1967. "Bureaucracy and Political Development." In *Bureaucracy and Political Development,* 2d ed., edited by Joseph LaPalombara, pp. 34–61. Princeton: Princeton University Press.

Larangeira, Sônia M. G. 1996. "Gestão pública e participação: a experiência do orçamento participativo em Porto Alegre." *São Paulo em Perspectiva* 10(3): 129–137.

Latinobarómetro 1995: "Datos Preliminares." 1995. Ann Arbor: University of Michigan, Institute for Social Research, Survey Research Center.

Lawrence, Graham. 1987. "The Role of the States in the Brazilian Federation." In *Subnational Politics in the 1980s: Organization, Reorganization, and Economic Development,* edited by Louis A. Picard and Raphael Zariski. New York: Praeger.

Leal, Victor Nunes. 1977. *Coronelismo: The Municipality and Representative Government in Brazil.* Translated by June Henfrey. London: Cambridge University Press.

Leeds, Elizabeth. 1996. "Cocaine and Parallel Polities in the Brazilian Urban Periphery." *Latin American Research Review* 31: 47–83.

Lemgruber, Andréa. 1996. Interview by Kurt Weyland in Secretaria de Receita Federal, Ministério da Fazenda, Brasília, July 3.

Lenin, Vladimir. 1969. *What Is to Be Done? Burning Questions of Our Movement.* New York: International.

Lernoux, Penny. 1989. *People of God: The Struggle for World Catholicism.* New York: Viking.

Levine, Daniel. 1973. *Conflict and Political Change in Venezuela.* Princeton: Princeton University Press.

Libânio, Joao Batista. 1983. *Volta à grande disciplina.* São Paulo: Edições Loyola.

———. 1987. *Teologia da libertação.* São Paulo: Edições Loyola.

———. 1992. "VIII encontro intereclesial das CEBs (eventos no evento)." *Revista Eclesiástica Brasileira* 52 (December 1992): 789–800.

Lijphart, Arend. 1997. "Unequal Participation: Democracy's Unresolved Dilemma." *American Political Science Review* 91(1): 1–14.

Lima, Délcio Monteiro de. 1987. *Os demônios descem do norte.* Rio de Janeiro: Francisco Alves.

Lima, Olavo Brasil de, Jr. 1990. "Alienação eleitoral e seus determinantes: Nota de pesquisa." *Revista Brasileira de Ciências Sociais* no. 14 (October): 68–72.

————. 1993. *Democracia e instituições políticas no Brasil dos anos 80.* São Paulo: Edições Loyola.

Lima, Olavo Brasil de, Jr., ed. 1990. *O balanço do poder: Formas de dominação e representação.* Rio de Janeiro: Rio Fundo Editora.

————. 1991. *Sistema eleitoral brasileiro: Teoria e prática.* Rio de Janeiro: Rio Fundo Editora.

Lima, Olavo Brasil de, Jr., and Sérgio Abranches, eds. 1987. *As origens da crise: Estado autoritário e planejamento no Brasil.* São Paulo: Vértice.

Lima, Olavo Brasil de, Jr., Rogério Augusto Schmitt, and Jairo Marconi Nicolau. 1992. "A produção brasileira recente sobre partidos, eleições, e comportamento político: Balanço bibliográfico." *BIB: Boletim Informativo e Bibliográfico de Ciências Sociais* no. 34: 3–36.

Lima, Venício A. 1993. "Brazilian Television in the 1989 Presidential Campaign: Constructing a President." In *Television, Politics, and the Transition to Democracy in Latin America,* edited by Thomas Skidmore, pp. 97–117. Baltimore: Johns Hopkins University Press.

Linz, Juan J. 1978. *The Breakdown of Democratic Regimes: Crisis, Breakdown, and Reequilibration.* Baltimore: Johns Hopkins University.

————. 1994. "Presidential or Parliamentary Democracy: Does It Make a Difference?" In *The Failure of Presidential Democracy,* edited by Juan J. Linz and Arturo Valenzuela, pp. 3–87. Baltimore: Johns Hopkins University Press.

Linz, Juan J., and Alfred Stepan. 1996. *Problems of Democratic Transition and Consolidation: Southern Europe, South America, and Post-Communist Europe.* Baltimore: Johns Hopkins University Press.

Lobato, Elvira. 1995a. "Política marca história das telecomunicações." *Folha de São Paulo,* September 3, 1–13.

Lobato, Elvira, et al. 1995a. "Itamar promoveu festival de concessões." *Folha de São Paulo,* February 19, 1–14.

————. 1995b. "Um em cada 6 congressistas tem rádio ou TV." *Folha de São Paulo,* May 14, 1–12.

Löwy, Michael. 1996. "A teologia da libertação acabou?" *Teoria e Debate* 31 (April, May, June): 75–77.

Longo, Carlos Alberto. 1994. "Federal Problems with VAT in Brazil." *Revista Brasileira de Economia* 48: 85–105.

Lovell, Peggy. 1998. "Gender, Race, and the Struggle for Social Justice in Brazil." Paper presented to the American Sociological Association, San Francisco, August 20–25.

Lovell, Peggy, and Jeffrey Dwyer. 1988. "The Cost of Being Nonwhite in Brazil." *SSR: Sociology and Social Research* 72(2): 136–42.

Loveman, Brian. 1994. "'Protected Democracies' and Military Guardianship: Political Transitions in Latin America, 1978–1993." *Journal of Interamerican Studies and World Affairs* 36: 105–89.

Lowden, Pamela. 1996. *Moral Opposition to Authoritarian Rule in Chile, 1973–1990.* Basingstoke, Eng.: Macmillan.

Loyola, Gustavo. 1993. *Bancos Públicos Estaduais–Origens da Questão BE's e Perspectivas do Setor.* Serie Pronunciamentos No. 6. Brasília: Banco Central do Brasil.

Machado, J. Teixeira, Jr. 1968. "Fundo de participação: Aplicação, contabilização e prestação de contas." *Revista da Administração Municipal* 86: 32–47.

Machado, Maria das Dores. N.d. "Da teologia da prosperidade à participação no debate sobre a campanha de planejamento familiar–a Igreja Universal do Reino de Deus em perspectiva." Rio de Janeiro. Unpublished paper.

———. 1996. *Carismáticos e pentecostais: adesão religiosa na esfera familiar.* Campinas: Editora Autores Associados.

Mahar, Dennis J. 1971. "The Failures of Revenue Sharing in Brazil and Some Recent Developments." *Bulletin for International Fiscal Documentation* 225(3): 71–79.

Mainwaring, Scott. 1986a. *The Catholic Church and Politics in Brazil, 1916–1985.* Stanford: Stanford University Press.

———. 1986b. "The Transition to Democracy in Brazil." *Journal of Interamerican Studies and World Affairs* 28 (spring): 149–79.

———. 1989. "Grassroots Popular Movements and the Struggle for Democracy: Nova Iguaçu." In *Democratizing Brazil: Problems of Transition and Consolidation,* edited by A. Stepan, pp. 168–204. New York: Oxford University Press.

———. 1991. "Politicians, Parties, and Electoral Systems." *Comparative Politics* 24: 21–43.

———. 1992–1993. "Brazilian Party Underdevelopment in Comparative Perspective." *Political Science Quarterly* 107: 677–707.

———. 1993a. "Democracia presidencialista multipartidária: O caso do Brasil." *Lua Nova* 28–29: 21–74.

———. 1993b. "Presidentialism, Multipartism, and Democracy: The Difficult Combination." *Comparative Political Studies* 26: 198–228.

———. 1995a. "Brazil: Weak Parties, Feckless Democracy." In *Building Democratic Institutions: Party Systems in Latin America,* edited by Scott Mainwaring and Timothy R. Scully, pp. 354–98. Stanford: Stanford University Press.

———. 1995b. "Democracy in Brazil and the Southern Cone: Achievements and Problems." *Journal of International Studies and World Affairs* 37(1): 113–79.

———. 1999. *Rethinking Party Systems in the Third Wave of Democratization: The Case of Brazil.* Stanford: Stanford University Press.

Mainwaring, Scott, and Paulo Krischke. 1986. *A Igreja nas bases em tempos de transição.* Pôrto Alegre: L & PM Editores.

Mainwaring, Scott, and David Samuels. 1997. "Federalism and Democracy in Contemporary Brazil." Working paper, for International Studies, University of Notre Dame, the Kellogg Institute.

Mainwaring, Scott, and Timothy R. Scully. 1995. "Introduction: Party Systems in Latin America." In *Building Democratic Institutions: Parties and Party Systems in Latin America,* edited by Scott Mainwaring and Timothy R. Scully, pp. 1–36. Stanford: Stanford University Press.

Mainwaring, Scott, and Matthew Shugart. 1997. *Presidentialism and Democracy in Latin America.* Stanford: Stanford University Press.

Mainwaring, Scott, and Eduardo Viola. 1984. "New Social Movements, Political Culture, and Democracy: Brazil and Argentina in the 1980s." *Telos* 61: 17–52.

Mainwaring, Scott, and Alexander Wilde. 1989. *The Progressive Church in Latin America.* Notre Dame, Ind.: University of Notre Dame Press.

Malloy, James. 1987. "The Politics of Transition in Latin America." In *Authoritarians and*

Democrats: Regime Transition in Latin America, edited by James Malloy and Mitchell Seligson, pp. 239–57. Pittsburgh: University of Pittsburgh Press.

Manzetti, Luigi. 1990. "Argentine-Brazilian Economic Integration: An Early Appraisal." *Latin American Research Review* 25: 109–40.

———. 1994. "The Political Economy of Mercosur." *Journal of Interamerican Studies and World Affairs* 35: 101–41.

Maravall, José Maria, and Julián Santamaría. 1986. "Political Transition and the Prospects for Democracy in Spain." In *Transitions from Authoritarian Rule,* vol. 2, *Southern Europe,* edited by Guillermo O'Donnell, Philippe Schmitter, and Laurence Whitehead, pp. 71–108. Baltimore: Johns Hopkins University Press.

———. MARE (Ministério da Administração Federal e Reforma do Estado). 1996. *Boletim Estatístico Mensal,* May 1.

Mariano, Ricardo. 1995. "Neopentecostalismo: Os pentecostais estão mudando." Master's thesis, Department of Sociology, University of São Paulo, São Paulo.

Mariz, Cecília. 1994. *Coping with Poverty: Pentecostals and Christian Base Communities in Brazil.* Philadelphia: Temple University Press.

Martin, David. 1990. *Tongues of Fire: The Explosion of Protestantism in Latin America.* Cambridge, Mass.: Basil Blackwell.

Martínez-Lara, Javier. 1996. *Building Democracy in Brazil: The Politics of Constitutional Change, 1985–1995.* New York: St. Martin's.

Martins, Luciano. 1986. "The 'Liberalization' of Authoritarian Rule in Brazil." In *Transitions from Authoritarian Rule,* vol. 4, *Latin America,* edited by Guillermo O'Donnell, Philippe Schmitter, and Laurence Whitehead, pp. 72–94. Baltimore: Johns Hopkins University Press.

Martone, Celso L. 1996. "Recent Economic Policy in Brazil Before and After the Peso Crisis." In *The Peso Crisis: International Perspectives,* edited by Riordan Roett, pp. 49–70. Boulder, Colo.: Lynne Rienner Publishers.

Marx, Karl, and Friedrich Engels. 1978. "Manifesto of the Communist Party." In *The Marx-Engels Reader,* 2d ed., edited by R. Tucker, pp. 469–500. New York: Norton.

Matos Filho, José Coelho, and Carlos Oliveira. 1996. *O processo de privatização das empresas estatais brasileiras.* Texto para Discussão No. 422. Brasília: IPEA.

Mauceri, Philip. 1995. "State Reform, Coalitions, and the Neoliberal Autogolpe in Peru." *Latin American Research Review* 30(1): 7–37.

Maybury-Lewis, Biorn. 1994. *The Politics of the Possible: The Brazilian Rural Workers' Trade Union Movement, 1964–1985.* Philadelphia: Temple University Press.

McDonough, Peter. 1981. *Power and Ideology in Brazil.* Princeton: Princeton University Press.

McNee, Malcolm K. 1997. "From Isolated Land Occupations to the Occupation of the National Debate: The Landless Rural Workers' Movement and the Struggle for Agrarian Reform in Brazil." Master's thesis, Center for Latin American Studies, Tulane University.

MED/UNICEF/CENPEC. 1993. *Educação & desenvolvimento Municipal.* Brasília: Quantum.

Medeiros, Antônio Carlos de. 1986. "Politics and Intergovernmental Relations in Brazil, 1964–1982." Doctoral diss., London School of Economics. London: Garland Publishing.

Médici, André Cezar. 1994. *A dinâmica do gasto social no Brasil nas três esferas de governo: Uma análise do período 1980–1992.* São Paulo: IESP.

———. 1995. "Políticas sociais e federalismo." In *A Federação em perspectiva: Ensaios selecionados,* edited by Rui de Britto Álvares Affonso and Pedro Luiz Barros Silva, pp. 285–304. São Paulo: FUNDAP.

MEFP. (Ministério da Economia, Fazenda e Planejamento). Comissão Executiva de Reforma Fiscal (CERF). 1992. *Projeto de emenda à constituição.* Brasília.

MEFP. Secretaria Especial de Política Econômica (SEPE). 1991. *Propostas de emendas à constituição.* Brasília.

Mello, Diogo Lordello de. 1955. "Panorama da administração municipal brasileira." *Cadernos de Administração Pública* 26. Rio de Janeiro: Fundação Getúlio Vargas.

———. 1965. *Problemas institucionais do município.* Rio de Janeiro: Instituto Brasileiro de Administração Municipal.

———. 1971. *O município na organização nacional.* Rio de Janeiro: Instituto Brasileiro de Administração Municipal.

Mello, Zélia Cardoso de. 1995. Interview by Kurt Weyland with former economy minister (1990–91), Rio de Janeiro, July 7.

Melo, Marcos André B. C. de. 1995. "Ingovernabilidade: Desagregando o argumento." In *Governabilidade e pobreza no Brasil,* edited by L. Valladares and M. Prates Coelho, pp. 23–48. Rio de Janeiro: Civilização Brasileira.

———. 1996. "Crise federativa, guerra fiscal, e 'hobbesianismo municipal': Efeitos perversos da descentralização?" *São Paulo em Perspectiva* 10(3): 11–20.

Mendes, Antonio Teixeira, and Gustavo Venturi. 1994. "Eleição presidencial." *Opinião Pública* 2(2): 39–48.

Mendes de Oliveira Castro, Flavio. 1983. *História da organização do ministério de relações exteriores.* Brasília: Editora Universidade de Brasília.

Mendonça, Antônio Gouvêa, and Prócoro Velasques. 1990. *Introdução ao protestantismo no Brasil.* São Paulo: Edições Loyola.

Meneguello, Rachel. 1994. "Partidos e tendências de comportamento: O cenário político em 1994." In *Anos 90: Política e sociedade no Brasil,* edited by Evelina Dagnino, pp. 151–72. São Paulo: Brasiliense.

Menezes, Alexandre Queiroz de. 1995. "Estado, cooperação internacional, e construção da cidadania no Brasil." *Cadernos do CEAS* 158: 35–46.

Mesquita Neto, Paulo de. 1997. "Armed Forces, Police, and Democracy in Brazil." Paper presented to the Sawyer Seminar of the Military, Politics, and Society, New School for Social Research, New York, November 4.

———. 1998. "Police, Armed Forces, and Democracy in Brazil." Paper presented to the Twenty-first Congress of the Latin American Studies Association, Chicago, September 24–27.

———. MF (Ministério da Fazenda). 1996. *O Plano Real: Vigésimo quarto mês.* Brasília.

Miceli, Sergio. 1988. *A elite eclesiástica brasileira.* Rio de Janeiro: Editora Bertrand Brasil.

Minas Gerais, Government of. 1989. *Economia mineira 1989: Volumes I, II, and III.* Belo Horizonte.

Ministério da Administração Federal e Reforma do Estado. *See* Brazil. MARE.

Ministério da Economia, Fazenda e Planejamento. *See* Brazil. MEFP.

Ministério da Fazenda. *See* Brazil. MF.

Miranda, Napoleão. 1994. *Ação da cidadania: Memória: O comitê das empresas públicas na ação da cidadania contra a fome, a miséria, e pela vida.* Rio de Janeiro: ISER.

Moisés, José Álvaro. 1985. "Poder local e participação popular." In *Política municipal,* edited by Pedro Dallari, pp.11–26. Pôrto Alegre: Mercado Aberto/Fundação Wilson Pinheiro.

―――. 1993. "Elections, Political Parties, and Political Culture in Brazil: Changes and Continuities." *Journal of Latin American Studies* 25: 575–611.

―――. 1994. "Political Legitimacy in Brazil in the 1990s: A Study of Public Satisfaction with the Actual Functioning of Democracy." Paper presented to the Sixteenth World Congress of the International Political Science Association, Berlin, August 21–25.

―――. 1995. *Os brasileiros e a democracia: Bases sócio-políticas da legitimidade brasileira.* São Paulo: Editora Ática.

Montenegro, Marcelo. 1995. "Labor and Mercosur." *NACLA Report on the Americas* 28: 32–33.

Montero, Alfred P. 1997. "Shifting States in Uneven Markets: Political Decentralization and Subnational Industrial Policy in Contemporary Brazil and Spain." Ph.D. diss., Department of Political Science, Columbia University, New York.

Montero, Paula. 1992. "Tradição e modernidade: João Paulo II e o problema da cultura." *Revista Brasileira de Ciências Sociais* 7, no. 20 (October): 90–112.

Montoro, Eugênio A. Franco. 1974. "A organização do município na federação brasileira." Unpublished Ph.D. thesis, Pontíficia Universidade Católica de São Paulo.

Moraes, Marcelo de. 1998. "PFL e PMDB passam a ter as maiores bancadas." *O Estado de São Paulo,* October 10, 1.

Moreira Franco, Wellington. 1996a. Interview by Kurt Weyland with federal deputy PMDB, Rio de Janeiro, and rapporteur of constitutional amendment on administrative reform, Brasília, July 4.

―――. 1996b. *Relatório: Proposta de emenda à constituição.* No. 173-A, of 1995. Brasília. Câmara dos Deputados. Comissão Especial Destinada a Proferir Parecer à PEC. No. 173-A, of 1995.

Motta, Athayde. 1997. *Racial Issues and Politics: A Public Policy Experience in Brazil.* Policymaking in a Redemocratized Brazil series, Policy Research Report no. 119. Austin: Lyndon B. Johnson School of Public Affairs, University of Texas at Austin.

Müller, Geraldo. 1986. "O não direito do não cidadão." *Novos Estudos* 15: 44–55.

Muller, Edward N. 1988. "Democracy, Economic Development, and Income Inequality." *American Sociological Review* 53 (February): 50–68.

―――. 1995. "Economic Determinants of Democracy." *American Sociological Review* 60 (December): 966–82.

Musgrave, Richard A., and Peggy B. Musgrave. 1989. *Public Finance in Theory and Practice.* 5th ed. New York: McGraw-Hill.

Muszynski, Judith, and Antonio Manuel Teixeira Mendes. 1990. "Democratização e opinião pública no Brasil." In *De Geisel a Collor: O balanço da transição,* edited by B. Lamounier, pp. 61–80. São Paulo: Editora Sumaré.

Nascimento, Elimar Pinheiro do. 1994. "A exclusão social no Brasil: Algumas hipóteses de trabalho e quatro sugestões práticas." *Cadernos do CEAS* 152 (1994): 57–66.

Negrão, Lisias Nogueira. 1996. *Entre a cruz e a encruzilhada: Formação do campo umbandista em São Paulo.* São Paulo: Editora da Universidade de São Paulo.

Neira, Nestor-Humberto Martínez. 1996. "The Ten Sins of Judicial Reform . . . and Some Anathemas." Paper presented to the Tinker Forum on the Role of the State in Latin America and the Caribbean, Cancún, Mexico, October.

Nelson, Joan M. 1987. "Political Participation." In *Understanding Political Development,* edited by S. Huntington and M. Weiner, pp. 103–59. Boston: Little, Brown, and Company.

Nelson, Roy C. 1995. *Industrialization and Political Affinity: Industrial Policy in Brazil.* New York: Routledge.

Nelson, Sara. 1996. "Constructing and Negotiating Gender in Women's Police Stations in Brazil." *Latin American Perspectives* 23: 131–48.

Neri, Marcelo, Claudio Considera, and Alexandre Pinto. 1996. "Crescimento, desigualidade e pobreza: O impacto da estabilização." Série Seminários No. 28/96. Rio de Janeiro: IPEA.

Neto, Joviniano. 1996. "Assessoria aos movimentos sociais: Crise e alternativa." *Cadernos do CEAS* 162: 75–84.

Neto, Leonardo Guimarães. 1995. "Desigualdades regionais e federalismo." In *Desigualdades regionais e desenvolvimento,* edited by Rui de Britto Álvares Affonso and Pedro Luiz Barros Silva, pp. 13–59. São Paulo: FUNDAP.

Neunreither, Karlheinz. 1994. "The Democratic Deficit of the European Union: Toward Closer Cooperation between the European Parliament and the National Parliaments." *Government and Opposition* 29: 299–314.

Nicolau, Jairo Marconi. 1992. "A representação política e a questão da desproporcionalidade no Brasil." *Novos Estudos* 33 (July): 222–35.

———. 1993. *Sistema eleitoral e reforma política.* Rio de Janeiro: Foglio Editora.

———. 1996a. "A migração partidária na Câmara dos Deputados (1991–96)." *Monitor Público* 3(10): 41–45.

———. 1996b. *Multipartidarismo e democracia: Um estudo sobre o sistema partidário brasileiro (1985–94).* Rio de Janeiro: Editora Fundação Getúlio Vargas.

Nino, Carlos Santiago. 1996. *Radical Evil on Trial.* New Haven: Yale University Press.

Nogueira, Júlio Cesar de A. 1995. "O financiamento público e descentralização fiscal no Brasil." Texto para Discussão No. 34. Rio de Janeiro: Centro de Estudos de Políticas Públicas.

Nogueira, Oracy. 1962. "Contribuição à história do municipalismo no Brasil." *Revista Brasileira dos Municípios* 56/60 (July-December): 105–37.

Novaes, Carlos Alberto Marques. 1993. "PT: Dilemas da burocratização." *Novos Estudos* 35: 217–37.

———. 1994. "Dinâmica institucional da representação: Individualismo e partidos na Câmara dos Deputados."*Novos Estudos* 38: 99–147.

Nunes, Edson. 1995. "Conclusión." In *Municípios y servícios públicos: Gobiernos locales en ciudades intermédias de América Latina,* edited by Alfredo Rodríguez and Fabio Velásquez. Santiago: Ediciones Sur.

Nylen, William. 1992. "Small Business Owners Fight Back: Non-Elite Capital Activism in Democratizing Brazil (1978–1990)." Ph.D. diss., Department of Political Science, Columbia University, New York.

———. 1997a. "Popular Participation in Brazil's Workers' Party: 'Democratizing Democracy' in Municipal Politics." *Political Chronicle* (Journal of the Florida Political Science Association): 1–12.

———. 1997b. "Reconstructing the Workers' Party (PT): Lessons from North-Eastern Brazil." In *The New Politics of Inequality in Latin America: Rethinking Participation and Representation,* edited by Douglas A. Chalmers, Carlos M. Vilas, Katherine Hite, Scott B. Martin, Kerianne Piester, and Monique Segarra, pp. 421–446. New York: Oxford University Press.

———. 1998. "New Political Activists for Disillusioned Democracies: An Analysis of the Impact of 'Popular Participation' on Participants in the Participatory Budgets (Orçamentos Participativos) of Betim and Belo Horizonte, Minas Gerais, Brazil." Paper prepared for Fourth International Congress of the Unión Iberoamericana de Municipalistas, Córdoba, Argentina, October 12–16.

Oates, Wallace E. 1972. *Fiscal Federalism.* New York: Harcourt Brace Jovanovich.

O'Donnell, Guillermo. 1984. "'Y a mí, que mierda me importa?' Notes on Social Interaction and Politics in Argentina and Brazil." Revised version of Helen Kellogg Institute for International Studies Working Paper No. 9. Notre Dame, January.

———. 1988. "Transições, continuidades, e alguns paradoxos," and "hiatos, instituições, e perspectivas democráticas." In *A Democracia no Brasil: Dilemas e perspectivas,* edited by Fábio Wanderley Reis and Guillermo O'Donnell, pp. 41–90. São Paulo: Vértice.

———. 1992. "Transitions, Continuities, and Paradoxes." In *Issues in Democratic Consolidation: The New South American Democracies in Comparative Perspective,* edited by S. Mainwaring, G. O'Donnell, and S. Valenzuela, pp.17–56. Notre Dame, Ind.: University of Notre Dame.

———. 1993. "On the State, Democratization, and Some Conceptual Problems." *World Development* 21: 1355–69.

———. 1994. "Delegative Democracy." *Journal of Democracy* 5(1): 55–69.

———. 1996. "Illusions about Consolidation." *Journal of Democracy* 7(2): 34–51.

———. 1997. "Polyarchies and the (Un)Rule of Law in Latin America." Paper presented at the Annual Meeting of the American Political Science Association, Washington, D.C., August 28–31.

Oliveira, Eliézer Rizzo de. 1987. "Constituinte, forças armadas e autonomia militar." In *As forças armadas no Brasil,* edited by E. Rizzo de Oliveira et al., pp. 145–78. Rio de Janeiro: Espaço e Tempo.

———. 1994. *De Geisel a Collor: Forças armadas, transição, e democracia.* São Paulo: Papirus.

Oliveira, Fabricio Augusto de. 1995. *Crise, reforma, e desordem do sistema tributário nacional.* São Paulo: Editora da UNICAMP.

———. 1986. "O sistema fiscal brasileiro: Evolução e crise (1965/1985)." Texto para Discussão No. 9. São Paulo: IESP/FUNDAP.

Oliveira, Gesner. 1991. "Condicionantes e diretrizes de política para a abertura comercial brasileira." IPEA Research Project, CEBRAP. São Paulo, February.

———. 1995. "The Brazilian Economy under the Real: Prospects for Stabilization and Growth." Paper presented at the Nineteenth International Congress of the Latin American Studies Association, Washington, D.C., September 28–30.

Oliveira, Jane Souto de. 1993. *O traço da desigualdade social no Brasil.* Rio de Janeiro: IBGE.

Oliveira, Pedro A. Ribeiro. 1992. "Estruturas da Igreja e conflitos religiosos." In *Catolicismo no Brasil atual,* vol. 1, *Modernidade e tradição,* edited by Pierre Sanchis, pp. 41–66. São Paulo: Edições Loyola.

———. 1994. "CEBs: O que são? Quantas são? O que fazem?" *Revista Eclesiástica Brasileira* 54 (December): 931–34.

Olson, Robert. 1995. "Concepts for Future Defense and Military Relations with Counterparts." In *Hemispheric Security in Transition: Adjusting to the Post-1995 Environment,* edited by L. Erik Kjonnerod, pp. 205–11. Washington, D.C.: National Defense University Press.

Oro, Ari Pedro. 1994. "O 'expansionismo' religioso brasileiro para os países do Prata." *Revista Eclesiástica Brasileira* 54: 875–95.

———. 1996. *Avanço pentecostal e reação católica.* Petrópolis: Vozes.

Ottmann, Götz. 1995. "Movimentos sociais urbanos e democracia no Brasil—Uma abordagem cognitiva." *Novos Estudos* 41: 186–207.

Paiva, Vanilda, ed. 1985. *Igreja e questão agrária.* São Paulo: Edições Loyola.

Palermo, Vicente, and Marcos Novaro. 1996. *Política y poder en el gobierno de Menem.* Buenos Aires: Norma.

Pang, Eul-Soo. 1989. "Debt, Adjustment, and Democratic Cacophony in Brazil." In *Debt and Democracy in Latin America*, edited by Barbara Stallings and Robert Kaufman, pp. 127–42. Boulder, Colo.: Westview Press.

Paoli, Maria Celia. 1991. "As ciências sociais, os movimentos sociais, e a questão do gênero." *Novos Estudos* 31: 107–20.

Partido dos Trabalhadores. *See* PT

Pastoriza, Lila. 1996. "Los sospechosos de siempre." *El Caminante* 2 (June): 15–18.

Pattnayak, Satya, ed. 1995. *Organized Religion in the Political Transformation of Latin America*. Lanham, Md.: University Press of America.

Paul, Jean-Jacques, and Laurence Wolff. 1996. "The Economics of Higher Education." In *Opportunity Foregone: Education in Brazil*, edited by Nancy Birdsall and Richard H. Sabot, pp. 523–54. Washington, D.C.: Interamerican Development Bank.

Payne, Leigh. 1994. *Brazilian Industrialists and Democratic Change*. Baltimore: Johns Hopkins University Press.

———. 1995. "Brazilian Business and the Democratic Transition: New Attitudes and Influence." In *Business and Democracy in Latin America*, edited by Ernest Bartell, C.S.C., and Leigh Payne, pp. 217–56. Pittsburgh: University of Pittsburgh Press.

Pedone, Luiz, ed. 1993. *Sistemas eleitorais e processos políticos comparados: A promessa de democracia na América Latina e Caribe*. Brasília: Universidade de Brasília.

Peña, Felix. 1992. "Pré-requisitos políticos e economicos da integração." *Política Externa* 1: 122–31.

———. 1995. "New Approaches to Economic Integration in the Southern Cone." *Washington Quarterly* 18: 113–22.

Perani, Cláudio. 1987. "Novos rumos da pastoral popular." *Cadernos do CEAS* 107 (January–February): 37–46.

Pereira, Anthony. 1996. *The End of the Peasantry*. Pittsburgh: University of Pittsburgh Press.

———. 1998. "'Persecution and Farce': The Origins and Transformation of Brazil's Political Trials." *Latin American Research Review* 33: 1.

Peters, B. Guy. 1991. *The Politics of Taxation*. Cambridge: Blackwell.

Petersen, Douglas. 1996. *Not by Might nor by Power: A Pentecostal Theology of Social Concern in Latin America*. Oxford: Regnum.

Petry, André. 1998. "Atenção com eles." *Veja*, September 30, 38.

Pierucci, Antônio Flávio de Oliveira. 1996. "Liberdade de cultos na sociedade de serviços: Em defesa do consumidor religioso." *Novos Estudos* 44 (March): 3–11.

Pierucci, Antônio Flávio de Oliveira, and Reginaldo Prandi, eds. 1996a. *A realidade social das religiões no Brasil: Religião, sociedade, e política*. São Paulo: Editora HUCITEC.

———. 1996b. "Religiões e voto: A eleição presidencial de 1994." In *A realidade social das religiões no Brasil: Religião, sociedade, e política*, edited by Antônio Flávio de Oliveira Pierucci and Reginaldo Prandi, pp. 211–38. São Paulo: Editora HUCITEC.

Pierucci, Antônio Flávio de Oliveira, Beatriz Muniz de Souza, and Candido Procópio Ferreira de Camargo. 1986. "Igreja católica: 1945–1970." In *Historia geral da civilização brasileira, tomo III, O Brasil republicano*, vol. 4, *Economia e cultura (1930–1964)*, edited by Boris Fausto, pp. 343–80. São Paulo: DIFEL.

Pimenta, Carlos Cesar. 1995. Interview by Kurt Weyland with former executive secretary of the Ministério do Trabalho e da Administração Federal. São Paulo, July 4.

Pinheiro, Paulo Sergio. 1991. *Estratégias da ilusão*. São Paulo: Companhia das Letras.

———. 1996a. "Democracies without Citizenship." *NACLA Report on the Americas* 30: 17–23.

———. 1996b. "Préfacio: O passado está morto, nem passado é ainda" In *Democracia em pedaços: Direitos humanos no Brasil,* edited by Gilberto Dimenstein, pp. 7–45. São Paulo: Companhia das Letras.

Pinto, Céli Regina Jardim. 1994. "Mulher e política no Brasil: Os impasses do feminismo, enquanto movimento social, face as regras do jogo da democracia representativa." *Estudos Feministas* 2: 256–70.

Poletto, Ivo. 1995. "Desenvolvimento social: O bem-estar como prioridade absoluta." *Revista Eclesiástica Brasileira* 55 (March): 161–66.

Pope, Clara. 1985. "Human Rights and the Catholic Church in Brazil, 1970–1983." *Journal of Church and State* 27(3): 429–52.

Portes, Alejandro. 1989. "Urbanization during the Years of the Crisis." *Latin American Research Review* 24, no. 3: 7–44.

———. 1997. "Neoliberalism and the Sociology of Development: Emerging Trends and Unanticipated Facts." *Population and Development Review* 23(2): 229–59.

Porto, Walter Costa. 1995. "A nova lei eleitoral e as sugestões do TSE." *Monitor Público* 2(7): 19–25.

Power, Timothy J. 1991. "Politicized Democracy: Competition, Institutions, and 'Civic Fatigue' in Brazil." *Journal of Interamerican Studies and World Affairs* 33(3): 75–112.

———. 1996. "Elites and Institutions in Conservative Transitions to Democracy: Ex-Authoritarians in the Brazilian National Congress." *Studies in Comparative International Development* 32(3): 56–84.

———. 1997. "Parties, Puppets, and Paradoxes: Changing Attitudes toward Party Institutionalization in Postauthoritarian Brazil." *Party Politics* 3(2): 189–219.

———. 1998. "The Pen Is Mightier than the Congress: Presidential Decree Power in Brazil." In *Executive Decree Authority,* edited by John Carey and Matthew Soberg Shugart, pp. 197–230. New York: Cambridge University Press.

Power, Timothy J., and Mark J. Gasiorowski. 1997. "Institutional Design and Democratic Consolidation in the Third World." *Comparative Political Studies* 30(2): 123–55.

Power, Timothy J., and J. Timmons Roberts. 1995. "Compulsory Voting, Invalid Ballots, and Abstention in Brazil." *Political Research Quarterly* 48(3): 795–826.

Prandi, Reginaldo. 1996. "Religião paga, conversão, e serviço." *Novos Estudos* 45 (July): 65–77.

Prandi, Reginaldo, and André Ricardo de Souza. 1996. "A carismática despolitização da Igreja Católica." In *A realidade social das religiões no Brasil: Religião, sociedade, e política,* edited by Antônio Flávio Pierucci and Reginaldo Prandi, pp. 59–91. São Paulo: Editora HUCITEC.

Presidência da República. 1995. *Proposta de reforma tributária.* Brasília. Presidência da República.

———. 1996a. Câmara da reforma do Estado. *Plano diretor da reforma do aparelho do estado.* Brasília.

———. Presidência da República. 1996b. *Programa Nacional de Direitos Humanos.* Brasília: Ministério da Justiça.

———. Presidência da República. 1997. *Três anos de Real: Construindo um país melhor.* Brasília.

Pressburger, Miguel, and Maria Tereza de Araújo. 1989. "A conjuntura eclesial." *Cadernos do CEAS* 124 (November–December 1989): 42–55.

Przeworski, Adam. 1991. *Democracy and the Market.* Cambridge: Cambridge University Press.

———. 1995. *Sustainable Democracy.* Cambridge: Cambridge University Press.

———. 1996. "Democracy as an Equilibrium." Paper prepared for discussion at the New School for Social Research, New York, March 27.

Przeworski, Adam, and Fernando Limongi. 1993. "Political Regimes and Economic Growth." *Journal of Economic Perspectives* 7(3): 51–70.

PT (Partido dos Trabalhadores). N.d. "Curiosidades eleitorais." Boletim Nacional. Mimeograph.

———. 1990. "'Balanço' da atuação da bancada, 1990." Brasília: Câmara dos Deputados, Gabinete da Liderança do PT. Mimeograph.

———. 1992. "Informe especial: Balanço das atividades da liderança em 1992." Brasília: Câmara dos Deputados, Gabinete da Liderança do PT. Mimeograph.

———. 1993. "Prefeituras petistas–1993." São Paulo: Secretaría Nacional de Assuntos Institucionais. Mimeograph.

———. 1994. "Balanço da liderança do PT na Câmara dos Deputados, ano legislativo de 1994." Brasília: Câmara dos Deputados, Gabinete da Liderança do PT. Mimeograph.

———. 1995. "Principais temas debatidos na Câmara dos Deputados–1995." Brasília: Câmara dos Deputados, Gabinete da Liderança do PT. Mimeograph.

———. 1996a. "O que é o PT." April 15. Web site address: http://www.pt-rs.org.br/apres.htm

———. 1996b. "Projetos do PT para o Habitat II." Mimeograph.

———. 1996c. "PT Elege 115 prefeitos." November 21. Web site address: http://www.pt.org.br/result.htm

Puls, Mauricio. 1997. "Conservadores já somam 45% do PSDB." *Folha de São Paulo*, January 20.

Putnam, Robert D. 1993. *Making Democracy Work: Civic Traditions in Modern Italy*. Princeton: Princeton University Press.

———. 1995a. "Bowling Alone: America's Declining Social Capital." *Journal of Democracy* 6: 65–78.

———. 1995b. "Tuning In, Tuning Out: The Strange Disappearance of Social Capital in America." *PS: Political Science and Politics* 27: 664–683.

Putnam, Robert D., with Robert Leonardi and Raffaella Y. Nanetti. 1993. *Making Democracy Work: Civic Traditions in Modern Italy*. Princeton: Princeton University Press.

Quércia, Orestes, ed. 1986. *Municipalismo*. São Paulo: CEPASP/Cidade Press Editora.

Queiroz, Maria Isaura Pereira de. 1976. *O mandonismo local na vida política brasileira e outros ensaios*. São Paulo: Editora Alfa-Omega.

Ramos, Alcida Rita. 1995. "O Índio Hiper-Real." *Revista Brasileira de Ciências Sociais* 10: 5–14.

Reddy, Sanjay, and Anthony Pereira. 1998. *The Role and Reform of the State*. Office of Development Studies Working Paper No. 8. Bureau for Development Policy, United Nations Development Programme, August. New York.

Reis, Eliza, and Zairo Cheibub. 1997. "Elites' Political Values and Democratic Consolidation in Brazil." In *Classes and Elites in Democracy and Democratization*, edited by Eva Etzioni-Halevy, pp. 222–29. New York: Garland.

Reis Filho, Daniel Aarão, et al. 1997. *Versoes e ficções: O sequestro da história*. São Paulo: Editora Fundação Perseu Abramo, second edition.

Reis, Fábio Wanderley, and Guillermo O'Donnell, eds. 1988. *A democracia no Brasil: Dilemas e perspectivas*. São Paulo: Vértice.

Remmer, Karen. 1996. "The Sustainability of Political Economy: Lessons from South America." *Comparative Political Studies* 29(6): 611–24.

Revista Brasileira dos Municípios. 1965. "Reunião Municipalista." 71/72: 205–6.

Revista Eclesiástica Brasileira. 1993a. "Demônios do fim do século (Análise da prática do exorcismo na Igreja Universal do Reino de Deus)." 53 (September): 693–95.

————. 1993b. "'Palavra viva' na telinha." 53 (September): 684–85.

————. 1995. "Eras tu, senhor? (A fraternidade e os excluídos)." 55 (March): 198–200.

Rezende, Fernando. 1995. "O financiamento das políticas públicas: Problemas atuais." In *A federação em perspectiva: Ensaios selecionados,* edited by Rui de Britto Álvares Affonso and Pedro Luiz Barros Silva, pp. 241–59. São Paulo: FUNDAP.

Ribeiro, Ivete, and Ana Clara Torres Ribeiro. 1994. *Família e desafios na sociedade brasileira: Valores como un ângulo de análise.* Rio de Janeiro: Centro João XXIII.

Ribeiro, Lúcia. 1994. "A experiência do aborto entre as mulheres católicas." *Cadernos do CEAS* 153 (September–October 1994): 70–76.

Ribeiro, Renato Janine. 1994. "A política como espetáculo." In *Anos 90: Política e Sociedade no Brasil,* edited by E. Dagnino, pp. 31–40. São Paulo: Brasiliense.

Rio Branco, José Mário Paranhos do. 1989. Interview by author in Departamento Jurídico, Federação das Indústrias do Estado de São Paulo, São Paulo, December 20.

Roarelli, Maria Liz de Medeiros. 1994. *Análise das transferências negociadas por órgão e esfera de governo.* São Paulo: FUNDAP/IESP.

Roberts, J. Timmons. 1995. "Expansion of Television in Eastern Amazonia." *Geographical Review* 85(1): 41–49.

————. 1996. "Global Restructuring and the Environment in Latin America." In *Latin America in the World Economy,* edited by Roberto P. Korzeniewicz and William C. Smith, pp. 187–210. Westport, Conn.: Greenwood Press.

Rocha, Sonia. 1996. "Renda e pobreza: Os impactos do Plano Real." Texto para discussão no. 439. Rio de Janeiro: IPEA.

Rodrigues, Fernando. 1997. "Eleições: Programa de Lula prevê taxa extra sobre o lucro." *Fohla de São Paulo,* October 7.

Rodrigues, Leôncio Martins. 1990. *Partidos e sindicatos: Escritos de sociologia política.* São Paulo: Ática.

Rodriguez, Vicente. 1995. "Federalismo e interesses regionais." In *A federação em perspectiva: Ensaios selecionados,* edited by Rui de Britto Álvares Affonso and Pedro Luiz Barros Silva, pp. 431–448. São Paulo: FUNDAP.

Roett, Riordan. 1978. *Brazil: Politics in a Patrimonial Society.* 2d ed. New York: Praeger.

Rolim, Francisco Cartaxo. 1985. *Pentecostais no Brasil: Uma interpretação sócio-religiosa.* Petrópolis: Vozes.

————. 1994. *Pentecostalismo: Brasil e América Latina.* Petrópolis: Vozes.

Rosa, José Rui Gonçalves. 1988. "Impacto financeiro da reforma tributária nos recursos disponíveis da união, estados, e municípios." In *O sistema tributário na nova constituição,* edited by Roberto Bocaccio Piscitelli, pp. 101–27. Brasília: Editora da UnB.

Rosenberg, Luis Paulo. 1994. "The PT in Government." Cited in C. Pinto and F. Abrucio, "Surprises in 'Who's Who' of PT Administration." *Gazeta Mercantil,* May 21–23, 1, 5.

Rosenn, Keith. 1990. "Brazil's New Constitution: An Exercise in Transient Constitutionalism for a Transitional Society." *American Journal of Comparative Law* 38: 773–802.

————. 1991. "The Success of Constitutionalism in the United States and Its Failure in Latin America: An Explanation." In *The U.S. Constitution and the Constitutions of Latin America,* edited by Kenneth W. Thompson, pp. 53–93. Lanham, Md.: Miller Center of Public Affairs, University of Virginia/ University Press of America.

Rosetti, Fernando. 1996a. "Mais de 90% das crianças vão à escola." *Folha de São Paulo,* September 6, 1: 9.

————. 1996b. "MEC quer vincular recursos à produção." *Folha de São Paulo,* February 4, 1: 15.

Sá, Xico, and Abnor Gondim. 1996. "ONGs vivem fenômeno 'Chapa-Branca'." *Folha de São Paulo* June 9, 1: 10.

Sachs, Jeffrey, and Álvaro Zini, Jr. 1995. "Brazilian Inflation and the 'Plano Real.'" Paper presented at the Nineteenth International Congress of the Latin American Studies Association, Washington, D.C., September 28–30.

Sadek, Maria Tereza. 1995. "Reformas políticas e ordenamento institucional." In *Lições da década de 80*, edited by Lourdes Sola and Leda M. Paulanipp, pp. 225–40. São Paulo: Editora da Universidade de São Paulo (EDUSP).

Sader, Emir. 1995. *O anjo torto: Esquerda (e direita) no Brasil*. São Paulo: Brasiliense.

Sader, Emir, and Ken Silverstein. 1991. *Without Fear of Being Happy–Lula, the Workers Party, and Brazil*. New York: Verso.

Salem, Tânia, ed. 1981. *A Igreja dos oprimidos*. São Paulo: Editora Brasil Debates.

Sales, Teresa. 1993. "Caminhos da cidadania." *Reforma Agrária* 23: 45–58.

Sallum, Brasílio, Jr. 1996. "Federação, autoritarismo, e democratização." *Tempo Social: Revista de Sociologia da USP* 8: 27–52.

Samuels, David J. 1999. "Incentives to Cultivate a Party Vote in Candidate-Centric Electoral Systems: Evidence from Brazil." *Comparative Political Studies* 32(4): 487–89.

———. 1998. "Careerism and its Consequences: Federalism, Elections, and Policy-Making in Brazil." Ph.D. diss., UCSD.

Samuels, David Julian, and Fernando Luiz Abrucio. 1997a. "The New Politics of the Governors: Subnational Politics and the Brazilian Transition to Democracy." Paper prepared for annual meeting of the International Political Science Association, Seoul, South Korea, August.

———. 1997b. "Federalism and Democratic Transition in Brazil." Unpublished, University of Minnesota.

Sanchis, Pierre, ed. 1992. *Catolicismo no Brasil atual*. 3 vols. São Paulo: Edições Loyola.

Santana, Angela. 1996. Interview by author with the secretary of Reforma do Estado, Ministério da Administração Federal e Reforma do Estado, Brasília, July 10.

Santos, Boaventura de Sousa. 1998. "Participatory Budgeting in Porto Alegre: Toward a Redistributive Democracy." *Politics and Society* 26(4): 461–510.

Santos, Boaventura de Sousa, Maria Manuel Leitão Marques, and João Pedroso. 1996. "Os Tribunais nas Sociedades Contemporâneas." *Revista Brasileira de Ciências Sociais* 30, no. 11 (February): 29–62.

Santos, José Vicente Tavares dos. 1992. "Violência no campo: O dilaceramento da cidadania." *Reforma Agrária* 22: 4–11.

Santos, Milton. 1994. *A urbanização brasileira*. São Paulo: Editora Hucitec.

Santos, Wanderley Gulherme dos. 1985. "A pós-'revolução' brasileira." In *Brasil, sociedade democrática*, edited by Bernardo Sorj, pp. 223–335. Rio de Janeiro: José Olympio Editora.

Santos, Wanderley Guilherme dos, Violeta Maria Monteiro, and Ana Maria Lustosa Caillaux. 1990. *Que Brasil é este? Manual de indicadores políticos e sociais*. São Paulo: Vértice.

São Paulo. 1983. "Encontro de Vereadores." São Paulo: Secretaria do Interior, Fundação Prefeito Faria Lima–CEPAM.

Scherer-Warren, Ilse, and Paulo J. Krischke, eds. 1987. *Uma revolução no cotidiano*. São Paulo: Editora Brasiliense.

Schmitt, Rogério Augusto, and Simone Cuber Araujo. 1997. "Migração partidária, reapresentação e reeleição na Câmara dos Deputados." Paper presented to the Twenty-first International Congress of the Latin American Sociological Association, São Paulo, August 31–September 5.

Schmitter, Phillippe. 1973. "The 'Portugalization' of Brazil?" In *Authoritarian Brazil: Origins, Policies, Future*, edited by Alfred Stepan. New Haven: Yale University Press.

————. 1983. "Democratic Theory and Neocorporatist Practice." *Social Research* 50: 885–928.

————. 1992. "The Consolidation of Democracy and the Representation of Social Groups." *American Behavioral Scientist* 35: 422–49.

————. 1995. "Transitology: The Science or the Art of Democratization?" In *The Consolidation of Democracy in Latin America,* edited by Joseph Tulchin and Bernice Romero, pp. 11–41. Boulder, Colo.: Lynne Rienner Publishers.

Schneider, Ben Ross. 1991. "Brazil under Collor: Anatomy of a Crisis." *World Policy Journal* 8: 321–47.

————. 1995. "Democratic Consolidations: Some Broad Comparisons and Sweeping Arguments." *Latin American Research Review* 30: 215–34.

Schneider, Ronald M. 1971. *The Political System of Brazil: Emergence of a "Modernizing" Authoritarian Regime, 1964–1970.* New York: Columbia University Press.

Schwartzman, Simon. 1997. "The New Brazilian Transition." Working Paper no. 232, Latin American Program of the Woodrow Wilson International Center for Scholars. Washington, D.C. December.

Secretaria de Planejamento. *See* SEPLAN

Segato, Rita Laura. 1995. "Cidadania: Por que não? Estado e sociedade no Brasil a luz de um discurso religioso afro-brasileiro." *Dados* 38: 581–601.

Selcher, Wayne, ed. 1986. *Political Liberalization in Brazil.* Boulder, Colo.: Westview Press.

————. 1990. "O futuro do federalismo na Nova República." *Revista de Administração Pública* 24: 165–90. SEPLAN (Secretaria de Planejamento).

Secretaria de Recursos Humanos. 1989. *Quadro de antecedentes dos recursos humanos.* Brasília.

Serbin, Kenneth P. 1990. "Dom Antonio Celso Queiroz (entrevista)." *Comunicações do ISER* 9, no. 38: 77–79.

————. 1991a. "Brazil Bishops' Vote May Mask Future Power Shift." *National Catholic Reporter,* May 3, 12.

————. 1991b. "Igreja, estado, e a ajuda financeira pública no Brasil, 1930–1964: Estudos de três casos chaves." In *Textos CPDOC.* Rio de Janeiro: Fundação Getúlio Vargas, Centro de Pesquisa e Documentação de História Contemporânea do Brasil.

————. 1992a. "Os seminários: Crise, experiências, e síntese." In *Catolicismo no Brasil atual,* vol. 1, *Modernidade e tradição,* edited by Pierre Sanchis, pp. 91–151. São Paulo: Edições Loyola.

————. 1992b. "State Subsidization of Catholic Institutions in Brazil, 1930–1964: A Contribution to the Economic and Political History of the Church." Working Paper no. 181. Notre Dame, Ind.: Helen Kellogg Institute for International Studies.

————. 1993a. "Collor's Impeachment and the Struggle for Change." *North-South Focus* 2(2).

————. 1993b. "Latin America's Catholic Church: Religious Rivalries and the North-South Divide." *North-South Issues* 2(1).

————. 1993c. "Priests, Celibacy, and Social Conflict: A History of Brazil's Clergy and Seminaries." Ph.D. diss., Department of History, University of California, San Diego.

————. 1994. "Re-creating the Brazilian Church in the Post–Santo Domingo Era." Paper presented at the Eighteenth International Congress of the Latin American Studies Association, Atlanta, 10–12.

————. 1995a. "Brazil: State Subsidization and the Church since 1930." In *Organized Religion in the Political Transformation of Latin America,* edited by Satya R. Pattnayak, pp. 153–75. Lanham, Md.: University Press of America.

———. 1995b. "Simmering Abortion Debate Goes Public in Brazil." *Christian Century* (March 8): 266–71.

———. 1996a. "Brazilian Church Builds International Empire." *Christian Century* (April 10): 398–403.

———. 1996b. "Church-State Reciprocity in Contemporary Brazil: The Convening of the International Eucharistic Congress of 1955 in Rio de Janeiro." *Hispanic American Historical Review* 76(4): 721–51.

———. 1996c. "O diálogo secreto de bispos e generais nos anos da repressão." *O Estado de São Paulo,* March 3, Caderno X.

———. 1997. "Um episódio esquecido da repressão." *Folha de São Paulo,* March 30, Mais! 12.

———. 1998a. "Anatomia de um crime: Repressão, direitos humanos, e o caso de Alexandre Vannucchi Leme." *Teoria e Pesquisa* 20–23: 1–23.

———. 1998b. "The Anatomy of a Death: Repression, Human Rights, and the Case of Alexandre Vannucchi Leme in Authoritarian Brazil." *Journal of Latin American Studies* 30: 1–33.

———. 1998c. "Social Justice or Subversion? The Secret Meetings of Brazil's Bishops and Generals." Unpublished manuscript.

———. 1999. "Religious Tolerance, Church-State Relations, and the Challenge of Pluralism in Brazil." In *Evangelization and Religious Freedom in Latin America: The Challenge of Religious Pluralism,* edited by Paul Sigmund. Maryknoll, N.Y.: Orbis Books.

Serra, José, and José Roberto R. Afonso. 1991. "Trajetória e mitos." *Conjuntura Econômica* (October): 44–50.

Shah, Anwar. 1991. "The New Fiscal Federalism in Brazil." World Bank Discussion Papers No. 124. Washington, D.C.

Share, Donald. 1986. *The Making of Spanish Democracy.* New York: Praeger Publishers.

Share, Donald, and Scott Mainwaring. 1986. "Transitions through Transaction: Democratization in Brazil and Spain." In *Political Liberalization in Brazil,* edited by Wayne Selcher, pp. 175–215. Boulder, Colo.: Westview Press.

Sherwood, Frank P. 1967. *Institutionalizing the Grass Roots in Brazil: A Study in Comparative Local Government.* San Francisco: Chandler Publishing.

Shugart, Matthew Soberg, and John Carey. 1992. *Presidents and Assemblies: Constitutional Design and Electoral Dynamics.* New York: Cambridge University Press.

Sigmund, Paul E. 1990. *Liberation Theology at the Crossroads.* New York: Oxford University Press.

Silva, Ana Amília da. 1993. "Do privado para o público—ONGs e os desafios da consolidação democratica." *Cadernos do CEAS* 146: 36–46.

Silva, Carlos Eduardo Lins da. 1993. "The Brazilian Case: Manipulation by the Media?" In *Television, Politics, and the Transition to Democracy in Latin America,* edited by Thomas E. Skidmore, pp. 137–44. Baltimore: Johns Hopkins University Press.

Silva, Golbery do Couto e. 1967. *Geopolítica do Brasil.* Rio de Janeiro: José Olympio Editora.

Silva, Luiz Inácio Lula da. 1996. Interview by William Nylen, São Paulo, June 20.

Silva, Pedro Luiz Barros, and Vera Lúcia Cabral Costa. 1995. "Descentralização e crise da federação." In *A federação em perspectiva: Ensaios selecionados,* edited by Rui de Britto Álvares Affonso and Pedro Luiz Barros Silva, pp. 261–83. São Paulo: FUNDAP.

Silva, Zilda Pereira da. 1996. "O município e a descentralização da saúde." *São Paulo em Perspectiva* 10(3): 81–87.

Simpson, Miles. 1997. "Informational Equality and Democracy in the New World Order." In *Inequality, Democracy, and Economic Development,* edited by Manus I. Midlarsky, pp. 156–76. New York: Cambridge University Press.

Singer, André. 1990. "Collor na periferia: A volta por cima do populismo?" In *De Geisel a Collor: O balanço da transição,* edited by Bolivar Lamounier, pp. 135–52. São Paulo: Editora Sumarê.

Singer, Paul. 1989. "Democracy and Inflation in the Light of the Brazilian Experience." In *Lost Promises: Debt, Austerity, and Development in Latin America,* edited by William Canak, pp. 31–48. Boulder, Colo.: Westview Press.

———. 1995. "Poder público e organizações populares no combate à pobreza. A experiência do governo Luiza Erundina em São Paulo –1989/92." In *Governabilidade e Pobreza no Brasil,* edited by L. Valladares and M. Prates Coelho, pp. 267–311. Rio de Janeiro: Civilização Brasileira.

Sives, Amanda. 1993. "Elites Behaviour and Corruption in the Consolidation of Democracy in Brazil." *Parliamentary Affairs* 46(4): 549–62.

Skidmore, Thomas E. 1988. *The Politics of Military Rule in Brazil: 1964–1985.* Oxford: Oxford University Press.

Sklar, Judith. 1989. "The Liberalism of Fear." In *Liberalism and the Moral Life,* edited by Nancy L. Rosenbloom, pp. 21–38. Cambridge: Harvard University Press.

Skocpol, Theda. 1985. "Bringing the State Back In." In *Bringing the State Back In,* edited by Peter Evans, Dietrich Rueschemeyer, and Theda Skocpol, pp. 3–37. Cambridge, Eng.: Cambridge University Press.

Skowronek, Stephen. 1982. *Building a New American State: The Expansion of National Administrative Capacities, 1877–1920.* Cambridge: Cambridge University Press.

Smith, Christian. 1991. *The Emergence of Liberation Theology.* Chicago: University of Chicago Press.

Smith, Mitchell. 1996. "Democratic Legitimacy in the European Union: Fulfilling the Institutional Logic." *Journal of Legislative Studies* 2: 283–301.

Smith, William C. 1987. "The Political Transition in Brazil: From Authoritarian Liberalization and Elite Conciliation to Democratization." In *Comparing New Democracies,* edited by Enrique Baloyra, pp. 179–240. Boulder, Colo.: Westview Press.

———. 1989. "Heterodox Shocks and the Political Economy of Democratic Transition in Argentina and Brazil." In *Lost Promises: Debt, Austerity, and Development in Latin America,* edited by William Canak, pp. 138–68. Boulder, Colo.: Westview Press.

Soares, Glaucio Ary Dillon. 1973. *Sociedade e política no Brasil.* São Paulo: DIFEL.

Sola, Lourdes. 1988. "Choque heterodoxo e transição democrática sem ruptura: Uma abordagem transdisciplinar." In *O estado da transição: Política e economia na Nova República,* edited by Lourdes Sola, pp. 13–62. São Paulo: Vértice.

———. 1994. "The State, Structural Reform, and Democratization in Brazil." In *Democracy, Markets, and Structural Reform in Latin America: Argentina, Bolivia, Brazil, Chile, and Mexico,* edited by William C. Smith, Carlos H. Acuña, and Eduardo A. Gamarra, pp. 151–182. New Brunswick, N.J.: Transaction Publishers.

———. 1995. "Estado, regime fiscal, e ordem monetária: Qual estado?" *Revista Brasileira de Ciências Sociais* 10: 29–60.

Soler, Salvador. 1994. "Movimentos sociais urbanos populares na atual conjuntura: Agentes de transformação social?" *Cadernos do CEAS* 154: 53–63.

Solimeo, Marcel Domingos. 1989. Interview by Kurt Weyland with director of the Instituto de Economia, Associação Comercial de São Paulo, São Paulo, November 30.

Somarriba, Mercês, and Otávio Dulci. 1995. "Primeiro relatório de atividades da pesquisa: avaliação da experiência de implantação e atuação de foruns de participação popular na administração municipal de Belo Horizonte–Período 1993–1996." Belo Horizonte, Convênio UFMG/PBH. Mimeograph.

Sousa, José Geraldo, Jr., ed. 1993. *Introdução crítica ao direito série o direito achado na rua*, vol. 1, *Brasília: Centro de educação aberta, continuada, a distância/núcleo de estudos de direitos humanos*. Brasília: Universidade de Brasília.

Souza, Celina. 1996. "Reinventando o poder local: Limites e possibilidades do federalismo e da descentralização." *São Paulo em Perspectiva* 10: 103–12.

———. 1997. *Constitutional Engineering in Brazil: The Politics of Federalism and Decentralization*. New York: St. Martin's Press.

Souza, Herbert de. 1991. *Escritos indignados: Democracia x neoliberalismo no Brasil*. Rio de Janeiro: Rio Fundo Editora and IBASE.

Souza, Maria do Carmo Campello de. 1976. *Estado e partidos políticos no Brasil (1930 a 1964)*. São Paulo: Alfa-Omega.

———. 1989. "The Brazilian New Republic: Under the Sword of Damocles." In *Democratizing Brazil*, edited by Alfred Stepan, pp. 351–94. New York: Oxford University Press.

Stallings, Barbara. 1992. "International Influence on Economic Policy: Debt, Stabilization, and Structural Reform." In *The Politics of Economic Adjustment*, edited by Stephan Haggard and Robert Kaufman, pp. 41–88. Princeton: Princeton University Press.

Stanley, William. 1996. *The Protection Racket State: Elite Politics, Military Extortion, and Civil War in El Salvador*. Philadelphia: Temple University Press.

Stark, Rodney, and James C. McCann. 1993. "Market Forces and Catholic Commitment: Exploring the New Paradigm." *Journal for the Scientific Study of Religion* 32, no. 2: 111–24.

Steigenga, Timothy. 1997. "'Jesus Christ Is Lord of Guatemala': Religious Freedom and Religious Conflict in Central America's Most Protestant Nation." Paper presented at the conference Evangelization and Religious Freedom in Latin America, Princeton University, October 24–25.

Stepan, Alfred. 1971. *The Military in Politics: Changing Patterns in Brazil*. Princeton: Princeton University Press.

———. 1973. "The New Professionalism of Internal Warfare and Military Role Expansion." In *Authoritarian Brazil: Origins, Policies, Future*, edited by Alfred Stepan, pp. 47–65. New Haven: Yale University Press.

———. 1988. *Rethinking Military Politics: Brazil and the Southern Cone*. Princeton: Princeton University Press.

Stepan, Alfred, ed. 1973. *Authoritarian Brazil*. Princeton: Princeton University Press.

———. 1989. *Democratizing Brazil*. New York: Oxford University Press.

Stepan, Alfred, and Cindy Skach. 1993. "Constitutional Frameworks and Democratic Consolidation: Parliamentarianism versus Presidentialism." *World Politics* 46: 1–22.

Sternbach, Nancy Saporta, Marysa Navarro-Aranguren, Patricia Chuchryk, and Sonia E. Alvarez. 1992. "Feminisms in Latin America: From Bogotá to San Bernardo." In *The Making of Social Movements in Latin America: Identity, Strategy, and Democracy*, edited by A. Escobar and S. E. Alvarez, pp. 207–39. Boulder, Colo.: Westview Press.

Stokes, Susan. 1995. "Democracy and the Limits of Popular Sovereignty in South America." In *The Consolidation of Democracy in Latin America*, edited by Joseph S. Tulchin with Bernice Romero, pp. 59–81. Boulder, Colo.: Lynne Rienner Publishers.

Stoll, David. 1990. *Is Latin America Turning Protestant?* Berkeley and Los Angeles: University of California Press.

Straubhaar, Joseph D., Orjan Olsen, and Maria Cavaliari Nunes. 1993. "The Brazilian Case: Influencing the Voter." In *Television, Politics, and the Transition to Democracy in Latin America*, edited by Thomas E. Skidmore, pp. 118–36. Baltimore: Johns Hopkins University Press.

Stromquist, Nelly P. 1997. *Literacy for Citizenship: Gender and Grassroots Dynamics in Brazil*. Albany: State University of New York Press.

Suplicy, Eduardo Matarazzo. 1995. *Programa de garantia de renda mínima*. Brasília, Mimeograph.

———. 1997. "O reconhecimento da renda mínima." *Folha de São Paulo*, October 21.

Suplicy, Eduardo Matarazzo, and Cristovam Buarque. 1996. "A Guaranteed Minimum Income to Eradicate Poverty and Help Poor Children Go to School Instead of Being Forced to Work: The Brazilian Debate and Experience." Paper presented at the Sixth International Congress of the Basic Income European Network, Vienna, September 12–14.

Swatos, William H., Jr., ed. 1995. *Religion and Democracy in Latin America*, New Brunswick, N.J.: Transaction Publishers.

Tanner, Evan. 1994. "Balancing the Budget with Implicit Domestic Default: The Case of Brazil in the 1980s." *World Development* 22: 85–98.

Tarrow, Sidney. 1994. *Power in Movement: Social Movements, Collective Action, and Politics*. Cambridge: Cambridge University Press.

———. 1995. "Cycles of Collective Action: Between Moments of Madness and the Repertoire of Contention." In *Repertoires and Cycles of Collective Action*, edited by M. Traugott, pp. 89–115. Durham, N.C.: Duke University Press.

Tavares, José Antônio Giusti. 1998. *Reforma política e retrocesso democrático: Agenda para reformas pontuais no sistema eleitoral e partidário brasileiro*. Pôrto Alegre: Editora Mercado Aberto.

Tavares, Ricardo. 1995a. "Land and Democracy: Reconsidering the Agrarian Question." *NACLA Report on the Americas* 28: 23–29.

———. 1995b. "The PT Experience in Pôrto Alegre." *NACLA Report on the Americas*, 24(1): 29.

Teixeira, Faustino Luiz Couto. 1988. *A gênese das CEB's no Brasil: Elementos explicativos*. São Paulo: Edições Paulinas.

Tendler, Judith. 1997. *Good Government in the Tropics*. Baltimore: Johns Hopkins University Press.

Theije, Marjo de. 1997. "Conservative CEBs and Liberated Charismatics." Paper presented at the Fourth Congress of the Brazilian Studies Association, Washington, D.C., November 12–15.

Tilly, Charles. 1995. "Democracy Is a Lake." In *The Social Construction of Democracy, 1870–1990*, edited by George Reid Andrews and Herrick Chapman, pp. 365–87. New York: New York University Press.

Toledo, Caio Navarro de. 1994. "As esquerdas e a redescoberta da democracia." In *Anos 90: Política e sociedade no Brasil*, edited by E. Dagnino, pp. 127–36. São Paulo: Brasiliense.

Toledo, José Roberto de. 1996. "Eleitorado malufista aumenta em bases do PT." *Folha de São Paulo*, July 14, 1, 8.

———. 1998. "Balanço parlamentar: PSDB é o que mais cresce no legislativo." *Folha de São Paulo*. October 13, 1.

Toledo, José Roberto de, and André Lahóz. 1996. "Universidade paga é opção para privilegiar o 1° grau." *Folha de São Paulo*, May 5, 1: 12.

Turra, Cleusa, and Gustavo Venturi. 1995. *Racismo cordial: A mais completa análise sobre o preconceito de cor no Brasil*. São Paulo: Editora Ática.

Uchoa, Virgilio Leite. 1998. "Analise de conjuntura, julho-agosto de 1998." CNBB. Mimeograph.

UNESCO (United Nations Economic, Social, and Cultural Organization). 1995. *Statistical Yearbook 1995*. World Wide Web version, http://unescostat.unesco.org

United Nations Development Programme. 1994. *Human Development Report*. Oxford: Oxford University Press.

United States Senate. 1971. United States Senate Hearings before the Subcommittee on Western Hemisphere Affairs of the Committee on Foreign Relations. 92nd Cong., 1st sess., May 4, 5, and 11.Washington, D.C.: U.S. Government Printing Office.

Ustra, Carlos Alberto Brilhante. 1987. *Rompendo o silencio*. Brasília: Editerra Editorial.

Valenzuela, Arturo. 1997. "Paraguay: The Coup That Didn't Happen." *Journal of Democracy* 8: 43–56.

Valladares, Lícia, and Magda Prates Coelho. 1995. *Governabilidade e pobreza no Brasil*. Rio de Janeiro: Civilização Brasileira.

Valle, Rogério. 1995. "Tecnoestruturas e exclusão social." *Perspectivas teológicas* 27: 37–44.

Valle, Rogério, and Marcelo Pitta. 1994. *Comunidades eclesiais católicas: Resultados estatísticos no Brasil*. Petrópolis: Vozes.

Varas, Augusto. 1995. "Latin America: Toward a New Reliance on the Market." In *Global Change, Regional Response: The New International Context of Development*, edited by Barbara Stallings, pp. 272–308. Cambridge: Cambridge University Press.

Varsano, Ricardo. 1996. *De ônus a Bônus: Política governamental e reformas fiscais na transformação do estado brasileiro*. Texto para Discussão No. 417. Brasília: IPEA.

Vásquez, Manuel A. 1997. "Structural Obstacles to Grassroots Pastoral Practice: The Case of a Base Community in Urban Brazil." *Sociology of Religion* 58, no. 1: 53–68.

———. 1998. *The Brazilian Popular Church and the Crisis of Modernity*. Cambridge: Cambridge University Press.

Veja. 1994. "The PT Shines and Also Instills Fear." June 15, 38–45 (in FBIS-LAT-94-139, July 20, p. 32).

———. 1997. "Número alto em lama profunda." March 5, 22–29.

Ventura, Zuenir. 1994. *Cidade partida*. São Paulo: Companhia das Letras.

Vigevani, Tullo. 1989. "Movimentos sociais na transição brasileira: A dificuldade de elaboração do projeto." *Lua Nova* 17: 93–109.

Von Mettenheim, Kurt. 1995. *The Brazilian Voter: Mass Politics in Democratic Transition, 1974–1986*. Pittsburgh: University of Pittsburgh Press.

Wallerstein, Michael. 1980. "The Collapse of Democracy in Brazil: Its Economic Determinants." *Latin American Research Review* 15(3): 3–40.

Wanderley, Luiz Eduardo, and Clodovis Boff. 1992. "Os novos movimentos eclesiais." *Revista Eclesiástica Brasileira* 52 (September): 702–6.

Weber, Max. 1976. *Wirtschaft und Gesellschaft*. 5th ed. Tübingen: J. C. B. Mohr.

Weschler, Lawrence. 1990. *A Miracle, a Universe: Settling Accounts with Torturers*. New York: Penguin Books.

Weyland, Kurt. 1993. "The Rise and Fall of President Collor and Its Impact on Brazilian Democracy." *Journal of Interamerican Studies and World Affairs* 35(1): 1–36.

———. 1995. "Social Movements and the State: The Politics of Health Reform in Brazil." *World Development* 23(10): 1699–712.

———. 1996a. *Democracy without Equity: Failures of Reform in Brazil*. Pittsburgh: University of Pittsburgh Press.

———. 1996b. "How Much Political Power Do Economic Forces Have? Conflicts Over Social Insurance Reform in Brazil." *Journal of Public Policy* 16, no. 1: 59–84.

———. 1996c. "Neopopulism and Neoliberalism in Latin America: Unexpected Affinities." *Studies in Comparative International Development* 31(3): 3–31.

————. 1996d. "Obstacles to Social Reform in Brazil's New Democracy." *Comparative Politics* 29(1): 1–22.

————. 1996e. "Risk-Taking in Latin American Economic Restructuring: Lessons from Prospect Theory." *International Studies Quarterly* 40(2): 185–207.

————. 1998. "From Leviathan to Gulliver: The Decline of the Developmental State in Brazil." *Governance* 11(1): 51–75.

Whitehead, Laurence. 1986. "International Aspects of Democratization." In *Transitions from Authoritarian Rule: Comparative Perspectives,* edited by Guillermo O'Donnell, Philippe C. Schmitter, and Laurence Whitehead, pp. 3–46. Baltimore: Johns Hopkins University Press.

Williamson, John. 1990. "What Washington Means by Policy Reform." In *Latin American Adjustment: How Much Has Happened?* edited by John Williamson, pp. 5–20. Washington, D.C.: Institute for International Economics.

Winn, Peter, and Lilia Ferro-Clérico. 1997. "Can a Leftist Government Make a Difference? The Frente Amplio Administration of Montevideo, 1990–1994." In *New Politics of Inequality in Latin America: Rethinking Participation and Representation,* edited by Douglas A. Chalmers, Carlos M. Vilas, Katherine Hite, Scott B. Martin, Kerianne Piester, and Monique Segarra, pp. 447–468. New York: Oxford University Press.

Wood, Charles H., and J. A. M. de Carvalho. 1988. *The Demography of Inequality in Brazil.* New York: Cambridge University Press.

World Bank. 1995. *World Development Report 1995: Workers in an Integrating World.* New York: Oxford University Press.

————. 1996. *From Plan to Market: World Development Report 1996.* Oxford: Oxford University Press.

————. 1997a. "Crime and Violence as Development Issues in Latin America and the Caribbean." Paper prepared by the World Bank for the conference Urban Crime and Violence, Rio de Janeiro, March 2–4.

————. 1997b. *Decentralization in Latin America: Learning through Experience.* Washington, D. C.

Xavier, Rafael. 1948. *Pela revitalização do município brasileiro.* Rio de Janeiro: Centro Gráfico do IBGE.

————. 1950. *Campanha municipalista.* Rio de Janeiro: Serviço Gráfico do IBGE.

Yúdice, George. Forthcoming. *We Are Not the World: Identity and Representation in an Age of Global Restructuring.* Durham, N.C.: Duke University Press.

Zald, Mayer N. 1996. "Culture, Ideology, and Strategic Framing." In *Comparative Perspectives on Social Movements: Political Opportunities, Mobilizing Structures, and Cultural Framings,* edited by D. McAdam, J. D. McCarthy and M. N. Zald, pp. 261–74. Cambridge: Cambridge University Press.

Zaluar, Alba. 1995. "Crime, medo, e política." *Sociedade e Estado* 10: 391–416.

Zaverucha, Jorge. 1993. "The Degree of Military Political Autonomy during the Spanish, Argentine, and Brazilian Transitions." *Journal of Latin American Studies* 25: 283–99.

————. 1994. *Rumor de sabres: Tutela militar ou controle civil?* São Paulo: Editora Ática.

————. 1996. "A justiça militar no estado de Pernambuco: Um enclave autoritário dentro do aparato de estado." In *O desafio da democracia na América Latina,* edited by Eli Diniz, pp. 106–39. Rio de Janeiro: Instituto Universitário de Pesquisa do Rio de Janeiro-IUPERJ.

————. 1997. "Prerrogativas militares: De Sarney a Cardoso." *Monitor Público* 4, no. 12: 35–41.

Zero Hora. 1994. "CNBB diz que país sucumbiu à desordem." July 26, p. 13.

CONTRIBUTORS ▦

Jeffrey Cason (Ph.D., University of Wisconsin—Madison, 1993) is an assistant professor of political science and director of the Latin American Studies program at Middlebury College in Middlebury, Vermont. He is coauthor (with Christopher Barrett) of *Overseas Research: A Practical Guide* (Johns Hopkins University Press, 1997) and coeditor (with Michael Carter and Frederic Zimmerman) of *Development at a Crossroads: Paths to Sustainability after the Neoliberal Revolution* (Global Studies Program, University of Wisconsin—Madison, 1998). His current research examines the political economy of integration in South America.

Kathryn Hochstetler (Ph.D., University of Minnesota, 1994) is an assistant professor of political science at Colorado State University in Fort Collins, Colorado. She is the author or coauthor of articles in *World Politics* and *Studies in Comparative International Development*, as well as of several book chapters on environmental social movements and policy in Latin America. She coordinates the Working Group on Social Movements for the Brazilian Studies Association. She is now completing a book manuscript on environmental movements in Brazil and Venezuela, and continuing a collaborative research project on the role of NGOs in UN conferences.

Wendy Hunter (Ph.D., University of California—Berkeley, 1992) is an associate professor of political science at Vanderbilt University. She is the author of *Eroding Military Influence in Brazil: Politicians against Soldiers* (University of North Carolina Press, 1997). Her research on the armed forces of Brazil and the Southern Cone has been published in *Comparative Politics, Political Science Quarterly,* and *International Studies Quarterly.* Her current research deals with international financial institutions and the politics of social policy reforms in major Latin American countries.

Peter R. Kingstone (Ph.D., University of California—Berkeley, 1994) is an assistant professor of political science at the University of Connecticut, Storrs. He is the author of *Crafting Coalitions for Reform: Business Preferences, Political Institutions, and Neoliberalism in Brazil* (Pennsylvania State University Press, 1999) and the author of articles in the *Journal of Interamerican Studies and World Affairs* and *NAFTA.* He is currently at work on a comparison of privatization and pension reform in Latin America.

Alfred P. Montero (Ph. D., Columbia University, 1997) is an assistant professor of political science at Carleton College in Northfield, Minnesota. He is the author of articles on Brazilian political economy in the *Journal of Interamerican Studies and World Affairs* and *Current History*. Presently, he is working on a book that compares the politics of subnational industrial policies in Brazil and Spain.

William R. Nylen (Ph.D., Columbia University, 1992) is an associate professor of political science at Stetson University in DeLand, Florida. He is the author of chapters in Douglas Chalmers et al., *The Right and Democracy in Latin America* (Praeger Press, 1992), and Douglas Chalmers et al., *The New Politics of Inequality in Latin America* (Oxford University Press, 1997), as well as of articles in the *Journal of Latin American Studies* and *NACLA Report on the Americas*. He is currently working on a book about the experiences and comparative implications of popular participation in cities administered by the Workers' Party in Brazil.

Anthony W. Pereira (Ph.D., Harvard University, 1991) is an associate professor of political science at Tulane University in New Orleans, Louisiana. He is the author of *The End of the Peasantry: The Rural Labor Movement in Northeast Brazil, 1961–1988* (University of Pittsburgh Press, 1996), and his essay "'Persecution and Farce': The Origins and Transformation of Brazil's Political Trials" recently appeared in the *Latin American Research Review* (1998). He is presently completing a manuscript on the use of military courts by authoritarian regimes in Brazil and the Southern Cone.

Timothy J. Power (Ph.D., University of Notre Dame, 1993) is an assistant professor of political science and an affiliate of the Latin American and Caribbean Center (LACC) at Florida International University in Miami. He is the author of *The Political Right in Postauthoritarian Brazil: Elites, Institutions, and Democratization* (Pennsylvania State University Press, 2000), and his articles have appeared in *Comparative Political Studies, Political Research Quarterly, Party Politics, Studies in Comparative International Development*, and *Journal of Interamerican Studies and World Affairs*. He was a visiting professor at the University of Brasília in 1994 and is currently the contributing editor covering Brazilian politics for the *Handbook of Latin American Studies*, published by the Library of Congress.

J. Timmons Roberts (Ph.D., Johns Hopkins University, 1992) is an associate professor of sociology at Tulane University in New Orleans, Louisiana. His research includes comparative studies of political economy and the environment. He is coeditor with Amy Hite of *From Modernization to Globalization: Social Perspectives on International Development* (Blackwell Publishers, 1999). His articles have appeared in *World Development, Social Problems, Economic Development and Social Change, Journal of Developing Societies, Geographical Review,* and *Political Research Quarterly.* He is coeditor with David Barkin of the Environment in Latin America Network (ELAN@csf.colorado.edu), an information network with nearly one thousand subscribers.

David Samuels (Ph.D., University of California–San Diego, 1998), is an assistant professor of political science at the University of Minnesota. He is the author of articles in *Comparative Political Studies* and the *Journal of Politics.* He is currently working on a book manuscript on the relationship between politicians' career ambitions and the legislative policy-making process in Brazil.

Kenneth P. Serbin (Ph.D., University of California–San Diego, 1993) is an assistant professor of history at the University of San Diego, where he directs the TransBorder Institute. His research concerns the Catholic Church, politics, and social and reproductive issues in Brazil. He is completing a book on church-state relations from 1970 to 1974, and his articles have appeared in the *Hispanic American Historical Review* and the *Journal of Latin American Studies.* He has been a fellow of the Helen Kellogg Institute for International Studies at the University of Notre Dame and a research associate at the North-South Center at the University of Miami.

Thomas E. Skidmore (Ph.D., Harvard University, 1961) is the Carlos Manuel de Céspedes Professor of Modern Latin American History and Director of the Center for Latin American Studies at Brown University. A past president of the Latin American Studies Association, Professor Skidmore is the author of several of the most influential works on modern Brazil, including *Politics in Brazil, 1930–1964: An Experiment in Democracy* (Oxford University Press, 1967) and *The Politics of Military Rule in Brazil, 1964–1985* (Oxford University Press, 1988). The former title is now in its tenth printing in Brazil, where it is widely used as a text in schools and universities, and the latter book won the Latin American Studies Association's first Bryce Wood Award in 1989. Professor Skidmore is also a regular contributor to the *Folha de São Paulo,* Brazil's most prestigious newspaper. His newest book is *Brazil: Five Centuries of Change* (Oxford University Press, 1999).

Kurt Weyland (Ph.D., Stanford University, 1991) is an associate professor of political science at Vanderbilt University. He is the author of *Democracy without Equity: Failures of Reform in Brazil* (University of Pittsburgh Press, 1996) and of articles in journals such as *Comparative Politics, Comparative Political Studies, International Studies Quarterly, Latin American Research Review, Political Research Quarterly, Journal of Democracy,* and the *Journal of Interamerican Studies and World Affairs.* He is currently working on a book that analyzes the politics of neoliberal reform in Argentina, Brazil, Peru, and Venezuela.

INDEX ▒

Abertura: amnesty during, 223–24; Catholic church in, 147. *See also* Democratization

Abranches, Sérgio, 23

Abrucio, Fernando Luiz, 83–84, 272*n17*

Ação Empresarial (Business action), 51

Accountability: effects of decentralization on, 43, 61; of military and police, 106–07, 114, 231–34, 270*n14,* 285*nn33,35,36;* of NGOs, 180; of officeholders, 40, 92, 158, 171; of state, 23, 36, 57, 218; and universalistic values, 55–57

Affonso, Rui de Britto Alvares, 66

AfroBrazilians: and economic inequities, 248–49; religion of, 148, 154–55. *See also* Race

Agencies, state, 104, 179; under authoritarianism, 37–38; and clientelism, 37, 39–40; Collor's program for reducing, 44–45

Agüero, Felipe, 120, 125

Albuquerque, J. A. Guilhon, 209

Alfonsín, Raúl, 206–07

Alvarez, Sonia E., 174–75

Álvaros, Élcio, 116

Amazon, defense of, 115, 120–21

Amendments. *See under* Constitution

Ames, Barry, 29

Amnesty, 170; during *abertura,* 107, 114, 222–24

Argentina, 112; Brazil's relations with, 111, 115, 205–06, 281*n3;* Brazil's trade with, 206–08, 214; state violence in, 223–24

Argentine Brazilian Economic Integration Program (ABEIP), 206–08, 281*n8*

Arinos, Afonso, 20

Arns, Archbishop Dom Paulo Evaristo, 223

Authoritarianism, 43, 258, 282*n; abertura* under, 166, 223; and Catholic Church, 144, 146–47; civil-military relations after, 101–03, 106–16; clientelism under, 37–39; compensation for families of victims of, 106–07, 114, 224–28, 284*n23;* decentralization under, 58, 62–64; effects of, 29, 87–88; opposition to, as frame of social movements, 166–67, 171, 174; opposition to, 129, 144, 164–65, 170, 243; remnants of, 4, 20, 32, 41; state under, 38–39; state violence under, 217, 222–28, 231; subnational governments under, 78, 81–82; support for, 154, 158, 279*n4;* trends against, 261–62; and vigor of civil society, 256–57

Azevedo, Clovis Bueno de, 140–41

Baia, Paulo Fernando, 131, 140–41

Banks, 266*n29,* 268*n11;* central *vs.* states', 59, 66–68

Betto, Frei, 152

Bezerra, Fernando, 214

Bicudo, Hélio, 223

Bornhausen, Paulo, 212

Brasil: Nunca mais (Arquidiocese de São Paulo), 225–26, 228

Brasil: Sempre (Giordani), 226

Brazilian Democratic Movement (MDB), 87

Brazilian Forum, 173

Brazilian Workers' Party (PTB), 128

Brener, Jayme, 260

Bresser Pereira, Carlos, 207–08

Brizola, Leonel, 69

Buarque, Cristovam, 253

Budget, participatory, 135–37

Bureaucracy, 38, 54, 73, 98; effects of democratization on, 40–42; jobs in,

245–46, 255; lack of accountability of, 204–05; military *vs.* civilian, 104–05; streamlining of, 44–45, 51–52, 192–93, 266*n23*

Business, 188, 194, 280*nn4,5*, 281*n1;* and Cardoso's economic reforms, 51, 53–54, 199–200; concerns about fiscal reforms, 186–87; effects of democratization on, 40–42; response to Collor's economic proposals, 45, 47, 190; role in collapse of regimes, 186, 198–99; support for democracy, 203, 280*n5*

Cabinets: military representatives in, 104–05, 106, 110; under presidentialism, 23–24

Cardoso, Fernando Henrique, 20, 258, 266*n26*, 271*n4;* and churches, 151, 156; and economic inequities, 176, 248; economic measures of, 33, 70, 194–202, 280*n3;* effects of democratization under, 54–55; as finance minister, 48–49; and human rights violations, 168, 227–28; and institutional reform, 25, 34; reform by negotiation by, 49–54; relations with military of, 106–07, 109, 114–18, 120–21, 232; successes of, 22, 35, 199; support for education by, 253–54; and Workers' Party, 131, 138; working with business leaders of, 200–01. See also *Plano Real*

Cardoso, Ruth Correa Leite, on social movements, 162, 166, 278*n2*

Carneiro, Leandro, 160

Carneiro, Sueli, 168–69

Catholic Church, 3, 144–61, 225, 276*n16;* human rights activism by, 222–23, 225; and Pentecostals, 153–60, 278*n40*

Cavarozzi, Marcelo, 141, 272*n17*

Centralization. *See* Decentralization

Central Única dos Trabalhadores, 52

Chalmers, Douglas, 33, 125

Chamber of Deputies. *See* Congress

Chauí, Marilena, 221

Chaves, Aureliano, 43

Cheibub, Ziro, 272*n7*

Chile, state violence in, 223–24

Citizens' Action Against Hunger, Misery, and for Life, 167, 177, 179

Citizenship, 175, 244; conditions of, 150, 167, 177; effects of informal economy on, 246–47; effects of state violence on, 229, 234–35; as frame for social movements, 167–69, 171, 173; inequalities of, 220–21; in Workers' Party ideology, 132

Civil liberties. *See* Human rights

Civil service. *See* Bureaucracy

Civil society, 222; control over state officials, 36–37; effects of religious pluralism on, 145–46; military's relation to, 101–25; and trade policy making, 205, 214; vigor of, 4, 243, 256–57, 261

Class, social: inequalities of, 221–22, 252; in social movements, 169, 279*n6;* and state violence, 219, 222, 230, 233, 286*n38*

Clientelism, 7, 175; under authoritarianism, 37–39; and Cardoso, 49–54, 266*n26;* and Collor, 45–47, 191–92; in Congress, 137–38; and democratization, 37, 39–42, 54–55; of Pentecostals, 157–58; and social movements, 165, 180–81, 257; and social security reform, 52–53; in subnational governments, 59, 62, 64, 72–73; trends against, 257, 261; and urban *vs.* rural voters, 86–87; Workers' Party rejection of, 127, 134, 274*n29*

Cold War, 107, 128; effects of end of, 129, 208, 211

Collective action problems, 31; frames for, 165–67, 174; and state institutions, 18–19, 33; strategic repertoires for, 170–81

Collor de Mello, Fernando, 23, 266*n23*, 280*n1;* and churches, 149, 156–57; and democratization, 54, 104, 175; economic program of, 44–47, 67, 69, 190, 199, 209; election of, 43–44, 104; relations with military, 106, 109, 111–13, 115; and TV Globo, 258–59; and victims of repression, 226–27;

and Workers' Party, 131, 139. *See also* Corruption

Companhia Vale do Rio Doce, 53

Congress, 20, 26, 49, 86, 156; clientelism in, 137–38, 274*n29;* and Collor's economic plan, 46, 191–92; corruption scandal in, 21–22; ignorance of military matters in, 118–19; and institution building, 30–32; and presidency, 23–24, 185–86; reform of, 34–35; representation in, 27–28, 269*n2;* resistance to reforms, 191–92, 194, 197; and Sarney, 188–89; and social security reform, 52–53; weakness of, 4, 28–30, 33, 89–90; and Workers' Party, 130, 138–40, 274*n29*

Constituent Assembly. *See* Constitutional conventions

Constitutional Amendment No. 25, 20

Constitutional conventions, 19–21, 138, 178, 264*n15;* influence of churches at, 150–52, 156–57; influence of social movements on, 171–72, 174; and the military, 110, 117; and municipalities, 79, 82–85; pre-1988, 85, 150–51; regional interests at, 64–65

Constitutions, 68, 117, 220, 263*n5;* 1946, 79–81, 92–93; amendments to, 21–22, 177, 191–92, 194–96, 263*n6;* decentralization in, 42, 47, 58, 64–66; economic effects of, 51, 189, 191, 194, 268*n14;* human rights in, 226, 234; influence of social movements on, 171–72; municipalities under, 79, 82–85, 93–94; politics around writing of, 33–34; presidentialism in, 20–21; revision of, 19, 21–22, 33–34, 48, 52, 263*nn6,7;* vagueness on intergovernmental relations, 95, 98

Corruption, 43, 257; in Collor administration, 23, 30, 45, 47–48, 171; Collor's campaign against, 44; in Congress, 21–22, 31; public response to, 50, 56; Workers' Party rejection of, 134, 139–40

Costa, Sylvio, 260

Couto, Cláudio Gonçalves, 83–84, 141, 272*n17*

Crime: class and protection against, 233–34; fighting as military mission, 120–24. *See also* Corruption; Violence

Cruzado Plan, 188–90

Cuba, socialism in, 129

Dahl, Robert, 5, 218, 254

Dallari, Dalmo, 223

Da Matta, Roberto, 221, 233

Debt, 63, 189, 193; crises, 42–43, 66–67, 206

Decentralization, 47, 87; in Brazilian history, 58–76; effects of, 42–43, 71, 267*n4;* effects on municipalities of, 77–98, 85, 91–97; of health care, 39, 71–72; innovative leadership by subnational governments after, 72–75. *See also* Federalism

Delfim Netto, Antonio, 201

Democracy, 3–4, 282*n1;* business support for, 203, 280*n5;* consolidation of, 5–6, 118, 127, 142, 144–46, 210–12, 267*n31,* 280*n6;* definitions of, 132, 267*n1;* and economic integration, 204–06, 209–12; effects of economic inequities on, 249–51; effects of social movements on, 162–82; effects of urbanization on, 243–44; evaluating, 3, 5–8, 17–18, 163; ideal civilmilitary relations in, 103, 115; legitimacy of, 148, 186, 217; military role in, 105, 118–19, 122–24; participation in, 134–38, 166–68, 174–75; quality of, 212–15, 234–35, 250–51, 262; religious pluralism in, 145–46, 160, 278*n46;* role of electronic media on, 257–60; satisfaction with, 31–32, 124, 279*n4;* within social movements, 165, 168–69, 180; and state violence, 118, 217–19, 228–34, 282*n2;* sustainability of, 18, 186, 238, 244, 260–62; and trade liberalization, 215–16; within Workers' Party, 140–41, 271*n3,* 273*n27,* 274*n30;* Workers' Party as opposition in, 126–43

Democratization, 166; civilmilitary relations after, 101–03; clientelism during, 39–40; and decentralization, 58–76, 78; definition of, 267nn1,5; effects of, 36–57, 107; influences on, 218–20, 228, 272n7; and institution design, 18–22; in media, 258–59; military strength during, 104–05; and role of the state, 76, 167–68, 267n2; support for, 131–32, 147–48, 150, 211–12, 278n2; theories on, 4–8; and vigor of civil society, 256–57

Democratizing coalition, 19

Demographics: changes in Brazil, 236–62; population growth, 86, 239; urbanization, 78–79, 85–87

De Souza, Herbert ("Betinho"), 172, 279n8

Development: Cardoso's program for, 53–54, 198; Collor's program for, 44–47; state programs for, 65, 73; use of military in, 120–21

Dias, Marcio De Oliveria, 212

Dirceu, José, 132

Diretas já. See Democratization; Elections

Doimo, Ana Maria, 174, 181

Dornelles, Francisco, 201

Drug trafficking, 244; fighting, as military mission, 120–22, 229–30

Earth Summit, 172–73, 176, 178

Economic crises, 68, 113; causes of, 43, 63; and economic reforms, 33–34, 54–55; effects of, 4, 185–86, 266n14

Economic integration. *See* Integration, economic

Economy, 8, 132, 199, 268n14; budget process in, 108, 135–37; under Cardoso, 195–96, 280n3; changes in, 186, 244–46; under Collor, 44–47, 50; decentralization of, 62–64, 66–68, 94–96; economic integration to strengthen, 206–07; of education, 252–54; importance of stability in, 185–86, 202–03; inequities in, 70–72, 146, 220, 247–51, 282n6; internationalization of, 208–09; military budgets, 108, 110–11, 113; military involvement in, 108, 119; of municipalities, 80–84, 87–88, 91–92, 96–97; between regions, 64, 240–41;

under Sarney, 187–90; state and subnational governments in, 58–62; state spending, 41–43, 52–54. See also *Plano Real*

Education, 259, 287n6; levels of, 39, 251–54, 261; of voters, 152, 239

Elections, 104, 131; 1989, 43–44, 190, 199; 1994, 141, 195–96; under authoritarianism, 78, 87, 170; Cardoso's mandate through, 49–50; and churches, 152–53, 156; demographics of voters, 39, 239–41, 261; reform of, 34–35; subnational, 63, 79, 87, 269n9; voluntary *vs.* compulsory voting, 25–26, 28; voters in, 96, 134; Workers' Party in, 127, 129–31, 141

Electoral system, 5, 20, 86, 107; and institution building, 25–28; problems of, 185–86

Elites, 7, 164, 247; business, 4, 186; positions of, 4, 24, 177, 241, 271n1; role of, 108, 218; subnational, 63

Elitist liberalism, 217–18, 220, 222, 283n9; and state violence, 233, 235

Environmental movement, 174–76, 255

Erundina, Luiza, 133, 152, 253

Estado Nôvo, 80

Europe, 121, 128; and democracy, 211, 213; as trade competitor, 208–09

European Union, 204, 213

Executive branch. *See* Presidency

Farias, Paulo César, 45

Favelas, 121, 180; conditions in, 243–44; violence in, 169, 229–30

Federalism, 59; fiscal, 82, 267n9; revival of, 42, 76; state *vs.* subnational governments in, 60–62. *See also* Decentralization; Government, levels of; State

Federation of Industry of the State of São Paulo, 45, 200–201

Fernandes, Rubem Cesar, 169, 178

Ferraz, Caio, 169

Figueiredo, Argelina, 31

Finance Ministry, 41

Foreign Ministry (Itamaraty), 205, 213–14

Legislative branch. *See* Congress

Limongi, Fernando, 24, 31

Linz, Juan J., 22–23, 124, 271*n2*, 280*n6*

Lucena, Zenildo de, 212

Lula da Silva, Luiz Inácio, 196, 263*n7;* in 1989 elections, 43, 50; and religion, 152–53, 157; and Workers' Party, 129–30, 272*n9*

Maciel, Marco, 227

Magalhães, Antônio Carlos, 94, 258–59

Mainwaring, Scott, 20, 23, 28–29

Marighella, Carlos, 106–07

Mata, Lídice da, 259

Media, 21, 134; Cardoso's use of, 49–50; and Catholic Church, 153, 159; coverage of violence in, 227, 230, 286*n37;* on the military, 102, 110; Pentecostals in, 155, 158; presidentialism in, 24–25; role in Brazil, 257–60

Mello, Zélia Cardoso de, 45

Menem, Carlos, 209

Mercado Comum do Sul (Mercosul), 204–06, 209–15

Mexico, as trade competitor, 208–09

Military, 202, 285*n27;* attempted coup in Paraguay by, 211–12; and police forces, 229–31; relation with civil society, 101–25; use of violence by, 225–26, 270*n14*, 284*n18;* in war against drugs, 229–30

Military government. *See* Authoritarianism

Military police (PMs), 229–30

Ministério da Previdência e Assistência Social (MPAS), 39

Ministries of the Army, Navy, and Air Force, 104, 110–12, 116

Ministry of Communication, 258

Ministry of Defense, 104, 106, 111–12, 116

Ministry of Social Security, 39–41

Modernization, 190, 199, 209

Moisés, José Álvaro, 31

Montero, Alfred, 73–74

Moreira, Marcilio Marques, 191

Movimento dos Trabalhadores Rurais SemTerra (MST), 151, 176–77, 181, 256

Municipalities, 269*n1;* empowerment of, 77–98, 269*n8;* growth of, 241–42; problems of, 96–97; Workers' Party members governing of, 130–31, 272*n14*, 273*n20. See also* Urbanization

NAFTA, 214

National Constituent Assembly (ANC). *See* Constitutional conventions

National Renovating Alliance (ARENA), 87, 109, 166

National Security Council (CSN), military representatives in, 104–05, 111–12

Neoliberal economics, 131, 185; opposition to, 138, 151, 196; support for, 209, 260

Neopopulism, 247

Neves, Tancredo, 131, 149, 258

"New federalism." *See* Federalism

New Republic. *See* Democracy

Nobrega, Maílson, 189

Nongovernmental organizations (NGOs), 173, 177–81, 224; influence of, 255–56; and social movement networks, 175–76

Novaes, Carlos Alberto Marques, 140

Novo sindicalismo (new unionism), 3

O'Donnell, Guillermo, 6, 19

Oviedo, Lino César, 211–12

Paraguay, 209, 211–12

Parliamentarism, 53; support for, 24–25; in writing constitution, 20–21. *See also* Presidentialism

Parliamentary Front, 24–25

Partido da Frente Liberal (PFL), 40, 43–44, 46

Partido da Social Democracia Brasileira (PSDB), 25, 271*n4;* Catholic support for, 152–53

Partido do Movimento Democrático Brasileiro (PMDB), 3, 19, 39–40;

effects of Cruzado Plan on success of, 188–89; in 1989 elections, 43–44; on participation *vs.* democratization, 166–67

Party politics system: and institution building, 28–30; multipartism and presidentialism in, 23–24; reform of, 34–35; weakness of, 33, 185–86. *See also* Political parties

Patronage. *See* Clientelism

Payne, Leigh, 199, 280*n5*

Pensioners, 41

Pentecostalism, 255, 278*n46;* and Catholic Church, 148–49, 153–60; growth of, 145–46; neo, 277*n38,* 278*n40*

Plano Real, 33, 266*n29;* effects of, 67–69, 251; factors in success of, 195–96; opposition to, 138, 196

Política de Defesa Nacional (PDN), 114–15, 118, 120–21

Political parties, 25, 26, 172; and electoral reform, 20, 27, 34; similarity of, 260; of the state, 128; and urban *vs.* rural voters, 86–87; weakness of, 4, 31. *See also* specific party names

Politics, 86, 175, 188, 196, 214, 241; Catholic Church in, 144, 146–48, 160, 276*n16;* in economic integration, 206–08, 215; effects of urbanization on, 243–44; inclusion in/exclusion from, 127–28, 152–53, 166–69, 277*n29;* inequities of power in, 249–50; and media, 258–59; military in, 105, 107, 118–19; municipal, 86–91, 97; participation in, 127, 167–68, 172, 218; Pentecostals in, 145–46, 154, 156–58, 160; public distaste for, 135, 137, 140; repression of opposition in, 218, 222, 227; subnational, 63, 78–79; tactics in, 4, 24, 50, 265*n6;* Workers' Party as opposition in, 126–43, 271*n2*

Popular Church, within Catholic Church, 147–51

Popular sector groups, 36–37, 41–42, 56–57

Population growth, 86, 239

Postauthoritarian regimes, excluded middle of, 4

Poverty, 272*n7;* and education, 252–53; and inverted priorities, 132–33; persistence of, 4, 247–51; and quality of democracy, 260, 262; and religious pluralism, 145–46, 148–49, 154, 157; and state violence, 218, 222

Presidency, 218; economic reform through, 187–202; relation to legislature of, 185–86; strength of, 44–45, 202

Presidential decrees, 24–25, 30–31

Presidentialism: and inefficiency of Congress, 30–31; and institution building, 22–25; *vs.* parliamentarism, 263*n4,* 264*n9;* in writing constitution, 20–21

Presidentialist Front, 24–25

Private sector. *See* Business

Privatization, 53, 186; under Cardoso, 50–51, 52; under Collor, 44; under Franco, 48; goals of, 193; opposition to, 46, 108, 138, 151; by subnational governments, 69

Protestant churches, 225, 277*n32. See also* Pentecostalism

Public employee associations, 46, 52

Putnam, Robert D., 61, 256–57

Race and ethnicity: discrimination by, 168–69, 277*n30;* and economic inequities, 220–21, 248–49

Real Plan. See *Plano Real*

Reforms, 33–34, 146, 265*n3;* administrative, 44–47, 49–51, 70, 192–93, 268*n13;* agrarian, 146–47, 151, 168, 176–77; alternatives to government proposals for, 138–39; antiauthoritarian, 20, 62–63; civil service, 51–52; of controls on military police, 231–34; of electronic media, 259–60; fiscal, 62–63, 69, 185–87, 191; health care, 41; methods of, 46, 49–55; political, 25, 27, 29–30, 217–18; response to, 147, 186, 191, 196–97, 202–03; and response to state violence, 225, 228; social security, 41, 51–53, 70; and state building, 54–55; structural, 32–35, 48, 50–51; by subnational governments, 58–60, 72–75; tax, 45–47, 52, 68, 96–97, 197–98, 201, 267*n7*

Regionalism: and call for creation of special districts, 97–98; at Constituent Assembly, 64–65; distribution of population, 239–42; and economic inequalities, 70–72, 95–96, 220–21, 248

Religion: pluralism, 144–46, 150, 153–60, 255. *See also* Catholic Church; Pentecostalism

Rompendo o silencio (Ustra), 226, 284*n18*

Sales, Teresa, 167

São Paulo Commission for Peace and Justice (CJP), 223–24

Sarney, José, 20, 23, 62, 149, 258; and clientelism, 64, 265*n6;* democratization under, 3, 54, 175; economic measures of, 187–90, 206; relations with military of, 109–11, 115, 226

Schmitter, Philippe, 4–8

Schneider, Ben Ross, 5–6

Secretariat of Strategic Affairs (SAE), 112

Serra, José, 200

Socialists, 50, 52; decline of, 128–29; in 1989 elections, 43–44

Social movements, 129, 279*n12;* effects of, 7, 162–82, 278*n2;* and vigor of civil society, 255–57

Social policies, 167; of Catholic Church, 144–47, 149, 151–53; lack of centralized leadership in, 65–66, 70–72; of Pentecostals, 145–46, 161; of subnational governments, 72–75, 83–84, 95; Workers' Party promotion of, 127, 129, 131–34

Social security reform, 41, 51–53

Social structure: in comparisons between governments, 238–62; positive changes in, 4

Sola, Lourdes, 67

South America, 82, 214; state violence in, 217, 219

Souza, Mario do Carmo Campello de, 19

Souza, Paulo Renato de, 254

State, 173, 207, 244; under authoritarianism, 38–39; definition of, 265*n1;* effects of decentralization on, 58–59, 66–68; effects of democratization on, 36–57; effects of informal economy on, 246–47; in income redistribution, 70–72; influence of social movements on, 164, 171–75; interventionism of, 44, 191, 193; programs to strengthen, 44–47, 49–51, 54; relations with Catholic Church, 146–47, 149, 156, 275*n3;* relations with NGOs, 179–80; revenue transfers from, 71, 189, 194, 268*n14,* 269*nn5,15;* revenue transfers to municipalities, 80–84, 87–88, 91–92, 194–94; role of, 167–68, 199; spending by, 40, 42, 45–46, 54; and subnational governments, 267*n2,* 267*n9. See also* Government

State apparatus. *See* Bureaucracy

State violence, 168, 170, 217–35; accountability for, 270*n14,* 284*n23;* against Landless Movement, 151, 177; effects of, 218–20; levels of, 282*n2,* 283*nn12,14*

Stepan, Alfred, 107–08, 117, 124

Subnational governments, 64, 97, 226, 267*n2;* under authoritarianism, 78, 87–88; and Cardoso's reforms, 51–52; effects of decentralization on, 58–59; fiscal policies of, 267*n9,* 268*n14;* government councils of, 174–75; reforms by, 72–75; revenue transfers to, 71, 189, 194, 268*n14,* 269*nn5,15;* spending, 64–68, 268*n10;* strengths of, 7, 61; Workers' Party in, 130–38. *See also* Municipalities

Suffrage, 25–26, 239, 261; for illiterates, 39, 239